# Youth in Contemporary Europe

# Routledge Advances in Sociology

*For a full list of title in this series, please visit www.routledge.com*

# Youth in Contemporary Europe

### Edited by Jeremy Leaman and Martha Wörsching

First published 2010
by Routledge
270 Madison Avenue, New York, NY 10016

Simultaneously published in the UK
by Routledge
2 Park Square, Milton Park, Abingdon, Oxon OX14 4RN

*Routledge is an imprint of the Taylor & Francis Group, an informa business*

© 2010 Taylor & Francis

Typeset in Sabon by IBT Global.

*Library of Congress Cataloging in Publication Data*
   Youth in contemporary Europe / edited by Jeremy Leaman and Martha Wörsching.—
1st ed.
   p. cm.—(Routledge advances in sociology ; 52)
   Includes bibliographical references and index.
   1. Youth--Europe.  I. Leaman, Jeremy, 1947–  II. Wörsching, Martha.
   HQ799.E9Y668 2010
   305.235094—dc22
   2009046393

ISBN13: 978-0-415-87817-3 (hbk)
ISBN13: 978-0-203-85153-1 (ebk)

# Contents

# Tables and Figures

## FIGURES

# Introduction
## Youth Culture in Contemporary Europe

*Jeremy Leaman and Martha Wörsching*

The context of youth culture today differs markedly from that experienced by the editors of this book when they were making their transition from dependent childhood to independent adulthood. Youth, for us, coincided with a period of considerable change in world history. In particular, the political and economic supremacy of the United States, as the unquestioned leader of postwar recovery in the West, was becoming less and less self-evident. The consolidation of Soviet power, military setbacks in southeast Asia, growing civil rights tensions, the rising cost of maintaining the dollar standard and the Bretton Woods regime of fixed exchange rates suggested at the least a wounded hegemon which could and should be challenged domestically and internationally. One of the major vehicles of this challenge was arguably the emergence of a politically and culturally assertive younger generation which increasingly questioned received norms and conventions of social behaviour and—perhaps for the first time in the troubled twentieth century—became an identifiable, 'autonomous' generation, less clearly fixed in traditional class stratifications. Setting aside the often overblown romanticization of the youth 'rebellion' of the late 1960s, the period did generate an atmosphere in which cultural and intellectual experimentation could thrive and accepted beliefs and institutional arrangements could be radically challenged.

A distinctive precondition for the challenging by 'our' generation of the cultural and ideological certainties of our parents (real or imagined) was—ironically—the relative economic security of full employment and the expectation of life courses which could be assured by academic or craft qualifications and which would continue untrammelled through to retirement; for those without formal qualifications and attested skills, some form of employment was also fairly assured. In the 1960s and early 1970s, the undoubtedly productive and positive results of youthful challenges to the established order, affecting most developed economies of the West, was thus facilitated by the seemingly secure affluence of 'our' societies and 'our' futures. As this volume seeks to demonstrate, this security is in no way assured today, even though affluence has reached higher levels than ever before and has become an unquestioned common goal of the majority in society. The transition from youth to adulthood in the new twenty-first century is beset by a wide range of insecurities deriving above all from the structural economic and demographic changes and their combined social and political side effects.

While policymakers in past cyclical crises—at times of postwar inflations and the Great Depression, for example—were confronted with the particular problems of youth unemployment, youth criminality and political radicalization, *cyclical stabilization generally neutralized them*. Above all, the 'golden age' of reconstruction, consumerism and the stable growth of 'Fordist' national economies after the Second World War allowed the emergence of a set of optimistic expectations in advanced European economies which assumed secure educational and training pathways that facilitated easy (albeit generally class-specific) transitions to the adult world of work and family formation.

Notwithstanding the cultural differentiations which produced significant changes in the pattern of youth development from the 1960s onwards, it was the onset of mass structural unemployment throughout the OECD in the 1970s that generated the central and enduring problems affecting the transition to adulthood of significant sections of the young population, and compounded the existential issues of maturation, puberty, relationships, independence and self-image. The disparity between youth (15- to 24-year-olds) unemployment and general unemployment indicated in Figure I.1 started to emerge in the late 1970s and has, in most cases, widened to become a

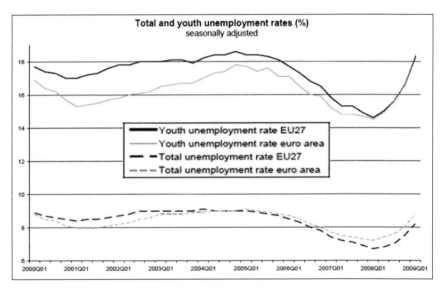

*Figure I.1*    Total and youth unemployment rates (%).
Source: Eurostat press release, 23 July 2009.
Note: The figures have been seasonally adjusted.

consistent feature of European societies in the first decade of the twenty-first century; the disparity is narrower in individual countries (Denmark, Netherlands, Germany) but it is consistent. The persistent structural disparity between disproportionately higher rates of youth unemployment and general adult levels of structural unemployment are additionally compounded by the effects of cyclical downturns, as Figure I.1 also illustrates. Thus, the severe Europe-wide recession of 2008–2009 has affected young people particularly badly, with a year-on-year rise of 3.7 percentage points from 14.6 per cent of the EU-27's youth cohort in the first quarter of 2008 to 18.3 per cent in 2009/I, while adult (15- to 64-year-olds) unemployment rose only 1.5 percentage points to 8.5 per cent in the same period. The particular vulnerability of young workers in the erstwhile 'tiger' economies of Ireland (youth unemployment up from 10.2 per cent in 2008/I to 21.5 per cent in 2009/I), Finland (15.9 per cent to 18.8 per cent), Estonia (7.6 per cent to 24.1 per cent) and Latvia (11.0 per cent to 28.2 per cent) is noteworthy, but so is the fact that almost a quarter (24.2 per cent) of Swedish and a fifth (19.1 per cent) of Luxembourg young people were registered as unemployed in the first quarter of 2009 (figures from Eurostat press release, 23 July 2009).

The removal of the material foundations of autonomous, comfortable adult existence for a significant proportion of young people and of the psychological expectation of material security for all has been the result of significant shifts in economic activity at both the global level and within the family of so-called advanced industrial countries. The *internationalization* of trade and production, initiated in the postwar 'tariff disarmament' programme, has been intensified by a further liberalization of commodity trade and the intense internationalization of capital flows, following the removal of exchange controls in the 1980s; this in turn has generated stronger competition between locations of production and service provision, intensified further by the end of the Cold War and the emergence of 'transition economies' in eastern Europe, south and east Asia and Latin America. *Global location competition* has put particular pressure on countries with higher wage costs and more generous welfare regimes. This pressure could be partly absorbed by higher levels of investment in both the productive and educational infrastructure, but this in turn reflected and reinforced the major *sectoral shifts* in all the advanced industrialized economies—away from skilled and unskilled manual labour in the primary and secondary sectors towards skilled and unskilled labour in the tertiary/service sector. These sectoral shifts have been accompanied by rising demands for formal academic qualifications and, in the majority of European countries, weakening demand for the broad range of craft skills typical of the first two thirds of the twentieth century, which provided lower academic achievers with safe pathways to training and employment; the results have been a general correlation between unemployment and low school achievement.

The skills profile of the working population has thus changed markedly, favouring those (young people) with specialist academic and scientific qualifications. The demographic composition of the working population has also (in part as a consequence) been subject to significant changes, firstly in the overall increase in the participation ratio since the beginning of the 1980s (i.e. the proportion of the population of working age in employment), and secondly in the marked increase in the *participation ratio of women* in employment, which has been one of the main factors in the rise of overall participation; the average rate of female participation in western Europe has risen from approximately 46 per cent in 1973 to 55 per cent in 2009 (source: OECD); in Scandinavian countries, the United Kingdom and the Netherlands the female participation ratio is considerably higher than the average, that of Mediterranean countries correspondingly lower.

The change in the skills profile of the working population is clearly reflected in the rise in the proportion of women in paid employment; however, the erosion of the 'male breadwinner' model of household development has been driven not simply by the shift from traditionally strenuous work in agriculture and industry to the physically less demanding activities in the service professions but also, on the one hand, by choice—the facility and desirability of family planning due to refined methods of contraception—and necessity, where households need the income of female partners either to sustain basic living standards or to enjoy a degree of affluence. There is no doubt that—in contrast to 40 years ago—the majority of young women now see employment as an important part of their life plan and that they hope that their (disproportionately high) educational qualifications will allow them to participate in the labour market on equal terms. Notwithstanding the exigencies of single parenthood or one-person households, in the context of structural unemployment, necessity often outweighs personal lifestyle preferences. The increased availability of female labour and skills has indubitably shaped the demand for labour and allowed/encouraged employers to exploit the advantages of short-term and part-time contracts, adjusting employment to capacity utilization. *Flexibilization* and *casualization* have clearly improved opportunities for generating or boosting household income but they have also reinforced the precariousness of employment and therefore the insecurities (real and psychological) that are associated with the lives of many people in the working population and with those of young people in particular. Part-time work, which at 3.9 per cent represented a minimal proportion of overall employment in the OECD in 1960, has become much more prevalent, averaging 18.2 per cent in the EU-27 in the last quarter of 2008; the gender ratios for 2008 differed starkly, with 7.7 per cent of men and 31.1 per cent of women in part-time employment; young people (26.3 per cent) were also more likely to have part-time jobs (Figures: OECD, Eurostat). Temporary contracts as a proportion of all employment contracts have also risen recently, from below 10 per cent in the early 1980s to 14 per cent in 2008, with a very high proportion of young people (46.1 per cent) in such employment (c.f. Eurostat 2009).

A crucial factor determining the material existence of all households dependent on income from employment has yet to be mentioned: notably, the share of income from wages and salaries as a proportion of national income and the related distribution of net household income (after taxes and transfer payments). The historic shift within the OECD from 'Welfare Keynesianism' to 'Neo Liberalism' in the 1970s and early 1980s as guiding orthodoxy of economic policy produced a corresponding and *dramatic* shift in the functional distribution of income from wages and salaries to profits throughout the OECD. Figure I.2, derived from the IMF's *World Economic Outlook* in the spring of 2007, demonstrates the truly astonishing changes in the distribution ratios of advanced states.

The decline in the wages ratio (the share of gross wages and salaries in gross national income) corresponds to the rise in the profits ratio (i.e. the income generated from corporate profits and personal financial wealth). The degree and speed of this redistribution in favour of the owners of capital is unprecedented in the history of the advanced industrial economies of Europe; 9.36 percentage points in just 25 years is worse than the average for advanced economies and for the United States and is only exceeded by Japan. It reflects first of all the advantage enjoyed by employers in an era of global mass unemployment where the supply of labour far exceeds the demand for labour; the *market incomes* of the employed population have thus been predictably depressed by the shift in the power balance of the labour market. However, it also reflects the economic 'wisdom' of the neo-liberal paradigm which has a more favourable view of (the advantages of) inequality and which, through the deliberate government policies of reducing both corporation tax rates and top marginal rates on income tax, have reinforced the market distribution of income. Thus, the net distribution

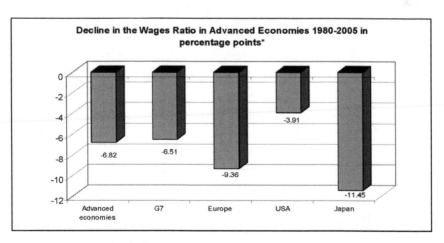

*Figure I.2*  Decline in the wage ratio in advanced economies, 1980–2005 (%); own caluclations.
Source: IMF *World Economic Outlook*, April 2007.

of income—after accounting for direct taxation and transfer payments—
has become overwhelmingly more inequitable than gross distribution; the
rising Gini-coefficients in European societies are a rough indicator of this
trend, but there are more refined studies of *net distribution* in individual
countries (c.f. Schäfer 2008).[1]

Growing income inequalities, above all the decline in the share of disposable household income enjoyed by the employed population, are a significant
factor in the shaping of young people's expectations of employment, career,
household formation, child rearing and social life in general. Thus it cannot
be emphasized enough—when considering the situation of the young generation today—that the maldistribution of income, even after state transfer
payments, also draws the observer's attention to other inequalities which
affect the life courses of the transition generation with which this volume
is concerned. The fairly robust correlation between income inequality and
health, life expectancy, obesity, educational performance, violence, imprisonment and social mobility (Wilkinson and Pickett 2009) would reinforce
the previous argument that the dramatic worsening of income distribution
in most European countries has increased the insecurities of young people
setting out on their adult lives.

This book looks at the challenges confronting both the transitional generation and policymakers in contemporary Europe, and at the opportunities
above all for neutralizing some of the problems outlined in the introductory
section. It is significant that the generational cohort studied in the fourteen
chapters of the book doesn't enjoy the convenience of a strictly defined age
range. Youth, in current scholarly literature and in official data collection,
varies in length with most analyses taking 29 years of age as the upper limit
for the category and where 15/16- to 25-year-olds comprise the common-
est dataset. The economic and social history of 'youth' certainly records a
gradual extension of the lower limit from the relatively short childhoods
of children under feudalism and early capitalism, when child labour was
commonplace and education minimal, to the era of compulsory secondary
education and extensive further and higher education in the twentieth century, when economic activity began increasingly later in the lives of 'young
people'. The new uncertainties of global neo-liberalism and postcommu-
nism have in turn rendered the problems associated with the transition to
independent lives palpable.

There are four core themes in this edited volume, covering (a) 'Life
Chances and Socio Economic Determinants of Youth Today', (b) 'Youth
and Socio Cultural Transformations', (c) 'Youth as a Problem Group?', and
(d) 'Youth and Political Culture'. The objective behind this organization of
the volume is to provide the reader with a multidimensional and interdisciplinary view of youth cultures in Europe, drawn from a variety of recent
research in several European countries. Some of the contributions are comparative studies, while others focus on single countries.

In the first part, three chapters address issues relating to the socio-economic situation of young people and the life chances experienced by particular groups. The first chapter, by the Estonian sociologists Kasearu, Kutsar and Trumm, investigates the relationship between perceived social exclusion and parental family background in Germany, Estonia and Britain, looking at the problems as they emerge in medium-sized towns. The authors conclude that the young adults' evaluation of their personal situation does not depend only on their current resources but is affected by earlier experiences and life chances, while parental involvement and support during adolescence can empower the young adults' human agency. Their analysis also reveals that the societal context noticeably influences the young adult's perception of social exclusion. A significant finding of the comparative study is that, in Estonia, with its middle-level objective indicators of social exclusion, where priority is given to the young age range, the perception of social exclusion and vulnerability of young adults is the lowest of the three countries compared.

The second chapter is by three Polish sociologists from the University of Łódź—Warzywoda-Kruszyńska, Rek and Rokicka—who investigate issues relating to poverty and unemployment affecting young Europeans from an intergenerational perspective, summarizing the results of a major eight-country comparative project funded by the European Union. The intergenerational transmission of inequalities through the transmission of cultural and social capital means that the low social (i.e. material, cultural and educational) status of parents severely limits the children's opportunities of education and social promotion which may lead to the transmission of a 'culture of poverty'. The analysis is comparative in nature and examines the impact of living in disadvantaged families during childhood (by the fourteenth birthday) on a wide variety of outcomes/attainments in young adulthood. It thus assesses the extent to which social disadvantage is transmitted across generations and across the life course of respondents by the age of 24–29. The chapter also seeks to assess the degree to which the social and socio-psychological characteristics of respondents facilitate processes of overcoming disadvantage. The authors proceed from the assumption that social mobility correlates with the ability to use, change and multiply the available resources.

The chapter by Leaman examines the emergence of youth unemployment in Europe, with a particular focus on Germany and Britain and the 'activation' policies adopted by the two social-democratic regimes of Blair and Schröder after 1997 and 1998 respectively. The comparison reveals, firstly, the degree to which the policy initiatives of New Labour influenced the policymaking of the 'Red-Green' coalition which was in power in Germany for eight years up to 2005. Secondly, the author concludes that the institutional and cultural advantages of Germany's extensive system of craft training, further and higher education cushion the younger generation from the disproportionate burdens which fall upon the young, less educated young people in the United Kingdom. In both cases, however, it is evident that extensive and expensive systems of 'activation' and welfare support have been unable to neutralize the structural and cyclical effects of volatile markets and employer preferences, nor to reduce the income inequalities which underlie the multiple disadvantages of a stubbornly high proportion of deprived young people.

The second part of the volume comprises four chapters, which focus on different features of youth culture and the strategies adopted to manage the problems and opportunities of transition. The first of these four chapters—by Brooks and Waters—examines the phenomenon of international educational mobility which, it is argued, is becoming an increasingly normal part of the life cycle of young people and a distinct preference in relation to 'biography building'; it has also been strongly promoted as part of the wider political project of forging a common European identity through the European Community Action Scheme for the Mobility of University Students (ERASMUS) programme, for example. The authors focus in particular on British students and explore the decision-making processes of those who choose to study abroad, comparing their motivations and experiences with their counterparts from mainland Europe.

Peter Kraftl, a human geographer specializing in children's geographies, examines the discourses of 'hope' and 'crisis' in relation to young people and children in Britain. His chapter looks at the 'event' of childhood and suggests that dominant modes of encountering British childhood and youth are enlivened by particular kinds of events. The 'event' is interpreted broadly, encompassing public displays, media reportage, interpersonal encounters and national-scale building projects. The author explores two case studies from the United Kingdom. First, he considers high-profile media coverage of 'crimes' against children and second, a major new education policy which is purportedly set to transform the landscapes of youth, education and (selected) local communities in the United Kingdom. He argues that each case study highlights the profound—and hitherto under-theorized—importance of events for the negotiation of childhood in contemporary Britain, and these events allow for a fuller theorization of the ways in which British childhoods are associated with an axis of 'crisis' and 'hope'. The latter ('hope') receives scant attention in principal social-scientific renderings of childhood. Kraftl concludes that an analysis of events *also* allows one to attend to the many hopeful sentiments attached to British childhoods.

The next chapter, by the educational sociologist Barbara Stauber from Tübingen, focuses on ways in which young people in their transition to adulthood deal with the paradoxical situation of having to plan their lives, while at the same time realizing that planning this period of uncertain transitions is highly problematic. Young people's agency is shifting into the foreground of sociological and pedagogical interest: Which strategies do young women and men develop to give this period between youth and adulthood their own 'Gestalt'? How do they use this insecure status of biographical uncertainty, this hardly defined yo-yo situation? What resources do they develop, what networks do they create, what self-concepts do they invent in the tension between consumerism and autonomous styles? It is through such questions that youth cultural activities start to uncover their fundamental role in the transitions of young women and men—although not for all of them to the same extent, and not always with the same intensity.

On the basis of a regional study carried out in southern Germany during the last few years, which involved interviewing young Goa trance activists in a rural area, the author analyzes modes of shaping (gendered) transitions. This then leads to a discussion of formal, nonformal and informal learning which is increasingly relevant within the political discourse on education in general.

The final chapter in this part by Vossler and Hanley compares the recent phenomenon of online counselling for young people in Britain and in Germany. The authors examine the growing trend in this type of provision, and ask whether we are truly ready for services that cross cultures so easily and create unprecedented technological challenges for therapists. The chapter discusses two online services that have been set up: Kooth in the United Kingdom and the Virtual Counselling Centre in Germany. Each service is briefly introduced with a particular focus on the context in which each has developed, secondly on the key features that they offer, and thirdly on evaluating the therapeutic work that has been undertaken. Following these descriptions, the similarities and differences between the services are discussed and the implications for the development of culturally sensitive youth friendly online counselling services considered.

The third part, which focuses on youth as a 'problem group', opens with a chapter by Lewis, Hales and Silverstone on violent youth crimes. The authors—all from the University of Portsmouth, United Kingdom—present results from interviews with English firearms offenders in London, Manchester, Nottingham and Birmingham. It sets these in the context of government crime policy in England and Japan. The interviews were conducted during a Home Office-funded study and the policy implications drawn from a comparative study funded by the Sasakawa Foundation. The main drivers of Gun Crime are covered, especially its relation to local drug markets and the availability of guns. Comparisons are made between England and Japan to show that, although the problems of young people are similar, the two countries have very different ways of dealing with them. Specifically the English approach of managing an inherently bad situation is contrasted with the Japanese approach of regarding the behaviour of young people as something that needs to be coped with by the whole of Japanese society.

The second chapter in this part—by social policy researchers, Alan France, Liz Sutton and Amanda Waring—bears the title 'Youth Citizenship and Risk in UK Social Policy'. In it the authors explore some of the tensions that influence and shape youth culture in contemporary (British) society, and in particular the political discourse of participation, with its emphasis on 'active citizenship'. This concept has underpinned much of New Labour's policies, and constructs certain expectations about how young people *should* behave which in turn can influence young people's experiences of growing up. It is argued that at the heart of the political discourse is a desire to control 'risky behaviours' and 'risk taking' and, despite the language of empowerment, what can be seen is a set of moral guidelines and prescriptions for living that creates new forms of governance of youth populations. Furthermore, the authors argue, by encouraging young people to be accountable and responsible for themselves and to avoid the 'risks' as identified through political channels, society is in danger of problematizing the everyday experiences of youth, giving little recognition to the wider context of how these risks shape their lives.

The chapter explores UK social policy responses to youth problems and illustrates the inherent contradictions in youth policy in contemporary society. It particularly focuses on the political discourse of participation, with its emphasis on 'active citizenship'.

The concluding chapter in this part, by the Spanish sociologist, Andreu López Blasco, examines the particular issues associated with the postponement of household formation by young people who choose or who are forced to stay in their parental homes. López Blasco interprets these issues with particular reference to the development of social capital. Postponing the time when young people in Spain leave their parental home is seen to be linked to social class and also gender. Those who leave at an early age seem to see little social advantage from staying, while those who postpone this decision wait for a good opportunity to leave or live as a couple. According to the author, family relations have changed in Spain over the last few decades, and in some cases—among the better-off middle classes and families with larger homes—young people can indeed have more personal freedom than earlier generations. However, under the changed socio-economic conditions of Spain today, it is still relevant to clarify why young people postpone the time of leaving their parents' home, even if the length of this period itself is not that significant. What is really important—and this was a central question in the Spanish Youth Survey of 2008—is what happens during those years when young adults stay on in the parental home and how they can benefit (e.g. how this period can prepare them successfully for full social and economic participation).

The fourth and final part of this edited volume contains five chapters dealing with young people and political culture. Gudrun Quenzel and Mathias Albert, from the University of Bielefeld, take data from the representative 'Shell Youth Survey' (2006) among young people in Germany, and identify significant shifts in attitudes towards European integration over a relatively short time span. Analyzing these changing attitudes in more detail and in relation to the 'Rome Youth Declaration' (European

Youth Forum 2007), the authors explore the idea that these changing attitudes among young Germans could signal not only short-term reactions to singular political events, but rather point to a reorientation towards the initial conceptualization of European integration as a peace project.

The sociologist Daniel Faas, from Trinity College Dublin, compares German and English young people in relation to issues surrounding national and European citizenship. Against the background of national education agendas being increasingly influenced by the processes of European integration, Faas examines the way in which educators have been encouraged to develop a European dimension in education and have in turn contributed to the institutionalization of education at the European level. Drawing upon qualitative data from documentary sources, focus groups and semi-structured interviews, the author compares German and English educational responses to Europe and discusses how these different historical engagements affect contemporary student responses. He shows that Europe has been central for the organization of the German educational system, whereas English policymakers and politicians have been more Euro-sceptic, and refrained from including a European dimension in the National Curriculum. This resulted, for instance, in English students having lower levels of knowledge about Europe than their German peers. However, student responses within one country also differ from school to school, depending on issues such as social class positioning and institutional interpretations of macro-level policies. Faas suggests that these knowledge gaps and disparities negatively affect young people's European citizenship as well as their employment and mobility opportunities.

Wolfgang Gaiser and Johann de Rijke, researchers at the German Youth Institute in Munich, analyze the political participation of German youth in the European context. The authors seek to qualify the general impression of young people's impatience with politics, lack of political commitment and the predominance of individualization by providing a more complex picture, where a basic willingness to become politically involved is in fact apparent. Indeed, many young people use the numerous and varied opportunities to express themselves politically. However, this usually only covers occasional activities. Not surprisingly, participation in traditional associations has declined. On the other hand, an affinity with and commitment to new social movements remain fairly consistent. Participation patterns differ according to gender, education level and also where young people live (in west or east Germany). The authors conclude that, if the comparison between eastern and western Germans is seen in a European perspective, the complex connections between the institutionalized political cultures of nations and the participation patterns of young people become apparent.

Martha Wörsching examines the extent and nature of political participation by young people in Britain. Her chapter discusses a number of recent studies and considers the reasons why there seems to be little interest in formal politics—much less than in many other European countries.

The focus on politics in general is then evaluated in relation to a potentially fuller concept of political participation and citizenship. The chapter engages with discussions which critique the narrow definition of 'the political' which is seen to ignore young people's own social experiences and definitions of civil engagement. Research on young people's own understanding of citizenship and their widespread experience of exclusion from public decision making is discussed in the context of social inequality, child poverty and levels of deprivation in contemporary Britain, where young people are all too often seen as objects of political intervention, instead of citizens in their own right.

The final chapter, by Stéphanie Dechezelles, focuses on the very specific political engagement of young neo-fascist activists in Italy. In contrast to most sociological research on political violence, which has focussed on the concept of relative frustration and the mobilization of resources, the author chooses a different perspective to focus on the culture of activist groups. This approach, it is argued, makes it possible not only to address the question of violent action as a reference, as a mode of justification and as the *modus operandi* of an activist organization, but also to deal with the consequences that the relinquishing of these references may have had on the militants and their political engagement. The objective is indeed to propose a tentative explanation of the reasons and mechanisms of the 'disuse' of violence, of its obsolescence, rather than study the mechanisms and reasons for the recourse to violence. In particular the author examines the case of young *Alleanza Nazionale* militants in Italy and sheds light on the modalities of the passage to a culture of nonviolence and on the consequences that such an apparent de-radicalization process may have had on the organization and institutionalization of players previously bent on violent activism. The starting point of her analysis is the fact that the main neo-fascist party has evolved in the space of a few years from political exclusion and marginalization to full participation in the exercise of power. Dechezelles advances the hypothesis that such an institutionalization process has necessarily implied some cognitive problems of identity among its members socialized and politically trained in a culture of violence.

\*\*\*\*\*\*\*\*\*

A problem that this book seeks above all to dispel is the demonization of youth, so rife in the popular print and broadcast media, so easy to evoke and mobilize as an 'other' to unsettle other, older generations and against which to construct a conformist social norm. What it seeks to underline, on the other hand, is the complex and ever-changing interdependence of societies, of their economic, political, social and cultural institutions and processes and the inescapable reality of shared experiences in every stage of every life course, within and between generations. The popular rhetoric of the new modernity stressing choice, consumption, individual preference, individual portfolios of commodified skills, self-presentation and marketization—factors which the state must above all seek to 'activate'—risks subverting the notion of interdependence and co-responsibility, unless the latter is kept alive with equal force. Above all, it risks destroying the cultural, intergenerational, international sense of solidarity with current and future generations of the world's inhabitants, upon which hard-won principles of social justice are based.

There is, without doubt, a clear and increasingly urgent awareness at the political level of the need to address the new structural uncertainties confronting young people, in particular in relation to employment and training. The Global Jobs Pact of June 2009, agreed under the auspices of the International Labour Organisation and involving governments, employers and trade union representatives, testifies to this, as do the countless special programmes launched by individual state ministries in Europe over recent years. The Director-General of the ILO, Juan Somavia, summarized the political and social challenges very succinctly in his statement, marking International Youth Day on 12 August 2009 :

> Helping young people to realize their productive potential and to harness their energies and talents to shape a better world is our challenge and our responsibility today, and our gift to *our* future (Somavia 2009: 2; our emphasis).

However, meeting the quantitative challenge of finding (any) employment for the one billion young people who will enter the global labour market over the next decade in no way exhausts the list of urgent tasks facing policymakers, enterprises and civil society in general, as the contributions to this volume reveal. Legitimizing the necessary political (re-)distribution of income, wealth, employment, access to vital resources, to education, health and a sustainable environment, must go hand in hand with an acknowledgement of Somavia's notion of a 'gift to our future' and a recognition of the need to help all young people enjoy the self-esteem that springs from the development of 'capability' (c.f. Sen 1999) or of 'craft' (Sennett 2009). Both Sen's 'capability' and Sennett's 'craft' are rooted in social relationships; they are not simply acquired as commodified, modular, individualized skills which make the (commodified, modular and separate) individual 'employable'. Rather they evolve slowly within social networks through trial and error, imaginative and innovative experiments in every context of human existence: activity in the household, the neighbourhood, the workplace, civil society involvement; contributing to the constantly changing stock of social capital. This is not the kind of capital that can be divided up into tradeable chunks or used as security against commercial risk. It is nevertheless fundamental to the shaping of social well-being. It can very easily be depleted, and many would argue that the deliberate promotion of inequality over the last three decades has contributed to a process of depletion and that poverty and social exclusion are the strongest evidence for this. However, it can also be enriched and sustained; the survival of solidaristic systems of welfare and human rights in Europe and beyond, the burgeoning of civil society organizations and global NGOs, the resilience of democratic aspirations worldwide all betoken the potential for restoring and advancing the stock of social capital and the survival of the spirit of hope, not just for young people, but 'for us'.

Martha Wörsching
Jeremy Leaman
August 2009

## NOTES

1. Schäfer calculates a decline in the gross wages ratio in Germany of 7.3 percentage points between 1991 and 2008 and a fall of 8.8 percentage points in the net wages ratio (the share of waged and salaried households as a proportion of disposable household income); Schäfer 2008: 587–588.

## REFERENCES

Eurostat (2009) 'Labour Market Latest Trends: 4th Quarter 2008 Data', *Data in Focus* 14/2009.
OECD (2009) *Employment Outlook*, Paris (OECD).
Schäfer, C. (2008) 'Anhaltende Verteilungsdramatik—WSI-Verteilungsbericht 2008', *WSI-Mitteilungen 2008*, (Nr 11+12), 587–96.
Sen, A. (1999) *Development as Freedom* (Oxford: Oxford University Press).
Sennett, R. (2009) *The Craftsman* (London: Penguin).
Somavia, J. (2009) Statement marking Internation Youth Day, 12 August 2009; http://www.ilo.org/public/english/bureau/dgo/speeches/somavia/2009/youth (Accessed 20 August 2009).
Wilkinson, R. and Pickett, K. (2009) *The Spirit Level: Why More Equal Societies Almost Always Do Better* (London: Allen Lane).

## Part I

# Life Chances and Socio-Economic Determinants of Youth Today

# 1 Determinants of Social Exclusion among the Young in Estonia, Germany and the United Kingdom

*Kairi Kasearu, Dagmar Kutsar
and Avo Trumm*

## INTRODUCTION

Young adulthood is identified as an initial period of adulthood, as a developmental stage of a person's life when transition processes from dependency on the family of origin towards independent life are most active. Young adults are 'no longer children—not yet mature adults', and so may have few legitimate means to make their voices heard. As Barry (2005) highlights, many young people lack status, rights and power in society. They are constrained by poverty, their prolonged dependence on the family and the state of transition towards adulthood, and the limited opportunities of access to higher education, employment, housing and citizenship make them vulnerable to social exclusion. In most European countries, young people's entry into the labour market is not without problems, thus compared to the other age groups they experience the highest risk of unemployment and socioeconomic precariousness.

According to MacDonald (1997: 186) the institutions, arrangements and policies which have previously structured youth transitions—in employment, training, welfare, education, housing, the family, the criminal justice system—have themselves undergone dramatic restructuring in recent decades. The combined effect of these changes has been to make youth transitions riskier and more insecure, which means that already disadvantaged youths are becoming more prone to social exclusion.

## YOUNG ADULTS AND INTERGENERATIONAL INHERITANCE OF SOCIAL EXCLUSION

Youth and young adulthood are key transition points that can determine a young person's future life chances. Empirical studies (e.g. Jenkins & Siedler 2007; Duncan et al. 1998) agree that people who fall into certain groups at these life stages experience poor outcomes and are at risk of facing a lifetime of social exclusion and poverty. Nevertheless, according to Ermich et al., 'family income and resources have no direct impact on children's outcomes, but instead reflect the explanatory power of other unmeasured characteristics . . . , like parents' personalities, family conflict and parental style' (2001: 14). In the Finnish study of inheritance of poverty and dependence, the authors found that the parents' lack of means and dependence on income support, unemployment and low educational qualifications contribute to the poverty of the current second generation and their reliance on income support (Airio et al. 2004).

The intergenerational inheritance of poverty and disadvantage can be explained by the transfer, extraction or absence of poverty-related capital, which is influenced by the broader socioeconomic environment. The main types of capital that could be transferred or extracted include human, financial/material, natural/environmental, sociocultural and sociopolitical capital (Moore 2001). The transmission of values, social norms, behavioural patterns, communication strategies—more generally, sociocultural capital—is well established by numerous longitudinal studies. In the current chapter we aim to answer the question of whether the status of exclusion as perceived by the young adult is inherited or the result of personal disadvantages.

## APPROACHING SUBJECTIVELY
## PERCEIVED SOCIAL EXCLUSION

The amount of research on social exclusion during the last decade has been enormous (Bergman 1995; Room 1995; Jordan 1996; Sen 2000; Tsakloglou and Papadopoulos 2002; Mickelwright 2002; Atkinson et al. 2002; Böhnke 2004; Williamson 2005; Marlier et al. 2007; Haisken-DeNew and Sinning 2007). However, there is no agreement regarding the meaning and central traits of social exclusion, or as Amartya Sen has concluded, 'the concept of social exclusion has been seen as covering a remarkably wide range of social and economic problems' (Sen 2000: 1). Social exclusion cannot simply be equated with poverty, multiple disadvantage or deprivation (Abrahamson 1995; Bergman 1995; Sen 2000; Vranken 2001). It is a concept that refers to a lack of social integration in the form of poor family support systems and/or lack of command over material resources (Alber and Fahey 2004: 19). As D'Ambrosio, Papadopoulos and Tsakloglou (2002) write, most importantly the concept of social exclusion deals with the 'inability of an individual to participate in the basic political, economic and social functioning of the society in which he/she lives'.

An individual is considered to be 'excluded' if—on the basis of a number of indicators—he/she cannot participate fully in a society. Kronauer (1998) lists six dimensions as central for the definition of social exclusion: exclusion from the labour market, economic exclusion, cultural exclusion, exclusion by social isolation, spatial exclusion and institutional exclusion. Eurostat (1998) outlines various indicators as the main components of a multidimensional social exclusion index: lack of financial resources, basic necessities, housing conditions, consumer durables, health, social contacts and general satisfaction.

Social exclusion has mainly been conceptualized in objective terms, and the research is aimed at registering evidence about restricted access or opportunities in specific life domains. Social exclusion is the opposite of social integration, which reflects the perceived importance of being part of a society and being integrated (Robila 2006). Several authors (Böhnke 2001a, 2001b, 2004; Robila 2006; Bude and Lantermann 2006) stress the importance of subjective indicators by measuring social exclusion. In order to get a comprehensive picture of social exclusion tendencies, the dimension of *perception* seems an important aspect to include (Böhnke 2001b: 9). Böhnke argues that the social exclusion debate on the European level concentrates more on socioeconomic precariousness and limited possibilities of social participation. In this context, the issues of hopelessness and the perception that there is no sense in changing one's circumstances can manifest themselves in fear, conflict and social-psychological distress. From a more general perspective, social scepticism, the lack of political interest and general trust, symptoms of anomie can arise, which might result in detachment from the moral and social consensus on which society is built. Finally, Böhnke concludes that 'issues of satisfaction and the self-assessment of individual living conditions and social integration offer reliable information on the consequences that material shortages have for perception of belonging' (2001b: 9).

The EU-25 level of analysis of low income and deprivation has revealed that low income alone is not associated with the higher rate of increased feeling of social exclusion (Russel and Whelan, 2004). Bude and Lantermann (2006) argue that even cumulative disadvantages do not necessarily lead to social exclusion because it depends on the subjective perception of the situation as well as opportunities, and objective indicators of social exclusion do not show whether and to what extent the person is excluded or perceives social exclusion at all. Thus, the measurement tool of social exclusion must include indicators which reflect the understanding of the marginalized social position of the specific individuals themselves.

Social exclusion is always relative, and 'feeling excluded' in different societies is determined by actual historical, cultural, social and economic developments. There are different understandings of social exclusion which might vary considerably from country to country and between social groups. The perception of social exclusion and how people feel about their lives may depend on what people regard as necessary for integration, what comparative yardsticks and reference groups are applied in evaluating living conditions or social networks (Böhnke 2004: 6). In addition, we assume that the individual's life stages play an important role in experiencing social exclusion. The process of positioning themselves within their society takes place as individuals compare themselves with their reference group. The subjective perceptions are mediated by personal as well as normative social standards. These processes of social comparisons acquire special importance at times of normative life transitions, as in the case of young adults. Multiple contextual factors can ease or trouble this process.

## THE OPERATIONALIZATION OF SUBJECTIVELY PERCEIVED SOCIAL EXCLUSION

Perceived social exclusion has been operationalized in several ways. The Quality of Life in the European Union and Candidate Countries project in 2002/2003 produced a summative index of perceived social exclusion from four statements: 'I don't feel that the value of what I do is recognised by the people I meet'; 'I feel left out from society'; 'I don't feel that I have the chance to play a useful part in society', and 'Some people look down on me because of my income or job situation' (Alber and Fahey 2004: 19). Bude and Lantermann (2006) assumed that perception of being excluded or included depends on coping strategies, resources for action and estimations of objective exclusion. In their theoretical model, the authors distinguish five determinants of perceived exclusion: objective situation, estimation of objective situation, expectation of situation in future, internal and external resources. External resources are, for instance, income, occupation, education, and family status. By internal resources they mean a sense of coherence or the feeling of insecurity.

## THE DATA AND METHOD

### The Point of Departure

In his work based on qualitative interviews with elite groups conducted in Estonia in the earlier stage of the PROFIT project, Trumm (2006) stresses the multidimensional nature of the inheritance of inequalities from generation to generation, where the values, material and nonmaterial resources were combined in the particular social environment. The main perceived risk factors for inherited disadvantage as perceived by the interviewed elite, were poor education, living in the peripheral area, unemployment, poor knowledge of the state language, insufficient social capital and poor social networks. Interviewees also admitted that ascribed social status and limited social mobility are unequally distributed within Estonian society—some social groups have higher risks of inheritance than others. It was felt that young people coming from families with low levels of material resources and educational attainments are more vulnerable to transmission of inequalities, compared with those who where raised in wealthier and more educated families.

In the following analysis we are interested in social exclusion as subjectively perceived by young adults of 24–29 years of age. The analysis is based on the data collected by face-to-face questionnaire method in middle-sized towns in Estonia (Pärnu), Germany (Giessen) and the United Kingdom (Loughborough) by national teams of the PROFIT project in 2006. The total sample contained 537 individuals (49.5 per cent were females and 50.5 per cent were males). After removing the missing cases, the final sample consisted of 473 individuals. We set out from the concept of social exclusion in general as a multidimensional construct as defined by Bude and Lantermann (2006) and look at its internal structures. Then we focus more precisely on subjectively perceived social exclusion.

## STRATEGY OF ANALYSIS

The respondents were asked to agree or disagree with fifteen statements concerning belongingness to society, social integration and empowerment. First we applied factor analyses to conceive the dimensions of social exclusion and reached five factors together explaining 41 per cent of the variance (Table 1.1).

*Table 1.1*  Factors of Perceived Social Exclusion

| Statements | F1 Perceived exclusion | F2 Support to redistribution | F3 Perceived lack of influence | F4 Concerned about welfare state | F5 Perceived distrust |
|---|---|---|---|---|---|
| I feel left out of society. | 0.68 | | | | |
| Life has become so complicated today that I almost can't find my way. | 0.51 | | | 0.25 | |
| I am optimistic about the future. | −0.43 | | | | |
| Things that happen to me are the results of my own decisions and action. | −0.39 | | | | |
| It is too difficult for someone like me to do much about improving my local area. | 0.38 | | 0.34 | | |
| It is a responsibility of the government to reduce differences in opportunities between people coming from wealthy and poor families. | | 0.61 | | | |

*(continued)*

*Table 1.1* (continued)

| Statements | F1 Perceived exclusion | F2 Support to redistribution | F3 Perceived lack of influence | F4 Concerned about welfare state | F5 Perceived distrust |
|---|---|---|---|---|---|
| The government should redistribute income from the better-off to those who are less well off. | 0.35 | 0.59 | | | |
| The government should spend more money on welfare benefits for the poor, even if it leads to high taxes. | | 0.56 | | −0.22 | |
| People receiving social security are made to feel like second class citizens. | 0.23 | 0.47 | | | |
| People like me don't have a say about what the local authorities do. | 0.24 | | 0.84 | | |
| I don't think the local authorities care much about what people like me think. | | 0.20 | 0.67 | | |
| The welfare state encourages people to stop helping each other. | | | | 0.76 | |
| The welfare state makes people nowadays less willing to look after themselves. | | −0.27 | | 0.53 | |
| If you are not careful other people will take advantage of you. | | | | | 0.74 |
| There are only a few people I can trust completely | | | | | 0.29 |

*Extraction Method: Principal Axis Factoring.*
*Rotation Method: Varimax with Kaiser Normalization.*

At the next stage of the analysis, we drew correlations between the received factors and formed five respective summated indices. The correlations between the indices of social exclusion were much lower than we initially expected. We found that the index of perceived exclusion correlates positively only with the indices of lack of influence and supportive attitude towards redistribution (correlation coefficients higher than 0.2). Next, we controlled it for the cultural differences and conducted separate correlation analysis for each respondent group selected by community (Table 1.2).

The results indicate that there are different patterns of social exclusion of young people in Giessen, Loughborough and Pärnu. In all communities, the perceived exclusion is most strongly positively correlated with the feeling that one has no influence on decision making at the local level. In the case of Pärnu, the index of perceived exclusion correlates positively also with the other subindices, with the exception of the index of distrust. Perceived social exclusion in Giessen is also positively connected to attitudes towards income redistribution, which is not the case in Loughborough. However, the Loughborough data reveal that perceived social exclusion correlates with the negative image of the welfare state (which is not the case in Giessen).

In the third stage of the analysis, because of diverse associations between dimensions of social exclusion across countries, we decided to concentrate only on the determinants of the perceived social exclusion and create

*Table 1.2*  Correlations of Factors of Perceived Social Exclusion

|  | 1 | 2 | 3 | 4 |
|---|---|---|---|---|
| **Exclusion** | | | | |
| Redistribution | | | | |
| *Giessen* | 0.26** | | | |
| *Loughborough* | 0.13 | | | |
| *Pärnu* | 0.26** | | | |
| Lack of influence | | | | |
| *Giessen* | 0.42** | 0.19* | | |
| *Loughborough* | 0.43** | 0.24** | | |
| *Pärnu* | 0.30** | −0.01 | | |
| Concern about welfare state | | | | |
| *Giessen* | 0.03 | −0.07 | 0.22** | |
| *Loughborough* | 0.24** | −0.16 | 0.33** | |
| *Pärnu* | 0.25** | 0.21* | 0.01 | |
| Distrust | | | | |
| *Giessen* | 0.13 | 0.06 | 0.19** | 0.12 |
| *Loughborough* | 0.20* | 0.05 | 0.30** | 0.22* |
| *Pärnu* | 0.07 | 0.18 | 0.01 | 0.20* |

\* Correlation is significant at the 0.05 level (two-tailed)
\*\* Correlation is significant at the 0.01 level (two-tailed)

respective regression models. The summated index of perceived social exclusion (the dependent variable) consists of five statements measured on the scale from 1 'strongly disagree' to 5 'strongly agree' ('I am optimistic about the future'; 'I feel left out of society'; 'Life has become so complicated today that I almost can't find my way'; 'Things that happen to me are the results of my own decisions and action'; 'It is too difficult for someone like me to do much about improving my local area'). The new variable had values from 5–25 (M = 11.38, SD = 3.04; Cronbach's alpha 0.69). Before compounding, items with negative loadings were recoded.

The explanatory (independent) variables entered into the model were divided into four groups. First, we assume that the current social position of a respondent is affected by the situation of the parental home when the respondent was a teenager. The socioeconomic status of parents is a characteristic of external resources. Therefore, the parents' education and occupational status when the respondent was a teenager were added to the models as dummy variables (for education, 1 = 'primary or lower education', 0 = 'other'; for employment, 1 = 'parent has been unemployed', 0 = 'no').

The second set of variables describes the situation of the parental home at the time the respondent was 14 years old. To assess the financial situation of a person's parental home, a single question was asked ('Which of the descriptions best describes the financial situation of your parental family then?') with the following categories: 'We could not satisfy the basic needs', 'We had to spend money very carefully', 'We had enough money for everyday expenses', 'We could afford much without special saving', and 'We could afford a certain level of luxury'. These categories were transformed into two dummy variables: 'poor situation' and 'well-off'.

Respondents were asked to evaluate the parental involvement and support in their lives when they were teenagers based on the two following statements: 'Parents encouraged me to read books' and 'Parents encouraged me to continue my education beyond compulsory level' (with the categories 'strongly disagree', 'disagree', 'neither agree nor disagree', 'agree', and 'strongly agree'). For regression analysis the categories were transformed to dummy variables (1 = 'agree'; 0 = 'other'). In addition, the parents' involvement and support in the child's educational path as dummies were included into the analysis. This set of variables includes also the assessments of whether the parents provided extracurricular classes to improve school performance and/or to expand knowledge, provided paid-for leisure activities and bought a computer.

The third set of variables represents achievement at school. The respondents were asked whether they had poor results during their schooling, problems with truancy, poor relations with teachers and classmates, and finally, whether they dropped out of school.

In addition, the current external resources such as education, occupational status of the respondent and estimation of current financial situation were entered into the model. Finally, the differences between findings from the respondents' towns were taken into consideration.

RESULTS

## The Baseline and Subjective Estimation of Being Socially Excluded

According to Eurostat (2006), the at-risk-of-poverty rate after social transfers (in general and for children under 15 years of age) is the highest in the UK and the lowest in Germany (Table 1.3).

The general unemployment rate was the highest in Germany and the lowest in Estonia, while it was relatively high also in Estonia in the case of young adults (based on EU SILC subjective data). This leads us to assume that the perceived social exclusion is also high in Estonia in the case of young adults, as compared to Germany and UK.

The factor analysis of 15 statements to measure social exclusion revealed five factors which together explained 41 per cent of the variance (Table 1.1). We compared youth perceptions by different factors of social exclusion in three different towns representing three different countries (Table 1.4). The mean score of perceived exclusion was the lowest in

*Table 1.3* Baseline Data of Estonia, Germany and the United Kingdom 2006

|  | At-risk-of-poverty rate after social transfers* | Unemployment rate* | Children's poverty rate after social transfers (0–15 years of age)* | Youth unemployment rate (24–29 years of age)** |
|---|---|---|---|---|
| Estonia | 18 | 4.7 | 20 | 7.4 |
| Germany | 13 | 8.4 | 12 | 8.5 |
| United Kingdom | 19 | 5.3 | 24 | 5.3 |

* *Eurostat database* (http://ec.europa.eu/eurostat)
** *EU SILC*, own calculations..

*Table 1.4* Factors of Social Exclusion by Towns

|  | F1: Perceived exclusion (score 5–25)[a] | | F2: Support to redistribution (score 4–20) | | F3: Perceived lack of influence (score 2–10) | | F4: Concerned about welfare state (score 2–10) | | F5: Perceived distrust (score 2–10) | |
|---|---|---|---|---|---|---|---|---|---|---|
|  | Mean | SD | Mean | SD | Mean | SD | Mean | SD | Mean | SD |
| Pärnu (Estonia) | 9.89 | 2.79 | 12.55 | 2.26 | 6.5 | 1.99 | 5.26 | 1.56 | 6.76 | 1.66 |
| Loughborough (UK) | 12.34 | 2.77 | 12.39 | 3.49 | 6.42 | 1.87 | 6.48 | 1.67 | 7.6 | 1.74 |
| Giessen (Germany) | 11.85 | 3 | 14.68 | 2.72 | 6.91 | 2.07 | 5.30 | 1.76 | 7.54 | 1.65 |

Pärnu compared to Loughborough and Giessen. The average support to income redistribution was the highest in Giessen, followed by Pärnu and Loughborough. Perceived lack of influence was highest in Giessen and negative aspects of the welfare state were more frequently mentioned by the young in Loughborough. Similarly, distrust towards other people was more common among youths in Giessen and Loughborough than among young people in Pärnu. Thus, these results indicate that youths in Giessen and Loughborough perceived their situation as more vulnerable compared to those in Pärnu.

Next we processed five separate models to estimate the association between the perceived social exclusion and characteristics of parental home and individual achievement (Tables 1.5 and 1.6). In Model 1, only the characteristics of parents and parental home at the time when respondent was a teenager were included in the analysis. The model indicated that those young people who estimated the financial situation at parental home to be poor were more likely to perceive greater social exclusion compared to those who estimated the financial situation at the parental home as sufficient to cope with everyday expenditure. However, the positive effect of the financial situation of the parental home did not come to the surface in cases where the young adults were raised in well-off families.

The unemployment status of parents had no effect on the perception of greater exclusion. Moreover, the analysis showed that young people from minority group families had higher risks of perceiving social exclusion. The father's education had no effect on the perception of social exclusion while in the case of the mother's education, the effect was slightly significant: mothers with no more than primary education increased slightly the level of perceived exclusion.

From different variables, which measured the parents' involvement in the child's educational path, only two were statistically significant (see Model 2 in Table 1.5). If parents contributed with extracurricular classes, the probability of perceiving social exclusion as a young adult was lower. Interestingly, the effect of the statement that parents had encouraged children to read books had no effect on perceiving exclusion. It could be explained by the societal context—in Estonia, parents encouraged children more to read books than in other countries. Finally, parental support and encouragement to make educational plans were also important here. Those young adults who found that their parents had not encouraged them to continue education beyond the compulsory level were more likely now to perceive social exclusion. The variables measuring the achievement at school were added to the model.

Although five aspects of relations and achievement at school were now in the models, only three factors—relations with teachers, relations with classmates and school performance—contributed to the model of perceived social exclusion for the young adult significantly. Respondents who reported poor relations with classmates or teachers were more likely to perceive social exclusion, compared to those who had good relations. From

*Table 1.5*  Linear Regression Models for Predicting Perceived Social Exclusion

| | Model 1 | | Model 2 | | Model 3 | |
|---|---|---|---|---|---|---|
| *Variables by groups of predictors* | B | *Std. Error* | B | *Std. Error* | B | *Std. Error* |
| *Characteristics of parental home, when respondent was 14 years old* | | | | | | |
| Poor financial situation at parental home | 1.61*** | 0.36 | | | | |
| Well-off financial situation at parental home | 0.03 | 0.36 | | | | |
| At least one parent was unemployed | 0.07 | 0.36 | | | | |
| Other language beside official language was spoken at home | −1.05*** | 0.33 | | | | |
| Father's education—primary or lower | −0.43 | 0.35 | | | | |
| Mother's education—primary or lower | 0.61* | 0.34 | | | | |
| *Parental involvement, support and school environment when respondent was teenager* | | | | | | |
| Parents provided extracurricular classes to expand knowledge | | | −0.72** | 0.27 | | |
| Parents encouraged respondent to read books | | | 0.11 | 0.29 | | |
| Parents encouraged continuing education beyond compulsory level | | | −0.59* | 0.32 | | |
| Poor performance troubles at school | | | 0.62** | 0.31 | | |
| Poor relations with classmates | | | 1.16*** | 0.40 | | |
| Poor relations with teachers | | | 1.54*** | 0.34 | | |
| *Respondent's current situation* | | | | | | |
| Unemployed | | | | | 1.63*** | 0.43 |
| Poor financial situation | | | | | 0.95*** | 0.34 |
| Well-off financial situation | | | | | −1.22*** | 0.33 |
| Secondary education | | | | | −1.12*** | 0.35 |
| Higher education | | | | | −0.56* | 0.32 |
| *Town* | | | | | | |
| Giessen (Germany) | | | | | | |
| Loughborough (United Kingdom) | | | | | | |
| Pärnu (Estonia) | | | | | | |
| Constant | 12.74*** | 0.87 | 11.31*** | 0.34 | 15.05*** | 0.85 |
| N | 473 | | 473 | | 473 | |
| R² | 0.072 | | 0.148 | | 0.148 | |
| Adjusted R² | 0.060 | | 0.137 | | 0.139 | |

Note: Un-standardized coefficients and standard errors are shown in the table.
*** p <0.01; **p<0.05; *p<0.1

school-related factors, poor performance at school increased the probability of perceiving exclusion.

Finally, in Model 3 (Table 1.5) the impact of the socioeconomic status of a respondent measured by the current occupational status and estimations of the financial situation was analyzed. When only considering the association between the achieved educational level, current occupational status, financial situation and perceived social exclusion, the model described 14.8 per cent of variance in perceived exclusion. Thus its predictive power was comparable to the effect of parental support and relations at school. The results indicated that the feeling of being socially excluded was less common among young people with higher and secondary education than among young adults with primary education. An important predictor was the estimation of the household's financial situation. Young adults who were financially well-off were less likely and those who had financial problems were more likely to perceive social exclusion. Moreover, unemployment was also relevant—the lack of a job had a significant effect on the perception of social exclusion.

This stage of analysis indicated that perceived social exclusion is related to parental home characteristics, parental support and school performance as well as the current situation of the individual. Therefore the next step of our analysis was to test whether the effect of parental home characteristics and support were mediated through the characteristics of the current situation and thus were not related to perceived social exclusion when the current situation is controlled for. Model 4 in Table 1.6 controls for this assumption by capturing the variables from previous models. The descriptive power of this model turned out to be the highest (R square 0.275) compared to the previous models. The assumption that parental home and support reduces its significance did not find strong support. Our model showed that the financial situation of the parental home and minority background were significant, even if the respondent's education, current occupation and financial situation were taken into account. It was similar in the case of parental support and relations with classmates and teachers at school.

And finally, the variable assessing the impact of local community/environment was added to the final model (see Model 5 in Table 1.6). This model clearly provided the best fit to the data. The descriptive power of the final model was the highest and the Model accounted for 32 per cent of the variance in perceived exclusion. If one adds the occupational status, estimation of the current financial situation and community variables, most of the parental home and school-related characteristics remain significant, but the poor performance at school loses its influence. Therefore, the impact of poor performance at school is mediated by the socioeconomic status of the respondent.

To conclude, the probabilities of perceiving exclusion were higher for young adults in Giessen and Loughborough and lower in Pärnu. This indicates that subjectively perceived social exclusion is dependent on the social context in which the young adult is currently living.

*Table 1.6*   Linear Regression Models for Predicting Perceived Social Exclusion

| Variables by groups of predictors | Model 4 | | Model 5 | |
|---|---|---|---|---|
| | B | Standard Error | B | Standard Error |
| *Characteristics of parental home when respondent was 14 years old* | | | | |
| Poor financial situation at parental home | 1.03** | 0.33 | 1.13*** | 0.33 |
| Well-off financial situation at parental home | 0.19 | 0.33 | 0.05 | 0.32 |
| At least one parent was unemployed | 0.16 | 0.33 | 0.01 | 0.32 |
| Other language beside official language was spoken at home | −1.17*** | 0.30 | −0.91*** | 0.30 |
| Father's education—primary or lower | −0.23 | 0.32 | −0.19 | 0.31 |
| Mother's education—primary or lower | −0.12 | 0.32 | −0.26 | 0.31 |
| *Parental involvement, support and school environment when respondent was teenager* | | | | |
| Parents provided extracurricular classes to expand knowledge | −0.62** | 0.26 | −0.69** | 0.26 |
| Parents encouraged respondent to read books | 0.28 | 0.28 | −0.01 | 0.27 |
| Parents encouraged continuing education beyond compulsory level | −0.39 | 0.31 | −0.07 | 0.30 |
| Poor performance troubles at school | 0.36 | 0.31 | 0.17 | 0.30 |
| Poor relations with classmates | 0.90** | 0.38 | 0.76** | 0.37 |
| Poor relations with teachers | 1.37*** | 0.33 | 1.29*** | 0.32 |
| *Respondent's current situation* | | | | |
| Unemployed | 1.29*** | 0.42 | 1.06** | 0.41 |
| Poor financial situation | 0.64* | 0.33 | .51 | 0.32 |
| Well-off financial situation | −1.18*** | 0.31 | −1.19*** | 0.31 |
| Secondary education | −0.49 | 0.35 | −0.37 | 0.39 |
| Higher education | −0.37 | 0.31 | −0.14 | 0.32 |
| *Town* | | | | |
| Giessen (Germany) | | | 1.31*** | 0.35 |
| Loughborough (United Kingdom) | | | 1.84*** | 0.35 |
| Pärnu (Estonia) | | | | |
| Constant | 15.62*** | 1.21 | 13.96*** | 1.26 |
| N | 473 | | 473 | |
| $R^2$ | 0.275 | | 0.320 | |
| Adjusted $R^2$ | 0.248 | | 0.291 | |

Note: Un-standardized coefficients and standard errors are shown in the table.
*** $p < 0.01$; **$p < 0.05$; *$p < 0.1$

CONCLUSION

The aim of this paper was to examine the young adults' perceptions of social exclusion in middle-sized towns of three countries of the European Union (Estonia, Germany and the United Kingdom) in order to answer the research question of whether the exclusion status as perceived by young adults is inherited or the result of personal disadvantages. The study allows the following conclusions:

First, the analysis revealed that the perceived status of being excluded is not directly inherited from parents. The regression analysis indicated that the parents' education and occupational status do not have an impact on the level of exclusion perceived by young adults, but it is instead determined by the wider situation and culture of the parental home. We can conclude that the parental home culture and the parents' involvement in a child's' life choices have more impact on the child's life outcomes or, at least, on subjective estimations of the current life situation than typical indicators, which measure social mobility. Here our findings are consistent with the findings of Ermich et al. (2001), who argue that some objective indicators (e.g. family income) reflect the impact of unmeasured parental family life characteristics on the child's life outcomes. Therefore, we do not deny the importance of the socioeconomic characteristics of parents, but see their impact mediated by parental support delivered to the respondent at fourteen years of age.

On the other hand, we consider the direction of association between perceived exclusion and parental home characteristics and ask whether the feeling of exclusion is determined by estimations given to the parental home situation or the other way around—the feeling of being excluded gives negative connotations to the subjective estimations of the parental home situation. The answer to this question stays open. We have to admit that to bring empirical evidence into these claims would require longitudinal data. Nevertheless, our analysis shows that there is a strong association between perceived social exclusion and estimations of parental involvement in the child's actions (e.g. extracurricular classes) and general parental home characteristics. Furthermore, the results also proved that the current feeling of being socially excluded was strongly associated with the earlier performance at school. Thus, it allows us to conclude that disadvantages experienced at home or school while being a teenager are transmitted to subjective evaluations of the current situation.

According to contemporary research on poverty and social exclusion, ethnic minorities tend to have poorer living conditions, experience more severe social exclusion and are economically more vulnerable than those who belong to the majority ethnicity (Fløtten 2006: 163). Our results confirmed that young adults from a minority background were more likely to experience feelings of being socially excluded. Consequently, the perceived social exclusion is not only built on the material background but is related also to the sense of belonging to a particular ethnic group (see also Kasearu and Trumm 2008; Haisken-DeNew and Sinning 2007; Aasland and Fløtten 2001; Kutsar 1997).

Although the poor material situation of the parental home was highly connected with the evaluation of the current situation, the current poor material situation had no impact on the subjective perception of social exclusion. This implies that the perceived social exclusion must not necessarily go along with deprived material living conditions. This observation finds support in the findings of Böhnke (2001a), who draws attention to the interrelation of poverty and social exclusion, showing that social exclusion must not be automatically connected with poverty, and poverty must not be the result of the social exclusion process. Our results confirmed that of young adults' socioeconomic characteristics, it was only unemployment which was an important determinant of perceived social exclusion, consistent with several previous findings (e.g. Chuprov and Zubok 2000; Böhnke 2001b; Kieselbach 2003), clearly referring to long-term unemployment as one of the sociodemographic characteristics of people experiencing social exclusion.

Secondly, our study underlined the impact of the societal context of perceiving social exclusion as a young adult. The analysis revealed higher levels of perceived social exclusion and vulnerability among young adults in Loughborough and Giessen, compared with the young people in Pärnu. This result could be surprising, considering the fact that baseline characteristics (general and children's poverty as well as youth unemployment rates) put Estonia in a middle position. However, this result can be explained from different perspectives. On the one hand, the studies have shown that in the countries with higher level of prosperity, people belonging to the materially disadvantaged groups suffer more from the perception that they are left out of the society—they are more affected by perceived social exclusion. Also Böhnke (2004) found that the polarization according to perceived social exclusion between employed and unemployed people in Estonia is lower than in the United Kingdom and Germany.

Estonia as a transitional society is more open than ever, and the possibilities of escaping from the poverty cycle are thus better (i.e. the field of choices for young people is wider). This assumption is based on an imaginary value hierarchy in which countries closer to the top (with higher living standards) look more attractive than the countries in lower positions. Consequently, in the case of Estonia, the field of choices between the countries by some imaginative value can be larger than in the case of the United Kingdom or Germany, which are higher up in the hierarchy of European countries. Thus, according to the imaginary value of countries, young adults perceiving social exclusion in the United Kingdom or Germany would do better to stay in their country as unemployed than move to markets that are lower valued.

On the other hand, the better position of young adults in Estonia is related to the context of a transitional society. The relative situation of young adults in Estonia has been more challenging—compared to that of the middle-aged and older generation in their country and young adults in the other two countries. The studies have shown that during the transition period social mobility was relatively high (Titma and Roots 2006) and young people were considered the 'winners of transition', given good chances to achieve personal success. The image of the 'winning generation' was also expressed in the follow-up in-depth interviews carried out with young people in Pärnu and selected from the survey sample, when they told the interviewer about their optimistic life plans and expectations (Ausna et al. 2007). Moreover, in the last few years the unemployment rate of young people has decreased rapidly from 23.9 per cent in 2000 to 10 per cent in 2007, and the decreasing risk of poverty has also been more significant in Estonia than in the United Kingdom or Germany.

In conclusion, the status of the poor and excluded young adults is not directly inherited from parents (the parents' education and occupational position did not have an impact on the perception of exclusion); it is rather the culture of the parental home (parenting style, norms and values) which shapes the process of inheritance. As the specific feature of a transitional country, from an intergenerational perspective at the micro-level, the former patterns of the transmission of material, social and cultural assets from parents to children were transformed and reconstructed according to new values and requirements of the society, individual adaptation and coping strategies. Children as active social actors are themselves mediators of positive and negative factors of life chances between two generations of adults, and they are active in building their own human, material and social capital. Young people's human agency can be empowered by effective educational policies that can reduce the lack of support of the parental family (access to education, supportive school atmosphere, etc.) and can be helped by specific measures given at a young age, which, together with society's openness, can all broaden the field of choice available to the young.

## ACKNOWLEDGMENT

This research was financed by the European Commission under the 6th FP Citizens and Governance in a Knowledge Based Society No. CIT2-CT-2004–506245. Any opinions, findings, and conclusions or recommendations expressed in this material are those of the authors and do not necessarily reflect the views of the European Commission. We are grateful to our partners Jeremy Leaman and Christina Kokoroskou from Loughborough University and Dieter Eissel and Christa Ludwig from Justus-Liebig-University, Gießen, for the supply of data and for effective academic cooperation.

# REFERENCES

Aasland, A. and Fløtten, T. (2001) 'Ethnicity and Social Exclusion in Estonia and Latvia', *Europe-Asia Studies,* 53 (7), pp. 1023–1049.

Abrahamson, P. (1995) 'Combating Poverty and Social Exclusion in Europe', in W. Beck, W. van der Maesen and A. Walker (Eds.) *The Social Quality of Europe,* pp. 145–175 (Bristol: The Policy Press).

Airio, I., Moisio, P. and Niemelä, M. (2004) *Intergenerational Transmission of Poverty in Finland in the 1990s,* Department of Social Policy, Series C: 13/ 2004 (Turku: University of Turku).

Alber, J. and Fahey, T. (2004) *Perceptions of Living Conditions in an Enlarged Europe* (Luxembourg: European Foundation for the Improvement of Living and Work Conditions, Office for Official Publications of the European Communities).

Atkinson, A. B., Cantillon, B., Marlier, E. and Nolan, B. (2002) *Social Indicators: the EU and Social Inclusion* (Oxford: Oxford University Press).

Ausna, A-R., Kasearu, K. and Trumm, A. (2007) 'Intergenerational Inheritance of Inequalities in Perceptions and Experiences of Young Adults in a Middle-Sized Town of Estonia', in W. Warzywoda-Kruszynska (Ed.) *European Studies on Inequalities and Social Cohesion, 1–2/2007,* pp. 31–59 (Lodz: Lodz University Press).

Barry, M. (2005) 'Introduction', in M. Barry (Ed.) *Youth Policy and Social Inclusion: Critical Debates with Young People,* pp. 1–8. (London: Routledge).

Bergman, J. (1995) 'Social Exclusion in Europe: Policy Context and Analytical Framework', in G. Room (Ed.) *Beyond the Threshold: The Measurement and Analysis of Social Exclusion,* pp.10–28 (Bristol: The Policy Press).

Bude, H. and Lantermann, E.-D. (2006) 'Soziale Exklusion und Exklusionsempfinden', *Kölner Zeischrift für Soziologie und Sozialpsychologie,* 58 (2), pp. 233–252.

Böhnke, P. (2001a) *Nothing Left to Lose? Poverty and Social Exclusion in Comparison. Empirical Evidence on Germany,* Discussion Paper FS III 01–402 (Berlin: Social Science Research Centre Berlin).

Böhnke, P. (2001b) *Reporting on Social Exclusion: Standard of Living and Social Participation in Hungary, Spain and Germany,* Discussion Paper FS III 01–407 (Berlin: Social Science Research Centre Berlin).

Böhnke, P. (2004) *Perceptions of Social Integration and Exclusion in an Enlarged Europe* (Luxembourg: European Foundation for the Improvement of Living and Work Conditions, Office for Official Publications of the European Communities).

Chuprov, V. and Zubok, J. (2000) 'Integration Versus Exclusion: Youth and the Labour Market in Russia', in *UNESCO 2000,* pp. 171–182 (Oxford: Blackwell Publishers).

D'Ambrosio, C., Papadopoulos, F. and Tsakloglou, P. (2002) *Exclusion in EU Member States: A Comparison of Two Alternative Approaches* (Working Paper, Bocconi University).

Duncan, G. J., Yeung, W. J. and Brooks-Gunn, J. (1998) 'How Much Does Childhood Poverty Affect the Life-Chances of Children? *American Sociological Review,* 63, pp. 406–423.

Ermich, J., Francesconi, M. and Pevalin, D. (2001) *The Outcomes for Children in Poverty* (Department of Work and Pensions Research Report, No 192).

Eurostat (1998) *Recommendations on Social Exclusion and Poverty Statistics,* Document CPS 98/31/2, (Luxembourg).

Fløtten, T. (2006) *Poverty and Social Exclusion—Two Sides of the Same Coin? A Comparative Study of Norway and Estonia* (Oslo: Fafo).

Haisken-DeNew, J. and Sinning, M. (2007) *Social Exclusion of Immigrants in Germany,* seminar paper http://www.vwl.uni-essen.de/dt/mikro/forschungsseminar/Social%20Exclusion.pdf.

Jenkins, S. P. and Siedler, T. (2007) *The Intergenerational Transmission of Poverty in Industrialized Countries*, Chronic Poverty Research Centre Working Paper 75, http://www.chronicpoverty.org/pdfs/75Jenkins_(Siedler).pdf.

Jordan, B. (1996) *A Theory of Poverty and Social Exclusion* (Oxford: Blackwell).

Kasearu, K. and Trumm, A. (2008) 'The Socio-Economic Situation of Non-Estonians', in *Estonian Human Development Report*, pp. 47–56 (Tallinn: Estonian Cooperation Assembly).

Kieselbach, T. (2003) 'Long-Term Unemployment among Young People: The Risk of Social Exclusion', *American Journal of Community Psychology*, 32 (1–2), pp. 69–76.

Kronauer, M. (1998) 'Social Exclusion and "Underclass": New Concepts for the Analysis of Poverty', in H.-J. Andreß (Ed.) *Empirical Poverty Research in a Comparative Perspective*, pp. 51–75 (Aldershot: Ashgate).

Kutsar D. (1997) 'Multiple Welfare Losses and Risk of Social Exclusion in the Baltic States During Societal Transition', in A. Aasland et al. (Eds.) *The Baltic Countries Revisited: Living Conditions and Comparative Challenges* (Fafo-report 230, Oslo, Fafo).

MacDonald, R. (1997) *Youth, the "Underclass" and Social Exclusion* (London: Routledge).

Marlier, E., Atkinson, A. B., Cantillon, B. and Nolan, B. (2007) *The EU and Social Inclusion: Facing the Challenges* (Bristol: The Policy Press).

Moore, K. (2001) *Frameworks for Understanding the Intergenerational Transmission of Poverty and Well-Being in Developing Countries*. CPRC Working Paper 8.

Mickelwright, J. (2002) *Social Exclusion and Children: A European View for a US Debate*, CASE Working Paper 51 (London: London School of Economics).

Robila, M. (2006) 'Economic Pressure and Social Exclusion in Europe', *The Social Science Journal*, 43, pp. 85–97.

Room, G. (1995) 'Poverty and Social Exclusion: The New European Agenda for Policy and Research', in G. Room (Ed.) *Beyond the Threshold. The Measurement and Analysis of Social Exclusion*, pp. 1–9 (Bristol: The Policy Press).

Russel, H. and Whelan, C. (2004) *Low Income and Deprivation in an Enlarged European Union* (Luxembourg: European Foundation for the Improvement of Living and Work Conditions, Office for Official Publications of the European Communities).

Sen, A. (2000) *Social Exclusion: Concept, Application and Scrutiny*. Social Development Papers No 1, (Asian Development Bank, Office of Environment and Social Development).

Titma, M. and Roots, A. (2006) 'Intergenerational Mobility in Successor States of the USSR', *European Societies*, 8 (4), pp. 493–526.

Trumm, A. (2006) 'Estonia', in W. Warzywoda-Kruszynska (Ed.) *European Studies on Inequalities and Social Cohesion, 1–2/ 2006*, pp. 35–84 (Lodz: Lodz University Press).

Tsakloglou, P. and Papadopoulos, F. (2002) 'Aggregate Level and Determining Factors of Social Exclusion in Twelve European Countries', *Journal of European Social Policy*, 12 (3), pp. 211–225.

Vranken, J. (2001) 'Unravelling the Social Strands of Poverty: Differentiation, Fragmentation, Inequality, and Exclusion', in H.T. Andersen and R. van Kempen (Eds.) *Governing European Cities*, pp. 71–91 (Aldershot: Ashgate).

Williamson, H. (2005) 'Young People and Social Inclusion—An Overview of Policy and Practice', in M. Barry (Ed.) *Youth Policy and Social Inclusion. Critical Debates with Young People*, pp. 11–26 (London: Routledge). Table 1 Factors of perceived social exclusion.

# 2 Poverty and Unemployment of Young Europeans from an Intergenerational Perspective

*Wielisława Warzywoda-Kruszyńska,*
*Magdalena Rek and Ewa Rokicka*

## INTRODUCTION

Children are vulnerable to poverty in European countries, although the degree of intensity varies. The degree of poverty seems to be related to the socio-economic and political context in which children live. Child poverty may result from a set of structural factors, such as income inequality, economic standing of the country, spending on social protection, family structure, employment of parents as well as the political approach towards preventing or alleviating poverty. Therefore, although poverty in childhood can predict the persistence in later life and intergenerational transmission of poverty, the risk of its perpetuation is not equally widespread across the European Union. This chapter aims to clarify the connection between child poverty and the socio-economic and political context at the national level and their impacts on poverty persistence as documented in research carried out in medium-sized towns located in different European countries[1].

## CHILD POVERTY—A FOCUS OF THE EUROPEAN UNION'S INTEREST

Though in the last decades of the twentieth century there was evidence that child poverty was increasing in some European countries, it was perceived as an experience of individual countries rather than a common feature of the European community. Opinion prevailed that with better parental education, lower numbers of children per family and increasing living standards would contribute to a rise in children's well-being. It was not until the publication of the first UNICEF Innocenti Report 'Child poverty in rich countries' (2000) that children became perceived as a vulnerable group in the process of economic and political changes. The report coincided with the adoption of the Lisbon Strategy which declared the 'Elimination of poverty' by 2010 a priority for the European Union. Since then social policy aimed at the eradication of poverty and social exclusion became one of the pillars of the European Union's development towards a better quality of jobs and life. It gave impetus to the improvement of statistics, allowing the monitoring of the process and comparison between Member States. Commonly agreed indicators have been defined to trace progress, and the Open Method of Coordination (OMC) based on exchange of good practice examples has been accepted for the transferability of measures and solutions across Europe. Since 2006, Member States produce their *National Reports on Strategies for Social Protection and Social Inclusion (NRSSP-SIs)* as part of the OMC every two years. Benchmarking countries' performance on a commonly agreed threshold (60 per cent of median equalized income) allows the identification of differences and commonalities in patterns of poverty among countries.

The focus on children's rights was expressed in Strategic Objectives 2005–2009 in the following words: '*A particular priority must be effective protection of the rights of children, both against economic exploitation and all forms of abuse, with the Union acting as a beacon to the rest of the world*', with the aim of putting the eradication of child poverty in the broader context of children's well-being. In March 2006, the European Council requested the Member States '*to take necessary measures to rapidly and significantly reduce child poverty, giving all children equal opportunities, regardless of their social background*'. In 2007 and 2008 fundamental reports were published, which document the extent of child poverty and children's well-being across the European Union (European Commission 2007a) and OECD countries (UNICEF Innocenti Research Centre 2007).

Hugh Frazer and Eric Marlier (2007) produced a synthesis report on tackling child poverty based on the National Reports on Strategies for Social Protection and Social Inclusion (2006–2008) which were delivered by 27 nongovernmental experts from each Member State. The authors of the report noted that, despite differences, there are also several factors which recur, though not to the same degree or intensity, in most EU countries. These factors include:

- the high number of poor and socially excluded children living in jobless households or households with a low work intensity;
- the high risk of poverty and social exclusion faced by children growing up in lone-parent families and in larger families with three or more children;
- the significant number of children living in households with one or both parents in work but with insufficient income to lift the family out of poverty (in-work poverty);
- the continuing impact of gender inequalities in terms of access to employment, levels of remuneration and the sharing of caring responsibilities;

- the low level of income support for families with children in some countries;
- the high risk of poverty and social exclusion faced by many immigrant children and by children belonging to some ethnic minorities (e.g. Roma children);
- the particularly high risk of extreme poverty and social exclusion faced by some groups of children such as children growing up in institutions, children with a disability, children who are victims of violence, abuse and trafficking, children who are unaccompanied migrants;
- the high levels of early school leaving and school failure amongst children growing up in poor and socially excluded families;
- the multi-dimensional nature of child poverty and social exclusion, which shows that income poverty and lack of resources are also frequently associated with poor health, living in inadequate housing and a dangerous environment and/or having poor access to key service such as health services, social services and child care services;
- the significant intergenerational inheritance of disadvantage, in particular educational disadvantage;
- the lack of opportunities for many children growing up in poverty and social exclusion to participate fully in society and in particular in normal social, cultural and sporting activities (Frazer & Marlier 2007: 5).

How much these conclusions apply to particular countries in the PROFIT project study is a matter of in-depth analysis provided next.

## STRUCTURAL FACTORS OF POVERTY IN
## SELECTED EUROPEAN COUNTRIES

The study of eight European countries was undertaken[2] with the aim of understanding better the impact of socio-economic and political contexts on child poverty and of childhood poverty impact on the achievements of young adults. We deliberately selected countries from both western and eastern Europe. For western countries the selection criterion was the type of social welfare regime. Thus, in the PROFIT project the United Kingdom represents the Anglo-Saxon social welfare regime, with Germany as an example of the Corporatist, Finland the Social-Democratic and Italy the Southern Social Welfare Regime.

For post-socialist countries involved in the study, the most important selection criterion was the degree of independence at the time of state socialism. Estonia and Lithuania were parts of the Soviet Union, while Bulgaria and Poland constituted separate nation states with relatively more independent central government and administration.

Western countries represent the affluent part of the European Union, while eastern countries are their poorer neighbours. As compared with the EU-27 average GDP per head in 2006 expressed in purchasing power parities (PPPs), Bulgaria (37 per cent), Lithuania (58 per cent), Poland (53 per cent) and Estonia (68 per cent) had the lowest values, while all western countries in the study were placed above the EU average: Finland (110 per cent), Germany (114 per cent), Italy (104 per cent) and the United Kingdom (119 per cent) (European Commission 2007b). Like all post-socialist countries, Estonia (1,625), Lithuania (1,448) and Poland (2,213) spent least on social protection, while all western partner countries spent more than the EU-25 average (6,188): Finland (6,897), Germany (7,230), Italy (6,257), the United Kingdom (6,994) (European Commission, 2007b: 207; data for Bulgaria not provided).

Lithuania and Poland are the most unequal countries in the EU (outdistanced only by Portugal), while Finland and Germany are the least unequal (see Table 2.1). At the same time Poland and Lithuania are countries with the highest risk of poverty in the EU, with one fifth of the national population having an income below the national poverty threshold set at 60 per cent of median equivalized income. Finland (12 per cent) and Germany (12 per cent) are below the average (16 per cent) for EU-25, whereas Estonia (18 per cent), the United Kingdom (19 per cent) and Italy (19 per cent) are above (see Table 2.2).

Poland (31 per cent) and Lithuania (27 per cent) are the least child friendly countries with the highest poverty rate among children in the EU. Estonia (24 per cent), Italy (21 per cent) and the United Kingdom (22 per cent) are above the EU average (19 per cent), while Finland (11 per cent) and Germany (12 per cent) are below. In Poland, Lithuania and Estonia, poverty rates decrease in subsequent age cohorts, with children being the most vulnerable. In Finland and Germany the risk of poverty is not differentiated substantially between age groups, while in the United Kingdom the elderly are the most vulnerable group; however, in Italy, children are more vulnerable than the elderly.

The proportion of age groups among the poor varies in the countries studied (see Table 2.3). In all countries, it is people of working age who prevail among the poor. Their proportions range from 52 per cent in the United Kingdom to 70 per cent in Poland. In Poland, Lithuania and the United Kingdom every fourth/fifth poor person is a child, while in Finland, Germany, Italy and the United Kingdom every fourth/fifth poor person is aged 65+. Poland is distinct in terms of the proportion of the elderly among the poor population—it is unusually low. In Poland, every twentieth poor person is older than 65; therefore, Poland can be described as an elderly-friendly country in terms of successful protection of the elderly against monetary poverty.

However, one has to bear in mind that the 'at-risk-of-poverty' concept is a relative one. This is why being poor means having different living standards in different Member States. Because of the varying levels of economic standing of countries, people considered poor in affluent countries are sometimes much better off in absolute terms than those in poorer countries. Differences between EU countries are substantial. The poverty threshold for two adults with two dependent children in Luxemburg (34,387), the country with the highest level in the EU, is more than ten times higher than in Romania (3,158), the country with the lowest poverty threshold. As regards the Profit project participants, in the United Kingdom, the poverty threshold is set in 2005 in PPS at 22,418, in Germany at 19,805, in Finland at 17,851, in Italy at 17,299, while in Poland it is 6,041, in Estonia 6,025, in Lithuania 4,916 and in Bulgaria 4,269 PPS. Therefore, it seems to be very reasonable to benchmark country position against the EU poverty lines expressed in relative and in absolute terms rather than against national relative poverty line (European Commission, 2007c, Chapter 3—The Risk of Poverty at EU Level).

The relative EU poverty threshold was set at 60 per cent of EU-24 (without Bulgaria, Romania and Malta) median income[3]. It amounts to EUR 670 a month, 'or more precisely to the purchasing power equivalent of this in the different countries'[4]. In 2004, some 100 million people living in the 24 EU Member States had an income below that poverty threshold, accounting for 22.5 per cent of the population of these countries. However, in Lithuania, Poland and Estonia (see Table 2.4) close to 80 per cent of these countries' populations live on income below 60 per cent EU median, as compared with less than 10 per cent in Finland, Germany and the United Kingdom and 16 per cent in Italy.

The same ranking of countries recurs when the poverty threshold is set at 50 per cent and 40 per cent of EU median income, though the relative number of the poor population decreases in both EU-24 and in given countries, amounting to 16 per cent and 11 per cent in EU-24. Lithuania, Poland and Estonia are again countries most affected by severe and extreme poverty, with three quarters of Lithuanians and two thirds of Poles and Estonians living below 50 per cent of the EU median and more than every second citizen in these countries living below 40 per cent of EU median income. Italy remains still below the respective EU-24 average, but it is affected by severe and extreme poverty twice as frequently as other western countries in the study.

The same result is obtained when poverty is expressed in absolute terms, having 10 or 5 Euro per day per person. Lithuania, Poland and Estonia again are shown to be the most affected, followed by Italy, while in other western countries the relative numbers of the poor are much lower. In Lithuania 40 per cent of the population and in Poland and Estonia more than 25 per cent live on 10 Euro or less per day.

Because of the different population size of particular countries, their share in the overall European poor population is different (see Table 2.5). Poland contributes heavily, while the impact of poverty in Lithuania and

Estonia is much less substantial in terms of the extent of the poor population in the whole European Union. Significantly, the impact of poverty in Poland is higher with the lower poverty threshold: while Poles constitute 16 per cent of the European population living on 60 per cent of EU median income, their share rises to 44 per cent among those living on 5 Euro per day. Whereas the same tendency is observed in Lithuania and Estonia, in the western countries studied the tendency is reversed: the lower the poverty threshold, the lower the share of the country in the overall European poor population.

Bearing in mind that child poverty very frequently results from parents' poverty, it is expected that children are most vulnerable to poverty in Lithuania, Poland and Estonia. On the other hand, in Finland and Germany children are expected to be better protected from poverty.

## EXTENT AND DETERMINANTS OF CHILD
## POVERTY IN SELECTED EU MEMBER STATES

Though poverty is painful and limits life opportunities at every age, it is particularly devastating in childhood. This is because poverty harms the individuals' development and also impacts on their relations with others in later life stages. There is no doubt that the family is the most important mediator of poverty transmission but, in the case of children, intervention by the state in the form of family benefits and institutions such as preschool, school, social assistance and health care can contribute strongly to reducing the damage of poverty to the individuals' intellectual and emotional development.

Among the countries in the study, Finland can be said to be the most children-friendly country, while Poland and Lithuania are the least. In Finland, the at-risk-of-poverty rate for children is low and lower than that for the total population (see Table 2.6). Yet the child poverty rates in Poland (29 per cent), Lithuania (27 per cent) and Bulgaria (18 per cent) are high and much higher than that for the total population. Germany, Italy and the United Kingdom differ in that in Germany, the child poverty rate—lower than average for the EU-27—is slightly higher than for the total population, whereas in Estonia, Italy and the United Kingdom higher poverty rates for children correspond with relatively moderate risks of poverty for children. Widespread poverty among children in Poland and Lithuania is accompanied by the highest child poverty intensity in the EU, or in other words, the highest poverty severity (see Table 2.7); the median equivalized income for poor children is 33 points lower than the national poverty threshold, as compared with 12 points lower in Finland and 23 points for the EU-25. Among the countries in the study, apart from Poland and Lithuania, also Bulgaria, Estonia and Italy belong to the cluster of countries with a high degree of poverty among children and a high median poverty gap for youngsters, higher than for the total population of the poor in these countries. Germany resembles Finland, and the United Kingdom differs in that a high risk-of-poverty rate among children is accompanied by a low poverty gap.

Children living in different household types are differently at risk of poverty (see Table 2.8). Those within lone parent and large families with more than three children suffer from poverty much more frequently than those having no more than one sibling and living with two adult persons. This applies to each country in the study. However, Finland performs best, in comparison with other PROFIT countries and the EU-25 average, regardless of household type. Germany is the second best performer, but the child poverty rate in lone parent families is higher there, though still below EU-25 average. Protection for children in lone parent families is worst in Lithuania, Poland and Estonia, and this also applies to large families in Lithuania and Poland.

However, differences in household structures in the countries under scrutiny result in different proportions of children living in various households (see Table 2.9). For instance, among poor children in Poland, those living in lone parent households are very heavily affected by poverty (poverty rate = 46 per cent) but their share (8 per cent) in the poor children population is the lowest in the EU-25, outdistanced only by Greece where children in lone parent households amount to 7 per cent of poor children. On the other hand, the poverty rate of children in lone parent families in Germany (33 per cent) is substantially lower than in Poland, although in Germany children from this type of household make up half of all poor children. Therefore, it is useful to examine whether countries differ as to how many children in different household types are overrepresented among poor children as compared to the proportion of children in these household types among all children in the country.

The analysis (see Table 2.10) confirms that in each country in the study child poverty affects lone parent and large family households. In Germany, Estonia and Lithuania the relative number of poor children in lone parent families is twice as high as it should be relative to the number of such children among all children. In Finland, Italy, Lithuania and Poland the number of poor children in lone parent households is 60 per cent higher than it should be relative to the share of children in such household types among all children, and in the United Kingdom it is 80 per cent higher.

Poor children in large families with more than three children are mostly overrepresented in Poland, Lithuania and Italy where their relative number among poor children is fifty points higher than it should be accordingly to the proportion of poor children among all children in the respective countries. Therefore, irrespective of the relative number of children living in lone parent and large families in each country in the study, the poor children living there are overrepresented.

Children are poor owing to low income of their families. However, sources of income of poor households differ substantially in countries in the study (see Table 2.11). While in Finland, Germany and the United Kingdom less than half of income comes from work, in Italy it amounts to 78 per cent and in Lithuania and Poland more than 60 per cent. This indicates that in the latter countries in-work poverty is widespread, while in the former countries jobless households are among the poor. It can be noted that in the United Kingdom more than two thirds of children in jobless households and nearly half in Germany live in lone parent families.

Family benefits are the second most important source of income for poor households with children. But again countries differ substantially in their contribution to total income. While in Estonia, Finland, Germany and the United Kingdom family benefit contributes 21–27 per cent to the total income, in Italy, Poland and Lithuania it is 6–12 per cent.

In Poland, Lithuania, Estonia and Italy, grandparents seem to support poor children financially, since pension income is a third income source for poor households in these countries. This may take the form of living together in the same household with grandchildren and their parent(s), which is the case in Poland, where every fourth poor child lives in a complex household, or it may be living apart, as seems to be the case in Lithuania where every eleventh poor child lives in a complex household.

Children living in jobless households, whether with one or two adults, suffer most from poverty as compared to children living with working adults (see Table 2.12).

In each country the increase in work intensity lowers the child poverty rate. But even if the lone parent works full time, poverty still affects more than every third child in Lithuania, every fourth in Estonia and every fifth in Poland. In the same countries full-time work of one adult and part-time work of another are not enough to protect one quarter of children in such households from poverty. Yet in the western countries studied this limits poverty among children substantially. Two full-time workers in Estonia and Lithuania, as in Finland, Germany, Italy and the United Kingdom are able to protect children from poverty more effectively, while in Poland 14 per cent of youngsters in such families still live in poverty. In-work child poverty increases with the number of children in the household (see Table 2.13). Families with two full-time workers and no more than two children are able to keep above the poverty threshold. This also applies to families with three or more children in Finland, Germany, Italy and Estonia. However, in Poland (30 per cent) and Lithuania (27 per cent) more than a quarter of children in multi-children families are not kept out of poverty, even though there are two full-time workers.

The impact of social transfers measured as a percentage of the reduction in the poverty rate once social benefits (excluding pensions) were taken into account differs in the countries studied. In each country social transfers reduce the poverty risk for both the overall population and children (see Table 2.14). In the EU-24 countries the reduction for children (44 per cent) is higher than for the total population (34 per cent). This applies to each country in the study with the exception of Poland where the reduction for the overall population is higher than for children. In Finland the social transfers (excluding pensions) alleviate child poverty by 68 per cent, in Germany by 55 per cent and in the United Kingdom by 50 per cent. The reduction in child poverty is lowest in Bulgaria (19 per cent), Lithuania (21 per cent), Italy (23 per cent) and Poland (26 per cent).

The authors of the report 'Child Poverty and Well-Being in the EU' (European Commission 2008a) have clustered EU Member States in four categories of determinants of child poverty, and it can be seen that the countries in our study are represented in all clusters. The report clusters countries according to three criteria: joblessness, in-work poverty and the impact of transfers:

- Group A: these countries 'reach relatively **good child poverty outcomes by performing well on all 3 fronts.** They combine relatively good labour market performance of parents (low levels of joblessness and in-work poverty among households with children) with relatively high and effective social transfers' (p. 48).
- Group B: these countries 'achieve relatively good to below average poverty outcomes. The main matter of concern in these countries is the **high numbers of children living in jobless households'** (p. 48).
- Group C: these countries 'record average or just below-average child poverty outcomes, despite **a combination of high levels of joblessness and in-work poverty among parents'** (p. 48).
- Group D: these countries 'record relatively high levels of child poverty . . . While they have low shares of children living in jobless households, they experience **very high levels of in-work poverty among families . . .** In these countries (apart from LU), **the level and efficiency of social spending are among the lowest in the EU'** (p. 48).

Of the countries in our study (see Table 2.15) Finland is classified in group A, Germany and Estonia in group B, the United Kingdom in group C and Italy, Lithuania and Poland in group D.

Comparing monetary poverty with economic deprivation in particular countries, the report on 'Child Poverty and Well-Being in the EU' (European Commission 2008a) underlines that more than 60 per cent of the poor in Lithuania, Poland and Estonia are concurrently deprived in economic terms. Thus, for instance, under the heading of 'Economic strain and enforced lack of durables', the following two sets of items are grouped together:

- Could not afford (if wanted to):
  - to face unexpected expenses
  - one week annual holiday away from home
  - to pay for arrears (mortgage or rent, utility bills or hire purchase installments)
  - a meal with meat, chicken or fish every second day
  - to keep the home adequately warm
- Enforced lack of:
  - Washing machine
  - Colour TV
  - Telephone
  - Family car (European Commission, 2008a: 51)

Comparing the overall population with households with children, it becomes clear that in each country in the study the percentage of children living in households that are concurrently monetarily poor and deprived in economic terms is higher than among the overall population. Also, the differences between countries are considerable. In Finland and Germany 6–8 per cent of children live under such conditions, while in the United Kingdom, Italy and Estonia the proportion is 13–16 per cent and in Lithuania and Poland 25 per cent (see Table 2.16).

Key results of the comparisons between eight European countries allow the assumption that in Poland and Lithuania the transmission of poverty across generations is most likely, while in Finland and Germany it is the least likely. Thus, we want to consider whether the results of studies at the level of medium-sized towns confirm this conclusion.

## INTERGENERATIONAL TRANSMISSION OF POVERTY AT THE MESO-LEVEL: THE CASE OF EIGHT EUROPEAN TOWNS

When the analysis of statistical evidence at the national level was aimed at a better understanding of the connection between child and youth poverty and its socio-economic background, our series of case studies conducted in medium-sized towns in eight countries (see Table 2.17) focused on achieving a deeper insight into the specificity of poverty reproduction at the level of the local community and its political context. Thus, the question to answer was whether and how the composition of social problems and the welfare regime at the national level influence the situation and life opportunities of children and young people. Furthermore, special attention was paid to the specific age cohort (25- to 29-year-olds), assuming that their representatives were particularly vulnerable to becoming 'victims' of deep social changes occurring in all eight countries and towns[5]. In each town, surveys among young adults were conducted. The main aim of the study was 'to estimate the incidence of intergenerational inheritance of inequalities and reveal its correlates. Randomly selected samples covered 130–250 young persons in each town (altogether 1680 respondents)' (see Table 2.18 and Rokicka 2007)[6].

It has to be underlined that, although many studies on social inequality and social mobility do exist, in this analysis a subjective measure of social status was applied. It was composed of two variables: the respondent's assessment of the parental family's or household's material situation and his/her current family/household material situation[7].

The analysis of survey data led to distinguishing correlates of poverty inheritance (see: Rokicka 2007), such as low education of father (VC = 0.20, p = 0.000), mother (VC = 0.18, p = 0.000) and respondent VC = 0.22, p = 0.000), frequent unemployment experienced by respondent's parents (VC = 0.22, p = 0.000), being supported at school due to financial hardship (VC = 0.15, p = 0.000) or poor housing at time of childhood (VC = 0.18, p = 0.000). Every fourth respondent among those inheriting poverty mentioned poor housing in childhood, as compared to every fifteenth among the whole population under study. Apart from poor housing, the previously listed factors are also important correlates of youth poverty revealed by national statistics and cross-country comparisons. Unfortunately, due to small samples in some towns, we were not able to examine similarities and differences in correlates of intergenerational inheritance of the low economic position between towns.

Another crucial question was the life opportunity structure available for young adults of different socio-economic origins. Hence, the measure of exchange mobility in particular town subsamples was implemented. However, it is well-known that exchange mobility is influenced by contextual factors, such as general changes in the social structure (e.g. changes as a result of the transition from industrial to postindustrial society) or the rate of economic growth. In order to reduce this influence, an odds ratio analysis was applied. This measure seems to be particularly useful when comparing the chance of certain events happening among two groups or categories. When the chance equals one, the event is equally likely in both groups. An odds ratio greater than one implies that the event is more likely in the first group; an odds ratio less than one implies that the event is less likely in the first group. It 'indicates the opportunity disparity that individuals with different origins face, and it is an index of the degree of social rigidity in society' (Farina and Savaglio 2006: 74); thus, the results of the odds ratio analysis was to show correlations between parents' and respondents' education (as one of the most crucial correlates of poverty), while the subjectively evaluated economic position suggests that inequality of opportunities remains a problem in the towns under study.

As shown in Table 2.19, people whose fathers had tertiary education were much more likely to achieve it themselves than those whose fathers only had a low or medium level of education. It seems that the chance of upward educational mobility in Pernik (Bulgaria) and Tomaszów (Poland) are particularly low, whereas Giessen (Germany) and Pori (Finland) seem to offer their young inhabitants more equal opportunity structures.

The *odds ratio* presented in Table 2.20 shows the probability of pursuing low economic status as compared with the probability of becoming poor among those who grew up in families with decent and high economic status. In all eight towns it is more probable that those growing up in poor families stay poor as adults than fall into poverty when born in relatively well-off families. Children born in families of low economic status as compared to those born in decent economic status families are in Giessen 2.2 times more likely and in Loughborough 6.5 times more likely to be poor as young adults. Poor children as compared with those originating from high economic status families are in Pori 5.6 times and in Loughborough 51 times more likely to be poor in their twenties.

Although young adults originating from families of different educational and economic background have different chances of attaining medium and high positions in both dimensions, there are substantial differences between particular towns. Parnu (Estonia) is the only town where the odds of being poor in early adulthood are the same for those originating from families of low and decent economic status. Loughborough (United Kingdom), followed by Tomaszów (Poland) and Pernik (Bulgaria) could be situated at the opposite end of the spectrum, as the probability of remaining poor for those born poor is many times more likely there than for those originating in more affluent families.

If we compare the odds ratio for a given town with the average for all studied towns, two clusters can be distinguished: one is composed of towns with an odds ratio lower than average and comprising Parnu (Estonia), Giessen (Germany), Pori (Finland), Jonava (Lithuania). The second is composed of towns with an odds ratio higher than average and comprising Loughborough (United Kingdom), Tomaszów Maz (Poland), Pernik (Bulgaria) and Rovigo (Italy).

In Parnu (Estonia) the parental economic status does not affect the odds of becoming poor for young adults who were born poor and born in families with a decent economic status, while in Pori (Finland) and Giessen (Germany) the probability of becoming poor for those born poor as compared to those who grew up in more affluent families is the lowest among the towns studied.

It has been assumed in the PROFIT project that inheritance of inequalities/poverty means the transmission of different kinds of disadvantages between parents and children resulting in low mobility flows of children born in low status families. Nevertheless, external intervention, in the form of specific welfare measures and children's internal abilities, like outstanding performance in school, may contribute to breaking the low status/poverty cycle.

## CONCLUSION

Although there are serious limitations in terms of the comparability of the presented data and many methodological limitations to be taken into consideration, some important conclusions can be drawn from the juxtaposition of statistical evidence at the national level and outcomes of small-scale survey research conducted at the level of deliberately selected local communities.

The risk of youth disadvantage can be observed at the national as well as at the local level in countries under scrutiny, but accessible data show that this differs between countries, with Finland predicted to be the best and Bulgaria, Poland, Italy, Lithuania and Estonia predicted to be the worst performers.

The risk of poverty reproduction is correlated with social welfare regimes represented by particular countries: Finland, in practising preventative measures, is effective in reducing poverty among children and the risk of the intergeneration inheritance of inequalities seems to be limited there to particular people or small groups suffering from specific deficits.

Germany, following the rules of the continental social regime, protects the majority of children from poverty relatively well. However, there are some 'pockets of poverty and social exclusion' which are beyond the effective protection of this affluent state. They are composed of immigrants who even in the second and third generation were unable to find a place in the labour market, having low educational qualifications.

The United Kingdom, following the priorities of New Labour, has shown progress in mitigating child poverty and improving education. However, a large proportion of all children still live below the poverty line. In the midst of an affluent society, deprived areas continue to exist which are populated by those who are not able to operate in the labour market.

Italy is the relatively most endangered western country in this study in terms of the intergeneration inheritance of inequalities resembling to some extent the situation in post-socialist countries. However, it is known that regional differentiations in Italy are very significant.

The risk of intergeneration inheritance of inequalities has to be of particular concern in post-socialist countries which are poor and cannot offer sufficient support to families with children. The results of the survey conducted with young adults in eight European towns may help clarify not only the mechanisms of intergenerational inheritance of social inequalities, but also the role and influence of social protection and institutional support systems at the local level, which are, to a large extent, shaped by the welfare regimes in particular countries. The highest range of upward social mobility could be observed in those towns/countries, which were previously identified as the best in fighting child poverty.

## NOTES

1. Research project PROFIT (Policy Responses Overcoming Factors in the Intergenerational Transmission of Inequalities) funded by 6th Framework Program (Contract No CIT2-CIT-2004–506245), was carried out in Bulgaria, Estonia, Finland, Germany, Italy, Lithuania, Poland and United Kingdom (www.profit.uni.lodz.pl).

2. The PROFIT project was coordinated by University of Łódź, Poland.
3. 'Income in the EU is the sum of equivalised household disposable income, measured in PPP terms in the 24 Member States covered' (European Commission 2007c: 73).
4. 'Once differences in prices levels are taken into account, EUR 670 is equivalent, to take the extremes, to EUR 507 in Denmark and EUR 1390 in Poland, while in Greece, it is equivalent to EUR 818, with the levels in the new Member States being in between the Polish and Greek levels, though in most cases closer to the former than the latter, and the level in Portugal being similar to that in Greece'(European Commission 2007c: 73).
5. In the 1990s, when the young adults were teenagers (hence, at the turning point of their educational career) Giessen (Germany), Loughborough (United Kingdom), Rovigo (Italy) and Pori (Finland) were dealing with deindustrialization, whereas Parnu (Estonia), Pernik (Bulgaria), Jonava (Lithuania) and Tomaszów Mazowiecki (Poland) were bearing the expenses of systemic transformation from state socialism to market society and political independence.
6. 'Young people aged 25–29 were asked about their childhood, school times and present situation to achieve insight into the policy impact on the life course of individuals living in the studied towns. Selection of respondents 25–29 year-olds was a consequence of the third assumption of the project, namely that the start of adulthood is a very important moment in the life course cycle of an individual determining future outcomes and occupational careers. This age cohort is very interesting for research purposes because it was the first generation entering adulthood in times of deepening changes in social structure of European societies marked by changing social mobility paths and uncertainty concerning professional and private life. They are at the beginning of their biographies as adults and at this point in the life cycle, nothing is definitive. But, with caution, it is possible to predict their future achievements' (Rokicka 2007).
7. Although '(t)here is a long-standing controversy in social indicators research about the advantages and disadvantages of "objective" and "subjective" approaches to measuring quantities of interest' (Rokicka 2007) following reasons decided about using both subjective and objective measures of social position: the researcher has to rely on respondents' memory when asking for 'objective' information, especially on his/her and parents' income (see the discussion in Veenhoven 2001). 'Ravallion and Lokshin [1999] show that total household income is a significant predictor of the answer to the subjective welfare question, although its explanatory power is lower ( . . . ). Only subjective indicators allow for truly comprehensive assessments of social position. Objective indicators can best assess details, but 'are typically less helpful in charting the whole' [Veenhoven 2001: 12]. One can objectively measure a person's income situation, accommodation, health status, social relations and so on, but there is no guiding rule on how to combine these pieces of information. Many of these problems can be avoided if people themselves, as experts, make an overall judgment of their lives [Delhey 2004] (Rokicka 2007).

## REFERENCES

European Commission (2007a) 'Tackling Child Poverty and Promoting the Social Inclusion of Children in the EU'. http://ec.europa.eu/employment_social/spsi/docs/social_inclusion/experts_reports/synthesis1_2007_en.pdf (accessed 6 January 2009).

European Commission (2007b) 'The Social Situation in the European Union'. http://ec.europa.eu/employment_social/spsi/docs/social_situation/ssr2007_en.pdf (accessed 6 January 2009).

European Commission (2007c) 'Social Inclusion and Income Distribution in the European Union: Monitoring Report'. http://ec.europa.eu/employment_social/spsi/reports_and_papers_en.htm (accessed 6 January 2009).

European Commission (2008a) 'Child Poverty and Well-Being in the EU: Current Status and Way Forward'. http://ec.europa.eu/employment_social/publications/2008/ke3008251_en.pdf (accessed 6 January 2009).

European Commission (2008b) 'Joint Report on Social Protection and Social Inclusion'. http://ec.europa.eu/employment_social/spsi/joint_reports_en.htm#2008 (accessed 6 January 2009).

Farina, F. and Savaglio E. (2006) *Inequality and Economic Integration* (London: Routledge).

Frazer, H. and Marlier, E. (2007) *Tackling Child Poverty and Promoting the Social Inclusion of Children in the EU: Key Lessons Synthesis* (Vienna: Peer Review and Assessment in Social Inclusion, European Commission).

OECD (2008) 'Growing Unequal? Income Distribution and Poverty in OECD Countries'.

Rokicka, E. (2007) 'Young Adults At Risk: Incidence of Inheritance of Low Economic Status and Constrains of Social Mobility', *Przeglad Socjologiczny*, Vol. LVI/2.

UNICEF Innocenti Research Centre (2007) 'Child Poverty in Perspective: An Overview of Child Well-Being in Rich Countries. A Comprehensive Assessment of the Lives and Well-Being of Children and Adolescents in the Economically Advanced Nations'. Innocenti Report Card 7, http://unicef-icdc.org/publications/pdf/rc7_eng.pdf (accessed 6 January 2009).

## APPENDIX

*Table 2.1*    Values of Different Inequality Indices in 2004 in PROFIT Project Participants

|  | *Gini* | *P90/P10* | *S80/S20* |
|---|---|---|---|
| Estonia | 0.334 | 4.455 | 5.543 |
| Finland | 0.249 | 2.906 | 3.478 |
| Germany | 0.267 | 3.204 | 3.915 |
| Italy | 0.324 | 4.126 | 5.366 |
| Lithuania | 0.359 | 5.271 | 6.599 |
| Poland | 0.352 | 5.122 | 6.446 |
| United Kingdom | 0.331 | 4.185 | 5.305 |
| Sweden—the most equal | 0.225 | 2.622 | 3.156 |
| Portugal—the most unequal | 0.412 | 6.003 | 7.950 |

Excerpts from: Social Inclusion and Income Distribution, Monitoring Report, 2007, Table A1, p. 30.

*Table 2.2*  Poverty Rates by Age (60%> National Median Equivalized Income)

|  | Population aged 0–15 | Population aged 0–17* | Population aged 16–64 | Population aged 65+ | Total population* |
|---|---|---|---|---|---|
| Bulgaria |  | 18.0 |  |  |  |
| Estonia | 24.5 | 21.0 | 19.0 | 16.3 | 18.0 |
| Finland | 11.1 | 10.0 | 10.2 | 12.3 | 12.0 |
| Germany | 12.4 | 12.0 | 11.4 | 14.6 | 12.0 |
| Italy | 21.2 | 24.0 | 15.4 | 22.2 | 19.0 |
| Lithuania | 27.1 | 27.0 | 19.7 | 13.8 | 21.0 |
| Poland | 30.9 | 29.0 | 22.4 | 8.1 | 21.0 |
| United Kingdom | 21.8 | 22.0 | 14.9 | 25.9 | 19.0 |

Excerpts from: Social Inclusion and Income Distribution, Monitoring Report, 2007, Table 4, p. 55; * from The Social Situation in the EU, 2007, Table 6.1a, p. 208 (SILC 2006).

*Table 2.3*  Composition of Poor Population in Given Countries

|  | Children | Working age | Elderly | Total poor population N = 100% |
|---|---|---|---|---|
| Estonia | 19.0 | 63.0 | 19.0 | 243,000 |
| Finland | 16.0 | 59.0 | 25.0 | 604,000 |
| Germany | 15.0 | 63.0 | 22.0 | 10,632,000 |
| Italy | 18.0 | 58.0 | 23.0 | 11,084,000 |
| Lithuania | 24.0 | 63.0 | 13.0 | 699,000 |
| Poland | 25.0 | 70.0 | 5.0 | 7,595,000 |
| United Kingdom | 23.0 | 52.0 | 24.0 | 9,353,000 |

Table created using graphs in: Social Inclusion and Income Distribution, Monitoring Report, 2007, p. 59–69.

*Table 2.4*  People Living Below Given EU Poverty Lines (% in each country)

|  | Poverty line relative to EU median income* | | | | |
|---|---|---|---|---|---|
|  | <60% | <50% | <40% | €10 a day | €5 a day |
| Estonia | 76.0 | 66.0 | 51.0 | 26.4 | 5.2 |
| Finland | 6.0 | <5.0 | <3.0 | 0.5 | 0.1 |
| Germany | 8.0 | <5.0 | <3.0 | 1.0 | 0.4 |
| Italy | 16.0 | 10.0 | 6.0 | 3.1 | 1.5 |
| Lithuania | 83.0 | 75.0 | 60.0 | 39.5 | 10.3 |
| Poland | 78.0 | 67.0 | 52.0 | 27.5 | 7.0 |
| United Kingdom | 9.0 | <5.0 | <3.0 | 2.0 | 0.9 |
| EU-25* | 22.5 | 16.0 | 11.0 | 5.2 | 1.5 |

Source: Social Inclusion and Income Distribution, Monitoring Report, 2007, Figure 1.

*Table 2.5* Division of People with Income Below Poverty Line at EU Level, 2004 (% of EU population below poverty line)

| | Poverty line relative to EU median income* | | | | |
|---|---|---|---|---|---|
| | <60% | <50% | <40% | €10 a day | €5 a day |
| Estonia | 0.6 | 1.0 | 1.2 | 1.4 | 1.5 |
| Finland | 0.9 | 0.3 | 0.2 | 0.1 | 0.1 |
| Germany | 13.0 | 6.7 | 4.7 | 3.6 | 3.6 |
| Italy | 11.7 | 9.1 | 7.9 | 7.4 | 7.6 |
| Lithuania | 1.5 | 2.8 | 3.6 | 4.5 | 5.7 |
| Poland | 15.9 | 29.0 | 34.6 | 39.8 | 44.2 |
| United Kingdom | 7.6 | 7.6 | 3.3 | 2.8 | 3.2 |
| EU-25* N = 100% | 100,000,000 | | | 23,758 | 6,898 |

* Household income equivalized for differences in household size and composition and shared equally between members, expressed in PPS terms in each country.
Excerpts from: Social Inclusion and Income Distribution, 2007, Table 1, p. 76.

*Table 2.6* Typology of EU countries: National child poverty rates vs. EU child poverty vs. overall national poverty rates (2005)

| | Children are at lower risk than (or equal to)the overall population | Children have a higher risk of poverty than the overall population (=<5pp) | Children have a significantly higher risk than the overall population (>5pp) |
|---|---|---|---|
| Child poverty is below EU average | DK, **FI**, SE, CY, SI | BE, **DE**, FR, NL, AT | CZ |
| Child poverty is above (or equal to) EU average | EL | ES, **IT, PT,** IE, **UK,** EE, LV | BG, HU, **LT, LU, MT, PL,** RO, SK |

Source: Child poverty and well-being in the EU, 2008, Table 1 p. 13.

*Table 2.7* Typology of EU Countries: National Child Poverty Rates vs. EU Child Poverty vs. Child Poverty Gap

| At-risk-of poverty intensity | At-risk-of-poverty headcount | | |
|---|---|---|---|
| | LOW | MEDIUM | HIGH |
| Low | DK, DE, FR, CY, AT, SI, FI, SE | CZ, LU, HU | MT, UK |
| Medium | NL | BE | EL, IE, RO |
| High | | SK | BG, EE, ES, IT, LV, LT, PL, PT |

Own elaboration based on Joint Report on Social Protection and Social Inclusion [2007]. Supporting Document, Annex 1C Table 1b (SILC [2005]), Income reference 2004. In countries marked grey poverty gap for children is higher than for total population.
Notes: Member States are classified as having a medium at-risk-of-poverty headcount (or rate) and at-risk-of poverty intensity (or gap) if the corresponding figure is respectively within +/- 1 point from the EU average

*Table 2.8*   At-risk-of poverty rates of children (%) by type of household, EU-25, 2005

| | All children | Lone parent | Couple with | | | Complex hh with children |
| | | | 1 child | 2 children | 3+ children | |
|---|---|---|---|---|---|---|
| Estonia | 21 | 44 | 13 | 13 | 26 | 16 |
| Finland | 10 | 21 | 7 | 5 | 12 | 13 |
| Germany | 14 | 33 | 10 | 7 | 14 | 7 |
| Italy | 24 | 38 | 15 | 21 | 35 | 24 |
| Lithuania | 27 | 57 | 14 | 18 | 44 | 16 |
| Poland | 29 | 46 | 17 | 23 | 47 | 26 |
| United Kingdom | 21 | 38 | 9 | 12 | 27 | 15 |
| EU-25 | 19 | 34 | 12 | 14 | 25 | 20 |

Excerpts from: Child poverty and well-being in the EU.2008. Table A2, p.145

*Table 2.9*   Distribution of poor children by type of households (%), EU-25, 2005

| | Lone parent | Couple with | | | Complex hh with children |
| | | 1 child | 2 children | 3+ children | |
|---|---|---|---|---|---|
| Estonia | 37 | 11 | 17 | 22 | 13 |
| Finland | 27 | 11 | 17 | 40 | 5 |
| Germany | 48 | 11 | 18 | 20 | 3 |
| Italy | 11 | 12 | 41 | 22 | 14 |
| Lithuania | 30 | 9 | 22 | 29 | 9 |
| Poland | 8 | 9 | 24 | 34 | 25 |
| United Kingdom | 44 | 6 | 19 | 26 | 5 |
| EU-25 | 23 | 10 | 28 | 27 | 11 |

Excerpts from: Child poverty and well-being in the EU.2008. Table A6a, p.150

*Table 2.10* Distribution of Poor Children as Compared with Distribution of all Children by Type of Household

|  | Lone parent | Couple with | | 3+ children | Complex hh with children |
|---|---|---|---|---|---|
|  |  | 1 child | 2 children |  |  |
| Estonia | 2.1 | 0.6 | 0.9 | 1.2 | 0.8 |
| Finland | 1.6 | 0.7 | 0.5 | 1.2 | 1.2 |
| Germany | 2.3 | 0.8 | 0.5 | 1.0 | 0.6 |
| Italy | 1.6 | 0.6 | 0.9 | 1.5 | 0.9 |
| Lithuania | 2.1 | 0.5 | 0.6 | 1.6 | 0.6 |
| Poland | 1.6 | 0.6 | 0.7 | 1.6 | 0.9 |
| United Kingdom | 1.8 | 0.4 | 0.6 | 1.3 | 0.7 |
| EU-25 | 1.8 | 0.6 | 0.7 | 1.3 | 1.0 |

Own calculations based on: Child poverty and well-being in the EU.2008. Table A6a and table A8a

*Table 2.11* Distribution of Gross Income by Main Sources of Income for poor households with children, %, EU-25, 2005

|  | Work income | Unempl benefits | Family allowance | Social exclusion | Housing allowances | Pension income | Sickness And disability | Other |
|---|---|---|---|---|---|---|---|---|
| Estonia | 52.2 | 0.8 | 27.7 | 0.1 | 2.7 | 5.8 | 6.9 | 3.8 |
| Finland | 34.4 | 17.2 | 24.2 | 4.7 | 8.4 | 1.1 | 4.7 | 5.3 |
| Germany | 47.5 | 12.2 | 22.4 | 4.5 | 3.7 | 1.3 | 1.5 | 6.9 |
| Italy | 77.8 | 2.5 | 6.0 | 0.3 | 0.4 | 5.5 | 2.4 | 5.1 |
| Lithuania | 61.2 | 1.0 | 11.8 | 4.9 | 0.6 | 9.2 | 6.2 | 5.1 |
| Poland | 64.0 | 3.5 | 9.9 | 1.2 | 1.2 | 9.1 | 8.5 | 2.6 |
| United Kingdom | 41.5 | 1.9 | 21.0 | 17.7 | 11.7 | 1.1 | 2.6 | 2.5 |
| EU-25 | 54.9 | 6.9 | 15.8 | 6.3 | 5.3 | 3.2 | 3.3 | 4.3 |

Excerpts from: Child poverty and well being in the EU. 2008.Table 6, p.28

Table 2.12   At-Risk-of-Poverty Rates of Children by Type of Household and Work Type of Adults in the Household, EU-25, 2005

| | Lone parent | | | Couple with children | | | | |
|---|---|---|---|---|---|---|---|---|
| | Jobless | Part-time only | 1 Full time | Jobless | Part-time only | 1 Full-time | 1 Full- time + part-time | 2 Full-time |
| Estonia | 82 | 41 | 28 | 94 | 51 | 23 | 25 | 6 |
| Finland | 53 | 30 | 8 | 64 | 38 | 17 | 7 | 3 |
| Germany | 68 | 23 | 13 | 64 | 20 | 10 | 4 | 3 |
| Italy | 77 | 47 | 19 | 81 | 68 | 33 | 5 | 5 |
| Lithuania | 89 | 89 | 37 | 87 | 59 | 46 | 25 | 9 |
| Poland | 77 | 66 | 22 | 77 | 71 | 39 | 28 | 14 |
| United Kingdom | 66 | 31 | 13 | 63 | 37 | 22 | 8 | 7 |
| EU-25 | 65 | 30 | 15 | 73 | 37 | 25 | 7 | 7 |

Excerpts from: Child poverty and well being in the EU. 2008. Table A14a-bis, p.168

Table 2.13  At-Risk-of-Poverty Rates of Children by Type of Household and Work Type of Adults of the Household, Couples with Children, EU-25, 2005

| | Couple with 1 or 2 children | | | | | Couple with 3+ children | | | | |
|---|---|---|---|---|---|---|---|---|---|---|
| | Jobless | Part-time only | 1 Full-time + part-time | 1 Full-time | 2 Full-time | Jobless | Part-time only | 1 Full-time + part-time | 1 Full-time | 2 Full-time |
| Estonia | 93 | 52 | 18 | 20 | 5 | 94 | 47 | 33 | 38 | 8 |
| Finland | 59 | 29 | 11 | 7 | 1 | 71 | 57 | 25 | 7 | 5 |
| Germany | 58 | 19 | 7 | 4 | 3 | 73 | 26 | 13 | 3 | 0 |
| Italy | 78 | 63 | 29 | 5 | 4 | 91 | 100 | 48 | 5 | 9 |
| Lithuania | 81 | 50 | 38 | 17 | 5 | 100 | 78 | 60 | 39 | 27 |
| Poland | 71 | 57 | 29 | 23 | 8 | 86 | 89 | 54 | 41 | 30 |
| United Kingdom | 75 | 34 | 17 | 5 | 6 | 43 | 40 | 32 | 17 | 14 |
| EU-25 | 68 | 32 | 21 | 6 | 5 | 82 | 47 | 33 | 10 | 13 |

Excerpts from: Child poverty and well being in the EU. 2008 Table A14b-bis, p.169

*Table 2.14*   At-Risk-of-Poverty Rate Before and After Social Transfers: Impact of all Social Transfers (excluding pensions) on Poverty Risk for Children and for the Overall Population (reduction in poverty rate in % of poverty rate before social transfers), EU-25, 2005, p.170

|  | *Total population* | *Children aged 0–17* |
|---|---|---|
| Bulgaria | 17 | 19 |
| Estonia | 25 | 32 |
| Finland | 57 | 68 |
| Germany | 46 | 55 |
| Italy | 17 | 23 |
| Lithuania | 19 | 21 |
| Poland | 30 | 26 |
| United Kingdom | 42 | 50 |
| EU-25 | 38 | 44 |

Excerpts from: Child poverty and well-being in the EU. 2008. Table 15, p.170

*Table 2.15*   Relative Outcomes of Countries Related to Child Poverty Risk and Main Determinants of Child Poverty Risk

|  | *Child poverty risk outcomes* | *Joblessness: children living in jobless households* | *In-work poverty: children living in households confronted with in-work poverty* | *Impact of social transfers (cash benefits (excluding pensions) on child poverty* |
|---|---|---|---|---|
| Estonia | — | — | + | - |
| Finland | +++ | ++ | +++ | +++ |
| Germany | ++ | — | +++ | ++ |
| Italy | — | ++ | —— | —— |
| Lithuania | — | + | —— | —— |
| Poland | —— | - | —— | —— |
| United Kingdom | + | —— | - | + |
| Bulgaria | — | —- | : | : |

Excerpts from: Child poverty and well-being in the EU. 2008. Table 11a, p.47

*Table 2.16*  Proportion of Overall Population and of Population Aged 0–17 Being at Risk-of Poverty and Economically Deprived

|  | *Total population* | *Children 0–17* |
|---|---|---|
| Estonia | 13.27 | 15.75 |
| Finland | 5.68 | 6.09 |
| Germany | 6.86 | 8.09 |
| Italy | 11.31 | 15.32 |
| Lithuania | 18.5 | 24.83 |
| Poland | 17.8 | 25.39 |
| United Kingdom | 8.01 | 13.27 |

Excerpts from: Child poverty and well-being in the EU. 2008. Table 13, p.56

*Table 2.17*  Description of Towns

**Towns in the study**

| *Country* | *Town* | *Population* | *Unemployment (in %)* | *Ethnic minorities (in %)* |
|---|---|---|---|---|
| Poland | Tomaszów Mazowiecki | 67,218 | 23.9% | Less than 1% |
| Bulgaria | Pernik | 81,674 | 8.8% | 5–6% |
| Germany | Giessen | 72,519 | 10.9% | 13.3% |
| Estonia | Pärnu | 43,528 | 4.3% | 25% |
| Finland | Pori | 76,144 | 14.7% | 1.3% |
| Italy | Rovigo | 50,883 | 6.42% | 3.8% |
| Lithuania | Jonava | 34,800 | 6.8 % | 13.8% |
| United Kingdom | Loughborough | 55,492 | 4.9% | 10.8% |

Source: Drabowicz 2007, based on town description forms filled in by national research teams using information published on websites, statistical year books, official reports elaborated by local authorities for different purposes etc.

Table 2.18    Respondents in Towns Under Study (frequency and %)

|  |  | Number of respondents | | % of female |
|  |  | Frequency | % |  |
|---|---|---|---|---|
| FIN | Pori | 258 | 15,4 | 63,6 |
| ITA | Rovigo | 251 | 14,9 | 48,2 |
| EST | Pärnu | 163 | 9,7 | 60,1 |
| UK | Loughborough | 133 | 7,9 | 40,6 |
| LIT | Jonava | 134 | 8,0 | 56,0 |
| GER | Giessen | 241 | 14,3 | 42,7 |
| BUL | Pernik | 250 | 14,9 | 50,0 |
| PL | Tomaszow Maz. | 250 | 14,9 | 48,8 |
| Total |  | 1680 | 100,0 | 51,3 |

Table 2.19    Probability of Attaining High Education as Compared with Low among those whose Fathers Achieved High Education

| father's education | Highest education attained by father | | | | | | | |
|  | Pori (FI) | Rovigo (ITA) | Parnu (EE) | Loughborough (UK) | Jonava (LIT) | Giessen (DE) | Pernik (BG) | Tomaszów (PL) |
|---|---|---|---|---|---|---|---|---|
| medium | 0,6 | 1,2 | 1,7 | 0,8 | 3,3 | 0,4 | 5,6 | 3 |
| High | 1,8 | — | — | 2,3 | — | 1,2 | 81,4 | 35 |

Note: Rovigo, Parnu and Jonava were too small national samples for calculation .

Table 2.20    Probability of Pursuing of Low Economic Status (poverty) as Compared with Getting Poor among those Growing Up in Families with Decent and High Economic Status, by Towns—Too Small National Samples for Calculation

| Family economic status | Pori FI | Rovigo IT | Parnu EE | Loughborough UK | Jonava LT | Giessen DE | Pernik BG | Tomaszów PL | Total |
|---|---|---|---|---|---|---|---|---|---|
| Decent | 2.6 | 6.1 | 1.1 | 6.5 | 2.7 | 2.2 | 5.2 | 5.3 | 4.4 |
| High | 5.6 | — | — | 51.1 | — | 9.1 | 32.7 | 36.4 | 19.5 |

# 3 Youth Unemployment Policy in Britain and Germany

## A Comparison of 'Third Way' Approaches

*Jeremy Leaman*

### THE CONTEXT OF POLICY TO COMBAT YOUTH UNEMPLOYMENT

It should be superfluous to underscore the centrality of work/employment to human welfare and the particular importance of work and career expectations for all new entrants into the adult world of economic activity. Work is the defining mundane quality of human existence: 'it is a necessary condition, independent of all forms of society, for the existence of the human race; it is an eternal nature-imposed necessity, without which there can be no material exchanges between man and nature, and therefore no life' (Marx 1954: 50). Work is an ontological given, be it in the individualized form of appropriating use values from hunting and gathering to sustain the family, or in the collective form of the massively complex division of labour currently operating in the global economy, alongside the (predominantly unpaid) labour required to maintain the household and the local community.

History nevertheless reveals fundamental changes in the nature of work, in the division of labour, in the general rates of participation in paid work and the specific role of men, women, children, younger and older generations in this core economic activity. These changes have been most dramatic since the end of feudalism and the development of dynamic, capitalist forms of production and service provision. Before the advent of capitalism, the bulk of economic activity (80–90 per cent) was in agricultural production; by 1900 only 40 per cent of the working population was occupied in the agricultural sector of advanced countries; by the middle of the twentieth century British agricultural employment represented only 6 per cent of all civilian employment (Germany: 25 per cent, France: 32 per cent, Italy: 42 per cent), but in the next 30 years economic modernization produced a rapid downward convergence of primary sector employment in all advanced European economies.

What is also revealed in Table 3.1 is the supplanting of industrial employment by service sector employment as the dominant provider of paid work in the second half of the twentieth century. The drastic marginalization of agricultural employment between 1950 and 1980 was arguably cushioned by the persistence of full employment up until the early 1970s and the corresponding

*Table 3.1*    Sectoral Distribution of Employment in Britain, France, Germany and
Italy, 1950–2000

|  | Britain (%) | France (%) | Germany (%) | Italy (%) |
|---|---|---|---|---|
| **1950** | | | | |
| Primary | 6 | 32 | 25 | 42 |
| Secondary | 48 | 35 | 43 | 31 |
| Tertiary | 46 | 33 | 32 | 27 |
| **1980** | | | | |
| Primary | 3 | 9 | 6 | 14 |
| Secondary | 39 | 36 | 45 | 38 |
| Tertiary | 58 | 55 | 49 | 48 |
| **2000** | | | | |
| Primary | 1.5 | 1.4 | 2.7 | 5.4 |
| Secondary | 25.4 | 25.7 | 33.4 | 32.4 |
| Tertiary | 72.8 | 72.9 | 63.9 | 62.2 |

Source: Organisation for Economic Co-operation and Development (OECD).

ability of the secondary and tertiary sectors to absorb the millions of redundant agricultural workers. In contrast, the deindustrialization of employment, which began to accelerate in the 1980s, coincided with the emergence of increasingly stubborn structural unemployment; the expansion of service sector employment was significant but still unable to cushion the shock of the disappearance of millions of manufacturing jobs, notably in the branches commonly associated with the first industrial revolution: coal and steel, textiles, shipbuilding, heavy engineering. Thus the rate of unemployment in Europe[1] doubled from just 3.2 per cent in 1972 to 6.4 per cent in 1980, peaked at 10.8 per cent in 1986, receded below 10 per cent until the recessions of the early 1990s, exceeded ten per cent for six years (1993–1998), but then averaged 8.3 per cent in the ten years after 1998. The latest Organisation for Economic Co-operation and Development (OECD) forecasts, in the wake of the 2009 global recession, envisage a sharp rise of the rate of unemployment in the euro area to 10.1 per cent in 2009 and 11.7 per cent in 2010. Structural unemployment has thus become an economic given in virtually all economies.

The patterns of both employment and unemployment in advanced economies have thus altered dramatically since the 1970s, with very particular effects on the expectations of young people preparing for and entering the labour market. The career pathways that seemed to have become firmly established in the 'golden age' (Hobsbawm) of postwar reconstruction, consumerism and increasing affluence, suddenly became far less secure and predictable. The stereotypical progression of working-class school-leavers into skilled or semiskilled trades and of middle-class school-leavers into 'the professions' was disturbed by the reappearance of job insecurity; there emerged the now typical mismatch in all advanced economies of too many job seekers and too few vacancies.

The particular vulnerability of young people to the new competition for scarcer job opportunities was only properly acknowledged in the second half of the 1970s. For example, the German Federal Statistical Office only started including disaggregated data on youth unemployment in its 1978 edition of the Federal Republic's Statistical Yearbook. The context matched that of the United Kingdom (and other European states), namely the coincidence of economic crisis (stagflation) and the entry of the demographic 'bulge' of the 1950s onto national labour markets. The well-documented complacency of the German state in not preparing for the educational and employment implications of the baby-boom years was illustrated dramatically by the sudden and high proportion of young people (aged 15–25) as a percentage of total unemployment. In 1977, 29.3 per cent of Germany's 911,000 registered unemployed were in this age group. With the doubling of unemployment by 1982—a year of deep recession—this proportion had risen to a record 30.3 per cent (Statistisches Jahrbuch der Bundesrepublik 1978).

It was thus only in the late 1970s that youth unemployment became a distinctive problem, attracting the interest of academics and policymakers alike because of its worryingly disproportionate level. Since then it has become a predictable pattern within a global economy characterized by structural unemployment. The International Labour Organisation has calculated ratios of youth-to-adult unemployment rates in 1995 of 2.3 : 1 for developed economies, including the EU, and 2.6 : 1 for central and eastern European and CIS economies, ratios which remained unaltered through to 2005 (ILO 2006: 18). In the group of developed economies the disparity persisted despite an absolute decline in the youth population of 1.6 per cent over the same period (ibid.: 13).

The disadvantage of youth in the labour market is even more marked at the global level. ILO figures estimate the youth share of total global unemployment at 43.3 per cent in 2005 against a youth share of the total working age population of just 25 per cent (southeast Asia at 58.8 per cent and sub-Saharan Africa at 59.5 per cent are the crass extreme of this already critical phenomenon; see ILO 2006 ibid.).

The analysis in this chapter is informed above all by the assumption that the experience of employment and/or unemployment is a key causal factor in the determination of individual (and group) life careers, in particular in relation to the degree of mobility out of poverty and social exclusion. Recent studies by labour economists (Arulampalam 2001, Gregory and Jukes 2001, Gregg and Tominey 2004) have introduced the concept of 'scarring', i.e. the long-term manifestation of an earlier negative experience, most notably in subsequent levels of earnings and a greater likelihood of further spells of unemployment:

Joblessness leaves permanent scars on individuals. They not only lose income during periods of joblessness they are also further scarred by these experiences when they find employment. A spell of unemployment is found to carry a wage penalty of about 6% on re-entry in Britain, and after three years, they are earning 14% less compared to what they would have received in the absence of unemployment' (Arulampalam 2001).

Gregg and Tominey (2004), using the National Child Development Survey (NCDS) of children born in 1958, claim robust results of a wage scar of between 8 per cent and 15 per cent at 42 as a result of youth unemployment, depending on the incidence of repeat unemployment in between. Rhum (1991)—in a study involving control groups in the United States—claims a wage disadvantage as high as 25 per cent which is persistent, while the employment disadvantage recedes with time. While the causal link between youth unemployment and later disadvantage is demonstrable, a more refined analysis—involving the psychology, motivation and expectations of both workers and employers—cannot hope to be as robust. A qualitative analysis of the nexus of factors affecting the initial process of labour market integration would nevertheless seem to be vital for a better understanding of the problem of persistent poverty and the better formulation of a preventive social policy.

The causes of this chronic structural disparity in patterns of unemployment—as opposed to the causes of general unemployment—are a subject of some contention, but it is clear that there are differences which relate to the national and regional contexts as well as to the levels of overall economic development. For the purposes of this analysis, it is important to distinguish between demand-side and supply-side factors in order to explain why youth unemployment rates are higher than adult unemployment rates. This will allow a more adequate assessment of the policy contexts and policy challenges of Germany and the United Kingdom.

On the demand side, the *last-in/first-out explanation* is frequently deployed; this reflects, among other things, the employer's perception of the value of longer experience and of the investment cost of in-house training which makes the older worker more attractive than the new recruit. This is further reinforced by the provision of employment protection rights in collective or individual contracts which accrue with the length of tenure. The cost of letting the younger worker go is thus lower than in the case of older tenured workers, particularly if the younger worker is subject either to a probationary period and/or to a short-term contract.

On the supply side, the skills profile of the younger worker may not match the requirements of the employer, either formally in the portfolio of qualifications or informally in the proven ability demonstrated by references from previous employers. The ILO also cites the *shopping-around explanation* as a supply-side factor, denoting the propensity of younger entrants to the job market to wait for preferred career opportunities in the earlier stages of job seeking, as well as the *lack of mobility explanation* which affects new entrants that do not have the resources to relocate away from the parental home to seek employment and are therefore limited in their geographical scope.

If it were necessary to justify the preoccupation with youth unemployment, one could deploy the insights of individual psychology, social psychology, sociology, politics, political economy, demography, micro- and macro-economics, anthropology and cultural studies, to name the main fields of youth research. The other chapters in this volume illuminate a broad swathe of disciplinary approaches to the problems that derive in large measure from the relatively recent but persistent phenomenon of disproportionately high levels of joblessness among younger generations.

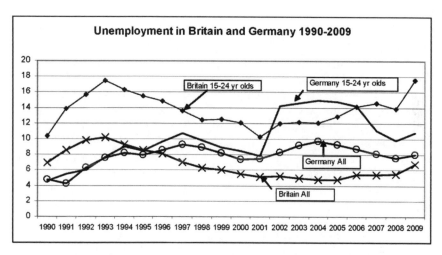

*Figure 3.1*   Unemployment in Britain and Germany, 1900–2009.
Sources: Eurostat, Organisation for Economic Co-operation and Development (OECD); ILO definition of unemployment; 2009 figures are for March.

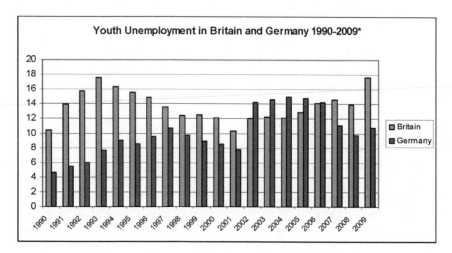

*Figure 3.2*   Youth unemployment in Britain and Germany, 1990–2009.
Source: Eurostat; ILO definition of unemployment; 2009 figures are for March.

The arguments most commonly deployed by policymakers include above all the security considerations of potentially delinquent young people without work.

Germany and Britain face similar challenges in relation to structural unemployment in general and youth unemployment in particular, as is shown by Figures 3.1 and 3.2; the United Kingdom's rate of youth unemployment since 1990 has been consistently higher than the rate of overall adult unemployment. Indeed, Britain's overall record of unemployment—which stayed below 5 per cent between 1999 and 2008—was widely regarded as a policy success story. Germany's pattern sees a parallel development of both youth and overall unemployment between 1990 and 2001 but then a less critical divergence in 2002, which has persisted, but with a narrowing of the gap since 2006 (Figure 3.1). However, the two countries have distinctive points of departure in terms of (a) the sectoral profiles of their economies, (b) the skill production regimes applying to new labour market entrants and (c) structural economic issues affecting the regional distribution of work.

As Table 3.1 shows, there is a significantly greater dependence of the UK economy on tertiary sector employment (72.8 per cent) compared to Germany (66.9 per cent)[2] and a correspondingly stronger presence of manufacturing and construction employment in Germany (33.4 per cent) compared to just 25.4 per cent in the United Kingdom. Secondly, German education and training is characterized by both institutional stratification—notably in the predominant three-tier school system—and by the long-standing formalized 'dual system' of skill-training, involving employer provision of some 1.8 million apprenticeships and parallel state-funded courses at further education colleges. In Britain, in contrast, state primary and secondary education are not tiered along vocational lines, but pursue general academic objectives centred around an extensive 'national curriculum'; apprenticeship training declined markedly in Britain after the Second World War reflecting both the predominance of 'Fordist' production methods and the marginalization of artisan trades on the one hand and the reluctance of British employers to invest in 'human capital' (Aldrich 1997: 71ff). The revival of apprenticeships has been almost entirely driven by UK government initiatives ('Modern Apprenticeships' [1994] organized by 'Sector Skill Councils' and the 'Learning and Skills Council'); the participation of employers in the United Kingdom is predicated on comprehensive state subsidies. The limited scope of this revitalized skills culture is evident in the modest ambitions of the Brown administration to reach a total of 250,000 apprenticeships by 2010 (as shown later). A third and significant distinction in the point of departure for current government policy in relation to youth unemployment is the very real issue of German unification in 1990 and the crass disparities this generated in the regional pattern of unemployment. The large scale deindustrialization of the five new eastern Länder in the early nineties produced not just an absolute level of unemployment in the eastern region which was consistently double the rate in the west of the united country (European Communities 2008: 86); it also produced a sectoral profile which differed markedly from the export-intensive economy of engineering production and industrial services that characterizes the old Federal Republic. Eastern Germany was and still is more strongly dependent on the service sector (Leaman 2009: 142f). With 17.9 per cent of young east Germans registered as unemployed in October 2005 (west: 9.8 per cent; see Stettes 2005), policies aimed at (re-)integrating young people into the labour market would always need to acknowledge this kind of structural disparity.[3]

## THE THIRD WAY AND YOUTH UNEMPLOYMENT

This chapter seeks to assess the particular policy responses of the social democratic regimes of Blair and Schröder to youth unemployment. A comparison between two cognate regimes in two similar advanced capitalist economies is illuminating, not least because much of the general comparative literature generates unfavourable conclusions about the quality of German employment policies and their quantitative effects (OECD 2003; OECD 2005; Bertelsmann-Stiftung [ed.] 2003; Knuth et al. 2004; Raines et al. 1999) whereas Germany's record of youth employment/unemployment is clearly better than that of the United Kingdom. By implication, therefore, the political economy of youth employment in Germany currently sits more favourably within a national comparison between different age groups, and also in a cross-national comparison.

## THE PROBLEM OF YOUTH UNEMPLOYMENT

Germany and the United Kingdom are by no means the only countries with a problem of youth (defined as 15- to 24-year-olds) unemployment. Within the group of European OECD countries, the average rate of youth unemployment (OECD Europe) in 1990 was 16.7 per cent when overall unemployment (OU) stood at just 8.7 per cent. The disparity in Europe has widened since then, with youth unemployment (YU) in the first quarter of 2009 rising to 18.3 per cent in the EU-27 and 18.3 per cent in the eurozone, with an overall unemployment rate of 8.2 per cent the ratio of youth to overall unemployment had thus risen from 1.9 to 2.2 (Figures: OECD 2005 and 2009; author's calculations).

Germany's relatively low ratio of YU to OU of 1.4 in 2008 compares favourably to countries like Belgium (2.6), Finland (2.6), France (2.6) , Greece (2.9), Italy (3.1), Luxembourg (3.7), Portugal (2.2), Spain (2.3) and Sweden (3.3) with YU rates in 2004 of between 17 per cent and 26.5 per cent. The performance of Germany in limiting the rise of youth unemployment to 11.7 per cent, when overall unemployment in the country was only less than two percentage points higher, is noteworthy and significant. YU in the United Kingdom in 2008 is also higher than in Germany at 15 per cent with a significantly higher YU : OU ratio of 2.7; first quarter results for 2009 from Eurostat show UK youth unemployment at 17.9 per cent, again contrasting with 10.5 per cent in Germany.

These data represent a condundrum for analysts, particularly for those that are all too eager to condemn the excessive levels of employment protection in Germany and the lack—until recently—of appropriately 'modernized' institutions and processes of political employment promotion. Conversely, the performance of the United Kingdom, commonly presented as paradigmatic for liberalized employment relations (low levels of employment protection) and for the reform of institutions and processes, poses another conundrum: how do 'modernized' employment practices and relatively low levels of overall unemployment fail to reach a high proportion of that generation, whose inclusion/exclusion from employment is a critical factor in the determination of social mobility and social cohesion, namely youth?

In their joint programme—published in 1999 under the title *The Way Forward for Europe's Social Democrats*—Gerhard Schröder and Tony Blair make an immediate distinction between the (old) politics of redistribution and the (new) politics of enablement. In old-style social democracy 'the promotion of social justice was sometimes confused with the imposition of equality of outcome. The result was neglect of the importance of rewarding effort and responsibility, and the association of social democracy with conformity and mediocrity, rather than the celebration of creativity, diversity and excellence' (Blair and Schröder 1999: Ch. 1). The rest of the document, mirrored in the work of their respective advisors, Giddens (2000) and Hombach (2000), represents an explicit rejection of welfarist Keynesianism and demand-side state interventionism and the explicit espousal of a 'new supply-side agenda for the left' as well as 'an active labour market policy for the left' (Blair and Schröder ibid.). The shift from a demand-side to a supply-side focus also represented a shift from a macro-economic to a micro-economic focus (c.f. Knuth et al. 2004). The direct or indirect fiscal stimulation of demand (for labour/consumption) and thus growth at the level of the macro-economy is accordingly to be supplanted by the improvement of the individual attributes of the job seeker as commodity on the labour market (qua human capital) which in accordance with a kind of Say's Law of the Labour Market generates demand for (employer interest in) that commodity.

State employment-creation programmes (public works) as core elements of 'active' employment policies are rejected in favour of the improvement of the 'employability' of the individual job seeker via 'activating' employment programmes:

> In the area of social and labour market policies "post-traditional", "neo-social democratic", "third way" policies put less emphasis on

classical concepts of social *security* and income compensation and more on social and labour market concepts that are built around concepts of inclusion (participation), activation and equality of opportunities (Siegel 2004: 6).

It is acknowledged that the transition from active to 'activating' labour market policies in Germany came much later than in Britain (Knuth et al. 2004; Büchs 2004; OECD 2005 etc.), despite a barrage of recommendations from organizations like the OECD (Zohlnhöfer and Zutavern 2004; OECD 2002). During the Blair administration (1997–2007) British politicians tended to assert Britain's pioneering, 'model' role in the development of policy initiatives, subsequently copied by other European nations (Denmark and Holland, for example) or by the EU in its European Employment Strategy (Büchs 2004). The hand-wringing by the OECD et al. over apparent German dilatoriness is thus in part disingenuous. Germany undoubtedly had identifiable structural deficiencies, evident from the early 1970s onwards (Leaman 1988; Leaman 2009). Nevertheless, the relative success of Germany's political economy in weathering global stagflation in the 1970s and 1980s, which gave it 'model' status for a brief time,[4] contrasted with the more long-standing 'English disease' and similar problems in Holland and Denmark (Knuth et al. 2004: 72ff); these three latter-day 'models' of modernization had far worse rates of unemployment in 1990 than Germany. The abandonment of Keynesian welfarism in Germany *in practice* was held up, despite strong ideological preferences of the ruling CDU/CSU/FDP coalition, by the transformation crisis following unification and Helmut Kohl's need to be an interventionist *malgré lui* (Leaman 2009: 120f). The real shift to supply-side 'activation' policies came—ironically—with the accession to power of the Red-Green coalition in 1998.

The provenance of supply-side labour market policies in Britain is ironic but in a different way, in that the policy agenda adopted under two Conservative administrations—Thatcher (1979–1990) and John Major (1990–1997)—was maintained, refined and in many respects intensified under Blair's 'New Labour' premiership, albeit with strong emphasis on the rhetoric of inclusion and social solidarity.[5] In any case, the British state had traditionally made much more limited use of 'active' labour market interventions than its European counterparts (OECD 2003; Siegel 2004: 42), relying instead on passive payments of low benefits to the unemployed and the incapacitated, and on market forces and decentralized collective bargaining agreements between employers and trade unions to shape the dynamics of the labour market. In contrast to Germany, the marketing of job vacancies was shared by the state-run Job Centres and a wide range of private recruitment agencies. Despite low levels of welfare benefits, British political and social culture stigmatized unemployment with frequent campaigns against benefit 'scroungers'; particularly under the Thatcher and Major administrations, when structural and long-term unemployment rose markedly and pauperization accelerated, the public political stigmatization of welfare recipients compounded the strong social stigma of unemployment in the deindustrialized regions of the Midlands and the North.

Although the focus of the labour market reforms of the Conservative governments between 1979 and 1997 was predominantly on the weakening of trade union power, the liberalization of market conditions and the reduction of job security—as negative incentives for both employed and unemployed workers—the 'activation' approach of the Blair governments was foreshadowed by the introduction of the Conservatives' 'Restart' programme in 1986 which was targeted at the long-term unemployed and involved interview training among other things; also the receipt of unemployment benefit was made conditional on the demonstrable, active search for work by the recipient. The ambiguous unemployment benefit was renamed 'job seeker's allowance' (JSA). Entitlement to the JSA, be it based on contributions to the comprehensive National Insurance scheme or calculated on need, is limited to six months and is paid as a flat rate, rather than on the 'equivalence principle' common to specific unemployment insurance schemes. The needs-based JSA has always been subject to means testing; entitlements currently fall incrementally with savings over £3,000 (ca €3,540) and are not paid to those with savings over £8,000 (€9,400). The low benefits of the JSA (current 2009 rates: £50.95 per week for 16- to 25-year-olds; £64.30 for those over 25) and the short period of entitlement frequently drive recipients to seek Disability Benefit, particularly when doctors (general practitioners) are sympathetically disposed to poor patients.

New Labour added to the inherited system of inducements to seek work in a variety of ways:

1. Increased resources for Jobcentres, notably in the appointment of an additional 5,000 personal employment advisors;
2. Staged reorganization of state employment and benefit agencies;
3. Prioritizing of macro-economic growth through supply-side measures designed to reduce costs of domestic and inward investors ("location competition") and counter-cyclical fiscal management;
4. A minimum wage for all adult workers was introduced in 1998, with different (lower) minima for young workers, in order to 'make work pay', to end sweatshop labour below welfare benefit levels and to prevent poverty traps for re-employed workers. By January 2009, the adult minimum wage had risen to £5.73 per hour, 18- to 21-year-olds receive £4.77 per hour, with a new minimum wage for 16- to 17-year-olds of £3.53 per hour.
5. Tightening of rules of entitlement to the JSA, in particular with the introduction of:
6. The New Deal for Young People (NDYP); this is the most far-reaching of all the New Deal schemes (there are others for the age groups 25+ and 50+), explicable in the main by the significantly higher rate

of youth unemployment in the United Kingdom and the government's own acknowledgement that long-term unemployment after leaving school impairs opportunities in later life.

7. Subsidies to potential employers to offer work experience and apprenticeship schemes; the chronically low level of apprenticeship starts (1996/97: 65,000) was almost trebled to 180,000 in 2006/07 (Department for Innovation, Universities and Skills 2008a: 15) but this still leaves the United Kingdom far behind Germany and many of its European partners. Indeed, apprenticeships 'are available today in just 10% of the country's stock of employers' (Department for Innovation, Universities and Skills 2008a: 33). The provision of apprenticeships within the United Kingdom's public sector is particularly poor (ibid.).

## THE NEW DEAL FOR YOUNG PEOPLE

The NDYP is targetted at those 18- to 24-year-olds who are unemployed for six months or more. It is compulsory for all; the refusal to participate leads to the withdrawal of benefit. The scheme operates on the basis of individual advice, training and subsidies to employers for fixed short-term employment.

In the *initial phase* of the NDYP, the so-called *Gateway*, individuals are allocated a personal advisor who provides guidance for seeking out suitable and available jobs and preparing them for interviews with prospective employers. Participants in this phase continue to receive the JSA.

If, after four months, the *Gateway* period has not resulted in a successful job application, participants move to a *second phase*, in which they are offered one of four options:

1. Full-time training or education for twelve months with continued payment of the JSA;
2. Employment within the voluntary sector for six months with continued payment of the JSA plus an additional £400 (£67 per month)
3. Work with the Environmental Task Force for six months with continued payment of the JSA plus an additional £400 (£67 per month)
4. Subsidized employment for six months with on-the-job training by the employer; the employer subsidy is £60 per week plus £750 to cover the costs of training.

In the event of further failure to find permanent full- or part-time employment, participants are obliged to enter a final 'follow through' phase, lasting up to 13 weeks, where they are again helped by Jobcentre advisors to look and apply for jobs.

Assessments of the NDYP have been mixed, both in terms of their quantitative outcomes and in terms of their value for money. Wilkinson (2003) produces findings from an extensive analysis of large sample groups which support the claim that the scheme has had positive effects on the reintegration of unemployed young workers into the labour market; however, these effects are greatest in the initial Gateway phase and in particular for men, but recede in the second Options phase and the follow-up final phase (Wilkinson 2003: 50ff). Millar (2000) took over 20 evaluation studies of the ND in general and concluded that the:

> programmes have made a real difference to a range of different groups. Of those who have been through the programmes, just under half of the young people, two fifths of the lone parents, and one in six of the long-term unemployed people have so far found work. . . . Just under 440,000 young people had been through the NDYP by February 2000 and in total about 200,000 people had found jobs. . . . It is projected that about 250,000 young people will find work over the four years planned for the programme (Millar 2000: 737–738).

Myck (2002: 3) notes the coincidence of the New Deal and the decline in youth unemployment between 1998 and winter 2000 but is careful to concede that 'some other factors apart from the New Deal, like the overall performance of the economy, may have been responsible for the recent reductions in unemployment'. This was a view shared by the opposition Conservative Party in the 2005 general election, when the party manifesto proposed to scrap what was considered to be a superfluous and expensive scheme.

McVicar and Podivinski (2003) find strong evidence of quantitative effects of exits from unemployment as a result of NDYP schemes in the United Kingdom's regions; unsurprisingly, they identify differences in outcomes, depending on the particular circumstances of the individual regions, with more participants proceeding to training schemes than to employment in high unemployment areas and more proceeding to employment in regions with lower levels of unemployment and more vacancies (ibid.: 40, Table 1).

Wilkinson's comparison of different sample groups (one NDYP group, one for nonparticipants 30–39 years of age) suggests at the very least a quantitative impact on both labour market integration of a significant magnitude (30,000 men, 9,000 women after the first six months of NDYP participation). However, a number of qualifications need to be made about the value of such findings: because of higher levels of structural unemployment among the 15- to 24-year-old age group, the calibre/potential employability of the cohort reserve is likely to be higher than the older group with a smaller reserve. Integration into the labour market, coming out of unemployment does not of itself mean escape from poverty or increased social mobility; the National Minimum Wage has not removed all poverty traps (Knuth et al. 2004: 28). Finally, the quality of training within the NDYP and the quality of subsequent employment has been brought into question.

Millar (2000) notes the relatively low emphasis on training within the ND programmes and concludes significantly that the programme 'has on the whole been better at serving people who need a bit of help than those who need a lot' (Millar 2000: 737). Given that the evidence shows that there is a 'close relationship between the quality of employment on the one hand and career development and social integration on the other' (Siebern-Thomas 2005: 203), this remains a key problem area of the ND programmes in the United Kingdom which require ongoing attention by researchers in terms of their long-term effects.

## YOUTH UNEMPLOYMENT AND 'ACTIVATION' POLICY IN GERMANY

Germany's performance in terms of growth and labour market reform became the object of increasing criticism in recent years, in particular from the Organisation for Economic Co-operation and Development (OECD 2002, OECD 2003, OECD 2005). Germany 'bringing up the rear', the *Schlusslicht* in GDP growth and in structural reform of labour markets has been meat and drink to headline writers for some time (Bertelsmann-Stiftung 2003). The absence/lateness above all of appropriate 'activation' measures of labour market policy are identified as critical deficiencies of Germany's political economy (OECD 2003, OECD 2005); reform has been urged upon Germany and other European countries by the European Commission following the launching of the European Employment Strategy (Büchs 2004).

However, as the urgency of introducing 'activation' measures has increased, so the concept itself has drawn some critical attention as 'fuzzy and ambivalent' (Siegel 2004: 23) or 'controversial' (Bothfeld 2005: 420). Taylor-Gooby (2004: 23) actually distinguishes between negative and positive activation which corresponds in part to Bothfeld's distinction between a *liberal* activation concept which motivates job seekers through the reduction in job and social security along 'workfare' lines and a *universalistic* concept of activation which addresses the needs of the unemployed/underemployed through high benefits and reintegration assistance through personal advice and subsidized placements (2005: 420). There was therefore little difficulty in establishing a consensus about the desirability of 'activation' strategies within the German discussions, encompassing both the neoliberal camp (Deutsche Bundesbank 2004) and the more worker-centred, universalistic camp (Bothfeld 2005, Trube 2005 etc.). The Bundesbank's espousal of activation has been typically linked to a catalogue of demands for the flexibilization of labour markets and the reduction of state expenditure on 'active' labour market measures (Deutsche Bundesbank 2004).

The history of recent 'activation' policies shows a preponderance of negative measures which have reduced job security for full-time employees and increased the scope of part-time, fixed-term and casual sub-contracted labour. It is noteworthy that the bulk of the measures have been introduced since 1998 (i.e. the inception of Schröder's 'Red-Green'coalition):

- Employment Protection: The Employment Protection Act was modified in 1996, raising the threshold for the applicability of the Act from six to eleven employees. This modification was reversed by the incoming Red-Green coalition in 1999 but restored in 2004. Germany, along with most European states—with the exception of Ireland and the United Kingdom—is considered to have a strong employment protection culture.
- Part-time employment: In 2001 the Act concerning Part-Time and Fixed Term Employment established a statutory right to part-time employment and the right to return to full-time employment. In 1999, the exemption from paying taxes and social security contributions for workers in low-paid part-time work (mini-jobs) was abolished but partly restored in 2003 for employees with a maximum of one additional low paid part-time job; reduced social security contributions for midi-jobs were introduced.
- Fixed Term Employment: Up until 1985 limited term employment contracts were only permissible for 'justified reason' through application. The Employment Protection Act of 1985 removed this restriction and introduced an 18-month maximum term. A revision of the Act in 1996 raised the maximum to 24 months and removed all restrictions for workers over 60 years of age. The Act concerning Part-Time and Fixed Term Employment of 2001 reintroduced justified reason for the bulk of adult workers but allowed limited term employment for new recruits and for all employees over 58 years of age; in the Hartz I and II Reforms of 2003, freedom from all restrictions was extended to all workers over 52 years of age. In 2004 the maximum period for standard limited term contracts was raised to four years.
- Sub-contracted labour: Until 1985, sub-contracting was heavily restricted (maximum of three months), which produced significant problems in the shape of a black economy, in particular within the building trades. Under the Kohl administrations (1982–1998) the maximum period was raised in stages to twelve months. In 2002 the Red-Green coalition raised the maximum period to 24 months but introduced the principle of equal pay for equal work for casual employees. In 2004 most restrictions on casual labour were removed, but provision for employment advice to affected workers was established with the creation of personnel service agencies.
- Self-employment: In 1999 the Act promoting Self-Employment outlawed pseudo-self-employment, rife in the construction industry (partly reversed in 2003). Start-up grants for unemployed persons

who become self-employed were introduced in 2003, with maximum duration of three years. In 2004, amendments to craft trade legislation removed the requirement of a Master Craftsman qualification from 53 out of 94 craft trades, allowing the possibility for qualified journeymen to become self-employed artisans.

These alterations to Federal Employment and Contract Law form the backdrop to the most radical of employment law reforms, associated with the Hartz-Commission reforms which were introduced between 2002 and 2005, but must be seen as having an activating function in the sense of permitting the expansion of employment opportunities that provide, by definition, less security—in terms of material gain, social security entitlements and length of job tenure. Notwithstanding the particular circumstances of German unification, there has been a marked increase in the incidence of part-time employment in Germany from 2.3 per cent of total employment in 1990 to 6.3 per cent in 2004; part-time work already accounted for 29.8 per cent of all female employment in 1990 and rose to 37 per cent in 2004, not far behind the United Kingdom, with just over 40 per cent, barely altered since 1990 (OECD 2005).

Activation, in terms of the targeted measures of advice, training, placements and employment subsidies, was promoted intensively in the first three phases of the Hartz reforms which also saw significant changes to the institutional arrangements for the delivery of employment policy measures and the provision of benefits.

*The First and Second Law for modern Services in the Labour Market* (Hartz I and II: 1 January and 1 April 2003 respectively) brought about:

- Reductions in benefits (for earnings-related Unemployment Benefit [*Arbeitslosengeld*] and Unemployment Assistance [*Arbeitslosenhilfe*] and *Unterhaltsgeld*, as well as stricter monitoring of need in the case of Unemployment Assistance;
- Stricter rules governing the degree to which job offers can be rejected on the grounds of quality (*Zumutbarkeit*) and periods when benefit is not paid (*Sperrzeiten*);
- The reorganization of continuing education, notably with the introduction of training vouchers;
- Establishment of *PersonalServiceAgenturen* (sic) as public, private or public-private agencies, operating as job agencies and advice centres; extension of temping agencies.
- Introduction of the so-called *Ich-AG* (individual joint stock company!) with grants and tax concessions for individual unemployed persons wishing to become self-employed.

*The Third Law for Modern Services in the Labour Market* (2004) involved above all:

- The restructuring of the Federal Institute for Labour in Nuremberg (renamed Federal Agency for Labour), extending its administrative role for delivering unemployment benefit to encompass Social Assistance, hitherto delivered by local authorities and allowing for the subcontracting of labour agency functions to the PSAs.
- Cuts in active job creation schemes and reductions in benefits (to be implemented between 2004 and 2006)

*The Fourth Law for Modern Services in the Labour Market* came into force on 1 January 2005 and involved arguably the most significant change in (negative) activation, namely the conflation of the hitherto earnings-related Unemployment Assistance, paid to long-term unemployed persons after the initial period of the more generous Unemployment Benefit (*Arbeitslosengeld* now re-termed *Arbeitslosengeld I*), with the flat-rate Social Assistance (*Sozialhilfe*) to produce the so-called Unemployment Benefit II, which is paid at a flat rate, generally at much lower levels than the discarded Unemployment Assistance. The Federal Agency for Labour is solely responsible for the delivery of both *Arbeitslosengeld I* and *Arbeitslosengeld II*, with help of increased federal government grants to supplement its revenue from Unemployment Insurance. The passage of this Hartz-IV Law was accompanied by large scale protests on behalf of the long-term unemployed, and the first year of its implementation brought further opposition and considerable hardship for the benefit recipients. The sheer magnitude of this break with the tradition of generous long-term social security for the unemployed—in terms of both the micro-economic fate of individual households and the macro-economic decline in effective demand—has arguably deflected attention away from the activation effects of the Hartz I–III reforms and partly neutralized the positive features of individual activation. Apart from its key objective of reducing Germany's comparatively high indirect labour costs, it is also clearly intended to alter the fundamental conditions of unemployment and the fundamental perceptions and expectations of the unemployed as the pre-requisite to accepting job offers of a lower quality, of limited extent (part-time or fixed term) and by definition with lower levels of job security.

The specific programmes targeted at reducing youth unemployment, which experienced sudden surges at the end of the 1990s, were conducted predominantly within the regulatory framework of the 'dual' system of training; substantively, they reflected the overall activation strategies of positive and negative incentives. Within six weeks of taking office, the first Schröder administration introduced an 'Action Programme to Reduce Youth Unemployment' on 9 December 1998 which was abbreviated to JUMP (*Jugend mit Perspektive*). JUMP was modeled on Labour's 'New Deal' but crucially directed its activation measures towards preparing long-term unemployed young people for participation in apprenticeships and other training programmes. It ran for six years up to 2003 with the banner objective of creating '100,000 jobs for young people' through:

- Increasing the supply of apprenticeships;
- Preparing young people to apply for apprenticeships;
- Providing training organizations outside enterprises and distinct from technical colleges (*Berufsschulen*);
- Providing further training to young unemployed people that had already completed an apprenticeship;
- Providing employment subsidies to private and public employers.

The JUMP programme was jointly run by the Federal Labour Agency and the European Social Fund; 40 per cent of the €1 billion budget was directed towards the five new Länder. The programme was extended for a further eighteen months by JUMP-Plus which promoted both the development of in-house training programmes at regional and local levels and training consortia involving groups of smaller employers. The monitoring of these new training programmes remained in the hands of the Chambers of Commerce and the education authorities at regional state level. The provisions of the Red-Green coalition's JUMP-programme—its primary vehicle for combating youth unemployment—were in part incorporated in the Job-AQTIV Law of 2001 and through this became part of general social security law. The 2001 Law tightened conditions for participation in training programmes, including the imposition of a 'duty of notification' (*Meldepflicht*) in the case of individuals threatened with redundancy. Young people were also subject to lower thresholds of *Zumutbarkeit*, as per the Hartz employment law reforms, which obliged job seekers or trainee applicants to accept positions of a lower quality if deemed necessary.

JUMP and its offshoots were wide-ranging and ambitious. Between January 1999 and December 2003, 663,296 young people participated in JUMP schemes, some more than once, such that total registrations amounted to 795,573; over 12,000 participants received mobility grants (Dornette and Jacob 2006: 11f). There were significant regional differences in the composition of the participants and the nature of the projects they took part in; in the west there was a high proportion of participants with non-German origins (15 per cent on average) while only one per cent of east German young participants were from a 'migrant background' (ibid.: 23). Many of the east German participants (60 per cent) had already completed apprenticeships, such that the programmes in the east were more strongly orientated towards employment subsidies, mentoring and profiling. Almost three quarters (73 per cent) of west German participants had no training qualifications at all. These disparities can be explained both by the much higher levels of unemployment in the east and the mismatch of existing qualifications and the markedly deindustrialized sectoral structure of the eastern economy. Thus 88 per cent of east German participants had been unemployed before joining a JUMP scheme, 27 per cent for more than six months; figures for west Germany were 79 per cent and 18 per cent respectively.

The assessment of the quantative impact of such a wide-ranging, multidimensional programme is, as in the case of its UK counterpart, problematic. Stettes notes that as early as 2002 it was clear that 'the placement rates of the various programmes were quite low. More than half of the former participants had, once again, become unemployed or had not been reintegrated into employment or training six months after they finished their programme' (Stettes 2005). The target of 100,000 new apprenticeships was not achieved in the operational period of JUMP and Jump-Plus; the Federal Labour Agency noted an additional shortfall of 27,000 apprenticeships in April 2004 (cited in: Gillmann 2004). This then clearly informed the pursuit of an *Apprenticeship Pact* by the Schröder government in June 2004, in which employers committed themselves to creating 30,000 new apprenticeships a year and also generating 25,000 work experience openings for young people deemed incapable of starting an apprenticeship (Stettes 2005). The signing of the Pact must be seen against the background of the coalition's threat to deploy a 'training levy' (*Ausbildungsabgabe*) on all enterprises, should the supply of training places not cover demand (Gillmann 2004). Be that as it may, the supply of apprenticeships rose sharply in 2004 (+59,500) and 2005 (+52,000); work experience opportunities also rose by 29,000 (figures in Stettes 2005).

## CONCLUSION

While the 'activation' initiatives epitomized by Labour's 'New Deal' programmes achieved a model status for both policymakers and labour market analysts in Germany, the performance of Germany's political economy in neutralizing the problem of youth unemployment and in turn mitigating its negative effects in the medium term has arguably been considerably greater than in the United Kingdom. The sudden surge in UK youth unemployment in 2009 and the increased emphasis on the need for improved apprenticeship provision (DIUS 2008a and 2008b) indicate a continuing failure to protect young people from the disproportionate effects of cyclical downturns and to anchor their training and career prospects in an economic culture that takes long-term skills needs seriously. The *World Class Apprenticeships* programme (DIUS 2008a) notes the particular urgency of engaging SMEs in apprenticeship schemes and encouraging training consortia among smaller companies. In Germany, in contrast, SMEs provide more than 80 per cent of all apprenticeships (Tatsachen über Deutschland 2007: 129); the bulk of these apprenticeships are in Industry and Commerce (59.9 per cent), Artisan Crafts (27.6) and the 'free' professions (7.1 per cent). Training consortia are also now an established feature of Germany's 'dual system'.

The comparison of British and German 'Third Way' policies to combat youth unemployment thus reveals significant contrasts: in the UK 'activation' can be seen to have been an attempt primarily to equip badly qualified school-leavers and young adults with basic skills of literacy, numeracy and self-presentation to allow an easier integration into a strongly liberalized and 'flexible' labour market; the emergence of a stronger craft skill dimension to New Labour policy—in the most recent emphasis on apprenticeships—has been later and less central to the overall strategy. Germany, in contrast, has *incorporated activation into an existing institutionalized system of apprenticeship training and education,* which has hitherto ensured that 80 per cent of the workforce has either vocational (ca. 60 per cent) or university (20 per cent) qualifications. The German system has involved significantly higher costs, born predominantly by employers, but with acknowledged benefits to corporate and overall macro-economic performance. Moreover, it has been able to cope—by and large—with the huge exogenous shock of unification, where success can be measured in the narrower disparity between youth and overall unemployment and in the provision of satisfactory—if not perfect— levels of apprenticeship training in both east and west.

In Germany the problems associated with youth unemployment are linked not to questions about the adequacy of the country's training culture, but predominantly to the structural weaknesses (regional and sectoral) of the eastern economy and the weaker educational performance of young people with a migrant background. These represent clear challenges to German policymakers seeking to reduce the dangers of social exclusion, but unemployment is a general problem, not one exclusive to young people; the minimization of the disparity between youth unemployment and overall unemployment in Germany is arguably a real measure of the success of an economic culture that views craft skills as fundamental to prosperity and social cohesion. It is also arguably strengthened by the system of mandatory social service for young men, be it in military training or in community service (*Zivildienst*).[6]

The skills culture in the United Kingdom compares very unfavourably with that of Germany; the virtual disappearance of apprenticeship training by 1970 and the subsequent decline in UK manufacturing was market-driven; increasingly skills shortages could be made up by either importing labour or, more recently, by extensive outsourcing. New Labour's 'activation' strategy thus lacked the infrastructural and cultural foundation which underpins German economic culture. Activation deliberately targets the individual because it is a short-term measure to prevent failure and social exclusion. What it has found much more difficult to achieve is the restoration of a deep-seated skills culture which provides the individual and the society with the social capital which allows the nonacademic and more deprived members of that society to feel real self-worth.

## NOTES

1. OECD data for the period 1972 to 1991 include Germany, France, the United Kingdom, Italy, Belgium, Ireland, Netherlands, Portugal and Spain; aggregate data from 1992 to 2009 refer to the euro area.
2. Figures for the year 2000.

3. In 1990, the year of economic and social union (July) and political unification (October), the overall rate of unemployment was just 4.9 per cent, compared to 6.8 per cent in Britain. In 2004, the rate had risen to 9.9 per cent in Germany, but fallen to 4.7 per cent in Britain. While there was an overall deterioration in structural unemployment throughout the OECD (1990: 6.4, 2004: 6.9), and other cases of significant increases in unemployment in this period, Germany's position was dramatically different and unrepresentative. The exogenous shock of absorbing the economic apparatus, the workforce and the wider population of a comparatively less advanced and structurally less favourable political economy was colossal. The initial conditions for east German enterprises were arguably worse than for any other transition economy, inasmuch as they were subject to an effective revaluation of their currency and therefore their liabilities, to significant increases in real wage costs and other costs of production, while levels of productivity were far lower than western standards. The resulting debacle—albeit made worse by haphazard and contradictory macro-policies—was in part predictable: the virtual halving of east German GDP by the end of 1991, the near deindustrialization of many east German districts, large scale redundancies and *official* levels of unemployment (between 15.7 per cent and 20.5 per cent) which barely concealed the effective halving of the east German workforce.

The effect on the fiscal and administrative resources of the German state and the para-public social insurance funds have also been colossal; approximately 4 per cent of German GDP continues to be transferred from West to East to plug the still wide gap between consumption and production (demand-output gap).

Any remotely fair comparison of employment policies within the OECD has to take the colossal effect of German unification into consideration before passing judgement on the comparative performance of its labour market policies. However, one of the major problems of the ongoing analysis of labour market policies and the policies themselves is that the impact of unification is either ignored or downplayed, so that Germany's poor performance can be seen more critically as the manifestation of a general structural malaise. This renders a frontal assault on the German social state much easier, if more dishonest.

4. Helmut Schmidt fought two federal elections with the slogan of 'Model Germany'; Zweig (1976), mirroring the views of many others, asserted that Germany provided an 'object-lesson in economic management'.

5. The first Blair administration explicitly committed itself also to maintaining the expenditure ceilings set for the two fiscal years 1997–1999 by the last Major government.

6. It is noteworthy that both the UK Labour Party (James Crabtree and Frank Field, *Prospect* March 2009) and David Cameron of the opposition Conservative Party (*Daily Mail* 29 October 2006) have raised the possibility of periods of community service for school-leavers; in February 2009 YouGov poll, 64 per cent of respondents supported such a scheme, See Crabtree, in *Prospect* March 2009: 156.

## BIBLIOGRAPHY

Aldrich, R. (1997) 'Apprenticeship in England: An Historical Perspective', in A. Heikkinen and R. Sultana (Eds.) *Vocational Education and Apprenticeships in Europe*, 71–97 (Tampere: Tampere University Press).

Arbeitsgruppe Alternative Wirtschaftspolitik (2004) *Memorandum 2004.*

Armingeon, K. and Beyer, M. (Eds.) (2004) *The OECD and European Welfare States* (Cheltenham: Edward Elgar).

Arulampalam, W. (2001) 'Is Unemployment Really Scarring? Effects of Unemployment Experiences on Wages', *Economic Journal*, Royal Economic Society, 111 (475), pp. 585–606.

Bertelsmann-Stiftung (Ed.) (2003) *Arbeitsmarktpolitik von 15 Ländern im Vergleich* (Gütersloh: Verlag Bertelsmann-Stiftung).

Blair, T. and Schröder G. (1999) *The Way Forward for Europe's Social Democrats* (London: The Labour Party).

Blanden, J., Gregg, P. and Machin, S. (2005) *Intergenerational Mobility in Europe and North America* (London: Sutton Trust, Centre for Economic Performance).

Bothfeld, S. (2005) 'Aktiv und aktivierend: Grundzüge einer zukunftsfesten Arbeitsmarktpolitik', *WSI-Mitteilungen,* August 2005, 419ff.

Breen, R. (2005) 'Explaining Cross-national Variation in Youth Unemployment: Market and Institutional Factors', *European Sociological Review*, Vol. 21/2, pp. 125–134.

Brenner, B. and Grüner, G. (2005) 'Personality and Profiling'. Fördernde und fordernde Arbeitsvermittlung—eine Oper in zwei Akten', Labournet Germany, http://www.labournet.de

Brogan, Benedict (2006), 'Cameron calls for "rite of passage" scheme for youngsters', *Daily Mail,* 29 October 2006, http://www.dailymail.co.uk/news/article-413318/Cameron-calls-national-rite-passage-scheme-youngsters.html (accessed 2 July 2 2009)

Büchs, M. (2004) 'Asymmetries of Policy Learning? The European Employment Strategy and Its Role in Labour Market Policy Reform in Germany and the UK', paper presented at ESPAnet Conference, University of Oxford, September 2004.

Bundesministerium für Bildung und Forschung (2006) *Berufsbildungsbericht 2006*, Berlin.

Bundesministerium für Bildung und Forschung (2009) *Berufsbildungsbericht 2009*, Berlin.

Bundespresse- und Informationsamt (2006) *Tatsachen über Deutschland*, Berlin.

Crabtree, J. (2009) The Prospect/YouGovPoll, 1 March 2009, in *Prospect*, Issue 156 http://www.prospectmagazine.co.uk/2009/03/theprospectyougovpoll/ (accessed July 2 2009)

Crabtree, James & Field, Frank (2009) 'Citizenship First: the case for compulsory civic service' in: *Prospect*, Issue 156, http://www.prospectmagazine.co.uk/2009/03/citizenshipfirstthecaseforcompulsorycivicservice/ (accessed 2 July 2009)

Dahrendorf (2004) 'The Third Way: An Epitaph', *Project Syndicate/Institute for Human Sciences*, (http://www.project-syndicate.org/commentary/dahrendorf24).

Department for Innovation, Universities and Skills (DIUS) (2008a) *World-Class Apprenticeships: Unlocking Talent, Building Skills for All* (London, HMSO).

Department for Innovation, Universities and Skills (DIUS) (2008b) *Draft Apprenticeship Bill July 2008* (London: HMSO).

Deutsche Bundesbank (2004) 'Mehr Flexibilität am deutschen Arbeitsmarkt', *Monatsbericht*, September 43–58.

Deutsche Bundesbank (2005) 'Rascher Wandel der Erwerbsarbeit', *Monatsbericht*, July 2005, 15f.

Dornette, J. and Jacob, M. (2006) *Zielgruppenerreichung und Teilnehmerstruktur des Jugendsofortprogramms JUMP*, Research Report Nr.16/2006 of the Institut für Arbeitsmarkt- und Berufsforschung.

European Communities (2008) *Eurostat Regional Yearbook 2008*, Brussels.

Giddens, A. (2000) *The Third Way and Its Critics* (Oxford: Blackwell).

Gillmann, B. (2004) 'Koalition beharrt auf Ausbildungsabgabe', *Handelsblatt* April 16.

Gorz, A. (1999) *Reclaiming work: beyond the wage-based society* (Cambridge: Polity Press).

Gregg, P. and Tominey, E. (2004) 'The Wage Scar from Youth Unemployment', CMPO Working Paper Series No. 04/097.

Gregory, M. and Jukes, R. (2001) 'Unemployment and Subsequent Earning: Estimating Scarring among British Men 1984–94', *Economic Journal*, 111 (475), pp. 607–25.

Haselbach, D. (1991) *Autoritärer Liberalismus und soziale Marktwirtschaft*, Baden-Baden.

Hillmert, S. (n.d.) 'Skill Formation in Britain and Germany: Recent Developments in the Context of Traditional Differences', Working Paper (06.1) Center for European Studies, Harvard University.

Hirsch, D. and Millar, J. (2004) *Labour's Welfare Reform* (London: Joseph Rowntree Foundation).

Hombach, B. (2000) *The politics of the New Centre* (Cambridge: Polity Press).

Huffschmid, J. (2002) *Politische Ökonomie der Finanzmärkte*, Hamburg (VSA).

Hyland, T. and Musson, D. (2001) 'Unpacking the New Deal for Young People: Promise and Problems, *Educational Studies*, 27 (1), 55–67.

ILO [International Labour Organisation] (2006) *Global Employment Trends for Youth*, Geneva.

Knapp, U. (2004), 'Die neuen Gesetze am Arbeitsmarkt aus frauenpolitischer Sicht', *Diskussionsbeiträge der Hamburger Universität für Wirtschaft und Arbeit*.

Knuth, M., Schweer, O. and Siemes, S. (2004) *Drei Menüs und kein Rezept. Dienstleistungen am Arbeitsmarkt in Großbritannien, in den Niederlanden und in Dänemark*, Friedrich Ebert Stiftung, March 2004.

Leaman, J. (1988) *The Political Economy of West Germany 1945–1985* (London: Macmillan).

Leaman, J. (2009) *The Political Economy of Germany under Kohl and Schröder* (Oxford: Berghahn).

Leaman, J. and Daguerre, A. (2004) 'Employment', in H. Compston (Ed.), *Handbook of Public Policy in Europe: Britain, France and Germany*, 110ff (London: Palgrave).

Marx, K. (1954) *Capital*, Volume One, London: Laurence & Wishart.

McVicar, D. and Podivinski, J. (2003) *How Well has the New Deal for Young People Worked in the UK Regions?*, Belfast, Northern Ireland Economic Research Centre, Paper No.79.

Millar, J. (2000) 'Keeping Track of Welfare Reform: The New Deal Programmes', Joseph Rowntree Foundation, *Findings* Ref: 740.

Myck, M. (2002) 'How the New Deal Works' in: *Economic Review*, Volume 19 No. 3 (Southampton University) pp. 1-4. http://www.soton.ac.uk/socsci/economics/ecreview/labour.html (accessed 26 June 2009)

Nicoletti, G. and Scarpetta, S. (2003) 'Regulation, Productivity and Growth. OECD Evidence', *Economic Policy*, April 2003, 9–72.

Nordström Skans, O. (2004). 'Scarring Effects of the First Labour Market Experience: A Sibling Based Analysis', *Working Paper Series* 2004:14, IFAU—Institute for Labour Market Policy Evaluation.

Organisation for Economic Co-operation and Development (OECD) (2002) *Policy Brief: Economic Survey of Germany* (Paris: December).

Organisation for Economic Co-operation and Development (OECD) (2003) *Employment Outlook: Towards More and Better Jobs* (Paris: OECD).

Organisation for Economic Co-operation and Development (OECD) (2005) *Employment Outlook: 2005* (Paris: OECD).

Organisation for Economic Co-operation and Development (OECD) (2006) *Employment Outlook: 2006* (Paris: OECD).
Raines, P., Döhrn, R., Brown, R. and Scheuer, M. (1999) *Labour Market Flexibility and Inward Investment in Germany and the UK*, Anglo-German Foundation Report (London: Anglo-German Foundation).
Rhum, C.J. (1991) 'Are Workers Permanently Scarred by Job Displacement?' *American Economic Review*, 81 (1), pp. 319–24.
Scharpf, F. (1991) *Crisis and Choice in European Social Democracy* (Ithica, NY: Cornell University Press).
Siebern-Thomas, F. (2005) 'Zum Stellenwert der "Qualität der Arbeit" in der europäischen Beschäftigungspolitik', *WSI-Mitteilungen*, April 2005, 193 ff.
Siegel, N. (2004) 'The Political Economy of Labour Market Reforms: Changing Paradigms, Ambivalent Activation and Re-commodification at the Margins', paper presented at ESPAnet 2004 Conference, Oxford.
Statistisches Bundesamt (1978) *Statistisches Jahrbuch der Bundesrepublik*, Wiesbaden.
Stettes, O. (2005) 'Youth and Work: The Case of Germany', *EIRO Comparative Studies*.
*Tatsachen über Deutschland* (2007) http://www.tatsachen-ueber-deutschland.de/de/head-navi/impressum.html (accessed 27 June 2009)
Taylor-Gooby, P. (2004) *New Risks, New Welfare: The Transformation of the European Welfare State*, Oxford: OUP.
Thoma, G. (2003) 'Jugendarbeitslosigkeit bekämpfen—aber wie?', *Aus Politik und Zeitgeschichte*, 06–07/2003.
Trube, A. (2005) '"Besser irgendeine Arbeit als keine Arbeit?"—Kritik einer qualitätsblinden Arbeitsmarkt- und Sozialpolitik', *WSI-Mitteilungen*, April 2005, 179ff.
Wade, R.H. (2005) 'Globalization, Poverty and Inequality', in J. Ravenhill, *Global Political Economy* (Oxford: Oxford University Press).
Wilkinson, D. (2003) 'New Deal for Young People: Evaluation of Unemployment Flows', PSI Research Discussion Paper 15, London, Policy Studies Institute.
Zohlnhöfer, R. and Zutavern, J. (2004) 'Too Many Rivals? The OECD's Influence on German Welfare Policies', in K. Armingeon and M. Beyeler (eds), *The OECD and European Welfare States* (Cheltenham: Edward Elgar).
Zweig, K. (1976) *Germany through Inflation and Recession: An Object Lesson in Economic Management*, London: Centre for Policy Studies.

# Part II
# Youth and Socio-Cultural Transformations

# 4 Young Europeans and Educational Mobility

*Rachel Brooks and Johanna Waters*

## INTRODUCTION

It is increasingly argued within the literature on migration and mobility that a period spent living abroad (studying, working or travelling) is becoming a normal part of the life cycle. Indeed, Conradson and Latham (2005) suggest that it is often a feature of the 'biography-building' associated with societal individualization, evident particularly amongst the young. Within Europe, educational mobility has also been promoted strongly in relation to the wider political project of forging a common European identity (through the European Community Action Scheme for the Mobility of University Students [ERASMUS] programme, for example). Nevertheless, we know relatively little about why students decide to study abroad for the whole or part of a degree, and the impact such experiences have on their lives after they graduate.

To address this gap in our knowledge, this chapter draws on 85 in-depth individual interviews collected as part of a British Academy-sponsored project on 'International Higher Education and the Mobility of UK Students'. In it, we explore the decision-making processes of British young people who chose to study abroad for the whole of their undergraduate or postgraduate education, and compare their motivations and experiences to those of their counterparts from mainland Europe, documented in the wider literature. The chapter begins, then, with a discussion of this literature, which has focussed on European mobility policy, patterns of student mobility across Europe, and the motivations and experiences of European students. We then proceed to discuss the particular case of UK students in relation to our study findings, examining trends in student mobility, before focussing on their motivations and experiences. Throughout, comparisons are drawn with what we know about the educational mobility of European young people more generally.

## EUROPEAN MOBILITY POLICY

Studies of student migration within Europe tend to draw a distinction between 'spontaneous' mobility on the one hand and 'organized' or 'integrated' mobility on the other. The former refers to students who make their own arrangements to move abroad for their higher education, typically for the whole of an undergraduate or postgraduate degree. The latter, as the name suggests, refers to educational mobility under the auspices of some institutional, national or international scheme. While spontaneous mobility characterizes the dominant forms of student migration in many parts of the world, in Europe it is the organized form which is prevalent. In large part, this can be explained by the key role played by European Union (EU) policy in fostering student mobility from the late 1980s onwards. Indeed, it has been argued that while spontaneous mobility for the whole of a degree was originally considered to be a possible focus for European initiatives, it was dropped as a goal in the face of objections from individual universities that were determined to retain firm control over their own admissions processes and national governments that did not want to have to offer social assistance to students from other countries.

In analyzing changing patterns of mobility across the continent over the past few decades, it is possible to identify three distinct stages of internationalization: the first lasted until the mid-1980s and was largely spontaneous and *individual* (i.e. higher education institutions, national and regional bodies played no particular facilitative role); the second stage (mid-1980s until 2002) was characterized by a shift towards organized mobility as a result of the ERASMUS programme, initiated in 1987, and bringing universities across Europe into much closer co-operation; the third stage was heralded by the signing of the Bologna Declaration in 2002, and is characterized by an explicit commitment to creating a European higher education space and to furthering mobility—amongst teachers, researchers and administrative staff, as well as students (Prague Communiqué 2002). The Bologna process is not, however, restricted to members of the European Union, and encompasses 'the wider Europe, stretching from Azerbaijan to Iceland' (Birtwistle 2007: 182).

Although there is some disagreement amongst scholars about this periodization (Wachter 2003; Teichler 2001), most agree that the inauguration of the ERASMUS programme in 1987 was a defining moment in the internationalization of higher education across the continent (Maiworm 2001) in terms of both encouraging many more young people to spend time studying in another country and privileging organized (and short-term) forms of mobility over the spontaneous (and, typically, longer-term) alternative. The ERASMUS programme provides funding for students to study in another EU country for a period of three months to a year, within a department recognized by the scheme and which is part of an interinstitutional network. Emphasis is placed on 'curricular integration' between departments, and the home department is expected to recognize the academic achievements of students during their period abroad (Teichler 1996).

The aims of the ERASMUS programme, while sometimes expressed in rather vague and inconsistent terms (Papatsiba 2005), are generally considered to be threefold, encompassing economic, political and personal objectives. The economic goals underpinning this initiative are, perhaps, the least ambiguous and have been spelt out clearly by the European Commission.

These include: achieving a significant increase in the number of university students spending an integrated period of study in another Member State 'in order that the Community may draw upon an adequate pool of manpower with firsthand experiences of economic and social aspects of other Member States'; and developing a pool of graduates with experience of intra-Community co-operation 'thereby creating the basis upon which intensified co-operation in the economic and social sectors can develop at Community level' (Commission of the European Communities 1989: 1–2). The main political goal was originally specified as 'consolidating the concept of a People's Europe' through strengthening international interaction of citizens and accelerating the formation of interuniversity networks (ibid.: 1–2). However, scholars have argued that this political and cultural goal was downplayed during the process of policy formation as a tactic to ensure the acceptance of the programme by the Commissioners (Papatsiba 2005). At the personal level, the ERASMUS programme aims to broaden students' horizons, stimulate intellectual curiosity and thus raise both the general level of learning and individuals' prospects for employment (ibid.). Beyond these three explicit goals, King (2003) contends in relation to UK studentsthat EU-managed student migration is also driven by the desire to produce a European elite, comfortable working across borders and committed to the European project. In support of this thesis, he argues that the 'students who are internationally mobile during their studies and thereafter are disproportionately likely to come from family backgrounds where there is a history of professional activity and cosmopolitan experience' (166) and are, therefore, well suited to taking up positions of influence across Europe. While this analysis may hold in relation to UK students, it is not necessarily supported by data from other European countries, as will be discussed next.

Although there is now a considerable body of knowledge about the ERASMUS programme and the students who take part in it, we know much less about other forms of European student mobility. There are a small number of national studies of European students pursuing spontaneous mobility within the continent (Araujo 2007; Guth and Gill 2008; Wiers-Jenssen 2008) and further afield (Haug 1996), but these do not yet provide a comprehensive picture of the motivations and experiences of students who move abroad for all or part of their higher education outside of an organized scheme. For this reason, when discussing patterns of student mobility across Europe and the experiences of mobile students, we refer mainly to those on short-term 'integrated' visits of up to a year, facilitated by the ERASMUS programme.

## PATTERNS OF STUDENT MOBILITY ACROSS EUROPE

As noted earlier, the number of European students who move abroad for the whole of an undergraduate or postgraduate degree, on their own initiative, is relatively small. Indeed, Teichler (2004a) estimates that only 5 per cent of European students enrol at an institution abroad and emphasizes that these students are not spread evenly across the continent: those from countries too small to offer a complete higher education such as Luxembourg and Liechtenstein are overrepresented, as are students whose parents lived and worked abroad while they were at secondary school. Greek students are also more likely than their counterparts in other European nations to complete the whole of a degree in another country as a result of the limited access to tertiary education in Greece (Raikou and Karalis 2007). In contrast, the number of European students who have participated in organized mobility programmes is significantly larger. In 1987, the first year of the ERASMUS programme, 3,000 students received grants and eleven countries participated in the scheme. By 2003–2004, the number of ERASMUS students had grown to 135,586, and thirty-one countries were taking part (Birtwistle 2007). However, while most commentators have argued that this particular EU initiative has played a central role in stimulating student mobility within Europe, the ERASMUS programme has failed to achieve the 10 per cent mobility by 1992 that was an original aim of the programme—instead, the actual level was around 4 per cent (King 2003). The rate of growth also slowed considerably from about 30 per cent on average until 1995–1996 to less than 10 per cent in the following years (Maiworm 2001)—although numbers in the UK have risen very recently, since the introduction of a work placement option (Baty 2009). Moreover, there are also stark disparities between participating countries. In general, there is a net flow from less wealthy, southern European countries to their more wealthy northern neighbours. There are also important differences by language: it appears that the more widely the host country language is spoken, the more attractive it is as a destination for ERASMUS students (Teichler 1996, 2004a). Ireland and the United Kingdom suffer from a particular imbalance between inward and outward mobility, taking in approximately twice the number of students they send out (King 2003).

While most countries have seen a steady increase in levels of ERASMUS mobility over the last two decades, until very recently the United Kingdom has witnessed dropping numbers. Indeed, its year of highest mobility was 1994–1995 (Birtwistle 2007). However, it is not the case that this is indicative of a more general decline in the mobility of UK students: researchers at the Sussex Centre for Migration Research (2004) have argued that the decline in outgoing ERASMUS students has been largely offset by an increase in students moving to Anglophone countries and other destinations. In attempting to explain the decreasing attraction of European countries, scholars have pointed to the declining linguistic abilities of British students (as a result of the smaller number of students pursuing languages at A Level), the limited opportunities for paid work placements in Europe, and the perceived high standards and marketability of American and other Anglophone education systems (Sussex Centre for Migration Research 2004).

Studies that have explored the characteristics of students who become internationally mobile through ERASMUS programmes have come to very similar conclusions: women are generally overrepresented, typically accounting for around 60 per cent of participating students (Teichler 1996; Maiworm 2001; Sussex Centre for Migration Research 2004), as are language students and those who have lived abroad before (Teichler 2004a). However, in terms of the social background of mobile students, there appears to be some national variation. Studies of ERASMUS students in general have suggested that they are not a particularly privileged group. Drawing on his analysis of various relevant surveys, Maiworm (2001) claims that around one third of ERASMUS students stated that their fathers and 28 per cent of their mothers had a degree. This, he argues, is broadly in line with the characteristics of the total population of European higher education students. Teichler (1996) reaches a similar conclusion, contending that 'there is no indication that ERASMUS students are a socially select group among the European students' (160). Data from the United Kingdom paint a rather different picture, however, with those from higher socio-economic groups overrepresented amongst outgoing students (Sussex Centre for Migration Research 2004). Indeed, Findlay et al. (2006) found that having a mother in professional or managerial employment was the strongest predictor of European mobility amongst the UK students they surveyed. Indeed, they go on to claim that 'students from working class and non-white backgrounds stand much less chance of engaging in international student mobility because of the financial and linguistic constraints on the environment in which they are embedded and because of the socio-economic and mobility cultures from which they are drawn' (313). In developing this argument, they suggest that, within the United Kingdom at least, such inequalities are exacerbated by considerable differences in the support given to students by the higher education institution they attend. The UK universities that send most students abroad are the more prestigious institutions, typically attended by more socially advantaged young people.

## MOTIVATIONS AND EXPERIENCES OF EUROPEAN STUDENTS

While the statistical data outlined in the previous section give us some idea of broad trends in European mobility and highlight some significant disparities between countries, they tell us little about young people's reasons for pursuing overseas education, nor about their experiences studying outside their country of citizenship. In this section of the chapter, we draw upon the relatively small number of qualitative and quantitative studies conducted in this area to highlight the meanings attached to educational mobility by European students, before we go on to explore how these compare with the motivations and experiences of UK students, in particular.

Again, these focus largely, although not exclusively, on 'integrated' mobility through ERASMUS programmes.

## Reasons for Pursuing Overseas Education

Motives for embarking on an 'integrated' period of study overseas seem remarkably constant across Europe. Indeed, the various evaluations of the ERASMUS programme have come to similar conclusions that students typically choose to embark on a programme of study overseas because of the benefits they believe will accrue in terms of their academic studies; understanding of another country and culture; linguistic competence; and professional preparation (Maiworm 2001; Teichler 2004a). In relation to professional preparation, Murphy-Lejeune (2002) suggests that what distinguishes young European students from other nomads is 'the qualitative investment in their futures' (100). She goes on to claim that 'aware of economic competition, they appreciate the professional stakes of an international position' (ibid.) and believe that overseas education develops the 'mobility capital' which may help them to obtain such employment. Reasons such as these tend to suggest that participation in the ERASMUS programme should be seen as an example of what Rivza and Teichler (2007) call 'horizontal mobility'—to neighbouring countries, where systems of higher education are seen as broadly similar and cultural differences are likely to be relatively small. Indeed, Teichler (2004b) argues that such mobility is particularly suited to some of the wider aims of the ERASMUS programme: 'destructive culture shocks are less likely than anywhere else and rapid insight into the international diversity as well as learning based on that insight are more likely to be achieved' (14).

Research that has focussed more explicitly on independent movers—those moving 'spontaneously' and typically for the whole of an undergraduate or postgraduate degree—indicates that this kind of mobility may have more in common with what Rivza and Teichler (2007) term 'vertical mobility', mobility which is undertaken to secure what students perceive to be a better education. For example, Guth and Gill's (2008) study of Polish and Bulgarian doctoral students in the sciences suggests that such mobility was economically driven—but not only in terms of income (through grants, studentships and part-time work). Many were also keen to move to research centres that were funded better than their domestic equivalents, and thus offered better facilities for their doctoral projects. Araujo (2007) argues that many Portuguese students move to other European countries for doctoral studies for similar reasons. Indeed, she explains that for many of her interviewees mobility was essential 'because the lack of equipment to perform tests and other experiments in Portugal would have forced them to do a more theoretical thesis or to take much more time to complete it' (395). In addition, the perceived lack of employment opportunities within the Portuguese higher education sector also contributed to a decision to move abroad: an overseas qualification was believed by some to make more likely employment outside Portugal in the future. A small number of studies in individual European countries have suggested that while an overseas education was not necessarily perceived as *better*, in some cases it was viewed as more accessible than a degree from a domestic institution. Wiers-Jenssen (2008) makes this argument in relation to Norwegian students who fail to gain entry to very competitive medical courses in Norway: instead of choosing another degree programme in their home country, they often choose to pursue medicine elsewhere. Similarly, and as noted earlier, Raikou and Karalis (2007) claim that the restricted opportunities for higher education in Greece often motivate Greek nationals to move abroad for degree-level study.

## Reflections on Experiences

Studies that have focussed more explicitly on students' experiences abroad and on return home have painted an extremely positive picture. Murphy-Lejeune's (2002) work is typical of most research in this area in concluding that 'the main research outcome is that practically everything in the European student experience may be assessed as a benefit' (23), and that even negative aspects are eventually perceived by students as enriching. The various evaluations of the ERASMUS programme have, however, revealed specific problems, such as inadequate preparation of students by their home institution before their period abroad (Teichler 2004a). The most commonly cited problems, however, were related to: administration (particularly in Greece, France and central and eastern European countries); accommodation (most common in Italy and central and eastern European countries); and financial issues. To some extent, financial problems can be seen to be related to the country of origin rather than of destination: Greek students, for example, often report financial difficulties because of the low cost of living in their home country when compared with many other European nations (Raikou and Karalis 2007). Nevertheless, in most cases, these reported problems do not seem to have detracted from a generally positive experience.

When students' accounts of their time abroad are compared with their initial motivations and expectations, some interesting contrasts emerge. In relation to the academic progress that students hoped to make as a result of their mobility, survey data suggest that most are successful in this endeavour (Sussex Centre for Migration Research 2004). Indeed, a majority of ERASMUS students claimed that their academic progress during their time abroad had been better than during a corresponding period at home (Maiworm 2001; Teichler 1996). Nevertheless, it appears that for many such students, by the time they return home, academic progress is valued considerably less than the cultural benefits gained through overseas study. However, Teichler (2004a) argues that the two are, in many ways, inextricably intertwined:

When describing the value of the study experience abroad, many ERASMUS students refer to the eye-opening and horizon-broadening effect. Contrasts in academic paradigms, modes of teaching and learning, communication styles, cultural environments, daily life of students—all contribute to a better understanding of the field of study, the culture and the host country (406).

In relation to the EU's own objective of strengthening a sense of common European identity, data from students are not conclusive. Studies of participants from the United Kingdom (King and Ruiz-Gelices 2003) and Greece (Raikou and Karalis 2007) indicate that those who have spent a year abroad tend to be more favourably disposed to European integration, have more interest in European affairs and are more likely to see their identities as at least partly European than their peers who remained at home. Similarly, on the basis of her work with mobile students from across Europe, Murphy-Lejeune (2002) suggests that, as a result of their experiences, these 'new strangers' come to 'question the notion of borders and the meaning of home' (234). However, Papatsiba's (2005) research with French participants came to different conclusions. Indeed, he remarks that 'if the topic of European integration constituted a "politically correct" motivation to support one's application for studies in Europe, it seldom constituted the object of an explicit awareness at the end of the stay' (181). Instead, he suggests that the cultural impact of the stay was experienced at an individual level, rather than as a collective experience. Indeed, cultural difference 'was treated like a new situation that stretched individuals' limits and potential for adaptability rather than as an opportunity to learn how to understand a foreign symbolic system and how to position themselves in it' (183).

There is similar ambiguity about the impact of a period abroad on young adults' employment prospects. Teichler (1996) argues that there is no evidence to suggest that overseas study has any obvious advantage or disadvantage for students' subsequent labour market experiences, although it may help to ease them into jobs that require an understanding of other countries. However, King's (2003) research with UK students comes to the conclusion that 'the official discourse that the year abroad provides students with tools that aid employability seems to be backed by survey findings' (170). Further research is needed to determine whether this is an effect specific to the United Kingdom (perhaps related to the privileged profile of the UK students who are internationally mobile), or has been replicated in other European countries since Teichler's study was published.

We now turn to the findings of our research project examining the motivations and experiences of international students from the United Kingdom. As already noted, our study involved in-depth interviews with 85 individuals seriously considering embarking on or having completed the whole of an undergraduate or postgraduate degree overseas. It differs from the majority of studies on European students in that it is concerned with 'spontaneous' (as opposed to 'integrated') and 'independent' forms of international mobility. Our study has therefore attempted to broaden and deepen knowledge of spontaneous and independent educational mobility amongst European young people, with a focus on students from the United Kingdom. Before discussing our findings in terms of the motivations and experiences of overseas education, we first provide an overview of some broad patterns to have emerged from our sample, beginning with the geography of UK students' mobility.

## THE OVERSEAS MOBILITY OF UK STUDENTS

### Trends in Student Mobility

A very small number of destination countries are heavily represented in our sample. At undergraduate level, the United States was overwhelmingly the preferred country of study, corresponding to what we know of patterns of international student mobility more generally, where the United States captures over half of the total global share (British Council 2004). Whilst a number of our respondents had also considered, or were considering, studying in Canada, our interviews revealed that in some cases this was because Canada was seen as a cheaper (but similar) version of the United States. Only three students had completed undergraduate degrees outside North America—in France, Ireland and Japan. These patterns reflect a number of factors: first, the overwhelming propensity for UK students to study in English—only the most obvious English-speaking countries were considered potential study destinations. In some ways, this again coincides with what we know about international students more generally, preferring an English-language medium education (British Council 2004). For most international students, however, this decision is motivated by a desire for proficiency in a *second* language (Balaz and Williams 2004), whereas for UK students, this is clearly not a factor and reflects in part, as noted earlier, a general decline in the linguistic competencies of British students (Findlay et al. 2006). Second, the cultural appeal of the United States for UK students was undeniable. Interviews revealed the strong influence of exposure to Hollywood films and television programmes imported from the United States, leading students to imagine and desire a certain 'lifestyle' attached to study in North America. A third reason for the geographical patterns that we have observed relates to what we have identified as 'global circuits of higher education' (Brooks and Waters 2009). UK students (like international students more generally) are increasingly cognisant of how different higher education institutions rank globally, reflecting the heightened importance given to published international league tables. For UK students, mobility is largely 'horizontal' (rather than vertical) (Rivza and Teichler 2007). Whilst King and colleagues have stressed the perceived 'marketability' of an *American* education system (Sussex Centre for Migration Research 2004), it was notable that many individuals did not seem to select their overseas destination by country, but rather by *institution* and particularly institutional status (Brooks and Waters 2009). For several students, North American institutions (notably Ivy League institutions) offered an acceptable alternative to an Oxbridge education in the United Kingdom. These factors will be expanded upon in the following section.

At postgraduate level, study destinations were slightly more diverse and included some European countries such as Italy, Sweden, Finland, Belgium, the Netherlands and France. However, despite this apparent diversity, half of those in our sample who had completed a postgraduate degree overseas had studied in North America (Canada and the United States). Some of the reasons for these patterns are similar to those at undergraduate level—particularly the desire for an English-medium education (only two students in our sample had studied in a language *other than English*) and the importance of institutional status. However, postgraduates were also concerned with the resources and staff available at particular institutions/academic departments overseas (not necessarily those with a high 'global' ranking), and academic staff in UK institutions often served to 'link' students with particular academic supervisors overseas, acting as 'feeders' for postgraduate study abroad (Brooks and Waters 2010). For those looking to complete a postgraduate degree overseas, financial factors were also often an important consideration.

More generally, in terms of the geography of UK students' mobility, our findings support other work by the Sussex Centre for Migration Research (2004), which notes that although the mobility of UK students to European destination countries declining, it is more than compensated for by rising numbers seeking study in other destinations, notably North America. This, alongside the observation that only two individuals in our sample reported having studied for their degree in a language other than English, raises important questions about the quality and nature of UK students' 'overseas' experiences (Waters and Brooks, forthcoming). To what extent is such spontaneous, horizontal mobility exposing students to potentially enriching forms of cultural difference?

The issue of socio-economic diversity provides another interesting comparison with extant literature on European student mobility. In contrast to some of the claims made with respect to the ERASMUS programme (e.g. Teichler 1996; Maiworm 2001), but corroborating Findlay et al. (2006), the individuals represented in our study were on the whole a highly privileged group of young people. This was particularly true of our 'undergraduate' sample, where almost two thirds of those interviewed had attended a private school at secondary level. Nearly all reported high levels of parental support, financially and in other less tangible ways, and many attended schools that actively encouraged overseas study (through the provision of various resources) at degree level. Our 'postgraduate' sample was more diverse and included some individuals that had followed less conventional routes through education (such as mature students). Fewer individuals within this sample had attended elite private secondary schools and more had therefore received less direct support for their decision to study overseas. Diverging again from what is known of ERASMUS students (Teichler 1996; Maiworm 2001; Sussex Centre for Migration Research 2004), our sample comprised slightly more men than women (48 compared to 37).

As described previously, and in contrast to some of the work reviewed on 'integrated' mobility, King (2003) has suggested that mobile students generally emanate from family backgrounds where 'professional activity' and 'cosmopolitan experiences' are the norm (166). Our findings support these observations, not just in terms of the relatively privileged socio-economic backgrounds of UK students but also with regard to 'cosmopolitan' experience. We have found a strong association between international travel and the decision to study for a degree overseas. The vast majority of our research participants had travelled a lot, either as a child, with parents, or as a young adult with family or friends, prior to attending university. Undoubtedly, these experiences of travel had exposed individuals to the possibility of going overseas for education. Several participants had visited family members residing abroad when growing up. Many had also experienced overseas travel and living abroad as part of a 'gap year' between tertiary and higher education and/or a 'placement' as part of an undergraduate degree programme. Having reviewed the most prominent patterns in our data, in the sections that follow we draw upon these further to examine, first, the motivations underlying overseas study, and then, secondly, students' reflections on the nature of their experiences.

## MOTIVATIONS AND EXPERIENCES OF UK STUDENTS OVERSEAS

### Reasons for Overseas Study

Amongst our sample, motivations for 'spontaneous' and independent overseas study were diverse, although recurrent themes are clearly apparent. These are: (a) financial considerations (an overseas education being seen as cheaper than an equivalent degree in the United Kingdom); (b) employment and career-oriented factors (concerns with securing 'positional advantage' in a competitive graduate labour market); (c) status considerations (the importance of choosing a highly ranked institution); and (d) enjoyment and self-gratification, over and above concerns about employability and careers. In what follows, we examine each of these in turn, using illustrative examples from the data.

Financial motivations for considering education overseas were most pertinent for individuals studying at postgraduate level, where self-funding was more widely apparent. Some European destination countries were seen as significantly cheaper than the United Kingdom, as the following quotations illustrate:

> To study in Europe is cheaper, to study in North America is more expensive. So therefore I'll study in Amsterdam. [ . . . ] I feel like I'm getting a quality education for a fraction of the price [ . . . ] I was considering doing a similar course in London but, as I say, the fees are more expensive in London and the cost of living is a lot more expensive. *(Eamon, undergraduate considering studying for an MA in the Netherlands or Sweden)*

Idris, another undergraduate student, had had very similar financial concerns, motivating the decision to look overseas for master's level study:

> It's a lot cheaper to do a master's in Holland, say, than it is in the UK, for law. And I think it's about £900 on average over there and here, like, the cheapest would be three grand. [ . . . ] I looked at America briefly and the fees are so high that it would be quite difficult. *(Idris, undergraduate considering studying for an MA in the Netherlands)*

Such sentiments—that fees for postgraduate study in the United Kingdom are prohibitive—were expressed by several interviewees, and reflect recent media coverage of the international mobility of British students (Clark 2006). The low cost of study in countries such as the Netherlands and Sweden have made these attractive destinations for UK students seeking postgraduate qualifications. One individual mentioned an additional, unexpected financial advantage of studying in parts of Europe, saying: 'It's effectively the same price for me to travel back from somewhere like France or Holland as it would from here [Surrey] to Birmingham' *(Jamie, undergraduate considering studying for an MA in France or the Netherlands)*. The growth of discount airlines offering cheap airfares to European destinations have, inadvertently, made study in Europe a more appealing prospect for some British students.

However, although European destination countries were attractive to a minority of UK students, choices were fundamentally constrained by language. With only a couple of exceptions, students only considered degree programmes offered wholly in English. Idris here describes the appeal of the Netherlands:

> Well, they normally teach in English. I mean, that would be a big factor for me. [ . . . ] I'd really only consider countries where I'd be taught in English, which would mean, like, Scandinavia or Holland really [ . . . ] That's why I haven't really considered much of, like southern Europe because it's a lot harder to get by if you don't know the language.

Such sentiments were extremely common amongst UK students.

In line with claims in the literature about young European students, some research participants viewed overseas study as an 'investment in their futures' and were cognisant of the 'professional stakes' of pursuing a degree abroad (Murphy-Lejeune 2002: 100). For a few individuals, an international master's degree was seen as a way to offset the effects of 'credential inflation' in the United Kingdom, where an undergraduate degree is becoming, increasingly, the 'norm'. Maxwell's view illustrates well this perception of the overseas degree:

> So many people get degrees now, it's harder to get jobs, and even so, lots of people are starting master's now because it's harder to get jobs. So I think, if I did a master's from somewhere else it makes you stand out that little bit more and gives you something a bit more to talk about in an interview.

Other individuals talked more generally, although in fairly vague terms, about how an overseas degree would enhance their employability several years down the line, giving them something 'different' that will make them stand out from the crowd.

For those seeking an undergraduate degree abroad in particular, status considerations were often paramount. The perceived international status of an overseas institution was a crucial factor in the decision-making process. In several cases, an overseas degree was seen as an 'acceptable alternative' to a prestigious Oxbridge education in the United Kingdom. Consequently, high ranking Ivy League institutions in the United States featured prominently in sixth-formers' accounts of why they were pursuing an overseas education. Darren's views, as expressed here, were typical of our sixth-former cohort. He said: 'I'm going to wait and hear from Oxford! Depending on what Oxford say, I'll decide whether or not I'll apply there [the US] . . . And so, if I don't [get into Oxford], then I'll probably apply to Harvard.' In many cases, Ivy League institutions offered privileged and high-achieving UK students a 'second chance' at success (Brooks and Waters 2009). This finding is not unlike Wiers-Jenssen's (2008) claims that Norwegian students who failed to get accepted on to their preferred medical course in Norway chose, instead, to pursue a 'second-best' medical degree course overseas.

Although some students, then, were quite strategic in their choice of overseas destinations and institutions, with status and career considerations in mind, many others appeared almost to shun planning altogether (Brooks and Everett 2008). For these students, overseas study was perceived as a way of pursuing pleasure, prolonging an enjoyable student experience, and forestalling the inevitable onset of full-time employment (Waters and Brooks 2010). Many individuals that we interviewed described the excitement and adventure associated with study overseas—offering the chance to 'try something different', to 'experience the world', or simply to 'have fun'. For sixth-formers seeking an undergraduate degree overseas, the US liberal arts system enabled them to try their hand at lots of different subjects, unlike the UK system, which forces students to decide on a single or combined degree programme from the outset. This opportunity for 'shopping around' offered the freedom and the extension of youth that many so desired.

## Reflections on Experiences of Overseas Study

Studies of international student mobility have been significantly concerned with identifying the advantages of an overseas education, whether viewed in terms of academic studies, cultural experiences, linguistic competences or specific professional preparation (Maiworm 2001; Teichler 2004a). We have already noted the insignificance of 'languages' in motivating British international students, and have also suggested that, due to the dominance of North America as a destination country, exposure to cultural difference may be limited. Here, we focus on UK students' and graduates' reflections on specifically 'labour market advantages'.

We have noted previously that the literature on European students is equivocal when it comes to employment prospects resulting from a period spent abroad (compare Teichler 1996 and King 2003). Our findings paint a similarly mixed picture. Advantages noted by participants included 'gaining confidence' and providing 'something different to talk about' during job interviews, increased cultural awareness, and the ability to work with people from diverse social backgrounds. Lillian, who currently works for a law firm after pursuing postgraduate studies at the European University Institute in Florence, was particularly (and unusually) emphatic in describing the many positive advantages she saw in her overseas education:

> I had that international focus. They were a very international firm and you know I was a prime candidate for them. [ . . . ] I do think it has actually given me opportunities I wouldn't have had otherwise. I think I stood out from the crowd in a big way.

Despite all of these advantages, however, she admits to being 'behind' her peers in terms of standard career progression.

Perhaps more common were the *disadvantages* mentioned by participants, particularly in relation to the UK labour market. Leo here refers to the lack of recognition often given to overseas credentials in the British context. He said: 'I thought it would help me more than it did . . . I suppose it's a bit frustrating that more people hadn't heard of where I'd studied.' Doug works in Maastricht as a lecturer and MBA programme director. Although he feels that his overseas degree has been an advantage for him *working in Europe*, he imagines it would hold him back, should he decide to return to the United Kingdom. He has been running an international MBA programme in the Netherlands for over ten years, and has observed a general lack of interest from UK students. In fact, he said:

We don't have one single British student and we have tons of students from Germany, from France, from Italy—countries where they struggle with the English language but they come and they do our MBA. We do not attract anyone from the UK, and my feeling is that people in Britain, why would they want an international MBA programme? Why would they want to meet somebody from France? [ . . . ] I wonder if people in the UK really care about that. [ . . . ] I think the UK is very sort of inward looking or looking towards the US but it's not interested in the, in culture, in international culture much.

Here he draws attention to a wider perception of the insularity and assumed superiority of British culture, resulting in a failure to recognize and appreciate overseas credentials and experience. Other students with qualifications from mainland Europe made similar observations—an international education is beneficial but only if you want to work in Europe. It is disadvantageous in the British labour market:

Oh, I think it's a plus. I think it looks good on your CV, particularly for the jobs in Brussels, because it [the international MA] really does have a good reputation in Brussels. In the EU world it's very highly regarded. I don't think people in this country [UK] really know what it is. It's not like saying, 'oh, I went to Cambridge' or somewhere! I don't think people really appreciated what it is [ . . . ]. I don't think most people [in the UK] have heard of it, to be honest. *(Faith, MA European Studies at the College of Europe)*

This brings us to a more general observation about the geography of overseas credentials and labour market outcomes—an international education was undoubtedly most beneficial for a number of individuals who had decided to seek permanent employment and residency abroad. Study had enabled them to get a 'foot in the door' when it came to local overseas labour markets—a door which may otherwise be effectively shut to foreigners. For a few individuals, studying was always seen as a means to living abroad and gaining permanent settlement. One participant, for example, said that having a degree from Australia 'allowed me to stay in Australia— it's as simple as that . . . [It] ticked a lot of boxes for me for other things like immigration and job prospects'.

In terms of labour market advantages, then, our findings paint a mixed picture. Whilst some participants talked of the benefits of overseas study, others talked of explicit disadvantages, and more still decided that their overseas education had had no discernable impact on their career to date. We would suggest that, in general, it is not the overseas nature of the educational experience *per se* but the particular (high status) institutions preferred by our sample that has offered them the greatest advantages.

## CONCLUSION

In this chapter we have examined the nature of educational mobility amongst young Europeans, providing a review of the extant literature on this topic, before offering our own critical reflections on the patterns, motivations and experiences of UK students, based on a recently completed in-depth qualitative study. The existing literature has, on the whole, focussed on 'organized' or 'integrated' movement, typical of the successful ERASMUS programme that promotes educational mobility on a sizeable scale within Europe. Consequently, whilst our knowledge of this is now quite considerable, much less is known about other, 'spontaneous' forms of mobility, involving a smaller number of individuals seeking education overseas, on their own initiative, for the whole of an undergraduate or postgraduate degree.

With regard to UK students, we outlined some expected and some less anticipated findings from our research. British students, unlike other European students but in common with international students more generally, demonstrated an overwhelming preference for study in North America over European destinations. As observed by Findlay et al. (2006), this reflects in large part the declining linguistic competencies of students with the United Kingdom, but it also, we have argued, indicates wider concerns with accessing educational institutions with 'global status'. This is most apparent from the trends that emerged in our sample with regards to the particular (Ivy League) institutions attended by individuals. We also noted the generally privileged nature of our sample and contrasted this with a more socially diverse cohort of European students involved, for example, in the ERASMUS programme. One of the main concerns of the literature to date on European student mobility has been with identifying the labour market advantages associated with overseas study, and we have discussed these in relation to UK students. Mirroring the complicated picture painted by the literature, we found that overseas study offered advantages *and* disadvantages whilst also having no obvious impact on the careers of some individuals.

## ACKNOWLEDGMENTS

We would like to thank the British Academy for funding the research; Helena Pinloff-Wilson for conducting the fieldwork; and all our respondents who gave up their time to be interviewed.

## REFERENCES

Araujo, E. (2007) 'Why Portuguese Students Go Abroad to do Their PhDs', *Higher Education in Europe*, 32 (4), pp. 387–397.
Balaz, V. and Williams, A. (2004) '"Been there, Done that": International Student Migration and Human Capital Transfers from the UK to Slovakia', *Population, Space and Place*, 10, pp. 217–237.

Baty, P. (2009) Mobility slows but EU wants many more to join Erasmus, *Times Higher Education*, 29th October.

Birtwistle, T. (2007) 'European and European Union Dimensions to Mobility', E. Jones and S. Brown (Eds.), *Internationalising Higher Education* (London: Routledge).

British Council (2004) *Vision 2020: Forecasting International Student Mobility*. Report produced with Universities UK and IDP Education Australia.

Brooks, R. and Everett, G. (2008) 'The Prevalence of "Life-Planning": Evidence from UK Graduates', *British Journal of Sociology of Education*, 29, pp. 325–337.

Brooks, R. and Waters, J. (2009) A Second Chance at 'Success': UK students and global circuits of higher education, *Sociology*, 43, 6, 1085-1102.

Brooks, R. and Waters, J. (2010) Social Networks and Educational Mobility: the experiences of UK students, *Globalisation, Societies and Education*, 8, 1, 143-157.

Clark, T. (2006) 'A free lunch in Uppsala'. *The Guardian,* 24 October 2006.

Conradson, D. and Latham, A. (2005) 'Friendship, Networks and Transnationality in a World City: Antipodean Transmigrants in London', *Journal of Ethnic and Migration Studies*, 31 (2), pp. 287–305.

Commission of the European Communities (1989) *ERASMUS Programme. Annual Report 1988* (Brussels, COM (89) 192 final).

Findlay, A., King, R., Stam, A. and Ruiz-Gelices, E. (2006) 'Ever Reluctant European: The Changing Geographies of UK Students Studying and Working Abroad', *European Urban and Regional Studies*, 13 (4), pp. 291–318.

Guth, J. and Gill, B. (2008) 'Motivations in East-West Doctoral Mobility: Revisiting the Question of Brain Drain', *Journal of Ethnic and Migration Studies*, 34 (5), pp. 825–841.

Haug, G. (1996) 'Student Mobility between Europe and the US', *European Journal of Education*, 31 (2), pp. 181–192.

King, R. (2003) 'International Student Migration in Europe and the Institutionalisation of Identity as "Young Europeans"', in J. Doomernik and H. Knippenberg (Eds.) *Migration and Immigrants: Between Policy and Reality*, pp. 155–179 (Amsterdam: Askant).

King, R. and Ruiz-Gelices, E. (2003) 'International Student Migration and the European "Year Abroad": Effects on European Identity and Subsequent Migration Behaviour', *International Journal of Population Geography*, 9, pp. 229–252.

Maiworm, F. (2001) 'ERASMUS: Continuity and Change in the 1990s', *European Journal of Education*, 36 (4), pp. 459–472.

Murphy-Lejeune, E. (2002) *Student Mobility and Narrative in Europe: The New Strangers* (London: Routledge).

Papatsiba, V. (2005) 'Political and Individual Rationales of Student Mobility: A Case-Study of ERASMUS and a French Regional Scheme for Studies Abroad', *European Journal of Education*, 40 (2), pp.173–188.

Prague Communiqué (2002) *Prague Summit of the European Ministers of Higher Education*, May 18–19, 2002.

Raikou, N. and Karalis, T. (2007) 'Student Mobility from a Greek Perspective: Benefits and Difficulties as Expressed by the Participating Students', *Higher Education in Europe*, 32 (4), pp. 347–357.

Rivza, B. and Teichler, U. (2007) 'The Changing Role of Student Mobility', *Higher Education Policy*, 20, pp. 457–475.

Sussex Centre for Migration Research (2004) *International Student Mobility* (Brighton: Sussex Centre for Migration Research).

Teichler, U. (1996) 'Student Mobility in the Framework of ERASMUS: Findings of an Evaluation Study', *European Journal of Education*, 31 (2), pp. 153–179.

Teichler, U. (2001) 'Changes of ERASMUS under the Umbrella of SOCRATES', *Journal of Studies in International Education*, 5 (3), pp. 201–227.

Teichler, U. (2004a) 'Temporary Study Abroad: The Life of ERASMUS Students', *European Journal of Education*, 39 (4), pp. 395–408.

Teichler, U. (2004b) 'The Changing Debate on Internationalisation of Higher Education', *Higher Education*, 48, pp. 5–26.

Wachter, B. (2003) 'An Introduction: Internationalisation at Home in Context', *Journal of Studies in International Education*, 7 (1), pp. 5–11.

Waters, J. and Brooks, R. (2010) Accidental Achievers: international higher education, class reproduction and privilege in the experiences of UK students overseas, *British Journal of Sociology of Education* (forthcoming).

Waters, J. and Brooks, R. (forthcoming) 'Vive la différence'? The 'international' experiences of UK students overseas, *Population, Space and Place*.

Wiers-Jenssen, J. (2008) 'Does Higher Education Attained Abroad Lead to International Jobs?' *Journal of Studies in Higher Education*, 12 (2), pp. 101–130.

# 5 Events of Hope and Events of Crisis
## Childhood, Youth and Hope in Britain

*Peter Kraftl*

> As a faith-based organization, every project we have has a goal of
> giving needed physical, medical and humanitarian help to children
> [ . . . ], with the ultimate purpose of bringing spiritual life and accom-
> panying hope, with life-changing faith, strength and direction to all
> those who are served. [ . . . ] Children are our world's future and if
> they do not find hope, health and homes, their future—our world's
> future—is in jeopardy (Children's Hope International 2008).

This chapter is about the event of childhood. I argue that youth cultures
are not simply overwritten by dominant representations or constructions of
childhood. Nor are those cultures merely embodied by youthful practices,
identities or material artefacts. Rather, I want to suggest that dominant
modes of encountering British childhood and youth are also, on occasion,
enlivened by particular kinds of events. Those events may take diverse
forms. Events of childhood may emerge from mundane interpersonal
encounters; or they may explode from a criminal act of violence, repeated
endlessly on our televisions screens; or they may be constituted by a step
change in governmental policy. In each case, childhood is thrown into stark
relief at a particular historical-geographical moment: each event marks a
time and place where childhood *matters*. Each event is a constellation of
discourses, socio-historical constructions, materials and performances.
Events of childhood exceed their constituent elements—they are named, or
categorized, as moments where childhood bears the burden of scrutiny.

Considering childhood as event-al offers a further analytical frame for
understanding youth cultures in Britain. Quite understandably, childhood
and youth studies mobilize representations, materials and performances
as the principal objects of their study (for diverse examples, see Epstein
1998; Muggleton and Weinzierl 2003; Gelder 2005). I want to suggest that
a focus upon events might offer a different perspective on the articulation of childhood within contemporary British culture. This impulse is not
new. For instance, amidst the Centre for Contemporary Cultural Studies'
(CCS) emphasis upon the homology of performance, material culture and
identity, one may recall Stanley Cohen's (1967) iconic 'disaster sequence' as
tensions between Mods and Rockers *became* a seminal event of youth culture. Whilst Cohen relies heavily upon newspaper sources, he demonstrates
that press reportage was not simply geared to the representation of young

people: rather, those documents were in fact complicit in a violent event that exceeded their mere content. The event—the disaster sequence—became the principal object of analysis and the major vehicle through which contemporary British youth was made to matter at that historical juncture.

Cohen's work is viewed as an early exemplar of a gathering interest in the childhood/youth in 'crisis' thesis which has pervaded narratives about British childhoods for some years (Scraton 1997; Wyness 2000; Evans 2006; Katz 2008). As I argue in the third section of this chapter, these narratives do occasionally draw upon particular events (principally criminal acts) to illustrate their analyses. Yet, since Cohen, few have questioned the events themselves—or questioned, rather, why they *became* identifiable events in the social history of childhood. Instead, most writers focus upon representations *of* and reactions *to* particular events, integrating these with wider ranging examples of the social construction of childhood (Valentine 1996; Jenks 2005).

This chapter takes its conceptual inspiration from mounting social-scientific interest in events. I account—selectively—for this interest in the next section. The remainder of the chapter charts a selection of empirical examples that should be considered 'events' of childhood. Principally, this allows me to extend the affective register of crisis into one less commonly associated with childhood—*hope*. Whilst children have remained important symbols for very simplistic representations of both nostalgic and anticipatory hopes—as the prefatory quotation to this chapter alludes—the complex terrain surrounding childhood and hope has only been tentatively mapped (Kraftl 2008). This chapter develops a discussion of the axis of hope-crisis that impinges upon contemporary British childhoods—and does so through a series of identifiable 'events' of childhood.

## CONCEPTUALIZING THE EVENT

Common understandings of the term 'event' often refer simply to a named, spatiotemporally delineated happening (like a birthday party or sports match). Considerable academic energy has been directed towards sketching possible explanatory frames that the concept of the 'event' might offer (Bassett 2008). Whilst there are multiple understandings of the concept, I summarize three explanatory frames below, fleshing out some implications in the remainder of the chapter.

Media theorists have demonstrated how mass-mediated events have become critical to the constitution of Late Modernity. Heyer (1995) argues that the Titanic 'disaster' was one of the first events to capture a mass audience. Mass media representation of the Titanic's sinking ensured that this became an 'event' of Western Modernity. In fact, it was this mediatized process—this event-alizing—that ensured the Titanic's last moments *became* a named event—a 'disaster' (note the parallel with Cohen's later narrative about the Mods and Rockers). Since then, the intensification of mass communication has enabled the framing of certain happenings—such as the 9/11 attacks on New York and Washington, DC—*as* events. Live television has ensured ever-greater audiences as complex political praxes are reduced to the status of event-spectacles and news extravaganzas (Marriott 2007). For Baudrillard (1995) and Virilio (2000), events represent both the zenith of multi-mediated, hyper-real cultures *and*, more prosaically, a key frame for understanding the manipulation, selection and naming of particular occurrences as 'newsworthy'.

At a more intimate scale, human geographers have interrogated the events of interpersonal, embodied encounter via detailed ethnographies which recall the seminal work of Goffman (Goffman 1963). McCormack (2004: 219) opens out the 'event-full' geographies of a week spent participating in Dance Movement Therapy, using line maps to illustrate the animation of place by embodied movements. He advocates what he terms a fidelity to the 'singularity of the event' of interpersonal encounter—its gestures, emotions and dispositions (McCormack 2003: 501). Laurier and Philo (2006) articulate the momentary encounters through which urban (non-) convivialities are construed in coffee shops. Such 'passing encounters' are critical to the *doing* of public places like cafes and bars. Although banal, the events of daily encounter are key sites at which societal norms and expectations—including aged identities—are negotiated. Notably, interpersonal, embodied encounters are often the spark for the kinds of major legal and media events wherein childhood ideals, laws and assumptions are questioned (Lee 1999).

Most recently, architectural theorists have mobilized the concept of the event to destabilize the assumed obduracy of large socio-technical systems. Jacobs (2006) introduces the idea of 'building events' to open out the 'Black Box' of architectural materiality. Rather than taking a named building as an object of analysis, she distends a building so that it becomes a relational effect—a 'diverse network of associates and associations' (Jacobs 2006: 11). A building becomes an event—not simply a material thing—because it actively *takes place*. Relational effects de/compose building events. Thus, building *events* make claims upon the practices, policies and materialities of architecture until they are more or less stabilized as assumed forms—as this or that named piece of architecture. Critically, building events may also exceed a singular built thing. Jacobs (2006) rereads the diverse forms of the 'global high-rise' as a series of multi-scalar, spatially extensive events that emerged with mid-twentieth-century Modernity. In this reading, events exceed the representational and symbolic economies of the mass media *and* the close embodied encounters outlined in the previous frames. Events are not merely happenings; they can also be understood as relational, socio-technical *achievements*—whether buildings, landscapes or political praxes.

## CHILDHOOD AND HOPE/CRISIS

The remainder of this chapter considers childhood both as and via a series of specific, nameable events. The approaches in the preceding section provide a framework for understanding those events. I have confined the analysis to two examples. Each queries the axis of hope and crisis in respect of contemporary British childhoods and youth cultures. The first example comprises a rereading of the kinds of high-profile criminal cases that attract nationwide media attention—and, indeed, considerable academic scrutiny. Such cases could usefully be read as events of interpersonal encounter *and* mass-mediated 'disaster' whose effect is event-al as much as representational. The second example is a 'big thing' of a slightly different register than Jacobs' (2006) high-rises—the UK government's 'Building Schools for the Future' (BSF) programme. This, I argue, is an irrepressibly hopeful event of childhood that promises to embody a socio-technical achievement on the grandest of scales—a nationwide 'break' with the past that at the time of writing is set to transform the landscape of UK schooling. Yet BSF is literally taking place against the backdrop of UK youth policymaking which has, since 2000, in part responded to a slew of critical 'disasters' for British childhood. My intention is to juxtapose a number of instances at which childhood is negotiated via events of different registers and scales. In the process, the chapter begins to unravel the multiple forms of hoping—as well as of pessimistic doomsaying—that are associated with British childhood.

## LOST HOPE: CRIMINALIZED EVENTS

In 2002, two British school girls from Soham in Cambridgeshire were abducted and later found dead. The reaction of the UK media and public alike was purportedly symptomatic of two emergent trends in UK society. First, this case and others like it signalled a temporary sharpening of national (adult) consciousness about the vulnerability of children and, indeed, childhood (Valentine 1996; James and James 2004). The implications for British understandings of childhood and youth 'in crisis' need not be repeated here (Scraton 1997). Second, it constituted one of a series of 'national obsessions'—purportedly beginning with the death of Princess Diana in 1997 (Murphy 2007). These obsessions found their outlet (and their source) in 24-hour media coverage, vigils, conspiracy theories and, increasingly, in then-new Internet discussion forums.

In cases such as the 2002 abductions, it seems to me that three facets of media/public reaction have gone largely unwritten—at least in academic accounts that detail their implications for the social construction of British childhood. First, the banality of the encounters themselves. Strangely, perhaps, the make-up of the material act of abduction—what distinguishes that act from a noncriminal act; what 'went wrong'—remains solely the substance of press reportage. Second, the translation of that material act into a national obsession—a *public event*—is simply assumed. Yet the reimagining of such cases as national events matters nearly as much as their implications (in lawmaking or policy writing, for instance). Events of childhood like these provoke their own effects and affects—they do not *just* challenge us to rethink our assumptions about childhood. For, third, public events of childhood do certain things to their publics. They stir and are nourished by certain emotions and create affective bonds—of despair, outrage, grief, loss and, ultimately, an ambivalent kind of hope. Children— *en masse*—signify one of our greatest repositories for hope (Kraftl 2008). Against this backdrop, nothing works quite like the loss of a child's life to make the nation's blood boil.

In 2002, then, the British public feared the compromising of one of the most foundational sources of hope: childhood. Fuelled by these passions, the Soham case became an *event* of ever-intensifying scope, with rapidly multiplying effects, some constituting events (like lynch mobs) in themselves:

> The rightwing media have typically manipulated the tragic abduction and murder of Jessica Chapman and Holly Wells [the victims] in order to stir up a climate of mass hysteria. This resulted in the gathering of a medieval-style lynch mob outside Peterborough Crown Court, in which Maxine Carr [the perpetrator's partner] appeared last Wednesday, charged with perverting the course of justice. Seething with hatred, the mob carried placards reading 'Rot in hell' and 'Bring back hanging'. Police restrained them as they screamed obscenities and threw eggs at the van in which Ms Carr was being transported. Many brought their children along to witness the spectacle (Marsden 2002, un-paginated).

> At a time when society is bound by few common experiences or ideals, these moments of tragedy are reinterpreted as moral parables that can unite people. We can all agree that the murder of Holly and Jessica was an evil act. In our capacity to feel sorrow at this waste of human life, we are apparently reaffirming our bonds with others, and showing that we are not just out for ourselves (Appleton 2002, un-paginated).

> What an appalling tragedy. May God give Holly's and Jessica's parents the strength to cope, and may Holly and Jessica rest in peace. As the mother of an 8 year old boy, I'm now paranoid about letting him out of my sight—what is the world coming to? (BBC Cambridgeshire 2003).

As Appleton's excerpt signals, the extent of public reaction to the schoolgirls' murders installed a strongly affective—if spatially distant—bond between victims, their families, and the general public. Through the becoming-event of the Soham abductions, the very nature of childhood became not only a talking point, but an *event* in itself. The Soham case was an encounter between an adult and two children which became a criminal act, and which simultaneously—for a whole array of complex reasons—became a national event. That event—that moment of childhood—encompassed its own set of emotions. One of the most significant was hope: that fundamental human hope for children, for the next generation, for the most vulnerable, was severely dented through the Soham event. Hence: 'what is the world coming to?'

A more recent case stirred the interest of the British public and media as much as the Soham abductions, and warrants a little more sustained analysis. In May 2007, four-year-old Madeleine McCann went missing from her family's apartment during a holiday in Portugal. Her disappearance stimulated considerable moral debate about her parents' absence from the apartment when she went missing. I am more concerned, however, with the multiple kinds of event that both characterized and were constituted by this case. Principally, these events were orchestrated by and via the UK media and (certain sections of) the UK general public.

A key concern of the UK media was to pick apart the moments, people and materials that constituted Madeleine's disappearance. A number of newspapers mused about various clues: a man seen walking away from the McCann's apartment at 21:15 in a southerly direction; the colour of Madeleine's pyjamas; a description of her favourite toy; the movements of a family friend who checked upon the McCann's children at 21:30; etcetera (BBC Leicester 2008; Brown and Bird 2007). Later, the Daily Telegraph published a sketch diagram showing in fine detail the movements of the first man suspected of abducting Madeleine (Gammell 2008). Their investigations seemed to reflect a thirst for the intimate *details* surrounding Madeleine's disappearance. Paramount was knowledge of which details did and did not matter (or were not, in fact, 'true'). Only then could the vast array of possible people, movements, actions and materials be narrated as a coherent *event*—a story with a beginning and end. With the provisional naming of that event *as* the abduction of Madeleine McCann, moral debate about the case—and a whole array of subsequent acts—could proceed. There remained uncertainty about what precisely had happened: questions about whether this event constituted a case of 'abduction', of 'poor parenting', or even a 'cover-up' of some terrible accident. These different versions of the same event simply fuelled greater curiosity about the *event* of Madeleine's disappearance *per se*: both about the truth behind what happened on 3 May 2007, and the moral and social implications of that truth and any other versions thereof. Moreover, and more importantly, the ensuing controversy regarding the intimate details of this event rendered it a moment of adult-child contact—an *event of childhood*—which mattered far more than most. The very details of this event *became* central to heated, ongoing debates regarding the vulnerability of children, regarding adult care for children, and regarding the possible motivation for taking *this* (or any) child.

The details surrounding Madeleine's disappearance were not, however, the only elements of the case that were configured as an event. Further, mediatized events were crucial to the ongoing progress of the hunt for Madeleine. Many of these events were subsequently historicized in comprehensive 'timelines' (BBC Leicester 2008), or rather, lists of events which represented the progress of the case. In June 2007, Madeleine's parents appeared on the BBC television show *Crimewatch* to appeal for the British public's help in finding their daughter. In July 2007, *Harry Potter* author JK Rowling called for posters of Madeleine to be displayed worldwide, following a synchronized plan. In September 2007, Kate McCann (Madeleine's mother) was declared an official suspect in her daughter's abduction. In October 2007, Madeleine's parents appeared on Spanish television to highlight the effect upon them of allegations charging their involvement in their daughter's disappearance. In November 2007, congregations from four churches local to the McCann's home 'come together to pray for Madeleine and other abducted, trafficked or exploited children' (BBC Leicester 2008). Each entry on the timelines was an event of sorts: events mattered to the mediatized reality and later historical narration of the case. Each event was—and I do not mean this cynically—orchestrated to do something different: to publicize the case globally, simultaneously (the posters); to instil the briefest sense of hope and to recognize the plight of missing children (the church service); to set the record straight and to appeal for information (the television appearances). Some events were certainly *for* the media, carefully planned and presented by public relations consultants for the McCanns. Others were not, but were picked upon *by* the media as 'key moments' in the ongoing saga. Looking back through the narrative provided by the 'timelines', then, the disappearance of Madeleine McCann was given historical substance by a series of ostensibly diverse *events*.

Perhaps key to the constitution of Madeleine's disappearance as an *event* of childhood was the intense and ongoing attention afforded by the British public. Like the death of Princess Diana, public interest both signalled that this was an event that mattered to them, and enabled the whole affair to become ever more event-al in nature. Kim Murphy (2007: un-paginated), writing in the *Los Angeles Times*, contextualized public reaction thus: '[i]n Britain, an estimated 77,000 children go missing every year: kidnapped, runaway, grabbed by a former spouse, murdered, lost in the woods. But for some reason no one seems able to explain, the case of Madeleine McCann has become a national obsession'. Murphy's reflection upon the case is significant for two reasons. First, in that it underscores the visibility of the case and, particularly, attendant public reaction *itself* as a crucial moment in contemporary British culture. It was not simply the McCann case that was worthy of comment but rather the particularly notable reaction of the British public. Second, Murphy's piece confirms that the intimate, momentary encounter that comprised the event of Madeleine's disappearance had for some reason gained a resonance that 77,000 other, similar, cases did not.

Public interest in Madeleine's disappearance took various guises. Knight (2007: un-paginated) argues that—unusually—it was not the British media but the British *public* who were responsible for alleging the involvement of Madeleine's parents, and the subsequent barrage of ill-feeling towards them. Knight's refrain is one of 'blame': *blame* for thousands of bloggers, forum users and conspiracy theorists making use of the Internet to publicize their thoughts. And *blame* for their feeling such mysterious interest in the McCann's plight. For Knight (2007: un-paginated), this was a 'weird national seizure', an 'apparently seismic event' that the British public felt a desire to own, capitulating the increasingly blurred relationship between news, gossip and the truth about the events of Madeleine's disappearance. In other words, the becoming-public of the case was a becoming-*event* of quite different proportions from the potentially mundane materiality of what happened on 3 May (and what happens to 77,000 other children in Britain every year).

Madeleine's disappearance represented a two-fold crisis. On the one hand, many commentators urged a consideration of the negative, hyperbolic public response to the case, which represented a seemingly monstrous incarnation of Britain's penchant for serial national obsessions. On the other, the press and the media were—however loosely—united around an acknowledgment of the despair caused by the events of 3 May. This was *also* simply the latest in a long series of events (some similar, some not) indicative of an ongoing crisis affecting Britain's youth. Nothing more needed be said.

Amongst predominant feelings of despair and anger, hope figured less prominently. As I argued at the outset of this paper, hope—as adjective, noun, feeling or verb—is far less commonly associated with contemporary British childhoods. In a sense, Madeleine's was simply a case of lost hope. This was another setback for traditional images of childhood which emphasize nostalgia, futurity and innocence. Each day gone without finding Madeleine was figured as an incremental loss of hope for both the family and the public. Yet hope was also mobilized in more particular ways with respect to Madeleine's disappearance. Hope was a significant component of both particular events in the case, and of the event of the whole affair. Each event, however minor—each police press conference, each new lead—was figured as a moment of hope (Daily Mail 2007). Each event was both a private, pragmatic moment of hope for the McCann family and, increasingly, an incremental step in a less distinct sense of public hoping for a happy ending.

Hope was an adjective called upon to describe the private plight of the McCann family as it was rehearsed in public—a family who would 'never give up hope' (Liverpool Daily Post 2007). Each false lead was simply written out of the case as 'false hope' or 'a week of hope and heartbreak' for the family (Daily Mail 2007). Hope was simply a word—the best word—to describe how the events of Madeleine's disappearance were being played out and felt in the McCann family's lives, following a rhythmic cycle of hope, despair, new hope, etcetera. The word hope—as it embodied the spectre of hopelessness and powerlessness—was a hollow signifier for this event and the many smaller events comprising it.

In public, however, hope was *mobilized* in particular ways, *through* particular events. In the McCann's home village, so-called 'ribbons of hope', cards, flowers and toys were left on a war memorial. Hope literally took place in a material display of solidarity for Madeleine and her family. This was an event of display that demonstrated the almost universal hopefulness attached to children: 1,000 toys—that symbol of childhood—were sent from all over the United Kingdom to be left at the memorial (Williams 2007). Elsewhere, Internet message boards and social networking sites such as *Bebo* were filled with entries stating simply 'hope you're safe Madeleine'. Hope represented an appropriate term for the public to use in their efforts to display care and express their own feelings about the case.

Hope was not the predominant emotion in the event of Madeleine McCann's disappearance. Yet, as an adjective and an emotion, hope did three things. First, hope was an adequate term to describe the ongoing energy being dedicated by the McCann family, the media and the police to finding Madeleine. Second, hope came to characterize particular events (like the transformation of a village war memorial) with particularly poignant meanings. Hope denoted a sense that Madeleine's safe return would be a joyous moment for a whole country—that the return of a missing *child* would be a cause for (an event of) celebration and relief. Third, the couplet of despair/hope was mobilized repeatedly—if not comparatively often—in journalistic attempts to render the manifold twists and turns of this case.

## PLANNED HOPE: BUILDING SCHOOLS FOR THE FUTURE

I want to turn more briefly to a second kind of event of a quite different register: a policy event. I suggest that, although government policies are first and foremost documentary guidelines, some policies may also be conceived as events (den Besten et al. 2008). An example of this is the UK government's recent 'Building Schools for the Future' programme. Under this scheme, *every* secondary school (compulsory for 11- to 16-year-olds) in the United Kingdom will be rebuilt or refurbished in the next 15 years (DfES 2004a). Whilst purported as a significant step change in the history and material landscape of British schooling, BSF also embodies an event of childhood that is preeminently hopeful.

The BSF programme represents far more than simply a piece of documentary policy guidance. It constitutes the pinnacle of the UK government's commitment, since 1997, to pre-19 education. It is a programme of enormous scope. In one Local Authority alone, BSF will provide £330 million of development. BSF has required fundamental revision of the way in which architects, contractors and Local Authorities design and build schools. Although ostensibly a building programme, BSF promises to radically alter the school curriculum, children's experiences of schooling, and the lives of families and communities that surround schools:

> For the first time since the Victorian era, a Government has committed itself to bring together significant investment in buildings . . . with significant educational reform . . . [BSF will] ensure secondary pupils in every part of England learn in 21st-century facilities (DfES 2004b: 2).

> [BSF will] achieve a step-change in the quality of school buildings for every secondary pupil. We want to move from 'patch and mend' to 'rebuild and renew' . . . , to create an environment in which to achieve educational transformation and innovation . . . [BSF will] help LEAs to reform and redesign the pattern of education . . . to best serve each community for decades to come (DfES 2004b: 22).

BSF promises (or, rather, *hopes*) to replace schools—materially, figuratively, economically, culturally—at the centre of their local communities. In a series of 'waves', the programme will literally sweep across the country during the next 15 years. Building Schools for the Future *is* an event because it anticipates doing so much: philosophically and pragmatically, it will herald change to children's learning; materially, it will leave *every* secondary school (and every community around it) with a brand-new building; socially, it will symbolize new opportunities for deprived and well-to-do communities alike. As press coverage in Coventry City (in the English West Midlands) enthuses:

> BSF is far more than a building programme . . . [BSF will] raise standards and improve access and participation in learning at all levels. The programme will enable the city to accelerate its transformation plans for all secondary education across Coventry . . . to fulfil the council's aim of raising standards and promoting inclusion and motivation to learn . . . [BSF will] change the educational experience for pupils and teachers and increase opportunities for lifelong learning for the wider community. With schools a focal point in every community they serve, virtually every family in the city will be affected by BSF (Coventry City Council 2007).

So much hinges upon BSF because the programme embodies a very special historical juncture: *the* moment ('since the Victorian era') when educational practices and spaces break with the past. Swept along by celebratory proclamations of a new era (and the lure of a shiny new building), this is a national *event*. It has been covered by national and local media, attracting harsh criticism as much as local praise—all of which ensures that this policy event becomes a nationally acknowledged (r)evolution in schooling.

> Coventry City Council is celebrating after . . . its bid for the city's biggest school improvement plan in 50 years were approve. . . . [A City Councillor] said: 'The BSF project will provide world-class teaching and learning environments for all pupils and teachers across the city. But it is not just about bricks and mortar—the programme is about transforming education for generations, providing environments in which every young person can unlock their talents' (Coventry Telegraph 2008).

The UK government has succeeded (at least in Coventry) in installing an optimistic, hopeful, almost joyous reception for BSF at a local level, within certain media. Policymakers and journalists are agreed that BSF somehow represents *more* than a building programme, and more than a change in policy direction for education. Rather, if one revisits the quotations highlighted previously, BSF promises to instigate *community change* via the (ostensibly incontrovertible) goal of *change for young people*. Building Schools for the *Future* intimates the construction—in a building event lasting nearly two decades—of a more hopeful future for children, and UK society at large. That goal—that style of hoping for children on a grand, planned, *national* scale—has been an immutable, perhaps universal facet of Western culture since 1900 at least (Gagen 2004; Kraftl 2008). BSF is a knowingly hopeful policy event with massive potential scope.

In the case of BSF, the quotations presented earlier underscore a kind of universal, future-orientated hopefulness for young people via two specific motifs. The first is the 'unlocking of young people's talents' (Coventry Telegraph 2008). In an era of personalized education and unprecedented emphasis upon 'choice' in accessing public services, BSF rehearses an age-old utopian desire that education might somehow allow young people to develop to their full potential. It presumes—rightly or wrongly—that schooling enables a reflexive, individual project of selfhood (compare Giddens 1991). Were a child to unlock their talents, they would, presumably, be one step closer to a fulfilled adult life.

The second motif is one of community inclusion and lifelong learning. BSF schools are figured by Coventry City Council (2007) as *focal points* for their communities. Educational transformation figures a hopeful future for young people: yet it also does so for *diverse* groups of young people, their families, and their neighbours, via the mantra of lifelong learning. For Ruddick (2003), the idea of lifelong learning represents a late-capitalist move to extend youthfulness into adult life stages (see also Miles 2000). The promise of lifelong learning is one which enables individuals to adopt a flexible, personalized approach to their working careers. For Biggs et al. (2006), British social policymaking has, since 2005, attempted to embed an 'age-shift', imbuing increasingly older age groups with the characteristics commonly associated with the young. Biggs et al. (2006) argue that the tenet of lifelong learning diverts education *away* from young people, but reinstates an imagery and ideal of *youthfulness*. Hence BSF's commitment to inclusive, lifelong learning is both a function of hope for children (and their hidden talents) and a kind of hopeful optimism that situates a revitalized school at the centre of an extended culture of youthfulness.

Like Jacobs' (2006) 'building events', the sheer unprecedented force of BSF is, at the time of writing, allowing the programme considerable influence over Britain's schooling landscapes. It will constitute a socio-technical achievement and taking-place at a national scale, combining material, ideological and socio-economic change. Whilst it may not represent the radical change claimed by some commentators, BSF relies relatively heavily upon articulating and inculcating an emotional language of promise and, particularly, hope. In the face of contemporary pessimisms about young people in Britain, there is a sense that BSF offers an alternative, more positive future as part of a brighter future for the country:

> The [refurbished school] will be a flagship building in the heart of a revitalised part of the city centre—the young people in the community deserve the best, and that's what they will be getting (Coventry City Council 2007).

It is worth remembering that in policymaking terms, much of this kind of sentiment emerged via a slightly earlier, but no less major, policy event: the publication of the UK government White Paper *Every Child Matters* in 2004 (DfES 2004c). Despite the heritage of BSF in UK *education* policymaking, the resonance with *Every Child Matters* is relatively clear:

> Our aim is to ensure that every child has the chance to fulfil their potential by reducing levels of educational failure, ill health, substance misuse, teenage pregnancy, abuse and neglect, crime and anti-social behaviour among children and young people (DfES 2004c).

The kind of optimism and hopefulness inherent to *Every Child Matters* turns (and returns) to the intimate relationship between crisis and hope that suffuses the kinds of high-profile cases discussed earlier in the chapter. Although BSF does not explicitly play on the crisis debate, *Every Child Matters* also responded, in part, to another high-profile case: in that instance, the catastrophic failure of a local authority social services department to recognize and deal with an incidence of child abuse.

## CONCLUSION

I have argued that certain facets of what sociologists term the 'social construction' of childhood and youth take place via *events*. Discourses about childhood and youth are contested via events of different kinds. Those events may be media spectacles, revolutionary policies, architectural projects, community gatherings, memorials, and/or intimate, seemingly banal encounters between adults and children. Each constitutes an event (or part of an event) of childhood. Each embodies more than a material thing, a representation or a social practice. Rather, those elements are combined during particular happenings, situations and moments to constitute *events* where childhood comes to matter.

Whereas many authors take high-profile cases of child abuse, neglect or abduction as examples of particular understandings of childhood, I have argued that the very evental nature of those high-profile cases is significant. In particular, events are configured at the very heart of those cases: the details of the 'crime' or other incident; the media coverage; the poster campaigns; the television appearances; etcetera. The media and the public alike often have a thirst for knowledge of the intimate details of a case, and, somehow, to express their feelings about the case via (un-)related events of their own making, such as vigils and online discussions. High-profile cases of child abuse, neglect or abduction often have their own event-al logic. This seems to be particularly true of a more recent example (the disappearance of Madeleine McCann), coverage of which has extended for over a year and comprised multiple, in some cases global, events, mobilizing celebrities and public relations consultants. In Britain, the becoming-event of *some* cases of child abuse, neglect or abduction is also characterized by a complex configuring of an axis between crisis/despair and hope. These cases might be taken as events which exemplify, *par excellence*, the crisis of contemporary British childhoods (and an attendant loss of hope for childhood). Nevertheless, a closer look at some of the events surrounding Madeleine McCann's disappearance reveals more subtle, diverse kinds of hoping. These kinds of hoping were embodied in ongoing, key 'moments' in the case, and in events specifically organized to mobilize a sense of hope, and to spur on the search for Madeleine. Hope was both a key adjective through which the private feelings of the McCann family could be narrated, and a key axis for the organisation of events, vigils and displays generally designed to support the family—and to help members of the public make sense of the confusing moral implications of the case.

In the case of the current 'Building Schools for the Future' programme in the UK, one may discern both events and forms of hoping that differ markedly from the events surrounding high-profile crimes. I suggested that BSF represents a *policy event* that—according to its own supporters and local media coverage in one British city—will radically transform the landscapes of future schooling and their surrounding communities. BSF is no mere documentary guidance: it is comprised of massive funding changes, philosophical shifts and architectural projects. BSF offers optimism, promises change, and instils very particular kinds of hope. Those kinds of hope are embedded in a kind of future-thinking about young people that seeks to enable them to make choices and fulfil their as-yet hidden potential. Thus

BSF's brand of hoping is woven into late capitalist cultural-economic formations that embed 'lifelong learning' and 'flexible working' into a cultural *youthfulness* that is (or could be) colonizing the lives of people of all ages. BSF represents a radical rupture in schooling, yet promises and hopes for so much more. Yet, some of the political precursors upon which BSF draws— if only implicitly— rest upon a kind of hoping that in turn draws upon the childhood in crisis thesis (and high-profile cases of abuse).

It is important that we continue to understand the events that constitute childhood. This chapter has provided a relatively preliminary sketch of the kinds of affective, emotional registers—of crisis, despair and hope—that ensure that events of childhood *matter* to diverse communities of people, in the British context. In tandem with work which has explored young people's own encounters with hope (Kraftl 2008), and bearing in mind the historicization of the events attended to in this chapter, it seems timely to explore how hope moves and mobilizes events and people with respect to childhood and youth in Britain and beyond.

## ACKNOWLEDGMENTS

The research on BSF was supported by AHRC grant number AH/ E507026/1. For the relevant section of the chapter, the author would like to acknowledge the support of AHRC, and that of the other participants on the project: John Horton, especially, for the primary empirical research, and also Olga den Besten, Andrée Woodcock, Michelle Newman, Matthew Kinross and Peter Adey.

## REFERENCES

Appleton, J. (2002) 'The Grief Roadshow Moves On', http://www.spiked-online. com/Printable/00000006DA25.htm (accessed 10 October 2008).
Bassett, K. (2008) 'Thinking the Event: Badiou's Philosophy of the Event and the Example of the Paris Commune', *Environment and Planning D: Society and Space*, 26, pp. 895–910.
Baudrillard, J. (1995) *The Gulf War Did Not Take Place* (Bloomington, IN: Indiana University Press).
BBC Cambridgeshire (2003) 'Have Your Say—Holly Wells and Jessica Chapman— Condolence messages', http://www.bbc.co.uk/cambridgeshire/have_your_say/ holly_jessica_messages9.shtml (accessed 10 October 2008).
BBC Leicester (2008) 'Madeleine McCann: Timeline', http://www.bbc.co.uk/leicester/content/articles/2007/05/10/madeleine_mccann_round_up_feature.shtml (accessed 10 October 2008).
Biggs, S., Phillipson, C., Money, A. and Leach, R. (2006) 'The Age-Shift: Observations on Social Policy, Ageism and the Dynamics of the Adult Lifecourse', *Journal of Social Work Practice*, 20, pp. 239–250.
Brown, D. and Bird, S. (2007) 'Madeleine McCann: The Key Questions', *The Times,* 21 September 2007. http://www.timesonline.co.uk/tol/news/world/ europe/article2422967.ece (accessed 10 October 2008).

Children's Hope International (2008) 'Mission Statement'. http://orphan.children-shope.net/About-Us.2.0.html (accessed 10 October 2008).

Cohen, S. (1967) *Folk Devils and Moral Panics* (London: Paladin).

Coventry City Council (2007) 'Building Schools for the Future in Coventry', http://www.coventry.gov.uk/ccm/navigation/education-and-learning/schools-and-colleges/building-schools-for-the-future/ (accessed 10 October 2008).

Coventry Telegraph (2008) 'All Coventry Schools to Get £330 Million New Look', www.coventrytelegraph.net/news/coventry-news/2008/07/16/all-coventry-schools-to-get-330-million-new-look-92746–21349719/ (ccessed 10 October 2008).

Daily Mail (2007) 'The Search for Madeleine: A Week of Hope and Heartbreak', *Daily Mail, 10 May 2007*, http://www.dailymail.co.uk/news/article-453948/The-search-Madeleine-week-hope-heartbreak.html (accessed 10 October 2008).

Den Besten, O., Horton, J., Adey, P. and Kraftl, P. (2008) 'The Eevent(s) of School (Re)design', paper presented to the Royal Geographical Society (with IBG) Annual International Conference, London, 26–29 August 2008.

Department for Education and Skills (DfES) (2004a) *Five Year Strategy for Children and Learners* (London: HMSO).

Department for Education and Skills (DfES) (2004b) *Building Schools for the Future: A New Approach to Capital Investment* (London: HMSO).

Department for Education and Skills (DfES) (2004c) *Every Child Matters* (White Paper) (London: HMSO).

Epstein, J. (1998) *Youth Cultures: Identity in a Postmodern World* (Oxford: Blackwell).

Evans, B. (2006) '"Gluttony or Sloth": Critical Geographies of Bodies and Morality in (Anti)obesity Policy', *Area*, 38, pp. 259–267.

Gagen, E. (2004) 'Making America Flesh: Physicality and Nationhood in Turn-of-the-Century New York Schools', *Cultural Geographies*, 11, pp. 417–442.

Gammell, C. (2008) 'Madeleine McCann: Sketch Shows First Suspect's Movements', *The Daily Telegraph, 6 August 2008*, http://www.telegraph.co.uk/news/newstopics/madeleinemccann/2506154/Madeleine-McCann-Sketch-shows-first-suspects-movements.html (accessed 10 October 2008).

Gelder, K. (2005) *The Subcultures Reader* (London: Routledge).

Giddens, A. (1991) *Modernity and Self-Identity* (Cambridge: Polity Press).

Goffman, E. (1963) *Behaviour in Public Places: Notes on the Social Organization of Gatherings* (The Free Press, New York).

Heyer, P. (1995) *Titanic Legacy: Disaster as Media Event and Myth* (London: Praeger).

Jacobs, J. (2006) 'A Geography of Big Things', *Cultural Geographies*, 13, pp. 1–27.

James, A. and James, A.L. (2004) *Constructing Childhood: Theory, Policy and Practice* (Basingstoke: Palgrave Macmillan).

Jenks, C. (2005) *Childhood* (London: Routledge).

Katz, C. (2008) 'Cultural Geographies Lecture: Childhood as Spectacle: Relays of Anxiety and the Reconfiguration of the Child', *Cultural Geographies*, 15, pp. 5–17.

Knight, I. (2007) 'You Are All to Blame', *The Times, 16 September 2007*,
http://www.timesonline.co.uk/tol/news/world/europe/article2459924.ece(accessed 10 October 2008).

Kraftl, P. (2008) 'Young People, Hope and Childhood-hope', *Space and Culture*, 11, pp. 81–92.

Laurier, E. and Philo, C. (2006) Possible Geographies: A Passing Encounter in a Café, *Area*, 38, pp. 353–364.

Lee, N. (1999) 'The Challenge of Childhood: Distributions of Childhood's Ambiguity in Adult Institutions', *Childhood*, 6, pp. 455–474.

Liverpool Daily Post (2007) 'Madeleine McCann: Family Say They Will Never Give Up Hope', *Liverpool Daily Post*, 24 December 2007, http://www.liverpooldailypost.co.uk/liverpool-news/breaking-news/2007/12/24/madeleine-mccann-family-say-they-will-never-give-up-hope-64375-20286101/ (accessed 10 October 2008).

Marriott, S. (2007) *Live Television: Time, Space and the Broadcast Event* (London: Sage).

Marsden, R. (2002) 'This Sick Society', http://www.cpgb.org.uk/worker/445/soham.html (accessed 10 October 2008).

McCormack, D. (2003) 'An Event of Geographical Ethics in Spaces of Affect', *Transactions of the Institute of British Geographers*, 28, pp. 488–507.

McCormack, D. (2004) 'Drawing Out the Lines of the Event', *Cultural Geographies*, 11, pp. 211–220.

Miles, S. (2000) *Youth Lifestyles in a Changing World* (Milton Keynes: Oxford University Press).

Muggleton, D. and Weinzierl, R. (2003) *The Post-Subcultures Reader* (London: Berg).

Murphy, K. (2007) 'Girl's Abduction Tugs at Hearts of Britons', *LA Times*, 17 May 2007, http://articles.latimes.com/2007/may/17/world/fg-child17 (accessed 10 October 2008).

Ruddick, S. (2003) 'The Politics of Aging: Globalization and the Restructuring of Youth and Childhood', *Antipode*, 35, pp. 334–362.

Scraton, P. (ed.) (1997) *'Childhood' in 'crisis'?* (London: UCL Press).

Valentine, G. (1996) 'Angels and Devils: Moral Landscapes of Childhood', *Environment and Planning D: Society and Space*, 14, pp. 581–599.

Virilio, P. (2000) *The Information Bomb* (London: Verso).

Williams, M. (2007) 'Ribbons of Hope Greet Madeleine's Father', *The Herald*, 22 May 2008, http://www.theherald.co.uk/news/news/display.var.1415045.0.0.php (accessed 10 October 2008).

Wyness, M. (2000) *Contesting Childhood* (London: Falmer Press).

# 6 Youth Cultures as a Way to Tackle Insecure Transitions into Adulthood

*Barbara Stauber*

This chapter aims to highlight the agency facilitated by youth cultures, how it responds to the demands which late modern European societies impose on young people, and how these young women and men—via this agency—not only find ways to cope with such demands, but also manage to shape their transitions into adulthood. I will analyze the relevance of 'performing selves'— as I will call this agency, which not only, but above all can be observed in the context of youth cultures—within late modern transitions. I will take the perspective of the young actors themselves, using results of my study on a local Goa trance scene in a rural context (Stauber 2004). I will consider the modes of developing transitional careers, and I will regard this specific youth cultural context as a social relational context, in which gender (and other) beliefs will have some impact but also can be reworked (see Ridgeway and Correll 2004). Thus, some tensions which the young individuals experience between coping and shaping their own lives in transition can be made visible, as well as some option spaces deriving from a de-structured situation.

## UNCERTAINTY AND STRUCTURAL INSECURITY IN DE-STANDARDIZED TRANSITIONS INTO ADULTHOOD

When identities—individual or collective, psychological, social or cultural—are mobilized and problematized, both the ability and need to define oneself increase. Reflexivity is intense in the life phase of adolescence and youth, where childhood is to be reworked into adulthood. It is also intensified among sub- or microcultures, cultivating styles and forms of expression. And when epochal shifts are taking place, societal reflexivity is generally increased. In late modern youth culture, these focal points coincide (Fornäs 1995: 212).

There is some terminological looseness, even arbitrariness in qualifying contemporary societies, ranging from late modern or even postmodern and information societies to 'second modernity' and 'reflexive modernization' (see Beck et al. 1996; Beck and Bonß 2001) and 'fluid' or 'liquid modernity' (Bauman 2000). For the purpose of this chapter I will not make a clear terminological choice but shall make the use dependent on the context of the argument. As I am starting from the perspective of young people, I will characterize this late modernity by the effects it has on the life course: In the process of planning, clear rules, linearity and directedness, according to Zygmunt Bauman (1973), constitute key elements of the basic ideology of modernity (without representing a reality for all members of the society, notably not for women); it is exactly these assumptions which are less and less accurate under conditions of late modernity. Assuming this shift, one would first have to talk about structural insecurity—i.e. the end of status passages leading to any secure 'arrival' into a status which would deserve the term 'adulthood' (i.e. economic independence, professional prospects, ability to manage diverse tasks related to this age). Second, one would have to speak about changed basic existential feelings: a general feeling of uncertainty has become dominant—of course under very different circumstances—which directly results from this structurally 'refused arrival' (Blossfeld and Mills 2005). Uncertainty and insecurity can be called the subjective and the structural part of de-standardized life courses (Hurrelmann 2003). As a consequence, biographical transitions increase. They increase in number, simply because late modern life courses are characterized by frequent disruptions and breaks; they become longer, above all in transitions to adulthood, and they have a fundamentally different structure compared to some generations ago: Life course transitions no longer follow predetermined patterns or 'normalities', and they are more and more reversible due to impeded transitions to work, unemployment (already early in life), changes in the demands for qualifications, changed transitions within emotional life, changed transitions from the family of origin into one's 'own' family. The internal dynamics of these various transitions have to be taken into account, each of them implying another logic, following another rhythm, transporting other ascriptions of being 'young' or 'adult' (see Stauber and Walther 2006). Within the context of EGRIS (European Group for Integrated Social Research) we have called them yo-yo transitions, making use of the metaphoric quality of this toy (see EGRIS 2001; Walber et al. 2006). Yo-yo transitions imply—for the young women and men concerned—both risk and chance at the same time.

From the theoretical perspective of subject-oriented transition research, these transitions are not one-dimensionally regarded as potentially problematic. Moreover, they are regarded as potentially eventful: it is *in* transitions, where relevant things happen—relevant with regard to the individual biography as well as with regard to societal developments and societal meaning related to them (see Stauber et al. 2007).

## SOCIETAL DEMANDS ADDRESSED EQUALLY, TAKING DIFFERENT EFFECTS

Following the ideology of individualization, demands in these transitions to adulthood are seemingly made of all young adults in the same way. However, it is clear from discourses on equal opportunities, diversity management etc. that as soon as formally equal demands meet different contexts of social positioning, they can reinforce or even establish social difference—and this is true even if all participants are convinced about the justness of this procedure. It has been one of the most enlightening insights of interactionist gender theory that differences are products and results of processes of differentiation (Fenstermaker and West 2002). Thus, the interactive settings, in which demands are articulated (respectively received), can be decisive: are these settings affirming and supporting these demands, thus reinforcing their selective effects, or are they encouraging reflection and eventually critical scrutiny gender (and other) status beliefs? These status beliefs come into play most easily in situations with hierarchically unequal partners. They can activate respective self-concepts, which again are based on gendering (or differentiating) experiences (see Ridgeway and Correll 2004).

The following—necessarily incomplete—list of demands therefore has to be read with regard to potentially different effects on different structural and interaction contexts—without falling into the trap of reifying difference. In how far these processes then are really 'doing difference', is an empirical question.

Regarding de-standardized life courses, the *first* and basic demand would be to cope simultaneously with a multitude of challenges, questions and problems within the different transitions young women and men have to engage in. Here, the Janus face of individualization becomes obvious: this kind of coping is not only a demand which society makes on the individual, it is at the same time also a demand young women and men are making of themselves. This implies an individualized problem ascription if one is unable to cope with these demands. Doing gender (or doing difference) takes place, where young women and man already are differently involved (e.g. in social responsibility for family members etc.). The complexity of demands is gendering, as soon as young women find themselves in a dilemma of having too many responsibilities and cannot really opt for a specific training route.

*Second*, with regard to the future, young women and men increasingly have to deal with the paradox of planning: on the one hand, they are encouraged by all transitional institutions to plan their transitions and careers, while on the other hand they constantly—already during time at school—experience contingency, which effectively shows them the decreased feasibility of planning (Lecardi 2006). This impression is even reinforced in young women facing the challenge of making their educational investments pay off (Smyth 2004).

The *third* demand means responding to the permanent expectations of the whole social environment of young women and men (including their peers) to present and explain their biographical decisions and developments. The demand to present themselves as competent and tough—as an element of a general performativity of social life—is accompanied by the internal pressure to give reasons for their own transition steps.

The *fourth* demand is linked to the highly reversible processes of becoming autonomous from or again dependent on the family of origin. If intergenerational independence has ever existed in the past, then it is definitively over in the era of yo-yo transitions. Instead, there is semi-dependency and/or semi-autonomy resulting from staying longer and longer within the family of origin due to difficult transitions into work and the ever more precarious start of working life, which add to the basic ambivalence characterizing generational relationships (Lüscher and Pillemer 2004). Becoming autonomous therefore has to be negotiated again and again between the generations. Because these negotiations are very much linked with gendered expectations, this is at the same time a highly gendered and gendering topic.

*Fifth,* young people need to find subjectively adequate ways of, on the one hand, adapting to given opportunities and, on the other, realizing their own ideas. This refers to demands such as maximum flexibility—e.g. with regard to training courses—and maximum mobility in terms of space.

*Sixth,* increasingly, young men—and more women—have to cope with frustrations deriving from experiences with selective schooling systems (especially in Germany). They have to fight against these frustrations affecting their self-image too deeply—and instead try productively to introduce breaks into their transition biography, to use them as starting points in the search for new directions (see the notion of 'biographicity' raised by Peter Alheit and Bettina Dausien 2000).

This is related to the *seventh* demand, namely to safeguard motivation and to manage motivation successfully. This seems to be the core prerequisite for young people to equip them against the setbacks in their path to training and employment (Stauber 2007).

*Eighth,* there are new responsibilities the young have to take on in the context of family relationships; in contrast to the support which in the past was 'normally' given by the parent generation, now increasingly young men but above all young women are called upon to support their parents, all the more so if these are single parents.

*Ninth,* young people's responsibility for themselves is also growing; the core demands on the individual are self-organization, 'steering oneself' or even self-socialization (see Heinz 2002), and this includes recognizing one's own needs and organizing help individually.

In this respect, the *tenth* demand of developing network competence becomes increasingly relevant. Here, indeed, an anchor for the relevance of youth cultures can be found (see Raffo and Reeves 2000). Informal networks help young people to stay socially integrated, even if systemically they are in danger of being excluded. They can thereby also organize a kind of balance in individualized coping. In order not to fall into the trap of reproducing a limited scope of agency, it is important that these networks are heterogeneous and build bridges to other networks (see Walther et al. 2005).

As already mentioned, these demands—and others—are not only made of the individual by society, but in a way they correspond to the demands late modern individuals would make of themselves. This is the main reason for the power of the ideology of individualization: It fits completely into what late-modern individuals would regard as an autonomous and self-directed life. For the very same reason these demands sometimes go unrecognized as societal demands. As an effect, failing to meet these demands would be regarded as an individual failure. And this is the core aspect of individualization: to turn societal demands (and risks) into individual ones.

## COPING WITH DEMANDS, SHAPING YOUTH LIFE: YOUTH CULTURAL SPACES AND NETWORKS

Against the background of these late modern transitions with their multitude of demands on young women and men, one could now read the impact of youth cultures and the latitude for agency they provide the young. This perspective shows that young women and men do have a certain scope for (different kinds of) agency (Emirbayer and Mische 1998; Deutsch 2007) which they use above all in their youth culture environments.

I have gathered some results from a study I carried out a few years ago about young women and men engaged in Goa trance—a more psychedelic and soft version of electronic (techno) music. My snowballed sample included 14 active members aged between 20 and 31 who, in a local community in the countryside of southern Germany, engaged either in organizing outdoor parties or running small businesses for such parties (a male and female DJ, and a female artist) or in relation to the parties (young people as owners of small fashion shops). The sample was based on semi-structured interviews with narrative openings, guided by an open connecting thread; the method for interview analysis was thematic coding as a more structured version of the Grounded Theory Methodology. I asked how they saw their involvement in these communal activities as 'creating sense' from a biographical perspective. For some of them, this interview was already an opportunity to 'look back': being in their twenties or early thirties, they presented themselves as 'mature ravers', able to handle the risks of some night life practices, and distinguishing themselves from younger people whom they regarded either as immersing themselves completely in partying and losing sense of themselves, or as mere consumers of a lifestyle. They presented themselves as those able to identify a deeper meaning to this culture. I found a lot of interesting links between their consciousness as agents in a specific regional context (without any other attractive options for people like them), their community building, the bodily processes they went through while adopting new styles (of moving, dancing, dressing), their shaping of gender identities, and their identity work within the different transitions they had gone through (see Stauber 2004). This study has sharpened my understanding of 'performing selves' as a mode of coping with and shaping later modern transitions into adulthood. I regard it as a kind of practice which is especially profiled in youth cultures, but which can be generalized: Beyond clear and defined membership of youth culture communities, young people present themselves, invent styles, invent rites of communication, of greetings, of bodily cultures, and borrow elements from one or other youth culture.

For the purpose of this chapter, I will only pick out some aspects of my study which are more or less directly related to the earlier mentioned demands, and show the way these demands are met by the respondents, giving some hints regarding (de-)gendering practices within this youth culture.

In order to cope with a multitude of challenges, questions and problems within the different transition areas, it is necessary to simultaneously maintain a kind of coherence and keep diverse things together despite some contradictions within these diverse transition demands. Regarding these demands, the informal Goa trance community provided a frame of reference for the creation of an individual and collective sense in my respondents: out of their own styles, out of communal practices such as spending their weekends dancing, combined with the different structuring of time, there emerged support structures for insecure transitions.

This framework is iridescent with regard to gender. The group on the one hand is normative with regard to its self-perception as a gender-equal community. This also includes spaces for types of gender behaviour which are beyond hetero-normative rules—explicitly for androgynous styles.

> This has been deliverance for the girls, a great deliverance. Finally: going to the Discotheque without all this silly harassment from former days, this silly 'oh, are you here with somebody—no—do you want to have a drink with me'—this in a way very silly harassment, it simply disappeared. (DJ X, male, 32 years)

On the other hand, a gendered division of labour in organizing parties seemed to break through again, with young men largely in technical positions (such as DJing and technical logistics) and women in 'personal services' such as selling drinks and preparing breakfast in the early morning. Nevertheless, this means people interested in altering given gender roles would find an accepted space and opportunity, whereas for those active people included in carrying out these events, a set of gendered ascriptions of what would be female and male work was waiting—it of course was reworked, e.g. it was underplayed with the community's ideology that *'gender would not make any difference at all' (Lila, female, 22 years)*, but obviously much of the well-known division of labour between men and women emerged again.

With regard to the paradox of planning, being involved in these youth cultural communities means at least a short-term response—without of course dissolving the paradox as a whole. But being able to project one-self within a reliable context of a collective 'making sense' at least allows the paradox of planning to be manageable. Short-term plans replace the planning of one's life, and this is what the young women and men empha-sized in the interviews. Living for the moment, with short-term plans and the consciousness of the reversibility of time—this is the implicit ideology. Considerations of having a family begin to intervene in this open horizon, especially among young women.

However, without real planning, some of my respondents' short-term plans turned into longer-term options: they used their contacts within the community to start their own businesses and further developed their first steps by targeting the community for marketing their services or products. At least in two cases (female and male) this led to a long-term career as owners of fashion shops: the young man became increasingly successful and now owns two well-run fashion shops. The young woman, after hav-ing a child and becoming a single mother, and having a second child with another partner, suffered some business crises which she successfully over-came with the support of her mother and a couple of friends.

This refers to the importance of networking: these young people, instead of skipping old networks in favour of new ones, managed to have old and new networks at their disposal at the same time: although they are deeply involved in their youth culture environment, they managed to maintain fairly close contact to their (mostly supportive) parents. This meant active negotiations for some of them:

> *I really had some trouble with them, and I think it is time now to move out, in order to achieve another level within our relationship. (Storm, female, 27)*

It also meant taking over some responsibility for others (e.g. for parents):

> *I would not expect that they understand everything, and some things I would not tell them to make sure they didn't worry about me. (Drum, male, 31)*

It is the heterogeneity of networks which turns out to be extremely helpful: They use parental support (e.g. when setting up a small business), but also make use of all their contacts and insider expertise. They have indeed built up 'individualized systems of social capital' (Raffo and Reeves 2000), but with a high level of commitment and therefore not so individualized: Net-works only function in reciprocity, and indeed the young themselves reveal a high level of responsibility within these networks:

> *Take the clothes hanging there. They are part of the collection of a small dressmaker label. I will not make one Euro with this stuff,*

*because I cannot sell them as expensive as I should. It doesn't bother me though. The important point is that these women are doing a good job in designing and producing all this. Everybody should get a good start. (Su, female, 24)*

Such networks within the community can be strong, though more often they are weak and develop their strength within time (see Granovetter 1977). The ties are weak, but never cold. This is reflected in the commitment to warm encounters—against mainstream coolness:

*Oh, it is so fashionable to be cool. Today, everybody wants to be cool. Not showing his vulnerable points. I do not like to be cool, on the contrary: I am extremely uncool. (Su, female, 24)*

This internal ethic (or communal ideology) represents a big support for these young people. The community offers a complex system of real and symbolic anchorage, ranging from social bonds to style-related issues. Such anchorage is extremely relevant in what can be called the 'fundamental orientation problem' in late modernity.

Also important and related to this latter point, are the motivational resources these communities provide for their members: All these young people had to face frictions and problems within their school-to-work transitions, some of them had already become quite de-motivated in the course of their former educational development. To them, getting to know techno trance not only as new music, new styles and new moves, but also as a new way of life, reinstated their desire and motivation for actively dealing with their transitions:

*Before, nothing interested me any more. Getting to know this brought back so much energy. (Drum, male, 32)*

This statement points to an issue I have stressed elsewhere, using Bloomer and Hodkinson's concept of the learning career: 'a learning career is simultaneously subjective and objective; ( . . . ) (it) serves both to constrain and to enable future experiences. It is a career of events, activities and meanings, and the making and remaking of meanings through these activities and events, and it is a career of relationships and the constant making and remaking of relationships' (Bloomer and Hodkinson 2000: 590). Indeed, this idea could be developed further towards a concept of 'motivational careers', underlining that motivation on the one hand is decisive for any kind of personal development, and that on the other it depends on all kinds of encouraging and motivating experiences. Youth culture's 'making sense' could be a decisive aspect in this regard.

For young men, it was above all *the body* that represented a new area to be discovered as a source of energy and of identity work. This discovery considerably enlarged the male self-perception established up to that point. This is an example of results in the study of youth cultures rapidly becoming out-of-date: There has been so much development since 2000 with regard to (hetero) male body styles; thus, what was something new for the interviewed young men then would no longer be so special today.

Bodily practices and performing selves are aspects which are highly relevant from the perspective of individual 'creating sense'. This is partly linked to conscious *(de-)gendering practices*. As an example, female fashion shop owners conceive selling clothes and giving style counselling to young female clients as transporting new ideas about how to deal with the female gender role concept. They want to encourage their clients to leave their traditional girlish style in order to experiment and try out different roles when dressing up for the next party: they encourage them to use the space of freedom this youth culture has created. At the same time, they reject traditional female styles and represent a different type of female role model to their clients— and are very conscious of playing this role for the girls:

> *Some girls need this small push, and you notice it exactly: they originally would like to have a much more exotic style, but they still do not dare, and if you manage to give them this small package of self-esteem, then it works. (Storm, female, 27 years)*

When it came to the topic of dancing, all my respondents, whether male or female, stressed the new freedom which especially girls and gay boys would find at parties, when comparing this setting to the setting of a mainstream discotheque. No sexual harassment and a lot of free room to move in a freestyle way were the main points that were highlighted.

Are bodily practices and performing selves the answer, when it is a question of uncertainty? Certainly they do not represent a complete answer. But: they represent some kind of symbolic answer and could provide young people with the space to try out different roles. Together with this, hidden or overt gender ascriptions are reworked in performing selves, in a kind of ironic distance to these ascriptions. If gender competence has been identified as another important prerequisite to deal with (gendered) impositions, this playful attitude is of some theoretical and practical relevance, thereby not necessarily linked to a deeper consciousness regarding the issue of 'doing gender'. Nevertheless, gendered ascriptions and expectations to a certain extent are suspended for a while.

When addressing gender topics directly, I discovered how loaded these topics are and how much young men and above all young women reject this loadedness. They seem to prefer to define gender differently without making a big issue out of it. Moreover, they stress the soft and smooth— and somehow de-sexualized—atmosphere between women and men (e.g. on the dance floor), and thus implicitly talk about their own standards for gender relationships.

However, in many respects the community did not represent pure paradise—it also revealed itself as a relational field which had some disappointments in store, above all for those who had invested a lot of energy and work in organizing parties. Learning to cope with some frustrations and achieving a *'more realistic point of view' (male, 31)* was a big topic in this regard.

## YOUTH CULTURE INVOLVEMENT AND LEARNING CAREERS

All these processes could be regarded as elements of an informal learning career. Indeed, it would be an interesting follow-up to go into biographical interviews with the respondents and let them evaluate the relevance that the involvement in these youth culture communities had on their general biographical development. Instead, I have made a second tour through my material, prompted by the hot debate on 'education' in the aftermath of the OECD-PISA-studies, which on the one hand strengthened a rather narrow school-based concept of education, but as a counter-reaction also encouraged broader concepts within educationalist discussions. Such broader concepts stress informal, self-directed social processes of learning and education. They refer to a kind of self-reflexivity, by which the individual turns events into experiences, and learning into a subjectively relevant process. Such processes have the potential of leading to biographical change.

Out of this approach I found the study of Arnd Michael Nohl extremely helpful, in which he identified the relevance of spontaneity within such learning careers (Nohl 2006). He used a subject-related concept of 'Bildung' (education) in terms of 'transformation of life-orientation', and reconstructed stages of such transformation processes out of biographical interviews with middle-aged business starters, with young male breakdancers and older women having their first experiences with the Internet. In these stages he could locate tentative, spontaneous aspects as core elements of learning processes. It was fascinating how neatly these stages of learning processes fit in with my interviews. Without going too much into detail, I will name these stages, inserting my own material; thus, the biographical relevance of performing selves in youth cultures can be underlined. Nohl distinguishes a first phase of spontaneous encounter with a new mode of agency: in almost all my interviews the initial moment of coming into contact with new music, new styles, new movements, and above all new ways of socializing and spending weekends as a community have been stressed as a highly relevant and above all highly motivating experience, in which they started to reinvent themselves as young women or men.

A second phase follows in Nohl's model, in which this spontaneous agency is reflected, albeit not specifically. This is documented by the endeavours of my respondents to describe what they have experienced in this starting phase of a new youth culture. The need to identify and explain is a necessary step because of the changes of everyday life organization, as the prelude to involvement in this specific youth culture.

Then—thirdly—the new agency is explored and refined. My respondents identified this phase by distinguishing their own youth cultural habits from those of 'mainstream techno-kids'. The creative ambivalence of 'fitting in and sticking out', as Steven Miles and his colleagues have put it so deftly in order to characterize the driving forces of youth cultural development (Miles et al. 1998) could be observed in this distinction from the mainstream.

In a fourth phase the new agency achieves social acknowledgment—something which in youth cultural contexts is mainly organized internally. One young woman—an artist who designed the set for the outdoor parties—highlighted the acknowledgement she gets for her work, another stressed the well-functioning division of labour as a kind of mutual acknowledgment, one young man allocated acknowledgement within risk taking (the illegal parties).

The fifth phase is that of spontaneity, in which the agency achieves a deeper biographical relevance. Youth cultural involvement in this phase is really starting to 'write somebody's history', to reshape social contexts— *'almost all my friends belong to the group' (Lila, 22).*

The sixth phase again concerns social acknowledgment—this time in the broader sense than simply the internal group. And indeed: the group becomes more and more visible within their activities (organizing outdoor raves); professional careers are developing, and young owners of fashion shops start to achieve a regional reputation.

The seventh phase finally represents a more profound biographical reflection, in which ways of finding a new balance between the party life and everyday life have been the core topic—together with coping with some frustration which goes along with the diminishing engagement of group members, vanishing collective experiences etc.

It is this task of readjusting to life which defines the biographical learning process. 'Transformation' is of course a big word for these processes, because it suggests grand biographical changes. However, viewed more closely, it fits quite well with the micro-processes through which young women and men go and in which they rework their (gendered) identities. These youth cultural settings not only help to find answers to the above societal demands, but they have themselves some demands in store. Youth cultural involvement does not simply work as glue for destandardized transitions, but instead could introduce other breaks and turbulences. They then have even more to be caught up reflexively, which then impels education in a biographical sense.

What has been critically added to the above list of societal demands in transitions is also valid here: social inequalities may increase, thus again causing difference by the uneven distribution of resources in response to these demands. Youth cultures were not able per se to solve these problems, but could at least motivate those young people who have withdrawn from formal educational contexts: it was able to provide them with some sense of coherence, which would help them to reachieve a proactive attitude concerning their personal project (their transition into adulthood). This last aspect is highlighted in the concluding discussion.

## SUMMARY: POTENTIAL OF YOUTH CULTURE INVOLVEMENT

Within the framework of destandardized life courses and increasing transitions, involvement in youth culture and performing selves in youth culture settings can help specific strengths to unfold—which they share with other informal and nonformal learning settings:

They deliver experiences of *manageability*, and this is the very reason for the creativity and virtuosity which young women and men express within their youth cultural practices. Manageability is often used to rework gender identities, and if it is only at the level of styles (see the concept of imaginary solutions here). This manageability could also affect other areas in which these young people are in transition as well, and it is probably crucial against the background of setbacks in their transitions.

The youth culture community and its practices also deliver a sense of *belonging*, which again is oscillating between the symbolic and real—in fact, this is one of the 'secrets' of (youth) cultural activities: they are always of symbolic value, they represent symbolic solutions for real problems, but often, they also generate real ties, real experiences, and (in retrospect) could represent real turning points in young people's lives (see Abbott 1997).

Thus, through their cultural involvement young people create *sense* for themselves, even if it is only by turning an ordinary rural countryside into an area full of cool locations for outdoor parties (see Skelton and Valentine, 1998). This experience of making sense is the rarest and thus the most important resource in youthful transitions. In the transitions of my respondents, youth cultural experiences could bridge some gaps in their motivational careers, and could prevent them from withdrawing. And for some of them, youth cultural involvement even materialized in terms of a professional career.

These issues can be related to a concept formulated by the health sociologist, Aaron Antonovsky, when he developed his model of 'saluto-genesis'; he replaces the question 'Why are people getting ill?' with the question, 'What is keeping people healthy?' (Antonovsky 1987), and he stresses that maintaining a sense of coherence is crucial for individuals. According to his model, the development of a sense of coherence has to be achieved by young adulthood. Taking into account the characteristics of late modern transitions, this seems to be quite unrealistic. Moreover, it seems that young people have understood this message of late modernity: that this sense of coherence does not emerge automatically as individuals grow older, but they have to develop and organize it themselves. Thus, their agency—above all in youth culture activities—can be seen to be actively related to this sense of coherence.

Youth cultures represent an anchorage, which could provide this sense of coherence—by experiences of belonging, of coping, of an individual as well as collective *creation of sense*. They also provide experiences of de-constructing gender ascriptions and allow the invention of new images within and outside the hetero-normative framework.

Of course this anchorage is not forever—on the contrary, it exists within a heightened consciousness of the reversibility of time/transition stages, in which also a succession of different youth culture orientations could take place.

Nevertheless—or therefore—it would be interesting to come back to this group of young people, who once in their period of transition found anchorage in these youth culture communities, giving them the chance to reconstruct their learning careers to see if and how traces of their youth cultural involvement have survived to the present.

## REFERENCES

Abbott, A. (1997) 'On the Concept of Turning Point', *Comparative Social Research*, 16, pp. 85–105.

Alheit, P. and Dausien, B. (2000) '"Biographicity" as a Basic Resource of Lifelong Learning', in P. Alheit (Ed.) *Lifelong Learning Inside and Outside of Schools* (Roskilde).

Antonovsky, A. (1987) *Unravelling the Mystery of Health: How People Manage Stress and Stay Well* (San Francisco: Jossey-Bass).

Bauman, Z. (1973) *Culture as Praxis* (London: Routledge & Kegan Paul).

Bauman, Z. (2000) *Liquid Modernity* (Cambridge: Polity Press).

Beck, U. and Bonß, W. (2001) *Modernisierung moderner Gesellschaften* (*The Modernisation of Modern Societies*) (Frankfurt: Suhrkamp).

Beck, U., Giddens, A., Lash, S. (1996) *Reflexive Modernisierung, 4th edition* (Frankfurt: Suhrkamp).

Blossfeld, H.-P. and Mills, M. (Eds.) (2005) *Globalization, Uncertainty and Men in Society* (London: Routledge).

Bloomer, M. and Hodkinson, P. (2000) 'Learning Careers: Continuity and Change in Young People's Dispositions to Learning', *British Educational Research Journal*, 26 (5), pp. 583–597.

Deutsch, F. M. (2007) 'Undoing Gender', *Gender & Society*, 21, pp. 106–127.

EGRIS (2001) 'Misleading Trajectories: Transition Dilemmas of Young Adults in Europe', *Journal of Youth Studies*, 4 (1), pp. 101–119.

Emirbayer, M. and Mische, A. (1998) What is Agency? *American Journal of Sociology*, 103 (4), pp. 962–1023.

Fenstermaker, S. and West, C. (2002) *Doing Gender, Doing Difference: Inequality, Power and Institutional Change* (New York: Routledge).

Fornäs, J. (1995) *Cultural Theory and Late Modernity* (London: Sage).

Granovetter, M. (1977) 'The Strength of Weak Ties', *American Journal of Sociology*, 78 (6), pp. 1360–1380.

Heinz, W. R. (2002) 'Self-socialisation and Post-traditional Society', in R. A. Settersten and T. J. Owens (Eds.) *New Frontiers of Socialisation* (Oxford: Elsevier).

Hurrelmann, K. (2003) 'Der entstrukturierte Lebenslauf: Die Auswirkungen der Expansion der Jugendphase' ('The De-standardized Life Course: Effects of the Expansion of Youth'), *Zeitschrift für Soziologie der Erziehung und Sozialisation*, 23(2), pp. 115–126.

Leccardi, C. (2006) 'Redefining the Future: Youthful Biographic Constructions in the 21st Century', in M. du Bois-Reymond and L. Chisholm (Eds.) *The Modernization of Youth Transitions in Europe*, pp. 37–48 (San Fransisco: Jossey-Bass).

Lüscher, K. and Pillemer, K. (2004) 'Intergenerational Ambivalences: New Perspectives on Parent–Child Relations in Later Life', in *Contemporary Perspectives in Family Research, 4th edition* (Oxford: Elsevier).

Miles, S., Cliff, D., Burr, V. (1998) 'Fitting In and Sticking Out: Consumption, Consumer Meanings and the Construction of Young People's Identities', *Journal of Youth Studies*, 1 (1), pp. 81–91.

Nohl, A.-M. (2006) *Bildung und Spontaneität: Phasen biographischer Wandlungsprozesse in drei Lebensaltern (Education and Spontaneity: Stages of Biographical Transformation in Three Life Stages)* (Opladen: Barbara Budrich).

Raffo, C. and Reeves, M. (2000) 'Youth Transitions and Social Exclusion: Developments in Social Capital Theory', *Journal of Youth Studies*, 3 (2), pp. 147–166.

Ridgeway, C. L. and Correll, S. J. (2004) 'Unpacking the Gender System: A Theoretical Perspective on Gender Beliefs and Social Relations', *Gender & Society*, 18, pp. 510–531.

Skelton, T. and Valentine, G. (eds) (1998) *Cool Places: Geographies of Youth Cultures* (London: Routledge).

Smyth, E. (2004) Gender, Education and Labour Market Outcomes, 5th report of the ChangeEqual Project, http://www.nuff.ox.ac.uk/projects/ changequal/ papers.asp?selbut=2 (accessed 13 January 2005).

Stauber, B. (2004) *Junge Frauen und Männer in Jugendkulturen: Selbstinszenierungen und Handlungspotentiale (Young Women and Men in Youth Cultures: Performing Selves and Agency Potentials)* (Opladen: Leske and Budrich).

Stauber, B. and Walther, A. (2006) 'De-standardised Pathways to Adulthood: European Perspectives on Informal Learning in Informal Networks', *Papers—Revista de Sociología*, 32 (79), pp. 241–262.

Stauber, B. (2007) 'Motivation in Transition', *Young*, 15(1), pp. 31–47.

Stauber, B., Pohl, A. and Walther, A. (eds) (2007) *Subjektorientierte Übergangsforschung. Rekonstruktion und Unterstutzung biografischer Übergänge junger Erwaschsener* (Subject0oriented transition research. Reconstruction of support for biographical transitions in young adults). Weinheim and Munich: Juventa.

Walther, A., Stauber, B., Pohl, A. (2005) 'Informal Networks in Youth Transitions in West Germany: Biographical Resource or Reproduction of Social Inequality? *Journal of Youth Studies*, 8 (2), pp. 221–240.

Walther, A., du Bois-Reymond, M., Biggart, A. (Eds.) (2006) *Participation in Transition: Motivation of Young Adults in Europe for Learning and Working* (Frankfurt: Peter Lang).

Walther, A., Stauber, B. and Pohl, A. (2009) *UP2YOUTH - Insights in Youth as Actor of Social Change by an Agency-Perspective. Final Report for the UP2YOUTH Project.* http://87.97.212.72/ne/images/stories/Up2YOUTHFinalreportwithoutAnnex.pdf [accessed 05 02 2010].

# 7 Online Counselling
## Meeting the Needs of Young People in Late Modern Societies

*Andreas Vossler and Terry Hanley*

The conditions for growing up in Western societies have changed perceptibly over recent decades. Influential sociologists like Anthony Giddens (1991) in the United Kingdom and Ulrich Beck (1992) in Germany view these changes as key features of social modernization processes. They have utilized terms such as 'individualization' and 'pluralization' to refer to the increased importance of individual decision making and the emerging plurality of lifestyles in contemporary societies. The effects of these social changes form new demands and needs, and thus inevitably impact on the lives of children and adolescents (e.g. new development tasks, see Havighurst 1982). A closer look at these new challenges and changing living conditions will provide insights into the nature of the needs that online counselling services try to meet. They also help us to understand why such services prove to be attractive for the young generation.

## INTRODUCTION

The dynamic of social change and modernization has reached all areas of life and society. Traditional values and identities (e.g. in regard to gender roles or sexual behaviour) are increasingly losing their predetermining influence on individual attitudes, behaviour and decision making. In growing up, the decisions and actions taken by young people now offer more options and potential outcomes than one or two generations before. This leads on the one hand to more choices of action, but requires on the other hand more self-organization and increases the complexity of decision-making processes. This requires young people to take a very active role in the dynamic process of constructing their identity in a fluid and ambiguous environment, or as Giddens puts it, 'What to do? How to act? Who to be? These are focal questions for everyone in circumstances of late modernity' (Giddens 1999: 70).

To know what to do and who to be has become difficult for many children and adolescents. Individuals are confronted with growing uncertainties and discontinuities which have a significant impact upon their lives.

The rate of divorces and separation has risen over the last decades and therefore more young people experience 'broken families' and have to cope with complex and ambiguous family situations. Additionally, social networks and neighbourhoods no longer offer the same support and protection that they did in the past. Formerly clearly defined stages on the way to adulthood (e.g. first employment, starting a family) have become blurred and fragile. Many young people are dependent on their parents for longer periods, a factor which can make it difficult for them to experience themselves as fully fledged members of society. This is evident in survey findings on the 'subjective age status' of young people in Germany, showing that individuals start feeling like adults (and not as adolescents anymore) at a much later stage than two decades ago (Gille 2008). Therefore, developing a coherent and homogenous identity has become a new challenge for young people living in today's late modern societies.

Young people are a treasured target of media and market forces. They also have to cope with growing educational demands and performance expectations from schools, parents, peers and the public. Not only do they have to learn more, they also have to build up new skills and competences to get to grips with the complexity of the continuously changing world around them—and they also have to do this in a much shorter time than 20 years ago (Lüders 2007). With this in mind, the acceleration of developmental processes and everyday life, multitasking and poly-chronicity become late modern challenges for the society as a whole as well as for every single individual.

In line with the policy model that Giddens (1998) conceptualized as the 'social investment state', the governments in the United Kingdom and in Germany tend to invest actively in 'human capital' rather than just maintaining a social security net for their citizens. Thus, the implicit aim of various activating programmes and initiatives in both countries (e.g. 'Every Child Matters'—'National Academy of Parenting Practitioners in the UK'; 'Soziale Frühwarnsysteme'—'Nationales Zentrum Frühe Hilfen' [Social Early Warning Systems—National Centre for Early Support] in Germany) is to equip and prepare children and parents for the life in a highly competitive and consumer-oriented society. The preparedness to fund a nationwide online counselling service for parents and young people (as described later when considering the German situation) can also be seen as part of this social investment policy. However, along with preventive investments often comes the threat of restrictions for those who are not willing to cooperate and benefit from the programmes (Lüders 2007). This leaves the individual family/ young person with the responsibility for a possible failure in keeping up with the speed and complexity of demands in their everyday life. The described tensions inherent within late modern societies are further amplified by the spreading economic inequality between different sectors of society.

In light of the described risks and growing pressure in families, schools and peer groups, it is not surprising that the number of distressed and depressed adolescents has increased. In Germany and the United Kingdom this can be seen within surveys on the mental health of children and adolescents (respectively, Robert-Koch-Institut 2007, and the Mental Health Foundation 1999). In the United Kingdom, the British Medical Association (BMA 2006) has estimated on the basis of study findings that 20 per cent of children and adolescents have mental health problems at some point in time. The BMA also stresses that socio-economic factors play an important role in the onset of psychological problems and that children and adolescents from deprived backgrounds have a greater risk of suffering from mental health problems. It can therefore be assumed that—among other factors—issues related to the difficulties of identity construction in an uncertain context play an important role when considering the higher levels of psychological distress among adolescents and young adults that are reported.

Despite higher numbers of young people having psychological difficulties, statistics also show that only a minority of these young people find their way to the established counselling services in both countries. The institutional conditions at these traditional counselling centres, with their often adult-oriented 'counselling culture', may deter young people from accessing therapeutic services (Vossler 2004). This might be one of the reasons why politicians in the United Kingdom now call for young people to have easy access to counselling (e.g. McGinnis and Hodge 2004)—something that is hoped to be provided by those who develop services online (Hanley 2006).

The attractiveness of counselling via the Internet can be partly explained by the fact that young people are embracing and taking advantage of technological developments. Recent studies have begun to show the full extent of this phenomenon. In the United Kingdom it has been reported that 75 per cent of young people now have access to the Internet at home and 92 per cent have access at school (Livingstone and Bober 2005) and a survey of the American college class of 2001 suggested that 100 per cent of these students were connected to the Internet (Miller 2001). The representative JIM-study (JIM 2007: Youth, Information, Media) shows that in Germany 95 per cent of all young people (age 12 to 19) have Internet access at home (45 per cent even in their own bedroom) and that 83 per cent of all Internet users are online daily or several times a week. These are impressive figures that provide an insight into the influence that the present technological revolution is having upon adolescents in countries where the Internet is commonplace.

The question therefore shifts from 'Do young people access the Internet?' to 'Is it beneficial for young people to be accessing the Internet?' Interestingly, much research has focussed upon the search for evidence of negative effects (Buckingham 2002). This has been compounded by the numerous scare stories reported in the worldwide press and by some practical experiences showing that seeking advice on suicide or anorexia may be risky if not moderated by a professional (Livingstone 2006). However, this is only part of the story and increasingly there are reports of the Internet positively impacting upon youth centred professions. For instance, the Internet can offer personalized opportunities for safe and entertaining identity expression and peer-focused relationship exploration (e.g. Gross 2004). Additionally young people can find different forms of support and help online. Free chat rooms offer a space to meet and communicate with other people with no explicit support function. Self-help groups on the Internet provide an exchange of views and experience that involves support and advice by laymen/peers. Finally, many children's charities and youth support groups provide opportunities for young people to seek out personal advice and support from trained professionals. These easily accessible services normally offer individuals with the possibility to remain anonymous, a factor which allows for greater openness when speaking about difficult topics (Yager 2002).

In the next two sections of this chapter we intend to focus upon two examples of mental health support services that have been developed to support adolescents online. The first offers a view of the service within the United Kingdom and the second in Germany.

## ONLINE COUNSELLING WITHIN
## THE UNITED KINGDOM: KOOTH

Within the United Kingdom, mental health services for young people have developed a major presence online. National organizations such as the National Society for the Prevention of Cruelty to Children (NSPCC) and the Samaritans have set up services that young people have been able to access for a number of years (www.there4me.com and www.samaritans. org respectively). Complementing these more generic support services are a number of localized projects that provide more specialized support. One such project is Kooth, a free at the point of access online counselling service that has made significant inroads into a number of counties in the United Kingdom (for a more detailed description see Hanley 2007).

Kooth was set up in 2004 to provide an online service to young people in the Stockport area of the United Kingdom. Since then it has grown and spread, due to its popularity and success, to a number of other areas within the United Kingdom. In doing so it has attracted significant amounts of funding from the likes of local Primary Care Trusts, Child and Adolescent Mental Health Services, substance misuse groups and Xenzone, this latter group being the company who developed and now update and manage the technical aspects of the service. No doubt, with its growing success, the potential of this small scale enterprise has been increasingly recognized by others.

The service itself varies slightly from region to region. Despite having generic webpage access to each geographical area, each service has been specifically tailored to local needs. These needs differ due to the multitude of funding streams and service remits that exist in the United Kingdom. With this in mind, and for ease of reporting, the focus of this chapter will be upon the Kooth service provided within the County of Cheshire. Here it is also important to note that the figures about service usage only relate to this specific geographical area.

The Cheshire-wide service aims to support 11- to 25-year-olds throughout the county by providing a free at the point of access online support service. In 2006/2007—the first 12 months of this service—it recorded 1,353 registered users of which 578 (42 per cent) become active users; notably those who revisited the site after their initial registration. Of these registered users 59 per cent were aged between 11 and 15 and, despite initial hopes to attract more male clients, 69 per cent of these registered users were female. Additionally, screening the users once they registered to use the service would indicate that this client group may actually be in more need of support than users of similar face-to-face services (Hanley 2008). As a major aim of the service is to increase access to individuals who would not ordinarily access therapeutic services, individuals can use the service without providing any identifiable material. A self-selected user name and basic demographic information, as summarized earlier, is required, but nothing else. Such a way of working raises numerous ethical issues, particularly about ensuring the safety of the young users. In working with these dilemmas, service developers have looked towards UK-based telephone precedents (e.g. ChildLine) for guidance and where necessary entered into uncharted territory.

## Kooth: The Services Offered

The Kooth service is comprised of a number of components that include one-to-one counselling, direct access to other appropriate support agencies, moderated peer support and specially written self-help information. Each of these areas is briefly introduced next.

*One-to-one counselling*: Users of the service can directly contact a counsellor to talk about issues that may be troubling them. Individuals may choose to arrange a real time chat with a counsellor or work through the website's internal asynchronous messaging system. These sessions are facilitated by individuals who have appropriate therapeutic training and who have received additional training in offering online counselling. During the year 2006/2007, 885 hours of synchronous chat counselling were provided and 2,134 private messages were sent to counsellors (these received 2,211 responses from counsellors).

*Access to other support agencies*: The local nature of the service means that the counsellors who offer support and moderate the message boards have a good knowledge of the face-to-face services within the area. This knowledge can, with the consent of the young users, lead to referrals to more specialist services such as those that provide support around substance misuse or domestic violence. Additionally, in some instances, these organizations actually have a presence on the Kooth site. Thus, the young users can directly access a wide variety of professionals that they may not ordinarily be able to.

*Moderated peer support*: A very popular area of the website is the message board section—this received 41,537 visits in the 2006/2007 period. This provides a space for users to discuss issues with other young people and it is not afraid of tackling some very sensitive issues. For example, forum strands include discussions about self-harm, being a young carer and domestic abuse. To ensure the content of the message boards does not contain content that is personally offensive to others or include personal contact information, every posting is reviewed by a counsellor before it goes public.

*Self-help information*: The final element of the website that is provided is an online magazine. This aims to respond to the issues that young people raise in other areas of the site. It provides informed responses to issues identified by Kooth workers in the form of youth friendly articles. Like the static content of the message boards, these articles act as an informative resource for service users 24 hours a day.

## Kooth: Evaluating the Service

The Kooth service has been proactive in evaluating the work that it has been undertaking. This has included providing numerous feedback avenues and rating systems on the website and developing more systematic research projects. One project in particular has worked to consult with individuals who have been utilizing the counselling service about their experiences. This work has reflected the numerous opportunities and challenges that Kooth users identify in the therapeutic service. Some of the key elements reported are noted in the following paragraphs.

Initially it is important to note that a great proportion of the comments from service users prove to be positive. Individuals who were encountered commonly reported their liking for the service (e.g. 'KOOTH RULES!!!') and noted that they would not have accessed face-to-face equivalent services (e.g. 'i h8 spkin face 2 face i feel incomterbul'). Intrinsically linked to the attractiveness of Kooth was the control that they could exercise online. Service users are able to censor/edit/withhold the content that they share with a counsellor (e.g. 'noone needs to know your crying and don't know unless you say') and this proved incredibly important to some individuals.

Although this raises the issue of whether the young person is actually *connecting with* or *escaping from* the process, it is difficult not to view this as an empowering process for adolescents entering into relationships with adult professionals.

The quality of the therapeutic alliance that was attainable online was generally viewed to be of a moderate to high quality—this concept is often linked to successful outcomes in the therapeutic literature (e.g. Horvath and Bedi 2002). Such a finding was reflected in online quantitative measures and in interviews with the young users (Hanley 2008). Although there were exceptions, 21 per cent rating the alliance as low and some of the interview comments expressing frustration with elements of the service, these findings challenge the view that relationships of a sufficient quality to create change cannot be created online (e.g. Pelling and Renard 2000). Creative compensatory techniques were utilized to enrich solely text-based dialogues, and individuals described working proactively with miscommunications rather than being disabled by them. This proves an area for continued enquiry; however, the reports from Kooth users provide a fascinating insight into how young people pragmatically use the Internet to seek out support.

In contrast to the more positive elements that were reported by the young users were the challenges that they encountered whilst using the service. Practical problems, such as finding a quiet space to use a computer (e.g. 'sorry ma lil sis has started to cry got to go bye') and technical difficulties (e.g. 'i was talking to some one and it just cut off'), were regularly noted. Additionally, the factor that was reported most often proved to be the limited resources available on the Kooth website. Unfortunately, due to the limited number of counselling hours available, numerous individuals were not able to contact a counsellor when they wanted to (e.g. 'I find theres not people on very often'). Thus, almost reassuringly, the negative comments from Kooth users predominantly revolved around the practicalities and technical problems with accessing the service rather that the counselling relationships themselves.

## ONLINE COUNSELLING IN GERMANY: THE VIRTUAL COUNSELLING CENTRE

At present, young people in Germany find an abundance of support and help services online. Various Internet projects have been developed in the mental health area as well as in the context of youth welfare services in the last ten years. These services have been initiated and set up by a broad range of organizations. These range from charities and foundations (e.g. Caritas: www.beratung-caritas.de) to established youth welfare institutions and national associations (e.g. pro familia: www.sextra.de; Kinderschutz-Zentren e.V.: www.youngavenue.de). The services also differ in the way that support is provided to young people, with some projects working with a combination of professional and peer counselling—young people who are trained as peer counsellors (e.g. www.kids-online.de)—and others solely relying on counselling provided by professional counsellors (e.g. www.beratung-caritas.net). Finally, some of the bigger projects offer their services nationwide for a range of problem areas, whereas other smaller services operate exclusively on a regional and local level (e.g. www.helpMAils.de in Mannheim) or only address specific problem areas (e.g. www.nico-und-nicola.de: children in bereavement situations).

One of the nationwide operating online counselling services for young people is the Virtual Counselling Centre (Virtuelle Beratungsstelle) run by the 'Federal Conference for Child Guidance and Family Counselling' (Bundeskonferenz fűr Erziehungsberatung, bke). This service was inaugurated in October 2000 and has since developed into one of the biggest and most widely used online counselling service for young people in Germany. Funded mutually by the 16 German federal countries, the Virtual Counselling Centre embraces two separate services on its central Internet portal (www.bke-beratung.de). One service addresses parents and provides information and advice similar to a traditional child guidance centre. The other service, which will be the focus of this section, offers cost free and anonymous counselling services for adolescents and young adults between 14 and 21 years of age.

Counsellors for the Virtual Counselling Centre are recruited proportional to the size of each federal country from regional child guidance centres throughout the country. They are all qualified counsellors/therapists who have to undergo a specific training before they can start working online with young people. In 2007, 84 professional counsellors from 72 different local child guidance centres were participating in the project (Seus-Seberich 2007).

To get access to the service, users have to register on the central webpage by providing a self-selected username, their age and their gender—no other information is required. The number of registered users has been continuously increased over the last years, with 215 new registrations every month in 2006 (bke 2007) and more than 30,000 registered users at present. The popularity of the service is also reflected by the 2,434 visitors to the webpage counted on average per day and the cumulative 9,658 counselling contacts with users in the year 2006 (bke 2007). The average user age was 18 years in 2006, with the majority of users aged between 15 and 24 years. As reported for the UK service Kooth, the online counselling service offered by the bke is predominately attractive for girls and young women, especially for the age group between 16 and 19 years of age. More than three quarters of all new registrations in 2006 were female users (Seus-Seberich 2007).

## Virtual Counselling Centre: The Services Offered

The Virtual Counselling Centre service for adolescents and young adults comprises three different components; one-to-one counselling, moderated group chat and discussion forums. These three service components provide the user with different online counselling settings and allow them to decide how much they want to disclose and be engaged in using the service. In particular, each component varies in regard to the degree of peer support and professional help a user can expect. In the following sections brief descriptions of the different components are provided.

*One-to-one counselling:* This is probably the most 'private' of the three service components (Weißhaupt 2004). Users have the possibility to contact a counsellor directly without notification in the daily offered one-to-one chat hours that last between 90 minutes and three and a half hours. They can also arrange a time when they meet a counsellor online for a one-to-one chat. In 2006, altogether 1,605 individual one-to-one chats lasting on average 30 minutes were provided. Individuals also have the possibility to request support using an asynchronous internal messaging service comparable to e-mail counselling. Users are assured that messages submitted via this messaging service will be answered by a professional counsellor within 48 hours. Almost 90 per cent of the 886 young people who made use of this messaging service in 2006 were female users (Seus-Seberich 2007). The problems most frequently addressed in one-to-one contacts are 'development difficulties'/'difficulties with myself' (41.6 per cent) followed by 'relationship problems' (32.2 per cent) and 'other problems in and with the family' (12 per cent; bke 2007). In 30 per cent of the cases, counsellors recommended a referral to a face-to-face service (bke-Projektgruppe Online-Beratung 2004).

*Moderated group chat:* This service component—which consists of group chats moderated by a professional counsellor—is characterized by a high self-help and peer support aspect. The users and moderator meet in a chat room and synchronously discuss problematic issues. Group chats take place about every other day and are either dedicated to a specific problem area (e.g. 'young motherhood—a challenge', 'When (not) eating dominates your life') or are open for the topics raised by users in the chat. The number of chat participants is limited (on average between 9 and 16 users); it is possible to leave or enter the chat room during a session. The task of the moderator is to facilitate the group process and to make sure that users do not break the chat rules. He or she is also responsible for the dynamics developing during the group chat. Users have the chance to write about their difficulties and to get feedback from a professional counsellor and other young people in similar situations. In 2005 alone, the Virtual Counselling Centre organized and held 207 group chats with 2,000 users involved (bke-Projektgruppe Online-Beratung 2004).

*Discussion forum:* The third component is the most 'public' part of the service with a strong self-help focus—similar to the message board space Kooth is providing in the United Kingdom. In the discussion forum, users can communicate asynchronously with other users by posting questions, making statements and writing comments on other postings. It is possible for everyone to read the postings, but only registered users are able to make postings themselves. All postings are stored in the forum and can be read at any time. Moderators review the postings and, if necessary, add information and supportive ideas. The discussion forum is divided into several sub-forums addressing relevant discussion topics, like 'stress with the family', 'problems in school' or 'the open door'—the latter group being a space for young people to discuss issues with parents who use the parent service of the Virtual Counselling Centre.

## Virtual Counselling Centre: Evaluating the Service

Knowledge about how young people use and benefit from the Virtual Counselling Centre is informed by service statistics, various published reports from online counsellors working for the service and by some informal feedback from service users. There has been no systematic investigation of the experiences of young people with the service so far, although there are plans for a large-scale evaluation study to be undertaken by the German Youth Institute in future.

The general popularity of the Virtual Counselling Centre among young people is displayed by the remarkable number of users, as reported earlier. Counsellors' experiences indicate that the professional online counselling offered by the Virtual Counselling Centre is capable of reaching young people who may otherwise not be reached by traditional face-to-face counselling services (Thiery 2005; Weißhaupt 2004)—a phenomenon that can be attributed to the easy accessibility of the service and the possibility for the users to remain anonymous when contacting a professional counsellor. The same factors can also be seen to have an impact upon the presenting issues that clients bring to counselling. Observations from practitioners note that clients are more direct and divulge problems very quickly in this medium. In addition, users appear to disclose stigmatized problems like depression, eating disorders and self harming behaviour more frequently than in face-to-face counselling (Seus-Seberich 2007). For many young people the online group setting (group chat) is the place where they share an experienced trauma with others for the first time—this can often be a first step to enter and trust in a therapeutic relationship.

With regard to the different service components, user feedback and service statistics indicate that young online counselling users prefer the synchronous service components of the service (one-to-one chat/group chat). This contrasts to the asynchronous, e-mail-like communication. The reasoning behind this appears to be that it is important for many young users to get an immediate response when disclosing their difficulties (Seus-Seberich 2007).

Service experiences over the years show that young people are primarily looking for personal contact and exchange when using the service—whereas the user of the parent online counselling service are more interested in helpful information and advice. Young people not only benefit from the professional counselling component, but also from the peer support they receive in the group chat setting and in the discussion forum. Furthermore, the more frequent service users have a high identification with the service and tend to build an online service 'user-community' with a social network character. They start to contact each other outside the service via e-mail and telephone and in some cases they even meet up in the 'real world' (bke-Projektgruppe Online-Beratung 2004).

## DISCUSSION

This chapter began by outlining some of the contextual/societal issues that have led to the development of online counselling services for young people in the United Kingdom and Germany. Following this, two independent online counselling services (Kooth and The Virtual Counselling Centre) have been briefly described. At this juncture we begin to unpack the similarities and differences that can be observed between the two services which includes reflecting upon the practical nuances of the services. To end this chapter, a consideration of the implications for practice is presented.

### Similarities and Differences Between the Two Services

Whilst reviewing these two services it has become very apparent that they have many more similarities than differences. Despite each service developing in isolation to one another, broad societal factors appear to have provided fertile ground for such youth friendly mental health provision. Both the German and British cultures have been greatly impacted by technological developments and the youth of both countries have had to learn to cope within these fast moving societies. The online services described here therefore aim to meet adolescents in an environment that proves both popular and comfortable to them. Such a rationale is echoed outside of the European context, the Australian Kids Help Line service noting these as key reasons for development in this area, too (e.g. King et al. 2006).

Both the described services exist as part of a larger movement towards online health care provision. Within the United Kingdom, although Kooth is regionally limited, it can be viewed alongside more generic support services which cover a broader territory (e.g. the NSPCC's nationwide service www.there4me.com). In contrast, within the German context, the national Virtual Counselling Centre is complemented by a variety of more specific services. In much the same way that Kooth and the Virtual Counselling Centre differ, these are distinct in their slightly differing client remits and modes of delivery. In accounting for such a wide selection of services it is therefore difficult to draw direction comparisons between services on such a small scale. Future researchers and policymakers may therefore consider the need to map out existing services as a priority before engaging in new developments.

Although the online territory becomes difficult to navigate due to its relatively haphazard nature, there is a clear ethos which surrounds the development of online counselling services. At the heart of this appears to be the desire to increase access to therapeutic services. Both of the services in question are free at the point of delivery and aim to utilize technology that is familiar to adolescents. Additionally, there is a sense that the potential anonymity within online communication may attract individuals who would not ordinarily utilize such services. This manifests in both Kooth and the Virtual Counselling Centre only asking for a very limited amount of information from those using the services. Interestingly, despite these attempts to broaden access, it is noteworthy that both services were predominantly accessed by young female users. Such a finding would challenge an oft-cited view that technologically mediated counselling may attract more male clients.

The limitations and opportunities inherent within online communication are evident within the provision described. Each service has different components which vary in the contact time with professionals on the website—notably these do not extend beyond text-based provision at present. At the most intensive is the one-to-one counselling that is offered. This then moves on to a variety of moderated group interventions which allow for varying degrees of contact with other users. Finally, the potential for users to access self-help information (through reading forum postings or magazine articles) provides an important but low intensity intervention. In practice, this could almost be viewed as a self-selecting stepped care model of provision. In such a model it is the adolescents themselves who determine the level of response that is offered. In instances where online support is felt limited, and with the agreement of the young user, both services provide the potential for referrals to face-to-face support to be made. Given that not all young people will feel comfortable in this medium (e.g. they may not be competent computer users), such flexibility proves important in offering services that work with the hope of increasing access to as many young people as possible.

Both services have proven very popular with young people in the respective countries. Usage statistics clearly indicate that adolescents are using the services and the feedback presently available suggests that many individuals benefit from them. Once again similar trends have been noticed in the Australian Kids Help Line service (KHL 2007). To date, the formal evaluation of both services proves relatively limited. Inroads have been made, with practitioner reflections and client voices being cited in relation to the efficacy of the services; however, there is still much territory to cover. The research that has been undertaken (e.g. Hanley 2008) complements the limited pool of research that has already been conducted (e.g. Bambling et al. 2008; King et al. 2006) and adds important strands to our understanding of such practice.

## SUMMARY: IMPLICATIONS FOR THE DEVELOPMENT OF YOUTH FRIENDLY COUNSELLING

Reflecting upon the two services in question has provided useful insights into the developing field of online youth counselling. Most strikingly it is evident that there are numerous similarities between the two endeavours. Contemporary German and British societies present challenges for adolescents, and the Internet provides a phenomenon of great importance within this narrative. If there is a major learning outcome from this endeavour, it would be the importance of working across cultures to develop appropriate youth friendly counselling services. In particular, there seems little point in international colleagues reinventing the wheel when good examples already exist elsewhere. Some more specific implications that could be highlighted, include the following:

- As the services appear to be both popular and effective, service developers should be open to creating such provision—they do however need to consider how these services may become more attractive to male clients.
- Counsellors working online need to have special skills to work effectively using a variety of modes of communication.
- Appropriate self-help tools need to be continually developed to keep up with technological advances.
- More formal evaluation of online practice is needed—this includes examining the effectiveness of such services and consulting with counsellors and clients about their experiences of using them.
- As services develop in this medium, regulators of such practice need to remain up-to-date regarding such practice.

Online youth counselling is a relatively new phenomenon that, in many ways, embodies the fast-paced challenges of our late modern societies. In particular, it presents great opportunities to provide increased access to services which support the well-being of today's youth. In contrast, it provides great challenges that can best be tackled through joint working and pooled experience.

## REFERENCES

Bambling, M., King, R., Reid, W. and Wegner, K. (2008) 'Online Counselling: The Experiences of Counsellors Providing Synchronous Single-Session Counselling to Young People', *Counselling and Psychotherapy Research*, 8(2), pp. 110–116.

146    *Andreas Vossler and Terry Hanley*

Beck, U. (1992) *Risk Society: Towards a New Modernity* (London: Sage).
Buckingham, D. (2002) 'The Electronic Generation? Children and New Media', L.A. Lievrouw and S. Livingstone (Eds.) *The Handbook of New Media*, pp. 77–89 (London: Sage).
Bundeskonferenz fűr Erziehungsberatung, bke (Ed.) (2007) *Erziehungs- und Familienberatung im Internet. Die Virtuelle Beratungsstelle. Projektbericht 1 Januar 2006 bis 31 Dezember 2006* (Fuerth: Eigenverlag).
Bundeskonferenz fűr Erziehungsberatung, bke-Projektgruppe Online-Beratung (2004) 'Hilfe im Internet für Jugendliche und Eltern', A. Hundsalz und K. Menne (Eds.) *Jahrbuch für Erziehungsberatung, Band 5*, S. 205–226 (Weinheim: Juventa).
British Medical Association (2006). *Child and Adolescent Mental Health—A Guide for Healthcare Professionals* (London: BMA Publications).
Giddens, A. (1991) *The Consequences of Modernity* (Cambridge: Polity Press).
Giddens, A. (1998) *The Third Way: The Renewal of Social Democracy* (Cambridge: Polity Press).
Giddens, A. (1999) *Modernity and Self Identity: Self and Society in the Late Modern Age* (Cambridge: Polity Press).
Gille, M. (2008) *Jugendliche in Ost und West seit der Wiedervereinigung. Ergebnisse aus dem replikativen Längsschnitt des DJI-Jugendsurvey* (Wiesbaden: VS-Verlag).
Gross, E. (2004) 'Adolescent Internet Use: What We Expect, What Teens Report', *Journal of Applied Developmental Psychology*, 25(6), pp. 633–649.
Hanley, T. (2006) 'Developing Youth Friendly Online Counselling Services in the United Kingdom: A Small Scale Investigation into the Views of Practitioners', *Counselling and Psychotherapy Research*, 6, pp. 182–185.
Hanley, T. (2007) 'R u still there?', *Therapy Today*, 18 (4), pp. 37–38.
Hanley, T. (2008) *The Therapeutic Alliance in Online Youth Counselling*, Unpublished PhD Thesis (University of Manchester).
Havighurst, R.J. (1982) *Development Tasks and Education* (New York: Longman).
Horvath, A. and Bedi, R. (2002) 'The Alliance', J. Norcross (Ed.), *Psychotherapy Relationships that Work: Therapist Contributions Responsiveness to Patients* (New York: Oxford University Press).
JIM-Studie (2007) *Jugend, Information, (Multi-) Media* (Medienpädagogischer Forschungsverbund Südwest. Online at http://www.mpfs.de).
KHL. (2007) *Kids Help Line 2006 Overview: Issues Concerning Children and Young People* (Australia: Kids Help Line).
King, R., Bambling, M., Lloyd, C., Gomurra, R., Smith, S., Reid, W. and Wegner, K. (2006) 'Online Counselling: The Motives and Experiences of Young People Who Choose the Internet instead of Face to Face or Telephone Counselling, *Counselling and Psychotherapy Research*, 6 (3), pp. 169–174.
Livingstone, S. (2006) 'Reflections on the Games Families Play', *The Psychologist*, 19, pp. 604–606.
Livingstone, S. and Bober, M. (2005) *UK Children Go Online: Final Report of Key Project Findings* (London: LSE. Online at www.children-go-online.net).
Lüders, C. (2007) 'Entgrenzt, individualisiert, verdichtet. Überlegungen zum Strukturwandel des Aufwachsens', SPI im SOS-Kinderdorf e.V. (ed.) *SOS-Dialog 2007—Jugendliche zwischen Aufbruch und Anpassung*, pp. 6–10 (Munich: Eigenverlag).
McGinnis, S. and Hodge, M. (2004) 'Susan McGinnis Talks to Margaret Hodge', *Counselling and Psychotherapy Journal*, 4, pp. 36–37.
Mental Health Foundation (1999) *Bright Futures: Promoting Children and Young People's Mental Health* (London: Mental Health Foundation).

Miller, M. (2001) 'A Snapshot of the Class of 2001', *Public Relations Tactics*, 8(9), pp. 21–2.

Pelling, N. and Renard, D. (2000) 'Counselling via the Internet, Can it be Done Well?', *The Psychotherapy Review*, 2 (2), pp. 68–72.

Robert-Koch-Institut (ed.) (2007) 'Ergebnisse des Kinder- und Jugendsurveys', *Bundesgesundheitsblatt*, 50, 5/6.

Seus-Seberich, E. (2007) 'Du bist die Erste, die mir glaubt, dass ich mich ernsthaft mit meinen Problemen auseinandersetzen will!', SPI im SOS-Kinderdorf e.V. (ed.) *SOS-Dialog 2007—Jugendliche zwischen Aufbruch und Anpassung*, pp. 53–62 (Munich: Eigenverlag).

Thiery, H. (2005) 'Schnell wachsende Nachfrage. Online-Beratung breit angenommen. Die Entwicklung der Virtuellen Beratungsstelle der bke', *Informationen für Erziehungsberatung*, 25 (1), pp. 41–42.

Vossler, A. (2004) 'The Participation of Children and Adolescents in Family Counselling: The German Experience', *Counselling and Psychotherapy Research*, 4, pp. 54–61.

Weißhaupt, U. (2004) 'Die virtuelle Beratungsstelle: Hilfe für Jugendliche online', *Praxis der Kinderpsychologie und Kinderpsychiatrie*, 53, pp. 573–586.

Yager, J. (2002) 'Using E-mail to Support the Outpatient Treatment of Anorexia Nervosa', R.C. Hsiung (ed.) *E-Therapy. Case Studies, Guiding Principles, and the Clinical Potential of the Internet*, pp. 39–68 (New York: Norton & Company).

# Part III

# Youth as a Problem Group?

# 8    Some Insights into Violent Youth Crime

*Chris Lewis, Gavin Hales and Daniel Silverstone*

Gun and knife crime is a difficult problem for all law enforcement agencies and more and more affects the lives of young people, especially in cities. In most European countries it is low prevalence but high impact. However, despite England having the most severe gun crime laws in Europe (Squires 2000; Squires et al. 2008), the number of gun crimes is much higher than it was ten years ago (Povey et al. 2008). It has recently been shown that crime in England and Wales involving knives, especially committed by and against young people, is of the same order or magnitude as gun crime, if not slightly higher, although trends are not yet known (Home Office 2008). Serious incidents such as street murders involving the use of guns or knives are routinely given front page news by the media who at the same time press for more action on the authorities' part. The continuing high level of such crimes, around one or two each week, itself ensures that publicity remains at a high level. Young people are particularly involved, both as offenders and victims.

Most recent figures for gun crime in England and Wales show that all offences (excluding those using air guns) stayed about the same (9,600 in 2006/2007 and 9,800 in 2007/2008), with gun homicides falling from 56 to 52. There were few changes in the types of firearms used, namely about 600 shotguns, 4,200 handguns, 70 rifles, 2,500 imitations, 1,300 unidentified, and 1,100 other.

The traditional English response is demonstrated by the government's three-point plan to tackle gun violence and to keep teenagers from involvement with violent gangs (Home Office 2007).

This involved:

- Tougher punishments for those who use others to assist in gun crime;
- Improved technology to link weapons to crime;
- More funding for community groups working in underprivileged areas.

However, this response was as much based on attempts to reassure the public and the media as on research evidence of what worked in combating gun crime. Following general criticism of youth crime policies in England (see e.g. Solomon and Garside 2008) a more recent government review of youth crime policy seems to have moved towards emphasizing prevention and early intervention more than the justice approach (Home Office 2008). The government has also brought forward specific policies to deal with knife crime (Smith 2008), with the aim to raise awareness among both young people and their parents. Police will also be given more powers and hardware to detect knife carrying, including the use of intensive and directed stop-and-search powers and charging of those caught carrying a knife.

There has also been a growing debate about the ways guns are carried and used and whether this amounts to a developing 'gun culture' in the United Kingdom (Squires 2000; Squires et al. 2008). The contemporary connection between carrying guns, drug markets and violent gangs is a particular aspect of the problem. Although not confined to particular ethnic communities, age groups, or geographical areas, there is clear evidence that gun crime is particularly prevalent in inner cities, with young men and Black communities being particularly involved and community leaders themselves expressing concerns (John 2006).

Surveys of young people themselves (Roe and Ashe 2008) confirm extensive criminality, although over three quarters of young people aged 10 to 25 claim to be law abiding. Among those that said they had broken the law, many had done so only occasionally or committed relatively trivial offences. However, just over a fifth reported they had committed at least one offence in the previous 12 months and 6 per cent had committed six or more offences. Ten per cent had committed at least one serious offence with around 4 per cent being both frequent and serious offenders.

The most commonly reported offences were assault (committed by 12 per cent of all respondents) and 'other thefts' (10 per cent), i.e. not from the person. Criminal damage (4 per cent), drug selling offences (3 per cent) and vehicle-related thefts (2 per cent) were less common, while less than 1 per cent said they had committed burglary or robbery.

When young people are asked about weapons, a significant proportion say that they have carried a weapon of some kind in the previous 12 months, usually for personal protection: e.g., Hayden (2008) reports that 1 in 5 of a sample of Southampton school children claimed to have carried a weapon.

## INTERVIEWS WITH FIREARMS OFFENDERS

Most information on firearms offences is obtained from the routine statistics collected by the English Home Office (Povey at al. 2008) or from the very limited amount of English research (Marshall, Webb and Tilley 2005). The extensive US research is of limited value because of the very different gun culture there, especially the routine use of firearms by the police. As part of a wide Home Office study to improve the evidence base of gun crime research, the authors examined the market in firearms, attitudes of young people towards the use of firearms and the details of the supposed gun culture.

Interviews were conducted with 80 offenders who had been given prison sentences for firearms crime. These were all male, aged between 18 and 30, and drawn from the cities of London, Manchester, Nottingham and Birmingham. Interviews were conducted in prison, in such a way that openness of response was encouraged and the accuracy of the response kept as high as possible. Although the sample was not intended to be a fully representative statistical sample, it corresponded broadly with all young firearms offenders from the areas covered, showing that 45 per cent of the sample of 80 were White, 35 per cent Black, 14 per cent of mixed race and 6 per cent Asian. Full details of the methodology and the sample can be found in Hales et al. (2006).

The background of the 80 offenders was very different from that of the young population as a whole: 59 of the 80 had experienced a disrupted upbringing of some kind; 43 had been excluded from school at some time and 22 had been excluded permanently. Ten had never worked and another 49 had only ever experienced manual or unskilled work. An extremely high proportion (72 out of the 80 interviewed) had taken illegal drugs; of these, 21 were problem users. Their social lifestyles mainly involved music, drugs, nightclubs and an acceptance of violence as a normal part of their life.

The distinction between being a victim and an offender was clearly blurred. Fifty per cent of the 80 offenders had themselves been threatened with guns; 35 per cent had themselves been shot at and 45 per cent had been robbed; 33 per cent had had members of their family or friends shot dead; and a further 33 per cent had had family or friends shot at.

All in all, the interviews with firearms offenders showed them growing up in an environment that was quite extreme and very different from that normally recorded in England at the start of the twenty-first century as being the typical young person's environment.

## GUN CULTURES

The single most important driver of gun crime identified from those interviewed was their involvement with local illegal drug markets. These markets were seen as providing a legitimate 'career option' for young people who did not have any clear likelihood of obtaining good employment otherwise. They also provided a clear career path, with younger teenagers being recruited as lookouts and those who pass on messages, in due course graduating to drug ordering and selling. There were also no entrance requirements, in the way of qualifications or experience; the market for illegal drugs was likely to continue indefinitely under current government policies, and the only precondition was to retain the contacts for employment in this market, mainly obtainable through older siblings/relations or ex-school friends.

The downsides to this form of employment were the likelihood of imprisonment or even an early death and the general short-term nature of such a career: however, these were regarded as being worth running the risk for. Such employment was in clear contrast to the extensive service industry employment opportunities offered in most English cities at the start of the twenty-first century, drawing in many thousands of immigrants from other countries of Europe and beyond. Interestingly, those we interviewed regarded service sector employment as leading only to dead-end jobs with no future. Clearly, the 'glamour' of a risky, criminal lifestyle outbids security in the employment stakes for such young English people.

Guns tend to be used by drug offenders because of the very illegal nature of the drug market. Debts have to be paid in cash, which results in large amounts of money being carried about and guns being used to reduce the susceptible to theft and robbery. Drug debts themselves are not enforceable by normal invoices, court procedures, etc., but need to be collected with force itself, and guns, or at least the threat of guns, are seen to be the most effective way of doing this. This leads to the first type of gun culture, which is the use of guns as instruments, either to enforce drug debts, to threaten or inflict violence, as an agent for armed robberies, and other criminal purposes.

The second is a more complex gun culture, where there are three consistent themes: the ascendancy of criminal role models, the market in illegal drugs and cultures of gang membership, which themselves very often go hand in hand. Significantly, firearms appear to have become increasingly normalized in relation to systemic violence in the street-level criminal economy, including robberies against drug dealers, territorial disputes and informal sanctioning of drug market participants. This includes the possession of firearms for offensive and defensive purposes in the context of complicated offending and victimization histories. Firearms also appear to have assumed a symbolic significance, as they have become associated with criminal affluence related to activities such as drug dealing and robbery, and they have been conflated with respect, status and violent potential.

## MORALITY OF FIREARM POSSESSION

The interviews also gave a much clearer understanding of the unavoidable fact that young people involved in gun crime have an entirely different view of firearm possession than the law enforcement authorities would wish. Around half of the interviewed young people indicated that they felt firearms possession was acceptable under some circumstances, with a distinction drawn between acceptability and need:

> *I wouldn't say there is ever going to be a time when it's acceptable but there's always a need . . . The need is when you're under pressure and you're threatened.*

There was also a widely held belief that the young person needed to provide the protection that the police were unable to provide to them:

> *If your life was in danger . . . you know the police are not on your side and there's nothing you can do . . . that's self-defence . . . you have to protect yourself, any way you know of.*

> *I'd rather carry it with a chance of getting a prison sentence than getting killed, or something happen to me where I get badly hurt.*

The carrying of a gun also led to a sense of empowerment:

> *You feel like you got power when you got a gun . . . Yeah, you feel safer. 'Cos you know if anyone comes to harm you or anything, you know you can defend yourself properly.*

Nonetheless, in some cases there remained a sense of unease:

> *No, it made me feel edgy. Loads of things running through your head, like if you see the people these threats are coming from, if you're driving and a police car stops you, what you're going to do.*

## RISK FACTORS SPECIFIC TO GUN CRIME

Gun crime does not occur randomly across the English population—it is most evident in certain areas and age groups. Such groups need greater research, e.g. in samples matched for one or two key characteristics, such as age, gender or area of residence. While females would present certain research problems, especially that very few will have convictions for firearms, the inclusion of a sample of women is important as their pattern of offending is so different, implying that their pattern of risk and protective factors is also different.

There is very little research that considers risk factors specific to gun crime, but Marshall et al. have provided an analysis (Marshall, Webb and Tilley 2005.). As a result of our interviews, we would suggest that the risk and protective factors listed in Table 8.1 are relevant. However, these suggestions would need to be supported by more research collating data on the backgrounds of a sufficient sample, to discern whether the proposed gun risk factors were present statistically more in certain groups than others. The results of such research could inform prevention activities for young people (see Hayden et al. 2008).

*Table 8.1*   Possible Specific Risk and Protective Factors for Young Gun Criminals

**Risk factors**

- Having peers or family who are themselves gun criminals.
- Having an escalating 'career' of anti-social behaviour, crime and drug misuse.
- Having easy access to guns, e.g. through peers/family/recent military service.
- Contacts with countries in a recent conflict/part of an organized criminal group.
- Having been the victim of or having family/peers who were the victims of gun crimes.
- Having a major debt, drugs debt or being responsible for enforcing drugs debts.
- Protecting a position in the drugs market.
- Having a perceived need to defend oneself against threat of violence.
- Habitually carrying any weapon, such as a knife.
- Being male and in the highest risk age group
- Having a psychological profile demanding power over others through violence

**Protective factors**

- Good quality, nonpunitive drug treatment services.
- Sustained employment.
- Support from the family of origin.
- Strong values transmitted from family or a religious faith.
- Having children and support from a partner.
- Having regular support and advice from a trusted noncriminal adult.
- Moving out of a high gun crime area.

A more accurate picture of these risk and protective factors would enable more effective targeting of resources in efforts to address gun crime. Partnerships and individual prevention agencies are constantly seeking to direct their resources more effectively and assess which individuals should receive intervention. Assessments are regularly being made by Youth Offending Services using the ASSET framework; yet this currently contains no specific factors relating to gun crime. At an instinctive level most criminal justice and crime prevention professionals are making such assessments on a daily basis and many would welcome more evidence to inform their judgements.

The three likely groups needed for such a study would be:

1. Persons known to have been convicted of a firearms offence;
2. Persons known to have been convicted of an offence but not of a firearms offence;

3. Those who have no convictions.

The first two groups could be identified from police records, and their histories would yield data on the differences between those already in a pattern of offending who do progress to use of guns and those who do not. We argue that ideally the third group with no offences should be included as there are many (indeed a majority) in the population of high gun crime areas who never offend and who succeed in resisting a lifestyle that is affecting their neighbourhood on a daily basis. This group may show up the protective factors that counter those influences. The methodological difficulty would lie in finding a matched sample of such individuals and in the loss of statistical validity presented by a small or nonrandom sample. While there may be sampling frames that could be considered, such as school cohort data or electoral registers, it is suggested that in practice the only feasible route would be to take a purposive or quota sample finding matched individuals who had not offended and were willing to participate from youth groups and community organizations in the neighbourhoods concerned.

## YOUNG PEOPLE AND KNIFE CRIME

During recent years concern has been expressed in the English press about what is seen as the growing use of knives by young people in violent incidents (Sturcke 2006; Hulme 2008). Until recently there has been little information on the extent of such incidents but the latest crime figures include information on this for the first time (Home Office 2008). In 2006/2007 there were over 22,000 offences involving knives: these comprised about one in five of all offences of violence. Knife offences tended to be recorded more in urban areas than rural ones. About 5,500 of these offences involved wounding with intent to inflict grievous bodily harm (GBH), and made up over a third of all GBH offences.

More serious offences included homicide, where there were around 250 offences in 2006/2007 and attempted murder, which involved 231 offences. There were 2,400 offences of robbery against businesses that involved knives and 11,500 of robberies of personal property.

These statistics show that recorded knife crime is slightly higher than gun crime, but, in many ways is more severe in its outcomes, since the offences involving guns include about a half which concern air guns only and are to a large extent criminal damage and vandalism.

Other surveys show the extent of reported carrying of knives by young people. Over the country as a whole, 3 per cent of young people aged 10 to 25 had carried a knife in the last 12 months, mainly a pen knife, giving personal protection as the most common reason (Roe and Ashe 2008). Local surveys confirm this trend, for instance Hayden (2008).

## LAW ENFORCEMENT POLICIES TOWARDS YOUNG PEOPLE

These interviews have provided an important body of empirical evidence of how young people in England think and behave about gun crime. Although government policies must have in mind the need to reassure the public, they also need to allow for the 'alternative world' that potential firearms criminals live in, and not to rely on the authorities knowing all the answers.

One further source of information on gun crime policies can be the way that other countries deal with young people. Here the authors have found useful work in a related area, which is a comparative study of the English and the Japanese criminal justice systems. This study, taking place between 2005 and 2008, has been funded by the Sasakawa Foundation (GB) and involves co-operation between Portsmouth University and both the National Police Agency in Tokyo and the Ryukoku University in Kyoto.

In many ways the problems faced by Japan and by England with regard to the behaviour of young people are similar. In both countries, there are growing concerns about offending by children. This is partly because of common drivers of young persons' criminality.

Common to many countries such as Japan and England are such phenomena as drug-taking, night-clubbing, alcohol, gambling, the desire for new technologies (video mobiles, iPods, Blackberries, laptops), the thrill of speed in fast cars and bikes etc., the pressure for early sexual experiences, the decline of religion, the 24/7 society, the influence of globalization and the increase in the numbers of young people who have enough money to join in all these activities.

It is interesting to consider how the Japanese law enforcement agencies regard their responsibility towards young people. Table 8.2 shows a very simplified and broad-brush summary of the general approach the two countries

*Table 8.2*   Simplified Overview of Japan and English Policies for Young People

**Japan: Welfare approach**

- Treatment, care.
- Social work ethic.
- Society is responsible for juveniles until they are around 20.
- Local initiatives of education, training.
- Punishment as a last resort.

**England and Wales: Justice approach**

- People responsible for consequences of their own behaviour from the age of 10.
- Punishment: increased penalty towards young people.
- High emphasis on victim's rights.
- Central control and setting of parameters.

have taken in the past. Thus, Japan can be said to exemplify a welfare approach, with England adopting a justice approach. Whereas the English statistics talk about numbers processed by the system, Japanese law enforcement remains proud of the fact that Japanese police gave advice to around one and a half million juveniles in 2006, mainly for smoking in public (560,000) or being out in the street late at night (720,000) (National Police Agency 2007a.) It is relevant that the most current policy proposals in England and Wales (Home Office 2008) include extending the use of police powers to remove young people from the streets and parks to a place of safety, often their own home, following long-established Japanese police practice.

The net result is that the treatment of young offenders is very different. Although youth crime has recently fallen in both countries, the 2006 prison population of young people in Japan remains at extremely low levels compared to England and Wales (161 in Japan compared to nearly 1,900 in England and Wales, despite the Japanese population being double that of England and Wales).

Japanese youth crime figures tend to move in cycle, with little long term increase, e.g. the figures for the year 2000 were below those of 1966. After a few years of rising juvenile crime, the Japanese government has tended to react, not by increased penalty and new laws, but by putting a lot of effort into providing support mechanisms for juveniles and protective treatment for those who commit serious offences. As a result, the number of crimes committed by young people tends to fall. Most recent figures (National Police Agency 2007a) show that penal code offences committed by juveniles have fallen from 142,000 in 2002 to 113,000 in 2006, following a series of initiatives starting in 2000.

Recent thinking on Juvenile Justice Policy is also routinely published, including independent academic analysis. The most recent volume tackles the statistics of what is called the 'Fourth wave of juvenile delinquency' (since the Second World War): it considers the routine work of the Japanese police aiming to mitigate youth offending, the activities of the Juvenile Support Centres for protecting juveniles and the co-operative strategy for the agencies associated with the clinical psychology-based community support for juvenile delinquency (National Police Agency 2007b).

An indication of police thinking on this can be obtained from extracts from the latest ministry publication on Juvenile Justice Policy, where firstly the need to check growing tendencies towards anti-social behaviour is underlined:

> *The growing seriousness of the situation surrounding juveniles [in Japan] has given rise to the need for efforts to nip delinquency in the bud and prevent juveniles from perpetrating crimes, in addition to making arrests for juvenile-related cases by conducting criminal investigations. While drinking, smoking, late-night roaming and other acts of misconduct are often taken lightly as "just a misdemeanour,*

*not a crime", leaving problematic behaviour unchecked at that stage only serves to reduced juveniles' sense of social norms and may let it develop into full-blown delinquency.*

Secondly, there is the need to set up police structures against such anti-social behaviour, relying more on advice and guidance than on sanctions and punishment.

*To promote the healthy development of juveniles and help the recovery of those who have fallen victim to crime . . . by preventing juvenile delinquency and providing appropriate protection, it is necessary to put in place a mechanism that enables street guidance, juvenile counselling, ongoing guidance, counselling for juvenile victims and other activities to be undertaken properly* (both quotations from National Police Agency 2007b).

An indication of the reaction of the Japanese criminal justice system is seen in the setting up of Juvenile Support Centres and the revised Juvenile Law, involving Family Courts set with the purpose of sound development of juveniles to avoid re-offending. The main characteristics of Japanese Juvenile Support Centres are shown in Table 8.3. These centres take very seriously their role of working with all other agencies, including family and local agencies, to get the juvenile offender back to the right path, rather than simply reassuring the public.

The characteristics of the Japanese Family Court are set out in Table 8.4. In the same way as Japanese Support Centres, the Court concentrates on stopping the offender re-offending. In fact, it is not a court as known in England: there is no prosecutor; no victims attend; and the press and general public are excluded. The background to the offender is investigated and if risk factors are shown to exist, or protective factors shown not to be present, then the court will set in motion actions to try to rectify the situation.

*Table 8.3*   Japanese Juvenile Support Centres

- Part of a wide response to juvenile behaviour.
- Advice and guidance to juveniles and their families.
- Assistance where necessary.
- Work with educational, health, religious, culture, sport, volunteer agencies to enrich assistance and establish networks.
- Juvenile Support Centres give
  Information on drugs provided to schools by police.
  Information to parents as to how to bring up children properly.
  Structure will vary according to local problems and resources.
- Juvenile issues are addressed by the whole society.

*Table 8.4*   Role and Characteristics of Japanese Family Court

- Informal.
- Private.
- Court may order investigation into socio-economic circumstances and behaviour.
- Only 9 per cent are remanded in a form of custody.
- Social investigation collects data for the court and supports and educates the suspect.
- Family Court Judge decides on the need for a hearing; mostly this does not happen.
- No prosecutor, general public or victims.
- Accent on deciding on action to minimize the chance of the suspect re-offending.

This contrasts with the English situation. The problems of juvenile crime were recognized with the setting up of the Youth Justice Board in 1999, with—in theory—a similar sort of role to the Japanese situation. The main aims of the Board are to reduce re-offending of juveniles, very similar to the Japanese case. However, the idea has foundered due to a lack of resources, mainly because of the way that prison numbers for young people have grown in England. This means that most of the YJB money has to be spent on imprisonment. There has also been a much lower ability to work with volunteers than in Japan, and constant pressure from the government to maintain national standards and reassure the public with increased custody and new sanctions such as anti-social orders.

The 2007 initiative involved a new scaled approach to juvenile justice that concentrated on three aspects:

- Developing a tiered approach to interventions based on risk (primarily of re-offending) which supports the proposed new sentencing framework;
- Ensuring a coherent relationship between national standards, key elements of effective practice and practice guidance;
- Supporting case management as an end-to-end process, and improve practice in asset completion, pre-sentence report (PSR) writing and intervention planning (YJB 2007).

What was plain to see—and in great contrast to the Japanese position— was the emphasis on management-speak and concentration on fitting the juvenile into the practices of the authorities, rather than changing the way of thinking of the authorities to meet the needs of the juvenile.

A further contrast was the production, only a year later, of a new approach to Youth Justice in England and Wales, clearly long before the 2007 initiative could have had any lasting effect (Home Office 2008).

However, this new plan does seem to reflect some new thinking with less emphasis on justice and management speak and more on prevention: in this case the approach is one that the Japanese would recognize.

- **Enforcement and punishment:** setting clear boundaries of accept-able behaviour and clear consequences for those who over-step these, including zero tolerance for carrying weapons and underage drinking in public.
- **Prevention:** addressing root causes of crime such as unemployment and spotting problems early and intervening to stop them getting out of control.
- **Support:** offering nonnegotiable intervention to families at greatest risk of serious offending, with a £100 million of extra money.

However, it is not in law enforcement structures and behaviour that the main differences are seen. It is in the general belief that Japanese society as a whole feels responsible for its next generation until they are ready to take their place in society as educated adults. This is in contrast with the feeling that young people in England are themselves responsible for their own bad behaviour from an early age and must accept the consequences.

Moreover, in Japan, there is a recognition that all agencies, the family, school, religious bodies and sports clubs have a share in the responsibil-ity of bringing up children, rather than being an option that children can accept or reject as they choose. This is perhaps best summed up by an Eng-lish journalist talking recently about the behaviour of English youth and criticizing the centralizing control that he feels is the only current response of the British authorities. Writing in *The Guardian*, a liberal English news-paper, in June 2007, Simon Jenkins said:

> *Misbehaviour that would once have been handled at the family, street or community levels is now delegated upwards to agencies of the state. Young people whose discipline in other countries is a prime charge on schools, churches, sports clubs and communal authority, are in Britain left to the Police. . . . Crime has shifted conceptually from being an issue of social reform to being one of repression.*

Although this may be exaggerating to make his point, our interviews with 80 young gun criminals have shown negative attitudes to conventional employment, modern authority, drug-taking and violence that are so far removed from those of most English society that more is needed by way of government response than simply the further tightening of the gun laws and small amounts of community funding that are currently proposed. A new approach to the problem of youth violence is needed.

Other media outlets have gone further than this. The TV company Chan-nel 4 has financed a Street Weapons Commission chaired by the barrister

Cherie Booth, which reported in July 2008 (Channel 4 2008). Among its recommendations are:

- That a Violence Reduction Unit be set up in the Home Office and co-ordinate action across government departments to implement violence reduction strategies. It should adopt a public health approach to the problem and bring together professionals and experts from all relevant disciplines.
- This Unit should conduct an audit of prevention provision in national hotspots for gun and knife crime with a view to identifying gaps in provision and strategically allocating resources to fill them. It should make it easier for community groups engaged in prevention and diversion to work effectively and share best practice.
- The provision of meaningful activities and relationships for young people needs to be prioritized, at the right times and in the areas of greatest need.

However, these proposals have not been costed nor has any response been received at the time of writing.

## REFERENCES

Channel 4 (2008) Report of Street Weapons Commission, http://www.channel4. com/news/microsites/S/street_weapons_commission/index.html (accessed 23 September 2008)

Hales, G., Lewis, C. and Silverstone, D. (2006) 'Gun Crime: The Market in and Use of Illegal Firearms', *Home Office Research Study 298*. (London: Home Office).

Hayden, C. (2008) 'Staying Safe and Out of Trouble: A Survey of Young People's Perceptions and Experiences', University of Portsmouth, July 2008.

Hayden, C., Hales, G., Lewis, C. and Silverstone, D. (2008) 'Young Men Convicted of Firearms Offences in England and Wales: An Exploration of Family and Educational Background as Opportunities for Prevention', *Policy Studies*, 29 (2), June 2008, pp. 163–178.

Home Office (2007) 'Press Notice Three-Point Plan To Tackle Gun Crime', http://press.homeoffice.gov.uk/press-releases/tackle-gun-crime on 2 July 2007 (accessed September 2008).

Home Office (2008) 'Youth Crime Action Plan', http://www.homeoffice.gov.uk/ documents/youth-crime-action-plan/youth-crime-action-plan-08?view=Binary (accessed September 2008).

Hulme, J. (2008) 'Whitehall Can't Stop Knife Crime', *Daily Telegraph*, http:// blogs.telegraph.co.uk/james_hulme/blog/2008/07/07/whitehall_cant_stop_ knife_crime (accessed 23 September 2008).

John, A. (2006) 'Guns, Gangs and Ghosts: Normalising the Abnormal', speech to West Indian Community Conference, Manchester, June 2006.

Marshall, B., Webb, B. and Tilley, N. (2005) 'Rationalisation of Current Research on Guns, Gangs and other Weapons: Phase 1', Jill Dando Institute of Crime Science, University College London.

National Police Agency (2007a) 'Situation of Juvenile Delinquency in Japan in 2006', http://www.npa.go.jp/english/syonen1/20070312.pdf (accessed 2 July 2007).

National Police Agency (2007b) 'Current Juvenile Police Policy in Japan', http://www.npa.go.jp/english/seisaku3/20060424.pdf (accessed 2 July 2007).

Povey, D. (ed.), Coleman, K., Kaiza, P., Hoare, J. and Jansson, K. (2008) 'Homicides, Firearm Offences and Intimate Violence 2006/07', 3rd edition *(Supplementary Volume 2 to Crime in England and Wales 2006/07)*, http://www.homeoffice.gov.uk/rds/pdfs08/hosb0308.pdf (accessed 23 September 2008).

Roe, S. and Ashe, J. (2008) 'Young People and Crime: Findings from the 2006 Offending, Crime and Justice Survey', *Home Office Statistical Bulletin*, http://www.homeoffice.gov.uk/rds/pdfs08/hosb0908.pdf (accessed 23 September 2008).

Solomon, E., and Garside, R. (2008) 'Ten Years of Labour's Youth Justice Reforms: An Independent Audit', Centre for Crime and Justice Studies, Kings College, London, http://www.crimeandjustice.org.uk/youthjusticeaudit.html (accessed 23 September 2008).

Smith, J. (2008) 'Tackling Knife Crime', speech by the Home Secretary, June 2008, http://press.homeoffice.gov.uk/Speeches/knife-crime-speech (accessed 23 September 2008).

Squires, P. (2000) *Gun Culture or Gun Control? Firearms, Violence and Society.* London: Routledge.

Squires, P. with Grimshaw, R. and Solomon, E. (2008) *Gun Crime: A Review of Evidence and Policy* (Centre for Crime and Justice Studies, Kings College, London), http://www.crimeandjustice.org.uk/guncrime.html (accessed 23 September 2008).

Sturcke, J. (2006) 'Knife Crime', *Guardian On-line,*
http://www.guardian.co.uk/world/2006/jun/06/qanda.ukcrime (accessed 10 July 2007).

Youth Justice Board (2007) 'Youth Justice: The Scaled Approach',
http://www.yjb.gov.uk/en-gb/practitioners/youthjusticethescaledapproach/ (accessed 25 July 2007).

Youth Citizenship and
Risk in UK Social Policy

*Alan France, Liz Sutton and Amanda Waring*

In this chapter we explore the role of UK social policy in influencing the experiences of young people in relation to risk. Over the past ten years, the UK government has been active in constructing policies that aim to 'encourage' the young to be active citizens. In the discussion that follows we show how the concepts of 'risk' and 'risk- taking' have been central to the policy agenda and how this has shaped the choices, expectations and opportunities made available to the young. The focus will be on exploring the moral agenda that emerges from such an approach, which underpins the notion of a 'good society' (Etzioni 1995). We will also show how such policies can have a negative impact on young people, leading to greater regulation and control of certain youth populations and creating a situation where the actions of young people more generally are bounded by moral expectations.

## ACTIVE CITIZENSHIP AND PARTICIPATION
## IN UK YOUTH POLICY

It is well recognized that citizenship is a contested concept (Osler and Starkey 2003). Historically it was constructed as a status and set of rights and responsibilities given to individuals living within nation-states (Marshall 1950). In more contemporary times such a definition is seen as problematic, as where we 'belong' in a global world is fragmented. Nationhood and national identities are being challenged by external influences and developments (Giddens 1998). When it comes to youth and citizenship, the matter is further complicated. Youth as a social category has historically been constructed as a stage between childhood and adulthood (France 2007). It is a state of limbo where the young are in transition from one state of being to another. This 'inbetweenness' gives the young limited status as citizens, seeing them as 'citizens-in-waiting'.

Much of UK youth policy towards citizenship has been concerned about the lack of young people's participation and active involvement as citizens (Department for Education and Employment [DfEE] 1998; Home Office 2006). These anxieties are centred on the young not fulfilling or understanding their civic duties and responsibilities as citizens (Department for Education and Skills [DfES] 2005). As a result the UK government has constructed its youth policies around 'encouraging citizenship'. For example, in 2002 citizenship studies was introduced to the national curriculum in schools, and it became a foundation subject in all secondary schools. Pupils aged between 11 and 16 are now expected to have some form of citizenship education as a part of the Personal Health and Social Education (PHSE) programme. At its heart, this policy advocates that young people should develop and experience social and moral responsibility, community involvement and political literacy (DfEE 1998).

The focus on 'active' and 'participatory' citizenship is further illustrated by the UK government's investment in a large volunteering programme targeted at the young (Home Office 2006; Russell Commission 2005) which aimed to provide one million young volunteers over the next decade (Home Office 2006). Investment in volunteering can be seen as one way of encouraging young people to become active in their local community. Simultaneously, it is also a way of enhancing young people's future employment skills. There has also been an emphasis on the role of 'positive activities' as a way of empowering young people through the government's *Aiming High* ten-year strategy for young people (HM Treasury 2007) and particularly for the most disadvantaged young people (Bielby et al. 2008). This notion of 'positive activities' also underpins policy developments in leisure and sport (see for example DfES 2005). Sport is seen as making a significant contribution to citizenship education in that it is seen to help young people develop positive values and actively engage in community life (Eley and Kirk 2002).

Concerns about the lack of participation in civil activity has also seen UK policy target what is known as the 'political deficit' of the young (France 2007). For example, in 2001 the UK government helped establish the UK Youth Parliament as a means of tackling young people's lack of participation in political activity (DfES 2004). One important area in the quest to get young people involved in political activity has been the UK government's focus on increasing participation by 'giving voice' to young people in decisions that affect their everyday lives (Children and Young People's Unit [CYPU] 2001). This approach has been influenced by Article 12 of the UN Convention on the Rights of the Child. It states:

> State parties shall ensure to the child who is capable of forming his or her own views the right to express those views freely in all matters affecting the child, the views of the child being given due weight in accordance with the age and maturity of the child (Article 12 of the UN Convention the Rights of the Child).

Since 2001 the UK government has set out plans for creating an integrated strategy and cross departmental focus on giving young people voice. Many national initiatives have evolved and major resources have since been directed towards increasing opportunities for the young to participate in decision making and for new facilities to be developed in local communities that are built according to young people's decisions (Big Lottery Fund 2009; Department for Children, Schools and Families [DCSF] 2008).

## SHAPING THE LIVES OF YOUNG PEOPLE

The UK government's current emphasis on active citizenship and the drive to encourage young people's participation in a range of areas can be said to indicate a neo-liberal approach to youth policy. Until the 1970s, welfarism dominated the wider political arena, whereby the state assumed responsibility for ensuring the well-being of its citizens (Ashton and Seymour 1988). During this time the welfare state adopted a curative role, acting as a political safety net, waiting to 'catch' vulnerable individuals. However, the mid-1970s saw a shift towards the principles of neo-liberalism or advanced liberalism, marking a desire for minimal state involvement and consequently moving the responsibility for welfare back toward social citizens (Rose 1992). At this time it was thought that the state was a coercive power, controlling the behaviour of individuals and preventing freedom of choice and autonomy. Thus, neo-liberalism was regarded as a sound alternative in encouraging people to be self-reliant and rational in their actions, free from the shadow of state interference (Peterson and Bunton 1997). However, despite the emphasis on self-reliance explicit within a neo-liberal approach to social policy, neo-liberalism continues to promote the ideological position of the state, and in turn individuals are expected to act according to government guidelines. For example, in contemporary policy, much of the emphasis is on the prevention of negative outcomes. As part of this discourse, young people often find themselves in the spotlight, as they are encouraged to discipline themselves and regulate their activities to prevent negative outcomes, either in the present or as adults in the future.

The expectation is that, by disseminating political concerns, individuals will accept the information before them and act accordingly. An example of this can be found in the Department of Health (2004) White Paper 'Choosing Health: Making Healthier Choices Easier' which advocates a partnership between the state and social citizens whereby health risks are defined and guidance on how to prevent them is presented. In turn it is expected that individuals will somehow do the right thing and conform (Peterson and Lupton 1996). In the White Paper, the overall aim for children and young people is ' . . . to support development of a healthy framework for life' (Department of Health 2004: 41). The notion of a 'framework for life' implies that young people should act according to defined parameters, while simultaneously adopting lifestyle practices that they will continue with as they move into adulthood. In creating such a framework, the policy aim is to protect young people by encouraging them to manage their own risks and develop ' . . . responsible patterns of behaviour' (Department of Health 2004: 41). The partnership approach between the state and young people advocated as part of the Choosing Health (Department of Health 2004) agenda is illustrative of the Foucauldian concept of governmentality whereby the state emphasis on prevention becomes an expression of surveillance that is noncoercive, yet despite this arguably subtle approach, compliance is clearly an objective. Governmentality is not about dominating and controlling individual action, it implicitly depends on free will (Scrambler and Higgs 1998).

In this context therefore, it can be argued that the UK policy towards youth and citizenship has been shaped by a series of assumptions of what the transitions to adulthood *should* look like. In this sense youth policy can be located within the wider policy debates about the role of the state and welfarism. It is underpinned by a view of human nature that sees the individual as active, rational, responsible and moral in their behaviour. The notion of the 'responsible individual' making positive choices about their future has become central to this view. This highlights the political transition from government to governance where a set of guidelines, morals and values are defined through policy (Rose 1989). Citizenship is viewed as individuals taking responsibility for themselves (and their families) and the government's role is to provide opportunities and choices to help individuals make the transition into adulthood.

This approach is underpinned by a growing commitment to individualization (Beck and Beck-Gernsheim 2002) where traditional ways of managing life are not seen as appropriate for the late modern age. Individualism is seen as the new social structure where people seek biographical solutions to the contradictions embedded in late modernity. Policy is aiming to achieve a society consisting of responsible citizens who are taking control of their own lives. However, simultaneously, UK policy has also been shaped by communitarianism (Etzioni 1995), which contends that there is a need to link rights with responsibilities and for individuals to be responsible for their families and wider communities. This approach underpins the welfare-to-work policy agenda and the growing encouragement for more civic involvement as volunteers. These dual individual and communitarianism discourses produce tensions within UK policy for how best to frame and encourage youth citizenship.

## TACKLING RISK AND RISK-TAKING IN UK YOUTH POLICY

So far we have concentrated on exploring the discourses of citizenship that dominate political debate showing a strong moral picture, influenced by communitarianism and the expansion of individualization. What emerges is a view of behaviour that is defined by the state and its institutions. Yet

UK youth policy has also been shaped by concerns about risk and risk-taking. In fact the concept of risk has seeped into a wide range of policy areas and has become the foundation for how policy tackles social problems. The impact of this is to re-enforce models of 'acceptable behaviour' that dominate in debates about citizenship. An example of the prevalence of risk and policy responses can be found in the policy approach to youth crime (France 2008a), social work practice with young people (Sharland 2006), children's play policy (Ball 2007) and sexual health policy (Hoggart 2007). Across these areas there are two prevailing discourses of risk and risk-taking that have dominated the policy landscape, one being about the 'risk society' and its influence on social life, especially for youth transitions, and the other anxiety over the 'risk-taking' generation where, it is claimed, young people are taking more negative risks than ever before.

The notion of the risk society is not a new concept in UK policy (Giddens 1998). Social and public policy has, over the previous decade, been greatly influenced and shaped by the belief that, in late modernity, risk has increased as a part of everyday life. In this context governments therefore assume the role of assessing risk and helping people manage it (Kemshall 2002). Beck (1992) argues that Western societies are in a period of global and local changes that are creating uncertainty particularly over identities and social membership. The new 'risk society' is characterized by manufactured hazards and risks that create uncertainties about the future. Many of these can be seen in areas such as environmental hazards, anxieties over medicine and concerns over employment. The risk society is also characterized by long term processes of cultural change, what Giddens (1992) calls 'detraditionalization'. Society is losing its cultural norms and values that helped guide and steer collective life. In this context life is becoming more 'individualized' (Beck and Beck-Gernsheim 2002) and people are constructing more personalized biographies where 'risk choices' are becoming central features of the life course. In this post-traditional society, despite class no longer predicting a person's life chances, risks are still likely to be distributed on existing lines of inequality (Beck 1992).

The risk society is seen as having a fundamental impact on the lives of young people (Cieslik and Pollock 2002) in that it is claimed they are being offered greater choice and opportunity to have control over their own lives (Beck 1992). New Labour have developed social policies that aim to empower individuals and communities to manage risk but also to use it as a way of developing lifestyle pathways and futures (Kemshall 2002). Over the last decade, UK government has focused on policies that aim to get the young into work, to reduce the risk of future unemployment (Social Exclusion Unit [SEU] 1998). Having a job and being in employment is also seen as core to the UK government's strategy of encouraging active citizenship and participation. Being in work helps minimize the risk of other problems and is seen to reduce social exclusion (SEU 1998). Over the last ten years there have been a wide range of policy initiatives and programmes in education, training and employment (i.e. New Deal, Modern Apprenticeships, E2E, New Start, Education Maintenance Allowance). These strategies tend to target the most 'at risk' in terms of economic inactivity or social exclusion, especially in areas of high deprivation, and are seen as a way of improving young people's life chances and increasing their economic and social contribution. Young people who are not willing to take up their responsibilities (or take the risk) in trying to find work or keeping work when they find it, are penalized (Finn 2003). For example, in 1997 the New Deal Employment Programme introduced sanctions that stopped cash assistance. Recent welfare reform has re-enforced this position, arguing that benefits should be linked to 'contributions' and responsibilities (France 2008b).

Perspectives on the risk society have clearly shaped how UK youth employment policy has developed (Cieslik and Pollock 2002). For example, the New Deal employment programme aims to offer a wide range of 'choice' in quality training and employment placements. This aims to encourage the young to improve their own skills and credentials and to take greater responsibility for their own futures (Percy-Smith and Weil 2002). Similarly, the development of life-long learning as a UK policy initiative aims to increase young people's skills and knowledge and to develop their ability to make choices about their futures (Tomlinson 2005).

There is a growing research literature that explores what Du Bois Reymond (1998) calls 'choice biographies'. Evidence suggests that more and more young people are in a position to make choices about their futures (Wyn and Dwyer 1999). In this context young people see choice as real and a critical aspect of their everyday lives in that they see it as a positive step towards independent adulthood and a mechanism for taking control over their own lives. Furthermore, young people see it as a major factor in shaping how they get into future training and employment and improve their life chances (Furlong and Cartmel 1997).

The concept of governmentality is then central to the notion of the risk society. The government's preoccupation with the idea of an observable reality of risk masks the way that it is being developed as a strategy for control and regulation of populations, as Sharland notes:

> Risk, therefore, exists not as some external reality but as a 'calculative rationality' of governance, through which particular groups and individuals may be identified as 'at risk' or 'high risk' and thereby observed, managed and disciplined (Sharland 2006: 255).

As a result, UK youth policy—in helping the young 'manage risk'—is arguably concerned with subtly monitoring and disciplining the young. For example, as discussed earlier in policies related to unemployment, we see a strong emphasis on regulating and controlling 'risky populations'. Similar developments can be identified in youth justice where state driven interventions aim to control those most 'at risk' or those identified as problematic 'risk takers' (Kemshall 2007). In this context the commitment to the 'risk society' becomes yet another mechanism of defining acceptable and unacceptable behaviour, in line with neo-liberal models of the 'rational actor' and of controlling young people and managing the 'youth question' (France 2007).

## THE 'RISK-TAKING' GENERATION

Risk-taking by young people is not a new phenomenon, having been of concern in premodern as well as modern societies (France 2007). Young people have always been involved in such behaviours as rioting, drunken behaviour and crime and disorder (Griffiths 1996). What has changed, however, is the way that society responds to that behaviour. In premodern times, misbehaviour and crime tended to be dealt with locally and by young people themselves, regulating their own behaviour through such practices as 'naming and shaming' (Davis 1990). Today's young people, in contrast, are affected by unprecedented state levels of regulation and surveillance and are subject to an increasing government process of responsibilization (Garland 2001). This, Sharland (2006) notes, arises from the merger between care and control in UK policy.

Risk-taking, however, can be regarded as a 'normal' developmental phase of adolescence, where young people learn the consequences of their own actions. The paradox, as Sharland (2006) points out, is that in the desire to protect young people, we prevent them from learning from their mistakes. Changes in the very structure of society can have consequences for the risks that young people have to face. For example, young people are now encouraged to stay on at school and to live at home for longer than previous generations did and therefore taking a 'risk' and leaving home can be seen as a form of escape for some (Sharland 2006). Within policy, however, another dominant discourse sees young people's risk-taking as a predominantly negative cultural activity. It is perceived that urban and modern life in the United Kingdom has seemingly been transformed by the growth of a 'culture of risk-taking' among young people that is a signifier of social decline (France 2007). It is important to note that clear distinctions exist between the notion of 'children' and 'youth' in this debate. Generally, when risk-taking by children is discussed, the focus of policy tends to be on the need to protect the child from such behaviour and intervene in ways that will encourage more pro-social forms of behaviour (France 2008a). Alternatively, when the focus is on young people's risk-taking, the issue tends to be discussed in terms of the need to regulate or control their behaviour (Sharland 2006).

Young people are generally perceived as high risk takers who are the cause of many of today's social evils (Mowlam and Creegan 2008). In this context, risk is usually equated with 'danger', with the young seen to be behaving in such a way that they are perceived as a 'danger' to others or themselves. For example, in a recent research report published by the charity Barnardo's it was suggested by 49 per cent of adults that the young were a danger to adults or to each other and that 43 per cent thought government had to do more to protect adults from young people (*Times* Online, November 2008).

Anxieties over young people and risk-taking have grown around a whole range of behaviours. The major concern is their criminal activity and the perceived growth in anti-social and criminal behaviour, which helps to shape the general public's perception of young people (Barnardo's 2008). There are also worries over the 'increased intoxication' and 'binge drinking' of the young (Institute of Alcohol Studies 2005). Over the previous decades a large number of surveys have shown a growth of young people's alcohol consumption and the types of drinks they take (Richardson and Budd 2003; Fuller 2004). 'Binge drinking' is claimed to account for 40 per cent of all drinking episodes amongst men, and 22 per cent amongst women (Cabinet Strategy Unit 2004); with 16- to 24-year-olds more likely to 'binge drink' than any other age group (Richardson and Budd 2003; Office for National Statistics 2004). Similarly, it is also thought that drug taking amongst the young has increased (Beinart et al. 2002; Fuller 2004). Drug-taking is now seen as a normal part of youthful leisure (Parker et al. 2002). For example, national and international evidence suggests that 'drug-taking', especially of cannabis, is becoming a normal and accepted part of young people's everyday lives and a major leisure risk-taking activity (Parker et al. 2002; Fuller 2004).

A number of youth policies have been developed in response to these so-called 'risky' behaviours. For example, teenage pregnancy in the United Kingdom is the highest in Europe, and the number of new cases of sexual transmitted infections has doubled. This was higher amongst young girls (Office of National Statistics 2004) while the highest rates of chlamydia are amongst 16- to 19-year-olds. The growth of teenage pregnancy and sexual infections are believed to be because more young people are taking greater risks in their sexual practices (Office of National Statistics 2004). In a bid to improve teenage pregnancy rates and the incidence of sexually transmitted diseases, the government introduced the Children's Health Guides as part of the Child Health Promotion Programme (Department of Health [DoH] 2004). In developing the health guides in partnership with medical professionals, young people are expected to build health into their life, considering issues such as contraception for example, and they are generally expected to take responsibility for their own health (DoH 2004). Similarly, the recently launched Government consultation on the need to tackle the culture of drinking among the young emphasizes the need for clear guidelines on alcohol consumption in order to help parents and young people be responsible for their own alcohol intake and associated behaviour (The Stationery Office 2008). It can therefore be argued that anxieties and perspectives of youth as 'high risk takers' are shaping a public and social policy agenda that emphasizes and encourages young people to take responsibility for their own lives but which implicitly leads to greater regulation and control of the young (Sharland 2006; France 2008a).

## THE SOCIAL CONTEXT OF RISK-TAKING

Individualistic theories of risk-taking place great importance on the idea of young people weighing up the costs and benefits to them of their actions. The risk is perceived as worth doing if the potential benefits outweigh the potential costs, such as smoking and being accepted by friends (Gillen et al. 2004). Risk-taking therefore has to be understood in its social context, as it is influenced by a range of social factors, and people's perceptions of risks are varied and complex (Tulloch and Lupton 2003). As Ward and Bayley suggest:

> . . . risk behaviours are complex and bound up within peer relationships, status and identity. Unless these are confronted within a broader framework incorporating sociocultural, socioeconomic and social ecological perspectives, we will miss the contextual factors that shape risk behaviour development. (Ward and Bayley 2007: 52)

What is missing from much of the policy debate, are the views and experiences of young people themselves, and how they perceive and experience risk in their everyday lives. This is particularly important as many responses to young people's risk-taking are based on adult definitions of risk and 'risky' behaviour (Shucksmith and Hendry 1998). Research by Ward and Bayley (2007) highlights young people's own definitions of risk and those factors most relevant to their own lives. They show how young people conceptualize risk as an action associated with harm, as something they do not have to do and as having potentially negative consequences. However, they also show how young people recognize that some of these consequences can have positive effects in the longer term. They highlight the 'fun' and the 'buzz' associated with some risks and demonstrate how most young people are extraordinarily well-versed in the art of keeping themselves safe in terms of road safety, teenage pregnancy and drug taking. Importantly, though, they argue that for many young people, risks and anxieties abound concerning their own peer relationships, status and identities. Taking risks can be fundamental to feelings of inclusion and being accepted (France 2000; Ward and Bayley 2007). Risk-taking in this context can be specific to relationships and have important elements that give a young person status or belonging. Mitchell et al. (2001) for example, found that young people who did not engage in certain risk-taking activities could find themselves socially isolated and excluded.

The importance of social structures to young people's lives cannot be ignored, especially in relation to their transitions into adulthood (Furlong and Cartmel 2006). Young people are, of course, a heterogeneous group and as such, their risks and opportunities as well as how they manage them will vary depending on many other social characteristics including their age, class, ethnicity and gender. Risk-taking and risk management in the 'risk society' will also vary depending on young people's own local context. It is important therefore to take into account the wider context of young people's lives to include their home, their school, place of work, the street or roads around them and their leisure space such as pubs or clubs. Similarly, the risks that young women contend with and manage will vastly differ (Hoggart 2007) to those of young men (Ward and Bayley 2007), and the risks that young people face in negotiating street space in cities will be different to those dealt with in rural communities (Elsely 2004). Cartmel (2004) highlights for example the differences in young people's access to informal networks in rural compared to more urban communities, which help to mitigate the risks of unemployment within these communities. Young people who live in disadvantaged communities will also be exposed to different types of risks than young people from more affluent communities and areas (Farmer 2005; MacDonald 2006; Matthews and Limb 2000).

Young people living in these communities have been shown to be subjects of victimization and crime (Armstrong et al. 2005) and will be more likely to have to take responsibility for their own safety when using public space (Seaman et al. 2005, Sutton 2008). The risks that young people negotiate and manage are then rooted in their everyday experience and are not primarily concerned with their outcomes as future adult citizens.

The wider socio-cultural and socio-economic context that gives legitimacy to some forms of risk-taking over others is also crucial to our understanding of young people's risk-taking and risk management. One example can be taken from the work of Hollands and Chatterton (2003). They explored the drinking culture in the northeast of England. National and local policy expressed major concerns about the 'binge drinking' culture of the night time activity of young people. Hollands and Chatterton's work showed that what was important to this activity was the social context of the night time economy. Major developments had taken place in the northeast leisure industries with an expansion of night clubs, themed pubs, casinos, new music venues and café bars. Ownership of the cultural industries was concentrated in the hands of the few international conglomerates and nightlife was controlled by their desire to make profits. As a part of this process, the new industries created new ways of involving young consumers. The creation of 'happy hours' and the expanded marketing and encouragement of alcopops are examples of such targeting of young people. In this context, excessive drinking and consumption of alcohol is encouraged, as it increases profit margins (Hollands and Chatterton 2003). This restructuring of urban night spaces can then influence what is defined (and available) as leisure. In this context, risk-taking in terms of 'binge drinking' is normalized and encouraged as a part of being a young consuming citizen.

CONCLUSION

Our discussion of UK youth policy has highlighted that the discourse of active citizenship which runs throughout youth policy is inherently contradictory. For example, young people are encouraged to make their own choices, yet these so-called choices are constrained by the notion of 'good citizenship' which is prevalent in a wide range of youth policies. As part of the discourse of active and good citizenship young people are required and expected to take responsibility for their own actions and to undertake certain types of behaviours that are perceived to contribute to a better society. In this context the young may well, in late modernity, have to navigate risks, yet this is part of the responsibilities they are required to undertake to be regarded as active citizens. The role of the state and its agencies therefore exemplifies a process of governmentality whereby youth policies are developed to help the young undertake a process of decision making and to help them learn how to be responsible.

Risk-taking is therefore presented in UK policy as a negative activity that needs to be controlled, regulated and in some cases punished. The types of risk-taking that are encouraged and accepted by the state are shaped by *adult* perceptions of the type of activities young people should be involved in. How risk-taking is understood and valued in policy is, therefore, a moral and value judgement, mediated by the state which shapes our understanding of which risks are acceptable and which are not.

A similar conclusion can be made of the concept of choice. As we have shown, 'choice' has become a central feature across UK youth policy. In the 'risk society thesis' it is a critical component of the new responsibilities of citizenship. If individuals are to have greater autonomy and control over their futures, then they are to be encouraged to make the right choices and take risks, yet as we have shown, different groups encounter risks in a variety of ways. For some, managing risks is more straightforward and unproblematic, while others have less resources and opportunities which can limit their chances of success. Choice, therefore, is shaped by external factors and the resources individuals bring to the decision-making process. As a result there are 'winners' and 'losers' in obtaining successful outcomes. Being a loser can result in the state regarding it as an individual failing and can subsequently instigate regimes of control and regulation, especially in terms of access to welfare benefits and resources. It can also lead to certain populations becoming defined as a problem and one that needs greater intervention.

But as we have shown throughout the discussion, youth citizenship and risk-taking can only be understood in its wider social context. It is not a process of rational choice where individuals explore right and wrong and, and if well informed, come up with the right outcome. Young people's lives must be seen within the specific contemporary social context, as the socioeconomic, sociocultural and political conditions in which they grow up have a major influence on how they behave. This is not to deny personal choice or individual decision making as influencing a young person's trajectory, but it recognizes the importance of other factors that can shape outcomes.

## REFERENCES

Armstrong, D., Hine, J., Hacking, S., Armaos, R., Jones, R., Klessinger, N. and France, A. (2005) *Children, Risk and Crime: The On Track Youth Lifestyles Survey* (London: The Home Office).

Ashton, J. and Seymour, H. (1988) *The New Public Health* (Buckingham: Open University Press).

Big Lottery Fund (2009) Myplace information leaflet, www.biglotteryfund.org.uk/prog_myplace_leaflet.pdf (accessed 2 February 2009).

Ball, D. (2007) 'Risk and the Demise of Children's Play', in B. Thom, R. Sales and J. Pearce, *Growing Up with Risk* (Bristol: Policy Press).

Beck, U. (1992) *The Risk Society* (London: Sage).

Beck, U. and Beck-Gernsheim, E. (2002) *Individualization* (London: Sage).

Beinart, S., Anderson, B., Lee, S. and Utting, D. (2002) *Youth at Risk? A National Survey of Risk Factors, Protective Factors and Problem Behaviour among Young People in England, Scotland and Wales* (London: Communities That Care).

Bielby, G., Gelden, S., Judkins, M., Wilson, R. and Maguire, S. (2008) *Empowering Young People Pilot Interim Evaluation*, Research Report DCSF—RW065.

Cabinet Strategy Unit (2004) *Alcohol Harm Reduction Strategy for England and Wales* (London: Strategy Unit).

Cartmel, F. (2004) 'The Labour Market Inclusion and Exclusion of Young People in Rural Labour Markets in Scotland', in W. Mitchell, R. Bunton and E. Green (Eds.), *Young People, Risk and Leisure: Constructing Identities in Everyday Life* (Basingstoke: Palgrave MacMillan).

Cieslik, M. and Pollock, G. (Eds.) (2002) *Young People in Risk Society* (Aldershot: Ashgate Press).

Children and Young People's Unit (2001) *Learning to Listen: Core Principles for the Involvement of Children and Young People* (London: Department for Education and Science).

Davis, J. (1990) *Youth and the Condition of Britain* (London: Athlone).

Department for Children, Schools and Families (DfCSF) (2008) 'Youth Opportunity Fund and Youth Capital Fund', *Year End Report* (London: DfCSF).

Department for Education and Employment (DfEE) (1998) 'Education for Citizenship and the Teaching of Democracy in Schools' (London: DfEE).

Department for Education and Skills (DfES) (2004) 'Review of the UK Youth Parliament' (London: DfES).

Department for Education and Skills (DfES) (2005) *Youth Matters* (London: DfES).

Department of Health (DoH) (2004) *Choosing Health: Making Healthier Choices Easier* (London: DoH).

du Bois Reymond, M. (1998) '"I don't want to commit myself yet": Young People's Life Concepts', *Journal of Youth Studies*, 1 (1), pp. 63–79.

Eley, D. and Kirk, D. (2002) 'Developing Citizenship through Sport: The Impact of a Sport-Based Volunteer Programme on Young Leaders', *Sport, Education and Society*, 7 (2), pp. 151–166.

Elsely, S. (2004) 'Children's Experience of Public Space', *Children and Society*, 18 (1), pp. 55–64.

Etzioni, A. (1995) *New Communitarian Thinking* (Charlottesville, VA: University of Virginia).

Farmer, C. (2005) *2003 Home Office Citizenship Survey: Top-Level Findings from the Children's and Young People's Survey* (London: Home Office).

Finn, D. (2003) 'The Employment-first Welfare State: Lessons from New Deal for Young People', *Social Policy and Administration*, 37 (7), pp. 709–724.

France, A. (2000) 'Towards a Sociological Understanding of Youth and Their Risk-taking', *Journal of Youth Studies*, 3 (3), pp. 317–31.

France, A. (2007) *Understanding Youth in Late Modernity* (Buckingham: Open University Press).

France, A. (2008a). 'Risk Factor Analysis and the Youth Question', *Journal of Youth Studies,* 11(1), pp. 1–15.

France, A. (2008b) 'Being to Becoming: The Importance of Tackling Youth Poverty in Transitions to Adulthood', *Social Policy and Society*, 7(4), pp. 495–505.

Fuller, E. (Ed.) (2004) *Smoking, Drinking and Drug Use amongst Young People in England* (London: Health and Social Care Information Centre).

Furlong, A. and Cartmel, F. (2006) *Young People and Social Change: Individualisation and Risk in Late Modernity* (Milton Keynes: Open University Press).

Garland, D. (2001) *The Culture of Control* (Oxford: Oxford University Press).

Giddens, A. (1998) *The Third Way* (Cambridge: Polity Press).

Gillen, K., Guy, A. and Banim, M. (2004) '"Living in My Street": Adolescents' Perceptions of Health and Social Risks', in W. Mitchell, R. Bunton and E. Green (Eds.), *Young People, Risk and Leisure: Constructing Identities in Everyday Life* (Basingstoke: Palgrave MacMillan).

Griffiths, P. (1996) *Youth and Authority* (Oxford: Oxford University Press).

HM Treasury (2007) *Aiming High for Young People: A Ten Year Strategy for Positive Activities* (London: HMSO).

Hoggart, L. (2007) 'Young Women, Sexual Behaviour and Sexual Decision Making', in B. Thom, R. Sales and J. Pearce (Eds.), *Growing Up with Risk* (Bristol: Policy Press).

Hollands, R. and Chatterton, P. (2003) 'Producing Nightlife in the New Urban Entertainment Economy: Corporatization, Branding and Market Segmentation', *International Journal of Urban and Regional Research*, 27(2), pp. 361–385.

Home Office (2006) *The Respect Agenda* (London: Home Office).

Institute of Alcohol Studies (2005) *Binge Drinking: Nature, Prevalence and Causes: Fact Sheet on Binge Drinking* (St Ives: Institute of Alcohol Studies).

Kemshall, H. (2002) *Risk, Social Policy and Welfare* (Buckingham, Open University Press).

Kernshall, H., (2007) 'Risk Assessment and Risk Management; The Right Approach'. in Blyth, M. Solomon, E. and Baker, K., *Young People and 'Risk'* (Bristol: Policy Press).

MacDonald, R. (2006) 'Social Exclusion, Youth Transitions and Criminal Careers: Five Critical Reflections on "Risk"', *The Australian and New Zealand Journal of Criminology,* 39(3), pp. 371–383.

Marshall, T.H. (1950) *Citizenship and Social Class* (Cambridge: Cambridge Press).

Matthews, H. and Limb, M. (2000) 'Exploring the "Fourth Environment": Young People's Use of Place and Views on their Environment', in *Children 5–16*, Research Briefing Number 9, ESRC.

Mitchell, W. A., Crawshaw, P., Bunton, R. and Green, E. E. (2001) 'Situating Young People's Experiences of Risk and Identity', in *Health, Risk and Society*, 2 (2), pp. 399–422.

Mowlam, A. and Creegan, C. (2008) *Modern-day Social Evils: The Voices of Unheard Groups* (York: Joseph Rowntree Foundation).

Office for National Statistics (2004) *Health Survey of the UK* (London: ONS).

178    *Alan France, Liz Sutton and Amanda Waring*

Osler, A. and Starkey, H. (2003) 'Learning for Cosmopolitan Citizenship: Theoretical Debates and Young People's Experience', *Education Review,* 55 (3), pp. 243–254.

Parker, H., Williams, L. and Aldridge, J. (2002) 'The Normalisation of Sensible Recreational Drug Use: Further Evidence from the North West England Longitudinal Study', *Sociology,* 36 (4), pp. 941–964.

Percy-Smith, B. and Weil, S. (2002) 'New Deal or Raw Deal? Dilemmas and Paradoxes of State Interventions into the Youth Labour Market' in M. Cieslik and G. Pollock (Eds.), *Young People in Risk Society* (Aldershot: Ashgate Press).

Peterson, A. and Bunton, R. (Eds.) (1997) *Foucault Health and Medicine* (London: Routledge).

Peterson, A. and Lupton, D. (1996) *The New Public Health: Health and Self in the Age of Risk* (London: Sage).

Richardson, A. and Budd, T. (2003) 'Alcohol, Crime and Disorder: A Study of Young Adults', in *Home Office Research 263* (London: Home Office).

Rose, N. (1989) *Governing the Soul: The Shaping of the Private Self* (London: Routledge).

Rose, N. (1992) 'Governing the Enterprising Self', in P. Heelas and P. Morris (Eds.), *The Values of the Enterprising Culture: The Moral Debate* (London: Routledge).

Russell Commission (2005) *A National Framework for Youth Action and Engagement* (London: HMSO).

Scrambler, G. and Higgs, P. (1998) *Modernity, Medicine and Health: Medical Sociology Towards 2000* (London: Routledge).

Seaman, P., Turner, K., Hill, M., Stafford, A., and Walker, M. (2005) *Parenting and Children's Resilience in Disadvantaged Communities* (London: National Children's Bureau).

Sharland, E. (2006) 'Young People, Risk-taking and Risk Making—Some Thoughts for Social Work', in *British Journal of Social Work,* February 2006, 36, pp. 247–265.

Shucksmith, J. and Hendry, L.B. (1998) *Health Issues and Adolescents: Growing Up, Speaking Out* (London: Routledge).

Sutton, L. (2008) 'The State of Play: Disadvantage, Play and Children's Well-Being', *Social Policy and* Society, 7 (4), pp. 537–549.

Social Exclusion Unit (SEU) (1998) *Bridging the Gap: New Opportunities for 16–18 Year Olds Not in Education, Employment or Training* (London: HMSO Cm 4405).

The Stationery Office (TSO) (2008) *Youth Alcohol Action Plan,* Department for Children, Schools and Families, The Home Office and the Department for Health June 2008 Cm 7387.

Times online, 17 November 2008, http://www.timesonline.co.uk/tol/life_and_style/education/article5167811.ece (Accessed 17 November 2008).

Tomlinson, S. (2005) *Education in Post-Welfare Society* (Milton Keynes: Open University Press).

Tulloch, J. and Lupton, D. (2003) *Risk and Everyday Life* (London: Sage).

Ward, J. and Bayley, M. (2007) 'Young People's Perceptions of "Risk"', in B. Thom, R. Sales and J. Pearce (Eds.), *Growing Up with Risk,* (Bristol: Policy Press).

Wyn, J. and Dwyer, P. (1999) 'New Directions on Youth Transitions', *Journal of Youth Studies,* 2 (1), pp. 5–22.

# 10 Leaving the Parental Home or Staying On?
## Young People in Spain and the Development of Social Capital

*Andreu López Blasco*

## INTRODUCTION

Youth has been commonly seen as a time of preparation for a place in society as well as in the labour market. This is to be achieved by physical and psychological development, socialization, the development of the self, education, vocational qualifications and the acquisition of life experiences; all these developments are to take place in the period roughly defined as 'youth', which should appear as a linear process. At its end one is supposed to assume a more or less secure professional career, partnership, family, and all this without any breaks. Youth has been seen as congruent with phases of transition. However, in society today—the 'risk society' or 'liquid society'—the processes of transition for young people are no longer linear but de-standardized, precarious and also dependent on the young individuals' own decisions. We call this situation 'yo-yo-ization of transitions between youth and adulthood'.

This contribution considers the specific behaviour of young people in Spain in relation to the ways in which they leave their parental home; this behaviour is analyzed in the context of the welfare state model, the labour market and the existing familial culture of Spain, and the analysis of statistical data and of narrative biographical interviews is placed in the centre of the discussion.

Firstly, there will be a brief outline of important factors which influence the long path towards social and economic participation. There is evidence which shows that, provided that their families' social and economic situation allows this, young people in Spain try to prolong the time they stay in their parents' home, so that they can increase their social capital, save money, prepare themselves for independence and improve their chances of success. While delaying their departure from the parental home, they use the 'services' available there, and benefit from the contacts and social networks of their families. It is interesting to see that young people with low educational qualifications—or whose parents have low educational qualifications—are the ones who leave their parental household earlier than others, since staying on would provide no more benefits.

## YOUNG ADULTS IN THE 'ANTE-ROOM' OF STABLE OCCUPATION

In many developed countries there are problems associated with integrating young people productively into society and the labour market, if they have poor vocational qualifications, low aspirations, low levels of confidence and an inability to cope with stress. On the one hand there is increasingly less demand for employees with few or no qualifications; on the other hand, unemployed people are increasingly obliged to take on occasional and seasonal jobs for low pay. At the same time competition between qualified employees is increasing with new and higher demand for specialist qualifications, social competence and regional mobility. Generally, the education and social systems have not yet adapted to the demands of the new labour market conditions. These systems themselves often lack the required financial and political strategies as well as the means to reform.

There are many older employees who are made redundant as a result of radical changes in production (relocation, rationalization, merger, takeover, insolvency), often without any hope of further employment, while on the other hand there are many young people seeking work after already extensive periods of education and training, who are employed in the 'ante-rooms' of qualified and stable occupation: they are in jobs which have nothing to do with the qualifications they have gained, they spend periods doing 'work experience', occasional, part-time and temporary jobs.

Thus, the potential of the younger generation is not activated enough in the social and economic sphere, and a considerable percentage of young people depend on the social network of public transfers (unemployment, supplementary or incapacity benefits). This is particularly problematic for society in economic and social terms, considering that an increasing proportion of older people are no longer available for the production process, while their financial provision depends on the employment income of the younger generation. Academics as well as politicians refer to a 'weakness of the new generation', and this does not simply mean that there is a declining birthrate, but also that the productive capital of the young generation is not available to a sufficient degree or sufficiently early.

It is surprising that societies confronted with the problem of increasing numbers of older people do not make more efforts to equip as many young people as possible with a minimum of qualifications. Neither can one understand why they do not encourage and support the development of qualifications during the time of transition towards employment in such a way that the young generation's capital can be deployed earlier and better, to offer these people their place in society at an earlier stage.

What is also evident is that in western European societies the high proportion of older people reduces the political weight of the younger generation in the democratic process of interest representation. Their interests are particularly ignored—at the cost of the young but also society as a whole—as the states today are faced with further great challenges, such as the reduction in state expenditure, safeguarding the social system and energy resources, the fight against terrorism, reducing environmental pollution, encouraging multinational political cooperation, etc. (Hornstein 2007).

There is evidence that today a considerable number of young people, who are still in education or training, live in the parental household for many years or depend financially on their parents, in part or completely. Long periods of education, long transition phases into stable occupation, higher expectations on the standard of living and higher costs of modern living (accommodation, electronic equipment, leisure activities), unstable partnership relations etc. have contributed to a situation where prolonged financial support via the parental family is encouraged or becomes a necessity.

If today politicians and academics talk about 'youth', then this term usually includes the third decade of life. It thus includes a phase when young adults try to enter the labour market, with lengthy educational programmes becoming necessary for more qualified career positions.

The educational paths have become longer and need to be revised frequently, while professional qualifications have to be adapted to changing requirements; apart from the institutional demands of training and occupational paths, the orientation and disposition of the individual play a more important role in today's knowledge society. As a result of the increasing significance of personal disposition and the ability to make decisions, young people depend in particular on the resources available in their parental family—both as help or hindrance—and the resources available in their whole personal sphere of life. This means that the ways in which young people behave vary strongly according to the original conditions which exist in the familial and personal sphere.

The great challenge for young people today is the 'winner/loser' competition: those of them who have low or no educational qualifications have only limited chances of finding jobs with a secure income, as a result of the globalizing labour market and the constantly increasing rationalization of productive facilities. There are limited job offers for people with no or insufficient qualifications or motivations, while there is huge competition for such jobs; redundant workers are forced to move into badly paid, unattractive and insecure service areas. This means that there is a great risk of young people being caught between unemployment, occasional jobs, underpaid or insecure types of occupation; there is no guarantee of gaining qualified positions, and there is always the risk of redundancy.

Young people in Europe discover that a modern standard of living demands high expenditure for leisure activities, health, insurance etc. To make the most of all the opportunities on offer, which they do not want to miss out on, financial resources are necessary, which many young people do not have. Leisure has become so important that the young want to take part in it fully; it seems more important than employment or independence from the family—even if it needs the support of the parental family. The acceleration of life (e.g. in relation to qualifications and technology) and the uncertainty of the future mean that people's views are fixated on the here and now, and this perhaps explains why young people are often surprisingly optimistic about their future perspectives, ignoring the past or the future.

While the situation of many young people in the 'ante-rooms' of stable occupation is a wide-spread phenomenon, in some countries the situation is more problematic than in others, as there are consistently higher proportions of young people and young adults who are unemployed, in relation to other age groups. On the one hand the competition for income and employment in connection with the right to private social security (financed not by the state but by the employer), and the preparation for retirement on the other, increase the need for early security: the young need sufficient income. In the present situation people become increasingly aware of the costs which families, the social services and the taxpayer have to carry to cover at least the most essential needs of the young. At the same time what is ignored is the social capital which is wasted because the young are not given the opportunity for social and economic participation. We must stress that the increasingly late entrance of young people into the social and economic process carries the risk that they enter a situation of social exclusion where they may stay, and that this can have devastating effects on the social framework as a whole.

## THE PARENTAL HOME: A PLACE OF
## HARMONY AND AMBIVALENCE

From an existential perspective, there are different levels of conditions affecting the younger generation: modern independent life is expensive; for many young people, the process of finding work and the right qualifications is prolonged, particularly if this process is not based on clearly personal choices but rather on abilities which they master only just adequately. Often they have no clear expectation of finding stability in partnership and employment (Baumann 2004).

In Spain, among the factors affecting and contributing to young people remaining in the parental home for increasingly long periods is the changing concept of the family and young people's own attitudes, which mean that they do not seek independence as long as they do not find suitable conditions.

Of the number of correlations we have made, we want to highlight the congruence between opinions and attitudes and the educational qualifications of parents and children. Decisions within the family are increasingly made in the context of compromises with the young people and their expectations. The percentages show that the higher the father's educational level, the higher the degree of compromise and collective decision making between parents and children.

*Table 10.1*   How are (or were) Decisions in your Family made in Relation to Children?

|  | Father's educational qualifications | | | | |
| --- | --- | --- | --- | --- | --- |
|  | Primary education | Secondary education I | Secondary education II | Tertiary education | Total |
| Parents decide | 18.60 | 15.20 | 7.90 | 8.50 | 12.60 |
| Discussion, but parents decide | 31.80 | 30.30 | 35.00 | 26.30 | 30.90 |
| Compromise decision | 34.90 | 44.30 | 48.60 | 55.40 | 46.30 |
| Discussion, but children decide | 10.10 | 8.60 | 6.70 | 8.50 | 8.30 |
| Children decide | 4.70 | 1.60 | 1.80 | 1.30 | 1.90 |
| Total number | 100 | 100 | 100 | 100 | 100 |

Source: INJUVE-CIS (4th Survey 2007, 'Young and older people, family relations, gender equality'). Own calculations.

The most common form of decision making, the 'compromise decision', can be found mainly if the father has had higher secondary education and achieved university qualifications. The lower the respondents' educational level, the higher is the percentage of those who say that the decisions are made by the father.

Decision making as the result of compromise is high for all educational levels. If, in addition, the children's educational level is taken into account, then it can be seen that they have a greater influence on the decisions made at home if their educational level is higher.

*Table 10.2*   How are (or were) Decisions in your Family made in Relation to Children?

|  | Children's educational qualifications | | | | |
| --- | --- | --- | --- | --- | --- |
|  | Primary education | Secondary education I | Secondary education II | Tertiary education | Total |
| Parents decide | 16.6 | 12.4 | 9.2 | 3.0 | 13.1 |
| Discussion, but parents decide | 34.6 | 28.5 | 26.5 | 28.7 | 31.0 |
| Compromise decision | 39.2 | 49.1 | 53.4 | 58.4 | 46.0 |
| Discussion, but children decide | 7.9 | 6.9 | 10.0 | 8.9 | 8.1 |
| Children decide | 1.7 | 3.0 | 0.8 | 1.0 | 1.9 |
| **Total number** | 100 | 100 | 100 | 100 | 100 |

Source: INJUVE-CIS (4th Survey 2007, 'Young and older people, family relations, gender equality'). Own calculations.

*Table 10.3*   How Often is (was) there a Discussion Within the Family About Your Work or Education?

| | Father's educational qualifications | | | | |
|---|---|---|---|---|---|
| | Primary education | Secondary education I | Secondary education II | Tertiary education | Total |
| Very often | 23.40 | 23.30 | 34.30 | 45.10 | 29.70 |
| Quite often | 44.50 | 57.50 | 55.70 | 48.20 | 54.30 |
| Not often | 25.80 | 15.30 | 8.40 | 6.30 | 13.10 |
| Never | 6.30 | 3.90 | 1.50 | 0.40 | 2.90 |
| Total number | 100 | 100 | 100 | 100 | 100 |

Source: INJUVE-CIS (4th Survey 2007, 'Young and older people, family relations, gender equality'). Own calculations.

It is evident that there are 'quite a lot' of discussions about the children's work and education within the family. The percentage of those who reply 'very often' is higher if the father has a better and/or higher education.

One of the most common divergences between modernity and postmodernity is ambivalence: In today's postmodern cultural sphere people are confronted in their everyday life with differing attitudes, ways of behaviour and relations which appear and indeed can be contradictory, but which do not exclude each other, as Beck and Baumann underline, because they are characteristic of our society.

These new situations are reflected today mainly in the way in which people live together in the parental home. The harmony which exists, the good relationships between parents and children are marked by the great difference between the life of parents and that of their children. The difference lies in the life biographies which can be summed up in the following way: there is ambivalence between the 'normal' biography of the parents and the 'do-it-yourself' biography of the children.

The contradictions and ambivalences become more acute, because the great changes we have experienced in Spain in relation to social tolerance, women's emancipation and the liberation of the individual are not continuous; on the contrary, they seem to be regressive now. The new conditions of the labour market, the growth in social inequality and individual freedom still depend to a large extent on the social milieu into which a person is born as well as on the parents' social background. For part of society, it has become difficult to secure their living via the market, which means that outside the parental family this security depends on the chance of establishing a stable position within the labour market, and this is increasingly unattainable. After so many efforts the parents have made to adapt to the demands of today's society, they dream that in the end their children would have it better if they behaved in the way they themselves had behaved when they were young.

In this context children are forced to produce their own biographies, without being dependent on the stability of the context and the traditions which surround them. But they do not have the opportunity to employ the necessary means in order to master the situation, and thus they have to share life—or rather part of their life—with their parents, and longer than they would like. They have to 'make a claim on the solidarity of the family'. Their longer stay in the parental home becomes 'family life forced upon them'. This situation is the result of a clear understanding: The children know that, despite everything else, they themselves have to shape their own biography, and they must secure their existence always in relation to a labour market developing in ways they do not understand (López Blasco 2006).

At the same time this harmonious, peaceful familial context free of control is unstable and often no longer functions: both parents are in employment, working hours do not fit together (shop opening times etc.), the family members' different phases of work and rest prevent good communication; leisure, sport and health activities encourage a conduct of life which is individualized; people don't have the time or the inclination for deeper and longer communication; at the same time, market services allow an increase in individual independence.

Today, young people have to be ready and able to compete in the market, in a context of socialization which has failed to equip them with the necessary resilience. All of them have grown up in a period of prosperity. They need to be ready for competition and confident of achieving, and this in a context of unpredictability and insecurity. They need to be competitive, although most of them have not learned to make the most of themselves on their own.

Is it surprising then that, under these conditions, they rely on their parents' support for a long time? Politicians certainly offer nothing that would make this familial support superfluous. It seems that they are not particularly interested in the potential capital which the young between 20 and 30 could offer. They prefer to lament the ageing society and do not talk about the cost to society as a whole.

The way in which young people today move out of the parental home is in stark contrast to that of young adults in the period between 1940 and 1975, at the time of the Franco dictatorship and of internal and external emigration: The relatively early independent existence of young people at that time was the result of the parents' life situation, and was at the same time the necessary precondition for adult life and starting a family (cf. Bertram 2004).

The longer stay in the parental home also has consequences for the parents: After they have dealt with the problems of puberty within the family, there follows an often extended period where they provide solidarity to their adult children while the latter are planning their professional life, finding their own form of life and setting up their own household. The adult children who still benefit from this parental support can find themselves in a variety of situations: They may be at university close to their parents' home or in another town, they can be unemployed, with part-time, occasional or mini jobs, in full-time employment, as singles with or without a partner, as single parents, even as married couples with or without children.

It seems that in Spain transition households (people living as singles, in communal households with people of the same sex or mixed) are still relatively rare, while moving out from the parental home is usually the result of setting up home with a partner or getting married; in Spain, typically people also move to a place they own themselves.

For the parents, the period where they provide this family solidarity is not only a financial burden, as they provide for the larger household or 'support' the cost of living of their adult children's households; they also share the worries about the difficulties their children have trying to make a success of their education, employment and partnerships.

As a result of the children's longer stay in the parental home, parents not only experience the structural barriers which their adult children encounter in their attempt to develop their life successfully, but they also experience the negative and positive competencies and ways of behaviour based on their own socialization and friendships within their own generation.

## YOUNG SPANISH PEOPLE MOVING OUT FROM THE PARENTAL HOME[1]

A number of youth studies carried out in Spain in the 1990s[2] found that young people remain in the parental home increasingly longer, which has led to heated discussions in the media. In many headlines, young people are dismissed as lazy: They are judged to be exploiting their parents and using the parental home like a hotel. But at the same time the media are surprised that the predicted generational conflict has not materialized. In this discussion, few people mention the high unemployment rate among young people. In general, the high proportion of young people still living at home is always stressed, while other things are ignored. And this is despite the fact that studies have shown for some time (CIRES 1993) that a large proportion of young people under 29 are very happy with the quality of communication between parents and children[3].

For many years cross-national comparative studies have produced data on young people's extended stay in the parental home, attempting to find explanations for the clear differences from country to country. More recently the debate has subsided. The question is no longer new. Also, as a result of complex influences, the differences can be interpreted in diverse ways. In addition, one may question the factual significance of the empirical differences. Nonetheless, the established national differences in relation to staying on in the parental home and/or the time of transition to independent living—alone, with a partner, in communal living—within a more closely comparable framework of conditions (for instance when focusing on young adults who are in employment and no longer in education) can provide significant information on determinant factors.

In recent years, young people's longer stay in the parental home has been one of the 'special' topics when discussing southern European countries in comparative EU studies. Young people who still live with their parents are usually categorized as 'users of Hotel Mama'[4]. But this in general is not based on proper evidence and is often no more than a superficial comment on the answer to: 'Where do you normally live for most of the year?' Percentages are not correlated with further variables such as gender, age, education, financial situation, occupation, the place where people live or the parents' education. Many studies merely focus on the superficial changes in young people's behaviour, without considering the societal connections.

The answers to 'Where do you normally live for most of the year?'—a question which was recently used in two surveys (October/November 2007, cf. INJUVE-CIS 2007) show that the proportion of young people between 15 and 29 who still live with their parents is indeed very high, namely 63 per cent. This proportion is also high in comparison to neighbouring countries, even though these also show the trend towards young people remaining longer in the parental home[5]. However, the number of all young people from 15–29 as a whole is not really significant.

Thus, based on my more recent research in relation to the Spanish Youth Surveys 2004 and 2008, I firstly want to present the answers to 'Where do you normally live for most of the year?' in the context of variables such as age, educational qualifications, gender or the labour market situation. I will then focus on one of the six biographical portraits from the Spanish Youth Survey 2008 (López Blasco 2008).

a) Changes in the area of family, occupation and economy affecting young people, in particular women between 20 and 26:

Among the most important changes in relation to the pluralization of forms of life one can stress mainly the *earlier decision making of young people*:

- Young people now leave the parental home or the home of those they depend on at an increasingly early age.
- Living with a partner starts increasingly early.
- The number of young people between 21 and 24 who live with a partner has increased by 7.3 per cent in the period between 1996–2008.
- The age of the young persons' partners with whom they live has fallen consistently.
- The first baby is born earlier.

The changes between 1996–2008 in relation to family, employment and economic life of young people/young adults are particularly marked for young women between 20 and 26. It can be seen that changes in one area, e.g. the time of leaving the parental home, are connected to events in other areas, such as living with a partner, end of education and training, etc. Such changes can also be seen in the life of young men, but not as consistently and also in a less pronounced way.

In 2007, a clearly smaller percentage of women of 20 years and older no longer live with their parents (Figure 10.1).

In Spain—in contrast to northern and central European countries— there are hardly any young women who live alone. Thus the data from 2007 are confirmed showing a significantly larger proportion of 20- to 26-year-old people living with a partner, as compared to 2004, 2000 and 1996 (Figure 10.2).

In the particular 20–26 age group, in 2008 there were significantly more young women in employment, as compared to 2004, 2000 and 1996, while conversely there are fewer in education and training (Figure 10.3).

In addition to the higher proportion of the age group over 20 and especially over 24 who are in employment, there is also a higher proportion of young women living mainly or completely on their own income (Figure 10.4).

The young women in the 2004 survey had earlier sexual relationships with men than the women questioned in 1996 and 2000. This development has continued, as the data from 2007 show (Figure 10.5).

Information about the timing and frequency of starting a family can show that in 2008 a somewhat higher proportion of young women between 21 and 26 already have children, in relation to the earlier surveys, while women over 27 have fewer than in the previous surveys (Figure 10.6).

The correlation between age, gender, education and the place where people live shows the following findings (cf. López Blasco 2008: 195–201):

- Most young people between 21 and 24 with low educational qualifications (no more than up to the minimum school-leaving age) live in their own households.
- Sixty-three per cent of young people between 25 and 29, and among them (only) those women who have low or medium qualifications (post-secondary education) live in their own households.
- In contrast, 49 per cent of women in the same age group but with higher educational qualifications are still in their parental home.

In the 21–24 and 25–29 age groups, it is the young adults with lower educational qualifications (unless they are still in education) who already run their own household; the percentage of women among them is clearly higher than that of men, as women normally leave the parental home earlier and also have older partners.

b) Delaying independence or how to increase social capital: parental support and strengthening through personal and peer-group relationships

Here we consider excerpts from the biographical portrait of a young woman we call Marta. They are derived from biographical interviews based on the sociology of knowledge, Karl Mannheim's theories, Garfinkel's ethnomethodology, Bourdieu's concept of the habitus, etc.[6]

Marta is 25 and studied audio-visual communication in Madrid; she is currently employed as a social worker; during five years of study in Madrid she lived alone and after her studies moved back to the town where her parents live, moving in with them again. For several years, having lived an independent life where nobody could control who she went out with, when she came home or what she ate, she is nevertheless finding it quite natural living with her parents again. For her it is a question of age and affordability: *'I am 25 years old and I like living with my parents . . . when I am 27 or 28, then it'll probably be time to leave the nest.'*

She believes that during a possible phase of transition she may be dependent on her parents, but she does not expect her parents to finance her independence. Living with her parents is just something she does at the moment; at 27 or 29 she will want to move out, or she might move in with a partner. *'There will come an age when I will then want to live with him, when I will somehow leave behind the life I now lead.' (Interview 1: 471–475).* Her partner lives in the same town, he studies and works at the same time.

> *Question: When you came back, did you not think about living independently with other people?*
> *Answer: No (she replies with conviction). No, to be honest, I have never thought about it. If I leave to be independent, then with my partner, not with female friends or alone . . . no, I have never considered that. I really feel happy at home, I have never been under any pressure when I felt like saying: 'But now I really want my independence, no.' (Interview 1: 259–263).*

The biographical narrative shows that we find here a strategy or a pragmatic attitude aimed at preparing for independence more carefully, but not an expression of laziness or of not wanting to stand up to responsibilities. The interviewee declares that she is still in a 'period of transition' and that in this way *'I prepare myself for economic independence and . . . how shall I say, also emotional independence. But I don't know; where I live now, I feel happy' (Interview 1: 453–455).* To stay with her parents, she is able to increase her social capital: she attends courses and does not have to take any old job, *'for I don't have to work where I don't actually want to, just to pay for my food' (Interview 1: 563).*

> *You know, whether you like it or not, at home you get a lot free and you can expect support, if you say one day: 'OK, this year I won't work but I'll take this or that training course'. When you live at home,*

*you always get support and you can get hold of all necessary things. Last year I lived and studied away almost for the whole year, and at the weekends I had a job in a shop to finance my own expenses. When you have the support, then it is really a big advantage . . . lots of people don't have that, and they have to say some time: 'Now I do have to work, no matter where, otherwise I can't pay for food or anything else.' Yes, . . . I do think I have an advantage, and at any time. If next year I want to do a master's or something, then my family will support me . . . I could say, now I will stop working and I'll do something different'. I don't know (Interview 1: 558–567).*

When she came back from Madrid at the end of her studies, both Marta and her parents had to adapt slowly to the 'new' situation, after not having lived together for several years. Marta is finding out that to live with her family is not the same as coming back at the weekend or for holidays, when she returned again to Madrid; she is realizing that they want to control her, but both Marta and her parents are gradually getting used to it. *'They don't control me directly, but there is a certain control. When I go out, I have to say with whom and when I am coming back'.* Marta understands her parents' worries, for she is a single child. The family makes an effort to achieve harmony in their relationships, and all family members avoid conflicts/arguments. They adapt to each other. Marta accepts a degree of control, as from her standpoint there are many more advantages than disadvantages in living with her parents.

Staying longer in the parental home makes it possible to accumulate social capital and to prepare for when she eventually leaves under the best possible conditions. For her this situation is just temporary, and when she decides to become independent, she shows herself to be prepared to give up certain advantages which she currently enjoys in her parents' house. She would spend less on clothes, go out with friends less often, economize on petrol (at the moment, her parents pay for that, and they also bought her car). While she is still at home, she can make decisions about her future, she can count on her parents' support while looking for a better job: *'When you want to do a master's, you can also do that while you live at home. And if you want to buy a house, then you can start and save up or you can take it easy, without always being broke'.*

Her circle of friends has not changed since her school years. After returning from Madrid, she picked up the relationships again, and is also in contact with the groups of friends from the village where she used to spend her holidays with her parents when she was younger.

*We have known each other since school, we used to go to kindergarten together and now we still see each other. There are six of us. Then I also have my friends from the village where we always spent our summer holidays . . . they are all the same age, that's how it is in the village, all groups of friends always get together according to age (Interview 1: 679–-681).*

The relationship to her circle of friends is another important factor in Marta's biography and it corresponds to the concept of 'peer group'. In her biographical narrative we can recognize all the characteristics which youth sociology ascribes to 'peer groups', especially in relation to the security, the models of behaviour and the mutual recognition, which all provide the arguments confirming the individuals' customs and habits.

> *Actually we all have gone similar paths.* **None of my friends are already independent,** *or wanted to be yet. We are all thinking about* **getting a subsidized flat,** *because none of us can afford anything else.* **In relation to our situation in the labour market, we are all in very similar situations.** *There is one who is just learning to apply for a job in the public sector, two are looking for a job, because . . . well, so far they just have not found one yet and . . . the others,* **they are already working, but not in a job they really like . . . it's just not their dream job** *. . . just what they can find (Interview 1: 689–693).*

In the context of her biography, Marta is able:

- To confirm the traditional relationships in her part of the town, in the school, with the families she has known for a long time, and this gives her security;
- To interpret the difficulties, which she has to overcome, in order to gain independence, and this helps her to be calm;
- To ignore new experiences, new contacts and new horizons, which in fact makes social and geographical mobility more difficult to achieve, and this explains potential frustrations, while also having a calming effect.

## CONCLUSION

In conclusion, the key points of this chapter should be highlighted, at the risk of repeating some arguments outlined already. Also, some open questions may point to possible new directions for research.

First of all the context must be underlined relating to the lengthening of the period which young people stay in their parental home; this is followed by considering the significance of young people's decision making for or against remaining longer in their parents' home.

### Summarizing the Most Important Results

The Youth Surveys provide considerable in-depth information about the changed circumstances and ways of behaviour of young people and young adults. However, because of its social significance, one fact should be of central importance:

The data seem to indicate that the employment and social paths of the new generation in society are distributed in new ways—even if structurally this is not totally new:

- There is one group of people who, while evaluating their possibilities, resources, opportunities and costs, seek employment without further and better qualifications; thus they are more likely to leave the parental home:
  - whether this is as a result of their precarious economic situation, lacking the conditions that would allow them to conduct their life in a self-determined way, or because of repressive modes of communication in the home etc.
  - or whether they are deterred by the demands of educational effort and the fear that they might fail or that poorer performance would risk them being left behind in the competition for better jobs.

Young people can gain valuable support from their parental home on the path to personal maturity and professional qualification, if the following conditions are in place:

- an objective, mutually respectful style of communication; living conditions and a style of care which allows opportunities for independent arrangements;
- an economic framework which provides young people with the material equipment for successful qualification;
- economic support which—in view of the high costs of modern personal needs, adequate accommodation and living expenses—allows them enough 'breathing space'.

This chapter aims to stress that it is not enough just to state that the lives and employment paths of young people have been changing. It is important also to consider the potential significance of these changes in social context and in relation to the future. The young people who move along these paths are confronted by a society which makes two absolute demands that can hardly be ignored: firstly, that one needs to be 'good' in one's subject and genuinely competent, i.e. that learning in itself is not enough, one needs to deploy it with ingenuity, and secondly, that personal engagement is absolutely necessary.

Parental support depends—and this is no less important—on the parents' competencies and resources. If the parental role as a factor is considered in relation to the developments in the children's leaving, educational and employment behaviour, then the following options can be identified:

- There are young adults who, with the parents' communicative and material support remain longer in the parental home (and/or live in student accommodation away from home), are clearly successful in their educational and employment paths, achieving good positions.

- There are young adults who, with the same support, but for various personal or social reasons, only achieve medium or lower qualifications and positions.
- There are young adults who cannot rely to a similar degree on the advantages provided by the parental home, but who as a result of their personal efforts fight hard to gain educational qualifications and employment positions at medium and higher levels.
- There are young adults who also cannot rely on positive parental support, who leave the parental home relatively early and who, as a result of personal or social disadvantages, normally only gain lower or medium educational qualifications and employment positions.

Data from the latest Youth Survey Spain (López Blasco 2008) indicate quite clearly that women's employment participation is becoming more like men's, and also that their behaviour in relation to housing is becoming similar, though less strongly so: according to the 2008 study, 50 per cent of women aged 21–24 are already in the labour market (18 per cent being without employment or working for the family). Sixty-one per cent of these women still live in the parental home. Seventy-one per cent of women aged 25–29 are already in the labour market, compared to 70 per cent of men; 8.1 per cent are still in education. Thirty per cent of them still live with their parents.

Comparing the results of the Youth Surveys of 1996, 2000, 2004 and 2008[7], it becomes clear that the proportion of young women in the labour market has grown constantly over the years: in 1996 roughly 53 per cent of 29-year-old women were active, while it was 76 per cent in 2008. Correspondingly, the proportion of young women in education in the 20–26 age group has declined. The proportion of women aged 20 and above who mainly or completely earn their own living has increased disproportionately: in 1996 the figures were 12 per cent of 20-year-olds and 48 per cent of 29-year-olds, while in 2008 they were 41 per cent and 71 per cent respectively.

Between 50 per cent and 74 per cent of the women aged 27–29 who still live with their parents have university degrees. The proportion of those with low educational qualifications still living with their parents is almost constant for the age groups of 21–29, namely between 25 per cent and 32 per cent. Young women with medium educational qualifications are those who are determined to set up their own household from the age of 25; only 10 per cent of 29-year-olds in this educational group still live with their parents.

## What is the Significance of Young People's Decision Making for or against Remaining Longer in the Parental Home?

While analysing the data of the Youth Surveys, we have repeatedly asked ourselves questions about the significance and the consequences of the delayed social and economic participation of young people for themselves, their parents and society as a whole. The answers to these questions depend on the factors which influence their decision making.

194 *Andreu López Blasco*

Let us consider first the *significance for the young adults* themselves:

The insecurity and the strongly inductive search for perspectives—a step-by-step approach—in relation to the appropriate education, the appropriate job, the occupation and income opportunities characteristic of the careers of many young people is conducive to the provisional way in which they plan their lives. This leads to trying out partnerships and keeping options open longer, in situations where gender-specific role segments are not clearly defined and where life together needs to be negotiated again and again depending on changing circumstances; it leads to transitional and satellite households or staying in the parental home until an independent household can be set up.

The process of clarification in relation to one's job, partnership and household demands a high degree of personal decision making to work out clearly what the individual aims are and what can be achieved realistically. Young people with strong personalities can deal with these demands more successfully—if they have found a basis for their own competencies as a result of acquiring technical and/or communicative skills or indeed by finding a key or anchor for their own life in their individual dealing with the big questions relating to the meaning of life.

In parallel to the difficult and only gradually gained perspectives in career and partnership, in the area of consumption, there are, however, wide opportunities for the young in relation to information, communication and lifestyle choices. The young are the main consumers in this area.

Expenditure in this area can be added to the costs of housing and food. Such costs seriously prevent young adults making provision for and investing in future goals from their own income. It is more likely that it is the minority of young adults, those who have discovered their personal abilities early, having gained clarity and confidence in their future goals, who may decide to curtail their consumption, go without such commodities or use them instrumentally in relation to their profession.

On the one hand it is the lack of clarity about career perspectives, while on the other hand it is the cost of modern living as well as the chance to rely longer on parental support, and these factors together do not make for favourable starting conditions when it comes to developing investment interest in the form of capital provision or time investment. Instead, a high amount of leisure time and comfortable personal communication structures at work are a priority for young adults.

The *significance for the parents* must also be underlined: The phase of helping their adult children along is not only a financial burden, whether by providing for them while they still live at home or helping them with their separate household costs. They often accept the burdens which come with the irritations of their adult children's problems in achieving success in their education, career and partnership. Through the extended stay in the parental home, the parents experience at first hand not only the structural barriers to their children's successful life path, but also their own positive and negative competencies and modes of behaviour as a result of their own education and the friendships within their own age group.

Finally, the *significance for society* has to be considered fully:

Young people are innovative in their outlook; they understand and use the technical opportunities and the new goods and services on the market. However, with the historical background of a long phase of prosperity, there are today, apart from the parents, hardly any other social representatives who might show the young the 'seriousness of the situation' in respect of future developments and who could point out specific opportunities for action. Thus there is the risk not only that the 'seriousness of the situation' is not recognized, but also that incentives are not sufficiently and not clearly enough posed so that the young would face up to the new challenges.

For a dynamic development of society, a strong economic and political role for the young generation is of great significance. The long phase of transition with waiting times, insecurity of direction and the lack of proper planning criteria, before the young find their positions in career, partnership and household—una vida por su cuenta—is, from the perspective of society as a whole, a time when no social investment is taking place.

On the one hand it is legitimate to expect that the phase of youth and post-adolescence is a time for adventures and experiences, for discovering the world. This seems especially justified under modern social conditions in which increasingly each individual is expected to be the architect of his or her own career and life path, without the help of an institutional safety net. On the other hand, as a result of the provisional nature of the career and partnership paths, this period between the ages of 20 and 30 does not have the potential which could challenge society economically and politically in the process of setting goals and strategies for action.

## NOTES

1. The research group EGRIS studied the specific ways in which young people moved out of the parental home; this study—*Familien und Übergänge in Europa* (FATE—Families and Transitions in Europe) involved a number of EU countries with reference to the welfare state model, the labour market and the familial culture. See www.iris-egris.de

2. In 1993, the research centre CIRES undertook a survey of 1,200 people (26 per cent of them were between 18 and 29, while 74 per cent were over 30). This was a standardized survey on the topic of youth. Since 1984, the Spanish Youth Institute (INJUVE) has carried out studies on young people. Every four years a specific survey on the situation of young people is carried out which is published as *Youth Report Spain*.

3. This situation has been summarized in the study 'Erzwungene Harmonie. Junge Erwachsene—zufrieden, freundlich, aber ohne Zukunft?' [Enforced Harmony—Young Adults: Content, Friendly but without a Future?] (López Blasco 1996).

4. The 7th Family Report (2006), produced by the Spanish Ministry for the Family, Senior Citizens, Women and Young People, still states in II.2.1 'Partnership and Moving out or "Hotel Mama" as a consequence of extended financial dependence'.

5. See also the results of the 'Shell Studie Jugend 2006' in Germany which states that 73 per cent of young people between 18 and 21 are still living with their parents. ' . . . even for people aged between 22 and 25, the percentage is still 34%' (Shell Deutschland 2006: 16–17). In this context, the 'relatively bad

economic situation' and the 'many different demands by educational institutions and employers' are underlined.

6. The scope of these theories became clear to me in discussions with and publications of Jutta Stich from the German Youth Institute, Munich.

7. This comparison is an important part of the Youth Survey Spain 2008—see López Blasco (2008).

## BIBLIOGRAPHY

Bauman, Z. (2006) *Liquid Times: Living in an Age of Uncertainty* (Cambridge, UK: Polity Press).

Bauman, 2. (2004) "Fluchtige Moderne". Conferencia, Congreso de ANSE sobre "Die Werteproblematik als Herausfoderung fur Praxis und Konzept von Supervision und Coaching" 07/Mai/2004, Leiden/NL.

Bauman, Z. (2000) *Liquid Modernity* (Cambridge, UK: Polity Press).

Beck, U. and Beck-Gernsheim, E. (1993) 'Nicht Autonomie, sondern Bastelbiographie. Anmerkungen zur Individualisierungdikussion am Beispiel des Aufsatzes von Günter Burkart', *Zeitschrift für Soziologie*, 22 (June).

Beck, U. (1986) *Risikogesellschaft* (Frankfurt: Suhrkamp).

Beck, U. (1997) 'Demokratisierung der Familie', in U. Beck (Ed.) *Kinder der Freiheit*, pp. 195–216 (Frankfurt: Suhrkamp).

Beck-Gernsheim, E. (2006) *Die Kinderfrage heute. Über Frauenleben, Kinderwunsch und Geburtenrückgang* (Munich: C.H Beck Verlag).

Bertram, H. (2004) Nachhaltige Familienpolitik. Zukunftssicherung durch einen Dreiklang von Zeitpolitik, finanzieller Transferpolitik und Infrastrukturpolitik. BMFSFJ, Berlín.

Biggart, A., Walther, A. et al., FATE (2004) Families and Transitions in Europe: Comparative Report (Coleraine: University of Ulster, October 2004).

Bien, W., Weidacher, A. (ed.) (2004) Leben neben der Wohlstandsgesellschaft. Familien in prekären Lebenslagen. (Wiesbaden: VS-Verlag für Sozialwissenschaften).

Bohnsack, R. (1993) *Rekonstruktive Sozialforschung. Einführung in Methodologie und Praxis qualitativer Forschung* (Opladen: Leske+Budrich).

Bohnsack, R. (2003) 'Dokumentarische Methode und sozialwissenschaftliche Hermeneutik', in *Zeitschrift für Erziehungswissenschaft*, 6 (4), pp. 550–570.

Bundesministerium für Familie, Senioren, Frauen und Jugend (2006) 7. Familienbericht, Familie zwischen Flexibilität und Verlässlichkeit. Deutscher Bundestag 16. Wahlperiode. Drucksache 16/1360, 26th April 2006.

CIRES, Centro de Investigaciones sobre la Realidad Social (Centre for Research on Social Reality) Survey "Attitudes and Experiences with Respect to the Public Sector", April 1993, Madrid, Spain

Dannenbeck, C. and Stich, J. (2002) *Sexuelle Erfahrungen im Jugendalter. Aushandlungsprozesse im Geschlechterverhältnis* (Cologne: Bundeszentrale für gesundheitliche Aufklärung).

du Bois-Reymond, M. and López Blasco, A. (2003) 'Yoyo Transitions and Misleading Trajectories: From Linear to Risk Biographies of Young Adults', in A. López Blasco, W. McNeish and A. Walther (Eds.) *Dilemmas of Inclusion: Young People and Policies for Transitions to Work in Europe*, pp. 19–42 (Bristol: Policy Press).

FATE—*Families and Transitions in Europe (2001–2004): A comparative analysis in nine European regions*, http://www.socsci.ulster.ac.uk/policy/fate/fate.html

Gaviria, S. (2007) *Juventud y familia en Francia y en España* (Madrid: Centro de Investigaciones Sociológicas, Colección Monografías n° 234).

Hornstein, W. (2007) Jugend und Jugendpolitik im Prozess der Globalisierung. Vortrag im Rahmen des DJI-Symposiums, Jugend, Jugend-(hilfe)forschung und Jugendpolitik in der globalen Welt', May 2007.

INJUVE-CIS (4th Survey 2007) Sondeo de opinión y situación de la gente joven: Jóvenes y personas mayores, Relaciones familiares, Igualdad de género (Madrid: INJUVE, Spanish Ministry for Equality).

López Blasco, A. (1996) 'Erzwungene Harmonie: Junge Erwachsene—zufrieden, freundlich, aber ohne Zukunft?' in A. Walther (Ed.) *Junge Erwachsene in Europa* (Opladen: Leske + Budrich), pp.187–200.

López Blasco, A. (2003) *Families and Transitions in Europe—Qualitative Survey. National Report Spain* (Coleraine: FATE-EU Project, University of Ulster).

López Blasco, A. (2004) 'Familia y Transiciones: individualización y pluralización de formas de vida' in: INJUVE *Informe 2004 Juventud en España* (Madrid: Ministerio de Trabajo y Asuntos Sociales).

López Blasco, A. (2005) 'La trama de los itinerarios de emancipación' in: J.F. Tezanos (Ed.) *Tendencias de exclusión social y políticas de solidaridad*, pp. 530–554 (Madrid: Editorial Sistema).

López Blasco, A. (2006) La familia como respuesta a las demandas de individualización: ambivalencia y contradicciones, *Papers: Revista de Sociología*, No. 79; 263–284.

López Blasco, A. (2008) Jóvenes en una sociedad cambiante: demografía y transiciones a la vida adulta. Informe Juventud en España Tomo I. Madrid, INJUVE, Spanish Ministry of Equality (November 2008).

López Blasco, A., McNeish, W. and Walther, A. (Eds.) (2003) *Dilemmas of Inclusion: Young People and Policies for Transitions to Work in Europe* (Bristol: Policy Press).

Moreno Mínguez, A. (2004) Family and Welfare State in the Southern Countries. The Role of Family Policy. BMFSFJ, European Ministerial Conference, Statement.

Moreno Mínguez, A. (2007) *Familia y empleo de la mujer en los Estados del bienestar del sur de Europa. Incidencia de las políticas familiares y laborales* (Madrid: Centro de Investigaciones Sociológicas, Colección Monografías nº 246).

Shell Deutschland (Ed.) (2006) *Jugend 2006. 15. Shell Jugendstudie* (Frankfurt: Fischer Verlag).

## APPENDIX

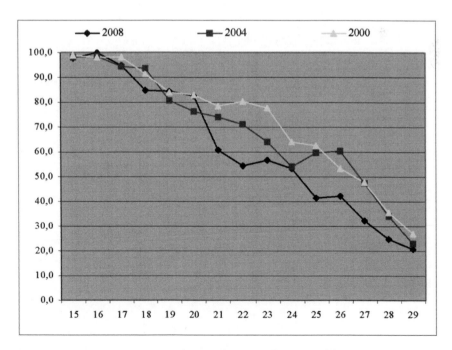

*Figure 10.1*   Young women aged 15–29 living in the parental home (%). Injuve 2000, 2004, 2008.

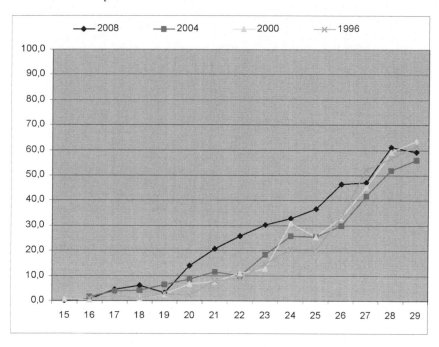

*Figure 10.2* Young women living with partners (%).
Injuve 1996, 2000, 2004, 2008

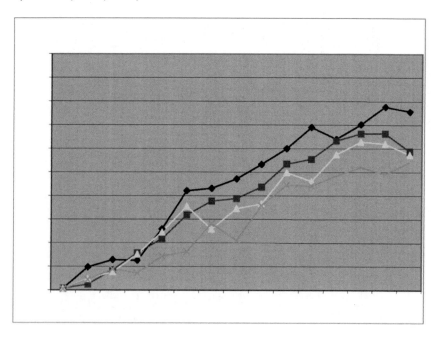

*Figure 10.3* Employment situation of young women (%)

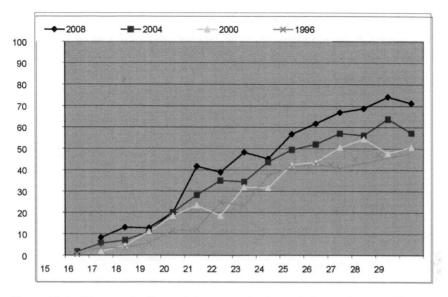

*Figure 10.4* Women who live mainly or completely on their own income (%).

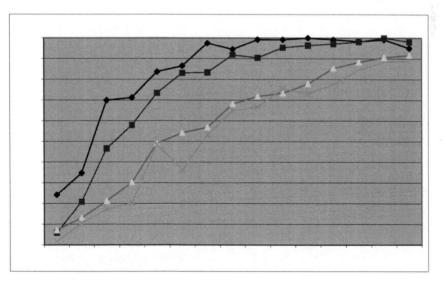

*Figure 10.5* Sexual relations of women (%).

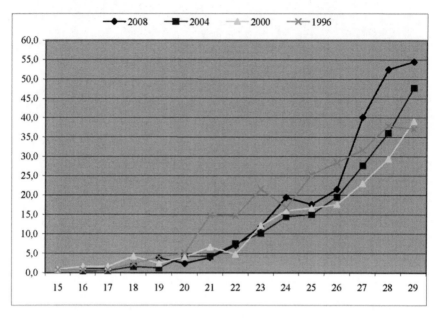

*Figure 10.6*    Young women with children, 1996–2008 (%)

# Part IV
# Youth and Political Culture

# 11 Youth Culture and European Integration in Germany

## Back to European Basics?[1]

*Gudrun Quenzel and Mathias Albert*

More than ever before, the project of European integration currently seems to be characterized by the European Union's feverish quest to find out who and what it is and who and what it wants to be. Questions of a 'European identity' loom particularly large in the context of the debates on further EU enlargement and particularly a possible accession of Turkey as an EU member. However, the debates on the depth of the integration process surrounding the proposed (and for the time being failed) project of a constitutional treaty, as well as the intensive debates on how the EU should assert and play its role on the stage of world politics (or as a 'normative power Europe'; see Manners 2002) can be seen as part of a discourse on a European identity.

As usual for symbolic constructions of collective identities, the discourse on a European identity is not always, and sometimes even not primarily, a discourse about what the EU wants to be in a 'positive' sense, but quite often also a discourse about who or what the 'Other' of Europe is (Diez 2004). It seems plausible to argue that on the level of meta-narratives the quest for a European identity can be characterized as a move away from the founding narrative which was primarily of a temporal nature: Europe's Other at the beginning of the integration project was Europe's own past as a conflict-ridden and war-torn continent (Diez et al. 2008). Much of the dynamics of the contemporary, multidimensional attempts to define a European identity can indeed be interpreted as anchoring a European identity not in the difference from a temporal, but from variably either a cultural (e.g. the Muslim world), a geographic ('Bosporus', 'Urals'), or, less pronounced, a geo-strategic other (the United States, Russia).

The present chapter neither seeks to survey the enormous body of literature which now exists on the subject of a European identity, nor does it attempt to make a conceptual contribution of its own in this respect. However, it does start from a central conceptual assumption which is that in the long run no (discursive) constructions of a European identity (and the policies which are legitimized and framed by it) can be successfully upheld if they do not find a significant degree of resonance in European public opinion—a lesson taught to policymakers quite forcefully in the Dutch and French referenda rejecting the constitutional treaty. Against this background, the aim of this chapter is not to add to the bourgeoning literature on European public opinion—a literature characterized by the two extremes of Eurostat surveys on the one hand and the theoretical discussion on whether there actually is such as thing as European public opinion which is more than the sum of individual national public opinions on the other hand. Rather, it is far more modest in that it will scrutinize attitudes towards Europe in but one European country, Germany, and in so doing only focus on attitudes among *young people*. The rationale for doing so is twofold: on a more general level, the attitudes and opinions of young people arguably have a seismographic function for future trends in society and can thus be taken as signposts of which discursive constructions can and which cannot be successful. On a more specific level, the data to which we will refer below signal a quite significant shift in the attitudes towards Europe and the European Union among young people in Germany over recent years. We suggest that this shift in attitudes could actually mean more than a simple surge or ebbing regarding opinions on specific issues. Rather, we argue that what we are witnessing here is a development which could indicate a reorientation towards more traditional constructions of a European identity, i.e. Europe as a 'peace project' and not as an identity primarily asserting itself against a cultural or a geographic Other. In developing this argument, we do of course not claim to refer to a trend which could be seen as representative of European—or even German—public opinion as a whole. Yet we would claim that what we are witnessing in the change of attitudes towards Europe among young people in Germany is a significant new development in terms of its *quality* which could—yet which by no means has to—serve as a role model for similar future developments in a broader European context as well. At the very minimum, what we are witnessing is a development which could point a way out of those logics of European identity construction which seek to construct a European identity primarily against ethnic, religious and geographic others, i.e. a development which could be seen to underpin more liberal and emancipatory pathways for the construction of a future European identity.

The present chapter will proceed in two steps. Primarily, based on the results of the 15th 'Shell Jugendstudie' (Shell Youth Survey) from 2006 (Deutsche Shell 2006), it will map attitudes of young people in Germany towards Europe and the European integration process, embedded also in the context of more general attitudes towards globalization and on Germany's role in the world. In a second step we will proceed in a more exploratory fashion, following the argument outlined so far and seeking to relate these attitudes of young people in Germany to the European integration process in particular and to the issue of the nature and contemporary state of this process in general.

## ATTITUDES TOWARDS THE EUROPEAN INTEGRATION PROCESS

Europe enjoys a good deal of popularity among young people in Germany. When asked about their opinion as to what in general young people consider to be 'in' or 'out', 64 per cent of the respondents stated that 'Europe' is 'in'. Even though the positive attitude towards Europe in general abated slightly in comparison with 2002, the majority of young people in Germany approve of Europe. The older the respondents, the more they consider Europe to be 'in'. Since the interest in politics also increases with age, this increasing interest in politics in general seems to have a positive effect on the identification with Europe.

Regarding more specific attitudes towards the European integration process, almost all of the respondents (94 per cent) related the European Union to the 'freedom to travel, study and work'. For 87 per cent, the European Union stands for 'cultural diversity', 82 per cent associate it with 'peace'. Thus the major associations with the European Union are clearly positive. It is only in the fourth place that we find the first negative evaluation of the EU. Of the respondents surveyed, 73 per cent associate it with bureaucracy, 72 per cent think that the EU implies an 'increasing influence in world politics', 64 per cent associate it with the 'dissemination of money' (i.e. the Euro), 58 per cent with a 'lack of border controls', 56 per cent with 'unemployment' and 53 per cent with 'more crime'. For less than half of the young people, the European Union stands for 'economic wealth' (47 per cent) and for 'social security' (33 per cent). Quite surprisingly, young people are least of all concerned that the European integration process would lead to an evaporation of local and national cultures.

In general, it seems that young people in Germany are most positively disposed towards the results of European integration on a *cultural level* as they value and enjoy the freedoms to travel around Europe, to study in

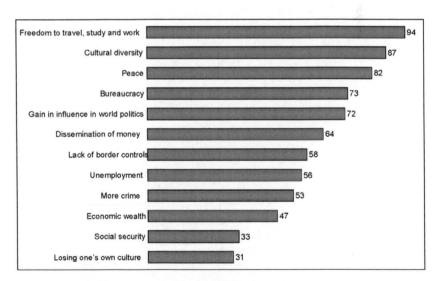

*Figure 11.1*   What young people in Germany associate with the European Union (%).
Source: Shell Jugendstudie 2006—TNS Infratest Sozialforschung.
Note: The respondents were young people aged 15–25.

another country, and to have the option to work in any EU member country they choose. Young people also cherish the increasing cultural diversity which results from these freedoms, i.e. the possibility of meeting people from other countries in their hometown, at school, the workplace, or university, as well as the greater variety of food, cultural events, languages and other products to be experienced in everyday life.

In contrast to this rather unequivocal appreciation of the cultural dimension of the European integration process, its results in the *economic* dimension are regarded more sceptically. Not even half of the young people associate the integration process with an increase in economic wealth—i.e. with one of the main goals of the common market. Quite to the contrary, they seem to consider European integration to be responsible for high unemployment rates, and think that the EU's budget could be spent more efficiently.

The *political* results of the European integration process are again evaluated more positively. The initial goal of the European project, i.e. to establish a lasting peace in post-World War II Europe, is valued highly. Particularly the recent war in former Yugoslavia has strengthened the consciousness among young people in Germany that war can still take place in Europe. A slight majority of 51 per cent even express a personal fear of another war in Europe (even though the current economic situation and the high unemployment rate are considered to be more pressing matters).

In comparison to the attitudes of young people, the population in Germany as a whole also primarily associates the EU with the freedom to travel, study and work within the EU (58 per cent) and with the opportunity to live in peace (53 per cent) (Eurobarometer 2005: 15). Yet the link between Europe and peace seems to be more pronounced among young people in Germany.

## PEACE TROUGH TRANSNATIONALIZATION

In order to judge the relevance of the findings above it seems worthwhile to contextualize them within more general attitudes of young people in Germany towards globalization and Germany's international orientation and role in the world.

Although globalization is primarily associated with the 'freedom to travel, study and work all over the world' (82 per cent) and with 'cultural diversity' (79 per cent), these two positive evaluations are immediately followed by two negative ones: a majority thinks that globalization will also result in 'unemployment' (66 per cent) and 'more crime' (59 per cent). While 57 per cent also associate globalization with 'peace', this link is clearly weaker than in the case of the evaluation of the European integration process as a peace project.

Almost three quarters of young people in Germany (72 per cent) believe that the European integration process results in an increasing influence of the EU and its Member States in world politics. The EU is also considered to be *the* political institution most likely to be able to control negative

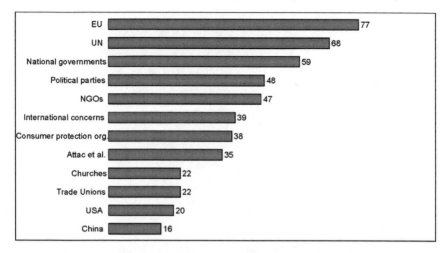

*Figure 11.2*   Confidence in the efficiency of providing solutions (%).
Source: Shell Jugendstudie 2006—TNS Infratest Sozialforschung.
Note: The respondents were young people (aged 15–25) familiar with the term 'globalization'. Respondents were asked 'Which of the following organisations or groups are you "altogether/to a certain extent" confident to handle the process of globalization correctly?'

impacts of the globalization process. When asked which organizations or groups they would trust 'altogether', 'to a certain extent', 'rather not' or 'by no means at all', to handle and respond to the challenges of the globalization process, the respondents put the EU in first place.

As Figure 11.2 shows, young people not only express great reservations about the role which China and the United States play in the globalization process. They also have the greatest confidence in the European Union as the institution most likely to manage the effects of globalization, even before the United Nations. One could, although in a highly preliminary fashion, conclude from these findings that young people in general value the EU's involvement in world politics and would support an even stronger involvement in the future. It is in this sense that it might also seem fair to say that in general the EU is increasingly perceived as a global *political* power rather than (merely) a global *economic* one. There would appear to be high expectations that the EU will exert its (growing) influence to help secure and establish peace, to find solutions for environmental problems, and to work against underdevelopment/inequality on a global level.

Even if abstracting from the EU in particular it seems to be highly noteworthy that despite the low interest young people take in politics in general and despite their rather sceptical attitude towards politicians, they express a high level of trust in governments and international governmental organizations to master the challenges posed by globalization—well before nongovernmental organizations or movements critical of the globalization process (e.g. Attac).

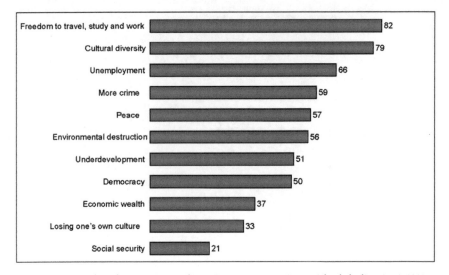

*Figure 11.3*    What do young people in Germany associate with globalization? (%).
Source: Shell Jugendstudie 2006—TNS Infratest Sozialforschung
Note: The respondents were young people (aged 15–25) familiar with the term 'globalization'.

## DECLINING EUPHORIA FOR THE EU AS A SINGLE STATE

Regarding the impression of the highly positive disposition towards the EU and its global role, it is remarkable that within the course of only four years we have witnessed a steep decline in the number of those who support the continuation of the European integration process in a 'deep' sense, i.e. in its resulting in a single European state (see Figure 11.4). In 2002, 49 per cent of the respondents supported the idea that the EU should develop into a single state in the future, while 28 per cent rejected the idea and 27 per cent were unsure whether to support the idea or not. By 2006, this attitude had changed dramatically: 45 per cent were now opposed to the idea of the EU becoming a single state in the future, only 32 per cent remained in favour and 23 per cent were still undecided. Even though the topic of further 'deep' unification will not be on the political agenda for the foreseeable future, given the failure of the first attempt to introduce a Constitutional Treaty, in general this shift in attitudes seems to signal a declining euphoria about the institutional aspects of the integration process in general.

We also find a growing scepticism towards further EU enlargement. Whereas in 2002 the big round of eastern enlargement, with the admission of 10 new Member States in 2005, was favoured by 44 per cent of the young people and opposed by 32 per cent, in 2006 only 19 per cent would support the accession of Turkey, while 61 per cent would oppose it.

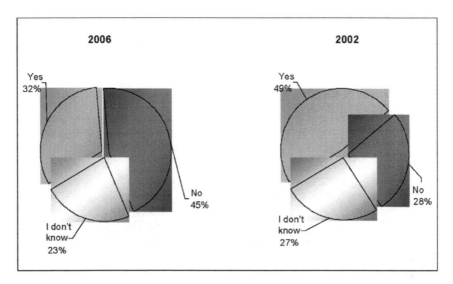

*Figure 11.4*   Attitudes towards Europe.
Source: Shell Jugendstudie 2006—TNS Infratest Sozialforschung.
Note: The respondents were young people aged 15–25.

## BACK TO EUROPEAN BASICS

Following the observations on attitudes towards further EU enlargement and particularly towards possible Turkish EU membership, analyses of the prevalent discourses on the Balkans and Turkey in relation to Europe demonstrate that the main arguments used to point out the 'incoherence' of the Balkans and Turkey refer to these states' claiming an 'anachronistic', 'heroic' identity, whereas western Europe had moved on to a post-heroic identity (Quenzel 2005). Heroic cultures differ from post-heroic cultures inasmuch as in heroic cultures social recognition can still be achieved through sacrifices made in armed struggle/war, while in post-heroic cultures the readiness to die for the fatherland is no longer of social significance. According to the heroic/post-heroic thesis, this acceptance of individual sacrifice as a means to gain recognition is absent in current EU member countries, particularly because of their negative relationship—strengthened by and through the European integration process—to Europe's past as a war-torn continent. Particularly in the case of Turkey it is thus, for example, not the genocide of the Armenian people which is held against the country, but the collective denial of guilt—and thus its self-exclusion from a European 'community of memory' with an associated negative relationship to the past (see, e.g., Winkler 2004 and Münkler 2004).

It is in this sense that Giesen (2002: 208ff) points out that many Western nations have replaced triumphant founding myths with references to a traumatic past, and that these memories include victims as well as perpetrators.

These new traumatic foundations of collective memory contrast sharply with some postwar attempts to clean up a nation's image by claiming the guilt of another nation or of specific groups within a nation. This common memory of a traumatic past now provides Europe with a 'tacitly assumed moral consensus: a European collective identity based on the horror of the past' (ibid.: 209). The strong reaction of and within the EU to the right-wing Freedom Party (FPÖ) joining the Austrian government in 2000 can in this sense be interpreted as a reaction towards a challenge to this conception of a European self. We would like to argue that it is exactly this tacit agreement which is in the process of gradually becoming part of a collective European identity, not only among young people in Germany, but also among young Europeans in general.

We would like to illustrate this observation using just one prominent example in the form of recent activities of the European Youth Forum, a federation of more than 90 national youth councils and international nongovernmental youth organizations which seeks to represent the interests of the young people in Europe. It would, of course, be wrong to see this forum as representative of all young Europeans. However, its activities provide important clues as to the interests of those young people in Europe who take an active interest in the future shape of Europe. Indeed, since politically active young people often serve as opinion leaders, we may consider the declarations of the European Youth Forum to be a potential seismograph for the attitudes of young Europeans towards the European integration process.

On the occasion of the 50th anniversary of the Treaty of Rome, the European Youth Forum in March 2007 published the 'Rome Youth Declaration' (European Youth Forum 2007), a postulate in the name of all young Europeans concerning the state of the European integration process. At its very beginning, the 'Rome Youth Declaration' refers to the founding intentions of the European project, to ensure 'peace' in a war-torn continent: 'We, the young people of Europe, gathered in Rome on the occasion of the 50th Anniversary of the Treaty of Rome to pay tribute to and continue the vision of those who made it possible for us to grow up in an environment of peace and prosperity, democracy and rule of law' (ibid.). Thus the Treaty of Rome is highlighted as the reason why young Europeans can live in a peaceful and democratic Europe, and indeed this vision of a peaceful Europe— or rather the continuation of it—serves as the rationale for the convention in Rome and the ensuing declaration. This means that the initial intentions of Robert Schumann—expressed in his declaration of 9 May 1950 (Schumann 1950), which is considered to be the founding speech of the European Community—to create a lasting peace in Europe through solidarity in the production of coal and steel between France and Germany that 'will make it plain that any war between France and Germany becomes not merely unthinkable, but materially impossible' are acknowledged by the young Europeans as the paramount achievement of the European Union.

In the following paragraph, the 'Rome Youth Declaration' states that the EU is 'a place of equality, freedom, tolerance, and solidarity' and that the process of integration preserves uniqueness and diversity. Of special interest for our argument here are also the following paragraphs connecting the failure of the Constitutional Treaty with the challenges of globalization. Read closely, they contain a rather complex argument. They ascribe to the European project a loss of direction and inspiration which has led to increasing uncertainty and dissatisfaction among the European people; as a consequence, the rejection of the Constitutional Treaty by the voters of France and the Netherlands is interpreted as a reaction to a lack of vision. The European Union is further accused of not dealing adequately with the opportunities and serious challenges of globalization. The European Youth Forum outlines its primary expectations towards a future European Union as follows: 'We want a European Union that promotes democratic values and Human Rights. We want a European Union that promotes sustainability, preserving our environment for future generations. We want a European Union that promotes the economic success and the social responsibility for all its citizens, especially the ones who are in greater need. We want a European Union that assumes its role in our globalised world' (European Youth Forum 2007).

Accordingly, one of the main aims of the 'Rome Youth Declaration' is to make the European Union fit for future challenges by giving it direction and inspiration. And interestingly enough, the promotion of democratic values and human rights are particularly stressed. Sustainability and environmental issues rank second on the agenda, followed by economic success and social responsibility. Similar to the results of the Shell Youth Survey 2006 it seems that young people from all over Europe do not consider European integration to be primarily an economic project. Here too the cultural and political achievements and especially the idea of Europe as a peace project are acknowledged as centre pieces of European integration.

## PEACE AND DEMOCRACY AS A CORNERSTONE OF A EUROPEAN IDENTITY

If we follow the idea that the formation of a collective identity requires a self-presentation of the community as an entity and hence the confinement of others not belonging to one's community (see for example Lepsius 1997: 949ff; Anderson 1983; Hall 1994: 196f, Laclau and Mouffe 1991: 164), then a European identity needs a *self-presentation* as an *entity* and ideas of what distinguishes Europe from *other* parts of the world. As Glynis Breakwell (2004: 34) points out: 'One main problem with describing the character of the identity element that might be generated by EU membership is that the EU as a category in itself is changing.' The history of European integration is also the history of its enlargement. The six founder states from 1958, Italy,

France, the Netherlands, Belgium, Luxembourg and Germany, were joined in 1973 by the northern countries Great Britain, Ireland and Denmark. The south of Europe followed with Greece in 1981 and Spain and Portugal in 1986. The EFTA-countries Sweden, Finland and Austria joined the EU in 1995. In 2004 came the so-called 'eastern enlargement' with Cyprus, Latvia, Lithuania, Estonia, Hungary, Malta, Poland, Slovakia, Slovenia and the Czech Republic. The newest members, Bulgaria and Romania, joined in 2007. The permanent change of the European Union's borders precludes a perception of the European Union as a fixed entity. And the discussion about the borders of the European Union is not likely to disappear over the coming years. Currently the accession of Turkey to the European Union dominates discussions. Yet the list of potential accession countries includes Albania, Bosnia, Croatia, Iceland, Macedonia, Moldavia, Norway, Russia, Switzerland, Serbia and Montenegro, the Ukraine, Belarus and also Israel. This list in itself demonstrates that the discussion about the borders of the European Union is unlikely to abate in the near future.

As Castano (2004: 41ff) demonstrated in a series of experiments, the perceived 'entity-ness' of a community is a critical factor for a positive identification with Europe. Presenting the EU as having fuzzy borders to the participants in the experiments did reduce their level of identification dramatically (ibid.: 48f). However, in order to perceive the European Union as an entity, it is not necessary for it to fulfil the criterion of cultural homogeneity. In contrast to many other political communities, cultural or even ethnic homogeneity is not considered to be the basis of the European Community. The European integration process was initiated to avoid the negative consequences that followed from strong nationalism based on the idea of cultural and ethnic homogeneity, thus consequently diversity and not homogeneity serves a basic principle underlying the European Union. Castano (2004: 43f) further argues that what mediates a common identity is not whether it is homogeneous or not, but the extent to which it acquires a *psychological existence*, in other words, a self-representation as an entity at a collective level. One way to acquire a psychological existence in the minds of the Europeans is to behave as an actor and to be recognized as such by other actors, like the United States, Russia, China, and the United Nations, etc.; this recognition first took place during the war in Yugoslavia, when the EU was acknowledged by the UN as a political actor (ibid.: 53).

More recently, the EU has acted increasingly as political actor on a global stage and could thus be perceived as an entity possessing intentionality and the capacity for action in world politics. The perception of the EU as a global political actor gaining influence, but also disillusion regarding world political events (e.g. the war in Iraq), could help to explain why expectations of the EU as an actor in global politics have risen among younger people.

CONCLUSION

As we were able to show with data drawn from the Shell Youth Survey 2006, Europe is widely appreciated by young people in Germany. Their main associations with the European Union are positive and refer primarily to the cultural and political impacts of the integration process, i.e. the freedom to travel, study and work within the European Union, cultural diversity and peace. This means that young people in Germany are more positively disposed towards the cultural and political achievements of the integration process than towards its results at the economic level, which are seen more sceptically. The representatives of the European youth organizations refer even more clearly to European integration as a peace project. In accordance with the attitudes of young people in Germany they also indicate cultural diversity as an important part of the European identity. Their vision for Europe is a European Union as a promoter of democratic values, human rights, sustainability, economic success, and social justice, and they support and indeed ask for an increasing role of the EU in world politics. Young people in Germany also consider the European Union to be *the* institution capable of controlling the negative impacts of the globalization process. Thus both groups agree in seeing the EU as a global political power rather than merely as an economic power, and they express their expectations that the EU will increase its influence in order to help secure and establish peace, find solutions to environmental problems and combat social injustice at the global level.

On the other hand (and here we only have data from young people in Germany), we are witnessing declining support for the 'deepening' process of European integration. This indicates a declining euphoria in relation to the further ceding of sovereign national rights to the European Union among young people. In addition we find a growing scepticism towards further EU enlargement.

Taken together, these attitudes towards the European integration process seem rather contradictory: Young people in Germany value the cultural and political achievements of European integration, they expect the EU to become more influential in world politics and to regulate the negative impacts of the globalization process, yet they disapprove of the 'deepening' as well as the 'enlargement' process.

However, the attitudes appear to be less contradictory if we accept Giesen's (2002: 208ff) concept of a moral consensus, based on European experiences of war and genocide, as a common European identity. Thus we can understand the importance of democracy and human rights as a dominant part of European self-presentation and also the demand that the European Union secure and establish peace, advance democracy and combat social injustice. The rejection of a homogeneous culture as the foundation of European identity and the distinct approval of cultural diversity and of tolerance as a dominant part of the European self-presentation may underlie some more sceptical dispositions towards the deepening process.

Yet the self-presentation of a community which has learned from its past and which took political action to prevent war and genocide, and which is committed to the values of democracy and tolerance as well as to human rights, is not only the foundation of the integration process. In contrast to a self-presentation as a continent with a shared ethno-cultural history, i.e., for example, as a Christian community, it allows people to perceive the EU as a political actor that had the capacity to establish lasting peace in a war-torn continent and that is able to exert its influence in this manner at a global level as well. In this way the European Union can be perceived as an entity even though its borders have changed frequently in the past and will change again in the future.

The self-presentation as a moral community also fulfils the symbolic need for a sense of transcendence. Peace, democracy and human rights are considered to be universal values. They are values in and for themselves. Even though these values were frequently violated during history, this does not diminish their validity. Thus the identification with Europe as a community of moral consensus allows the individual to be part of a concept that outlasts its own physical existence.

By way of conclusion we would like to emphasize once more that the argument presented here in no way claims to have extrapolated future trends of the European integration process from representative data covering European society as a whole. Rather, we have taken some remarkable empirical findings regarding the attitude towards Europe among young people in Germany as a starting point to engage in what can be little more than a theoretically informed speculation about a future European Union which might see its increasing role in world politics accompanied by a (re-) construction of its identity 'back to basics', i.e. a sharper focus on the EU as a peace project and a corresponding self-perception. This is not to argue that this is the best that the EU or the construction of a European identity can hope for. But if additional research could show that what we can suspect when looking at the young generation of the EU's largest member country can also claim validity on a wider European scale, then it is certainly not the worst it can hope for as well.

## NOTES

1. This chapter appeared as an article in *Asia Europe Journal*, Vol. 5, Nr. 4, January 2008, p. 529–540 and is reprinted here by kind permission of Springer Publishers.

## REFERENCES

Anderson, B. (1983) *Imagined Communities: Reflections on the Origin and Spread of Nationalism* (London: Verso).

Breakwell, G. (2004) 'Identity Change in the Context of the Growing Influence of European Union Institutions', in R. Herrman, Th. Risse and M. Brewer (Eds.) *Transnational Identities: Becoming European in the EU*, pp. 25–39 (New York: Rowman & Littlefield).

Castano, E. (2004) 'European Identity: A Social-Psychological Perspective', in R. Herrman, Th. Risse and M. Brewer (Eds.) *Transnational Identities: Becoming European in the EU*, pp. 40–58 (New York: Rowman & Littlefield).

Deutsche Shell (2006) *Jugend 2006: 15. Shell Jugendstudie*. Conceptualization and Coordination by K. Hurrelmann, M. Albert & TNS Infratest Sozialforschung (Frankfurt: Fischer Taschenbuch Verlag).

Diez, Th. (2004) 'Europe's Others and the Return of Geopolitics', in *Cambridge Review of International Affairs*, 17(2), pp. 319–335.

Diez, Th., Stetter, S. and Albert, M. (2008) 'Introduction', in Th. Diez, M. Albert and S. Stetter (Eds.) *The European Union and Border Conflicts* (Cambridge, UK: Cambridge University Press), pp. 1–12.

Eurobarometer 63.4 (2005) *Die öffentliche Meinung in der Europäischen Union*. http://ec.europa.eu/public_opinion/archives/eb/eb63/eb63_nat_de.pdf (Accessed 3 May 2007).

European Youth Forum (2007) *Rome Youth Declaration*, http://europa.eu/50/docs/ro-me_youth_declaration_en.pdf (accessed 17 May 2007).

Giesen, B. (2002) 'Constitutional Practice or Community of Memory: Some Remarks on the Collective Identity of Europe', in D. Sachsenmaier (Ed.) *Reflections on Multiple Modernities*, pp. 193–216 (Leiden: Brill).

Hall, S. (1994) *Rassismus und kulturelle Identität: Ausgewählte Schriften 2* (Hamburg: Argument-Verlag).

Laclau, E. and Mouffe, Ch. (1991) *Hegemonie und radikale Demokratie: zur Dekonstruktion des Marxismus* (Vienna: Passagen Verlag).

Lepsius, R.M. (1997) 'Bildet sich eine kulturelle Identität in der Europäischen Union?' *Blätter für deutsche und internationale Politik*, 8, pp. 948–955.

Manners, I. (2002) 'Normative Power Europe: A Contradiction in Terms?' *Journal of Common Market Studies*, 40(2), pp. 235–258.

Münkler, H. (2004) 'Helden wie nie', *Der Tagesspiegel*, 21 April.

Quenzel, G. (2005) 'Der Balkan im europäischen Identitätsdiskurs: Zur kulturellen Legitimierung der EU-Außengrenzen', in J. Meyer, R. Kollmorgen, J. Angermüller and D. Wiemann (Eds.) *Diskurse der Gewalt: Gewalt der Diskurse*, pp. 127–139 (Münster: LIT).

Schumann, R. (1950) *Declaration of 9 May 1950*, http://europa.eu/abc/symbols/9-may/decl_en.htm (Accessed 17 May 2007).

Winkler, H.A. (2004) 'Selbstzerstörung inbegriffen', *Frankfurter Rundschau*, 1 March 2004.

# 12 'Europe? Totally out of my Depth'
## National and European Citizenship among Young People in Germany and England

*Daniel Faas*

## INTRODUCTION

National political and educational agendas have been reshaped by the processes of European integration. Although a few educational issues were mentioned in the 1957 Treaty of Rome including provisions for vocational training and for the mutual recognition of diplomas and certificates (Phillips 1995), the birth of the European dimension in education dated back to the early 1970s (Hansen 1998; Ryba 2000). In 1971, education was first mentioned as an area of interest to the then European Community. It was in July of that year that the European Commission decided to set up two bodies which would work on educational issues: (a) a working party on teaching and education and (b) an interdepartmental working party on coordination. In November 1971, the Ministers of Education held their first meeting. In their resolution, they stated that the provisions on educational measures in the Treaty of Rome could be complemented by increasing cooperation in the field of education, and they argued that the final goal was 'to define a European model of culture correlating with European integration' (Neave 1984: 6f.), recognizing for the first time the close relation between educational policy and European integration. In June 1974, the Ministers of Education held their second meeting in Luxembourg, arguing for the need to institute European cooperation in the field of education. As a basis for cooperation, it was stated that the traditions of each country and the diversity of their education systems should be respected.

However, it was not until the mid-1980s that the institutionalization of education took on new forms with the introduction of several educational programmes including *ERASMUS* (higher education exchange scheme) and *Lingua* (pupil exchange scheme for language learning). Arguably, the most important intergovernmental agreement was the *Resolution of the Council and the Ministers of Education on the European Dimension in Education* (1988), prompting educators to 'strengthen in young people a sense of European identity and make clear to them the value of European civilization and of the foundations on which the European peoples intended to base their development today'

(Council of Ministers of Education 1988: 5). The Maastricht Treaty theoretically provided the EU with the legal framework of its involvement in all the educational levels of the national educational systems. However, Article 126 for general education (the Community 'contributes to the development of education') and Article 127 for vocational training (the Community 'implements policy') state that Community action is to complement and support action taken at national level (Council of the European Communities 1992). The linguistic differentiation between 'contribute' and 'implement' is due to the already existing involvement of the Community in vocational training. The *Green Paper on the European Dimension in Education* (1993) sought for proper enactment of Article 126 of the Maastricht Treaty. The third part focused on general education and suggested possible cooperation among students, parents, teachers and trainers (Council of Ministers of Education 1993). As a result, the Socrates programme was adopted in 1995. The Comenius strand of Socrates aims explicitly to foster the sense of citizenship with a European dimension both by curriculum development and exchange activities in schools.

Notions of a European dimension in education as well as European identity and citizenship have also been promoted by the Council of Europe. *Recommendation 1111 on the European Dimension of Education* regarded Europe 'as extending to the whole of the continent and in no way synonymous with the membership of any particular European organisation' (Council of Europe 1989). The document also stressed the importance of encouraging the European dimension in teacher training and teacher exchange; giving more emphasis to the teaching of history, geography, citizenship and modern languages; encouraging European school links by using the latest information technologies; and ensuring information exchange on activities undertaken by organizations involved in European cooperation in education. Two years later, a *Resolution on the European Dimension of Education: Teaching and Curriculum Content* was issued (Council of Europe 1991). This document considered the European dimension at all school levels and types (general and vocational), stating that 'all areas of the school curriculum can make a contribution to the European dimension in teaching and learning as part of education for international understanding' with the aim of making the younger generation 'conscious of their common European identity without losing sight of their global responsibilities or their national, regional and local roots[1] (Council of Europe 1991). The Council's activities also include the *Education for Democratic Citizenship* programme, launched in 1997 in response to Member States' requests for further information and assistance with this policy area (www.coe.int/EDC). The institutionalization of education is likely to continue, with the role of education becoming more important.

The aim of this chapter is to compare and contrast the German and English national political and student responses to these European-level education policy developments, and to show how as a result of the different historical engagements with Europe, national governments were setting the framework for schools and students in rather different ways.

## RESEARCH METHODOLOGY

The chapter draws on data from a larger study designed to explore how German and English national agendas and identities are reshaped by European and multicultural agendas at the government level and what implications these political agendas have for schools and young people (Faas 2010). The main argument of this chapter is based on a critical review of the relevant literature and policies as well as empirical evidence from four multiethnic, multifaith secondary schools, two in Inner London and two in Inner Stuttgart. With the help of local authorities, I selected two boroughs in Stuttgart and London on pragmatic grounds—including proximity to Cambridge and my home town of Pforzheim—and with a similar interest in European issues. I then formally approached schools with comparable achievement levels, inner-city locations and socio-ethnic intake; and met with the liaisons once prior to fieldwork. In early 2004, I distributed a questionnaire to 202 students in the two German schools and 208 students in the two English schools. The aim was to obtain broad insights into students' attitudes towards, and knowledge of, Europe. Then, I conducted six focus group interviews of four to five students in each school (native youths and youths of Turkish descent) to elicit information about what the different groups of young people thought about Europe, and I also interviewed eight students in each school (two boys and two girls from each of the ethnic groups). Purposive sampling was used in an effort to ensure a gender and ethnic balance. Additional interviews with the head, the citizenship coordinator, the head of geography and the head of religious education were conducted in each school to learn more about how school officers responded to European political and educational developments.

The interviewer, who is the author of this paper, is a native speaker of German, fluent in English and relatively young, which, in terms of age at least, resulted in a fairly balanced power relation during the interviews. The strategies I used to be a non-threatening 'other' included that I introduced myself as someone who would like to learn more about other cultures and ways of thinking about people and society. I also decided not to dress too formally so that students were not put off by the image of having a teacher-like adult in the room. Despite these strategies, there was a possibility that the respondents constructed their identities in response to my own identity (e.g. adult, German, middle-class) and the questions I was asking of them. It was difficult, of course, to determine the extent to which my own identity may or may not have interacted with the interviewees' self-perceptions. The choice to focus on Turkish youths makes this chapter particularly topical because (a) it is fascinating to explore the shifting identities of Turkish students as Turkey gets politically closer to Europe (Faas 2007); (b) this is the only minority ethnic group with sufficiently large numbers in both German and English schools; and (c) this is a particularly under-researched community. Before I look at the ways in which young people related to the nation-state and Europe, I shall examine the educational responses to European integration in Germany and England.


## GERMAN AND ENGLISH EDUCATIONAL RESPONSES TO EUROPE

Since the 1950s, as a founding member of the European Coal and Steel Community in 1951 and the European Economic Community in 1958, Germany has been of central importance to the processes of European integration and successive postwar governments promoted what could be called a 'Europeanised national identity' (Goetz 1996; Risse and Engellmann-Martin 2002). Because of the rather problematic nation-state identity during the first three decades following World War II, many Germans considered the goal of European unification so self-evident that they did not debate its advantages and disadvantages. German policymakers and politicians regarded the establishment of a lasting European peace as the ultimate aim of integration (Paterson 1996). It was not long before the European agenda also started to impact on education. In 1978, the Standing Conference of the Ministers of Education (Kultusministerkonferenz, KMK) published the document 'Europe in the Classroom' (*Europa im Unterricht*). This was republished in 1990 in response to the Resolution of the Council of Ministers of Education, mentioned earlier, and again in 2008. This not only underlined the enthusiastic approach German policymakers and educators have had towards Europe but also highlighted the role of education in shifting national political identities towards a more European agenda. The document stated that the goal of education must be 'to foster in young people the consciousness of a European identity' (KMK 2008; translated from German).

The KMK directive stressed the political justification for a European dimension, arguing that Europe was more than just a geographical term and that the painful experiences of two world wars as well as the developments in western and eastern Europe since 1945 had given Europeans every reason to reflect upon their common origins. The task of the school was also seen as conveying insights into geographical diversity, political and social structures, formative historical forces, and the history of the European idea. In 1992, the Standing Conference of the Ministers of Education published a further review of progress and recommendations. The particular areas for development were identified as foreign languages as part of vocational qualifications; political and cultural education; school exchanges; school links; and teacher exchanges (KMK 1992). Since 1990, European Schools (i.e.

schools that particularly emphasize the European dimension in education)
were set up across the country (Bell 1995). The impact of these directives
was investigated by educational researchers (e.g. Hauler 1994; Kesidou 1999;
Natterer 2001). Research on the European dimension in the curriculum and
school textbooks, for example, described how Europe and European integration became part of the German secondary school curricula and textbooks.
Youth studies focused particularly upon young people's attitudes towards
Europe and European integration. For example, Weidenfeld and Piepenschneider (1990) identified five different responses to Europe that were typical
of young Germans in the 1980s and early 1990s:

> The *enthusiastic European* (14%) who is in favour of a unified Europe
> and feels strongly addressed when people use the term 'the Europeans'
> in an ordinary discussion; the *interested European* (47%) who is in
> favour of a unified Europe and feels partly addressed by the term 'the
> Europeans' and would regret it if the European project failed; the *indif-
> ferent European* (14%) who is in favour of a unified Europe and feels
> partly addressed by the term 'the Europeans' and would not regret it at
> all if the European project failed; the *sceptical European* (8%) who is
> in favour of a unified Europe but feels not addressed when people talk
> about 'the Europeans'; and the *anti-European* (16%) who is against a
> unified Europe (ibid.: 117).

Although the pro-European attitude of German policymakers and politicians continued in the 1990s, reunification created new challenges for
the country which resulted in a less idealistic and enthusiastic approach
to Europe. With the costly addition of the poorer regions of eastern Germany, policymakers responded more cautiously to European initiatives but
remained ardent proponents of widening (i.e. enlarging) and deepening (i.e.
institutionally reforming) the EU. At the same time, several German federal
states, such as Baden-Württemberg in 1994, overhauled their curricula to
implement a European dimension indicating the connectedness between
political commitments and educational developments. The notion of
Europe was particularly integrated into subjects such as geography and history. For example, in the geography curriculum of Baden-Württemberg, the
entire Year 7 (ages 12 to 13) in extended elementary schools (*Hauptschule*)
was spent on Europe; in grammar schools (*Gymnasium*), three out of four
teaching units in Year 6 (ages 11 to 12) dealt with Europe.

Britain, by contrast, experienced Europe very differently. There was little
reason why the country should reconceptualize its national identity in European terms and the processes of Europeanization have not seriously affected
English schools. The politics of Europe, initiated by Germany and France,
were undercut by the special relationship with the United States, the geographical detachment from continental Europe and Britain's postwar role in
the Commonwealth (Katzenstein 1997). Consequently, Britain engaged little

with the European project until the 1960s when Prime Minister Macmillan realized that his country needed to reorientate as the Empire was rapidly falling apart (Woodard 1998). After the United Kingdom had joined the EC in January 1973, it spent the first decade of membership arguing about the terms of accession and seeking a budget rebate (Geddes 1999. Given Britain's more Euro-sceptic historical engagement with Europe, compared to Germany, the European dimension received little attention and, unlike multicultural education, did not specifically appear amongst the cross-curricular themes and dimensions of the 1988 National Curriculum (Department of Education and Science 1988). The national protectionist approach to Europe under Thatcher (1979–1990) meant that, until the 1988 Resolution by the Council of Ministers of Education, English schools received no encouragement to foster European citizenship among the young, whereas, by this time, the European agenda had taken over the issue of identity in Germany.

Arguably, when citizenship education was introduced as a new statutory subject for students aged between 11 and 16 (key stages 3 and 4) in the English National Curriculum in 2002, the ideas of European citizenship and identity were underdeveloped (Osler and Starkey 2001) although the Council of Ministers of Education recommended that 'education for citizenship should include experiencing the European dimension ( . . . ) and socialisation in a European context ( . . . ) because this enables each citizen to play a part on the European stage' (Council of Ministers of Education 1993: 6). The European guidelines sought to promote citizenship at a European level as part of a self-identity that included national and regional elements (Ross 2000). Despite the limited acknowledgement of the processes of Europeanization in citizenship education, which has become a key means of reasserting the concept of Britishness and national belonging, some schools in England developed a European agenda, such as the Anglo European School in Essex (www.aesessex.co.uk). The Department of Education and Science also responded to the 1988 Resolution of the Council of Ministers of Education on the European dimension in education, maintaining that the government's policies were aimed at 'promoting a sense of European identity'. Since the 1991 policy statement, the responsibility for the implementation of the European dimension in education rested with local education authorities and schools.

However, despite the fact that schools were asked to develop a European dimension and promote a sense of European identity, the presence of Europe in programmes of study of the National Curriculum was only marginally more than had previously been the case with examination syllabuses in subjects like art, music and history (Tulasiewicz 1993). Specific advice and curriculum guidance on precisely what content and form the European dimension should assume did not match official British concern with other parts of the National Curriculum (multicultural and global education). Convey and Merritt (2000) optimistically argued that although in some National Curriculum subjects (notably geography, history, art, music and modern languages) the programmes of study ensured that a European dimension was included, 'there is still no specific statement that such a dimension must be included, and of course an *awareness* of Europe goes beyond *knowing* about Europe' (ibid.: 396; original emphasis). Focusing on modern European language skills, the authors pointed out that the learning of one foreign language was compulsory from ages 11 to 16 in England and that a second language was always optional in English secondary schools. However, language learning beyond the age of fourteen (Key Stage 4) ceased to be compulsory in September 2005 (Department for Education and Skills 2005) despite the European Commission's recommendation that all students should master at least two European languages in addition to their own by the end of their compulsory education. Instead, the Department for Education and Skills published the guidance paper *Developing the Global Dimension in the School Curriculum* (2005) outlining aspects such as social justice, global citizenship, conflict resolution, diversity, human rights, sustainable development and interdependence. This global dimension has been one of seven cross-curricular dimensions (the others being creativity, enterprise and cultural diversity) since September 2008.

These national political developments set a very different framework for schools in Germany and England. I shall now compare young people's responses to Europe in each context.

## GERMAN AND ENGLISH STUDENT RESPONSES TO EUROPE

Given that the school system is more or less under direct control of the regional government, one might expect all schools and teachers within a German federal state to promote similar values. However, Tannberg Hauptschule mediated national agendas through a dominantly European and, arguably, at times a Eurocentric approach with the head of religious education arguing for instance that 'if a religious symbol was allowed in class then it should be the cross and not the headscarf; we are still Christian Occidental [white and European]'. On another occasion, while eating with the students in the canteen, I witnessed that the teacher on duty told a male German student who wanted to help himself to some beef sauce that this is 'Muslim sauce' (*Moslemsoße*) and that he should rather take some 'non-Muslim sauce'. By contrast, Goethe Gymnasium emphasized Europe as a common bond and thus interpreted the European dimension differently from Tannberg. The school prospectus stated that 'the ethos of our school is characterized by mutual respect and tolerance towards other people. Our students learn the manifoldness of European languages, cultures and mentalities and can thus develop their own identities within our school'. Young people within one country will have therefore experienced quite different messages about Europe.

Arguably, at Tannberg Hauptschule, the at times Eurocentric educational approach made it quite difficult for both ethnic majority and Turkish minority studentsto develop a sense of European citizenship. Their predominantly working-class backgrounds (about 56 per cent of students had skilled and unskilled parents) may have been another reason why many students engaged in local and national political discourses but did not perceive European and global issues to be particularly relevant to their lives (except for the war in Iraq). Their general knowledge about Europe seemed to be rather limited. The Turkish students listed some concepts including 'the Euro', 'the EU', 'Western world' and 'advanced rich countries', but were unable to engage in a wider discussion. Tamer, for example, alluded to the 'united in diversity' motto of the EU and Ugur referred to its peacekeeping role:

*DF [Daniel Faas]:* What do you know about Europe, about the European Union?
*TAMER:* It's a community.
*YELIZ:* That's what I think too.
*UMAY:* I don't know. I'm not so sure.
*TAMER:* It's a community of different countries.
*CARI:* EU, countries that belong together; they talk about politics of different countries; they have negotiations and debate what they can do. It's a strong, political team.
*YELIZ:* If a country needs help then the other EU countries will help. They have treaties with each other.
*UGUR:* The European Union is a good thing; we don't have war today.

Ethnic majority German 15-year olds also revealed some factual knowledge about Europe and the EU. For example, the group of boys and girls referred to notions of power as well as transatlantic and inner-European relationships. Not only was Sebastian aware of the strength of the common currency, but he and Tobias also alluded to the political and economic benefits of a united Europe. Drawing upon the dispute over the Iraq war in 2003, Jessica reminded the boys that Europe still does not speak with one voice:

*DF:* What do you know about Europe and the EU?
*FRANZISKA:* The euro.
*TOBIAS:* I think it's better now when it's Europe than when the countries were alone. We are too weak. We would have no chance, for example, against America. The euro strengthens everything, of course. And the English always say 'travel to Europe'; they still think they are on their own. That's a bit silly what they think, I just find that the wrong attitude.
*SEBASTIAN:* Well, I think the deutschmark used to be weaker than the dollar. Now the dollar's become weaker than the euro. And when

you're together, when you're a community, you're a lot stronger
than on your own.

JESSICA: Lots of languages, lots of cultures, well, I think that Europe
is really a comprehensive image, although the countries don't
always stick together. You could see that with the Iraq War and
America, some countries supported America. Germany didn't.
And that's where you can see that the countries don't really
always stick together.

Some of these glimpses of factual European knowledge amongst 15-year-
old interviewees might be the result of European teaching units in compulsory subjects such as geography, history and politics in Baden-Württemberg
secondary schools.

In contrast, as a result of the school's inclusive interpretation of Europe
and students' more privileged backgrounds (about 54 per cent of students
had professional middle-class and routine non-manual parents), young people at Goethe Gymnasium had a wider range of opinions when talking about
Europe and also made Europe part of their multidimensional identities.
For example, Andreas (a German boy) pointed to the expansion of the EU,
although he was not exactly sure how many and which countries will join:

ANDREAS: In a few weeks [referring to 1 May 2004], new countries will
join the EU, it's getting bigger and bigger which is good and bad.
I think that the idea of a European Union hasn't really worked
as it should have in the fifteen countries and now even more will
join. And in a few years, some more will join again. The borders
are open and it's called the EU but they don't really belong to it.
The new members slow down the integration process.

Leo (another German boy) argued that 'I think about the expansion, and I
also cast my mind back to Columbus. Europe used to be the centre of the
world; many things started here', thus alluding to the industrial revolution in eighteenth-century England as well as the 'discovery' of America
by Christopher Columbus in 1492. One of the groups of Turkish students
referred to the decade-long debate amongst policymakers about the future
structure of Europe:

DF: What comes to your mind when you hear the word 'Europe'?
SEMRA: Well, Europe consists of countries that have got together, a community with the same currency. But you can't say that that's a
giant country 'cos there are different languages and you can't
say that Europe is one culture. The people are kind of similar
but there are nevertheless other cultures, and France isn't like
Germany, and it's different in England. Europe just has the same
currency but not the same language and culture.

NILGÜN: For me, Europe is more geographical. It's also more simple that you can move from one country to another. There's the euro, but I don't really like it. I mean, people think that all Europeans are the same but, in reality, there are quite different cultures. I've got relatives in France and when we crossed the border it looked quite different. It's not one country.

SEVILIN: You can't change the cultures, only the laws. I don't think there'll ever be something like a United States of Europe. That's somehow not possible. Maybe it's just a term 'cos in America each state has its own laws, too, but the language and culture is the same, and that's not the case in Europe.

ZEYNEP: They all see themselves as Americans.

Fifteen-year-olds at Goethe Gymnasium also had significantly higher scores when asked to locate ten European countries correctly on a geopolitical map of Europe compared to both their counterparts at Tannberg Hauptschule and students in the two English schools.

Arguably, the fact that the average scores were higher in both Tannberg Hauptschule (62.6 per cent) and Goethe Gymnasium (77.3 per cent) compared with the two English schools (34.4 per cent Millroad School, 48.9 per cent Darwin School) was a result of both the schools' emphasis on Europeanness rather than German values and the aforementioned macropolitical account that Europe became a focal point for the organization of the German educational system. Nine out of ten students at Goethe Gymnasium located five countries correctly on the map, and over 80 per cent

*Table 12.1*  Students' *Correct* Location of Countries on a Map of Europe (%)

|  | Germany | England | Tannberg | Goethe | Millroad | Darwin |
|---|---|---|---|---|---|---|
| Britain | 85.6 | 85.1 | 76.8 | 93.5** | 81.3 | 89.1 |
| Germany | 89.6 | 51.0** | 85.3 | 93.5 | 37.4 | 65.3** |
| Spain | 86.1 | 52.4** | 78.9 | 92.5* | 38.3 | 67.3** |
| Finland | 25.7 | 8.7** | 15.8 | 34.6** | 4.7 | 12.9* |
| Italy | 94.1 | 64.4** | 89.5 | 98.1* | 54.2 | 75.2** |
| Turkey | 66.8 | 33.2** | 58.9 | 73.8 | 33.6 | 32.7 |
| Portugal | 81.2 | 37.5** | 74.7 | 86.9 | 28.0 | 47.5** |
| Poland | 58.9 | 14.4** | 48.4 | 68.2* | 11.2 | 17.8* |
| France | 85.6 | 56.7** | 75.8 | 94.4** | 43.0 | 71.3** |
| Ukraine | 30.2 | 10.6** | 22.1 | 37.4* | 12.1 | 8.9* |
| Average | 73.3 | 41.4** | 62.6 | 77.3 | 34.4 | 48.9 |

*Significance below 0.05, **significance below 0.01.

of students in the German sample correctly identified the location of six European countries. In contrast, only Britain was correctly identified by eight out of ten students in the English sample. Students in the middle-class dominated schools (Goethe and Darwin) were also significantly better at locating European countries than students in the working-class dominated schools (Tannberg and Millroad) which probably had to do with their privileged backgrounds allowing them to take part in school exchanges and travel across Europe.

Turning now to the English case, we see that young people struggled to talk about Europe in political terms, especially at Millroad School. As a result of the Euro-sceptic approach, European issues are a relatively low priority in schools. However, given that the English school system and curriculum is not in direct control of the (regional) government, there is considerable room for schools to develop rather different approaches to Europe. Millroad School, for instance, where over 65 per cent of students had skilled and unskilled parents, only had one European teaching unit in Year 8 (Italy: a European country) whilst highlighting the importance of an international perspective with units on Japan and Brazil in addition to local and national issues. The citizenship curriculum promoted notions of ethnic and cultural diversity with three teaching units (i.e. Britain: a diverse society; promoting interracial tolerance; debating a global issue) spent on the multicultural and global dimension, whereas only one focused on local, national or European topics. Not surprisingly, therefore, the group of British girls I interviewed did not appear to know much about the expansion of the EU on 1 May 2004, despite the fact that the discussion took place only days before this event:

*DF:* What do you know about Europe, about the European Union?
*ELLIE:* [laughing] Nothing!
*KATIE:* Nothing.
*DF:* What is happening at the moment in Europe?
*ELLIE:* Erm, there's a lot of disagreement about the Iraq War, whether it should have happened and stuff. Because, um, England was very go for it, and I know France was very very against it and I think that's, I dunno which other countries, but I think there were quite a lot more that were saying we shouldn't do it, and the English government, even though most of the people in England didn't want it to happen, decided to go ahead with it anyway.
*DF:* In the UK, they are now talking about this European Constitution; they want a referendum for that. Have you heard of that recently?
*KATIE:* Like, I read a lot of newspapers and I watch some news, but I've never heard of that. Well, they may not, you know, advertise it as much as they should do. None of us here heard that; so that must mean that they're not doing as much as they can to make people know that it's expanding.

The girls were not aware of the current debate about a European Constitution, and Katie pointed towards, what she perceived, as a low media representation of European issues in England. Other British students I interviewed, such as Robert, claimed that the political and educational marginalization of European agendas in England led to his poor knowledge about Europe and its institutions. 'The European parliament is never like televised, we don't know what they actually, if Parliament [Westminster] passes a bill, we'll know about it; I don't know what goes on in the European parliament'. Similarly, Turkish respondents had difficulties to make sense of how Europe and the EU work in political terms:

*DF:* What do you know about the European Union or Europe?
*BARIS:* European Union, what's that?
*SARILA:* Well, nobody knows nothing about it basically.
*BARIS:* What's the European Union?
*SARILA:* You think I know?
*BARIS:* I heard about it, but I don't know what it is.
*SARILA:* Me neither.
*HALIL:* Is it the power?
*BARIS:* I'm asking you.
*SARILA:* I don't really know, no.
*HALIL:* 'Cos the Union—
*BARIS:* The Union's a bunch of people that decides something, but I don't know.

Europe did also not fit easily with students' English or Turkish political identities at Millroad. Although geopolitical knowledge is not necessarily the basis of political identities, the evidence in the larger study suggests that it nevertheless affected identity formation. Students in the two English schools did not consider Europe part of their identities (Faas 2008a) whereas young people in the two German schools, particularly at Goethe Gymnasium, partially identified with Europe (Faas 2008b). It is, however, beyond the scope of this chapter to engage in a wider discussion about the complexities of youth identities.

Similarly, Darwin School (where about 57 per cent of students had professional middle-class and routine non-manual parents) made little efforts to integrate students on the basis of common European citizenship and instead emphasized similarity around notions of Britishness. 'The school strives to be a high-performing inclusive community school, fully committed to active citizenship and academic excellence. We value all who learn and work here; promoting a strong sense of community within and beyond the school' (School prospectus). The European context was also largely absent from Darwin's citizenship curriculum, and other subjects suitable for promoting a European dimension, such as geography and history, also offered only limited acknowledgement of the processes of European integration. For example, only one geography teaching unit in Year 8 dealt with Europe. The remainder of the geography curriculum was structured around local, national and global issues (e.g. international disparities, Brazil, Australia, UK climate, vine farm Lincolnshire); and the history curriculum centred on the two world wars as well as British national history. In their discussions about Europe and the EU, 15-year-old Darwinians struggled to talk about Europe:

*DF:* What sorts of things do you know about Europe and the European Union?
*ANNE:* Not much!
*VICTORIA:* It's really difficult,—
*ANNE:* I don't know anything.
*VICTORIA:* Europe? Totally out of my depth.
*ELIZABETH:* It's quite confusing 'cos it changes so much, that people—
*ANNE:* The euro.
*SOPHIE:* There's places part of it [indistinct]
*ELIZABETH:* Oh, isn't there a referendum or coming up for something or other?
*VICTORIA:* A what? What's that?
*ELIZABETH:* I dunno. I just heard it, walking through my house and the news was on somewhere, this whole thing about—
*VICTORIA:* What's a referendum?
*ELIZABETH:* I don't know.
*ANNE:* I know about the euro because I was in Ireland when it was going through.
*VICTORIA:* They don't have it in Ireland.

Arguably, the limited coverage of European issues in the British mass media and the failure of English schools to respond to calls for a European dimension alongside multicultural and global education (Tulasiewicz 1993; Convey and Merritt 2000) were all responsible for this low level of knowledge of, and interest in, European issues. Similar reasons can be deployed to justify the difficulties the sample of Turkish students had to engage in European political discourses. Some Darwin students referred to 'power', 'opposition to America' and 'community of countries'. Typically, however, Turkish interviewees neither knew the purpose of the EU nor how European institutions work. This can be seen in the following quotation from the discussion with a group of male and female students:

*DF:* What do you know about the European Union or Europe actually?
*ADEM:* It happened after World War II; France and Germany, they like made an agreement, and then loads of other countries joined or something.
*NEYLAN:* What happens when you're in the EU anyway?

*AFET:* Nothing, you're just—
*ADEM:* No, you get to, the United Nations.
*NEYLAN:* What do you get?
*ADEM:* You get into the United Nations.
*NEYLAN:* So what, who cares? Why can't the whole world be in it? That's not fair.
*ADEM:* 'Cos they're not.
*NEYLAN:* It's just stupid!

In contrast, both ethnic majority and Turkish minority students at Darwin frequently drew upon national citizenship discourses when talking about England's role in Europe and the wider world. Students frequently referred to notions of insularity, separateness and detachment and also portrayed the special partnership with the United States as a main factor undermining the Europeanization of British national identity ('we go and side off with the United States and stuff and beg from them and all the other countries think it's a bad idea'; 'in a way I think we are more similar to America because of the language'). Charles alluded to the level of national pride in England suggesting that it was 'quite strong', possibly stronger than elsewhere in Europe, and William referred to, what could be called, England's 'sitting on the fence' politics where policymakers and politicians have long been undecided whether to deepen their ties with Europe or America. Arguably, this exemplified the extent to which students' responses were affected by the national political context.

## CONCLUSION

European countries have responded rather differently to calls for a European dimension in education resulting in different levels of student engagement with Europe. Socio-economic factors and school interpretations of macro-level policies (e.g. Eurocentric education at Tannberg versus an inclusive concept of Europe at Goethe) also affected student responses and access to Europe, for instance in terms of travelling. Their limited, and at times inaccurate, geopolitical knowledge of Europe begs the question about the appropriateness of school curricula of subjects such as citizenship, geography and history, where countries like England currently only marginally include European topics while Europe has been central to curriculum development in countries like Germany. Arguably, insularity and complacency lead youngsters to reject learning foreign languages. Young people in England do not feel the necessity to learn a new language as in other European countries as they speak a world language. However, a foreign language is an important way to foster a sense of European citizenship among students, and poor language skills could mean for instance that young people in England are not only losing out on funding to study abroad but also decrease their employability and mobility opportunities in the European knowledge economy.

The EU clearly has no mandate to introduce European educational standards. Moreover, despite likely disadvantages in the labour market, policymakers in a country like England might not feel the necessity for strengthening the European political and educational dimension. In fact, the new global dimension was designed with a view of subsuming notions of Europe. Alongside these national discussions, the European Commission has recently stepped up their efforts to strengthen the European education area and knowledge economy and moved beyond the mere promotion of Community action programmes. Having hitherto largely focused on vocational education and higher education, in 2007, the Commission also recognized the need to assist Member States to adapt their school curricula. For example, the Communication *Improving Competences for the 21st Century: An Agenda for European Cooperation on Schools* (European Commission 2007) drew on the Open Method of Coordination (an intergovernmental means of governance in the EU, based on the voluntary cooperation of its Member States) in education and training, identifying key challenges for Member States which they may subsequently include in their national reform programmes. The document referred to eight key competencies students should acquire including cultural awareness and communication in the mother tongue and foreign languages. In addition, young people should get a sense of what is meant by active European citizenship and civic responsibility within a democratic, culturally diverse society. It remains to be seen however whether this top-down approach has any impact on future policies with regard to Europe.

## ACKNOWLEDGMENTS

I would like to thank Jeremy Leaman and Martha Wörsching for taking the time to edit this volume and for inviting me to contribute. I am grateful to Madeleine Arnot, Lynne Chisholm and Anna Triandafyllidou for commenting on earlier drafts of this chapter. I also thank the British Economic and Social Research Council, the Cambridge European Trust. Clare Hall College Cambridge and the European Comission Research Directorate-General for sponsoring the research on which this chapter is based.

## REFERENCES

Bell, G.H. (Ed.) (1995) *Educating European Citizens: Citizenship Values and the European Dimension* (London: David Fulton Publishers).
Convey, A. and Merritt, A. (2000) 'The United Kingdom', in C. Brock and W. Tulasiewicz (Eds.) *Education in a Single Europe*, pp. 377–403 (London: Routledge).

Council of Europe (1989) 'Recommendation 1111 on the European dimension in education', http://assembly.coe.int/Main.asp?link=/Documents/AdoptedText/ta89/EREC1111.htm (accessed 8 November 2008).

Council of Europe (1991) 'Resolution on the European dimension of education: teaching and curriculum content', http://www.coe.int/t/e/cultural_co-operation/education/standing_conferences/i.17thsessionvienna1991.asp#P11_353 (accessed 25 October 2008).

Council of Ministers of Education (1988) 'Resolution of the Council and the Ministers of Education: Meeting within the Council on the European Dimension in Education of 24 May 1988', *Official Journal of the European Communities*, C 177, pp. 5–7.

Council of Ministers of Education (1993) *Green Paper on the European Dimension of Education* (Luxembourg: Office for Official Publications of the European Communities).

Council of the European Communities (1992) 'Treaty on European Union', *Official Journal of the European Communities*, C 191.

Department of Education and Science (1988) 'Education Reform Act 1988', http://www.hmso.gov.uk/acts/acts1988/Ukpga_19880040_en_1.htm (accessed 31 October 2008).

Department for Education and Skills (2005) 'Developing the Global Dimension in the School Curriculum', http://www.dfid.gov.uk/pubs/files/dev-global-dim.pdf (accessed 10 November 2008).

European Commission (2007) 'Communication on Improving Competences for the 21st Century: An Agenda for European Cooperation on Schools', http://etuce.homestead.com/com425_en_2008.pdf (accessed 10 November 2008).

Faas, D. (2007) 'Turkish Youth in the European Knowledge Economy: Exploring their Responses to Europe and the Role of Social Class and School Dynamics for their Identities', *European Societies* 9(4), pp. 573–599.

Faas, D. (2008a) 'Constructing Identities: The Ethno-national and Nationalistic Identities of White and Turkish Students in Two English Secondary Schools', *British Journal of Sociology of Education*, 29(1), pp. 37–48.

Faas, D. (2008b) 'The Europeanisation of German Ethnic Identities: The Case of German and Turkish Students in Two Stuttgart Secondary Schools', *International Studies in Sociology of Education*, 17(1), pp. 45–62.

Faas, D. (2010) *Negotiating Political Identities: Multi Ethnic Schools in Europe.* Farmingdale: Ashgate.

Geddes, A. (1999) *Britain in the European Union* (Tisbury: Baseline Book Company).

Goetz, K. (1996) 'Integration Policy in a Europeanised State: Germany and the Intergovernmental Conference', *Journal of European Public Policy*, 3(1), pp. 23–44.

Hansen, P. (1998) 'Schooling a European Identity: Ethno-cultural Exclusion and Nationalist Resonance within the EU Policy of "The European dimension of education"', *European Journal of Intercultural Studies*, 9(1), pp. 5–23.

Hauler, A. (1994) *Die europäische Dimension in der schulischen Wirklichkeit: eine quantitative Analyse des Europa-Unterrichts im historisch-politischen Unterricht an baden-württembergischen Realschulen* (Weingarten: Forschungsstelle für politisch-gesellschaftliche Erziehung).

Katzenstein, P.J. (1997) 'United Germany in an Integrating Europe', in P.J. Katzenstein (Ed.) *Tamed Power: Germany in Europe*, pp. 1–48 (Ithaca: Cornell University Press).

Kesidou, A. (1999) *Die europäische Dimension der griechischen und baden-württembergischen Lehrpläne und Schulbücher der Sekundarschule: an den*

*Beispielen Geographie, politische Bildung, Geschichte und Literatur* (Frankfurt: Lang).

Kultusministerkonferenz (1992) *Zur europäischen Dimension im Bildungswesen: Beschluss der Kultusministerkonferenz vom Juni 1992* (Bonn: Sekretariat der Ständigen Konferenz der Kultusminister der Länder in der Bundesrepublik Deutschland).

Kultusministerkonferenz (2008) 'Europa im Unterricht: Beschluss der Kultusminister konferenz vom 08.06.1978 in der Fassung vom 05.05.2008', http://www.kmk.org/doc/beschl/555_Europa_in_der_Schule.pdf (accessed 29 October 2008).

Natterer, A. (2001) *Europa im Schulbuch: die Darstellung der europäischen Einigung in baden-württembergischen Schulbüchern für Geschichte und Gemeinschaftskunde der Sekundarstufe I* (Grevenbroich: Omnia).

Neave, G. (1984) *The EEC and Education* (Stoke-on-Trent: Trentham Books).

Osler, A. and Starkey, H. (2001) 'Citizenship Education and National Identities in France and England: Inclusive or Exclusive?', *Oxford Review of Education*, 27(2), pp. 287–305.

Paterson, W.E. (1996) 'The German Christian Democrats', in J. Gaffney (Ed.) *Political Parties and the European Union*, pp. 53–70 (London: Routledge).

Phillips, D. (1995) 'Introduction', *Oxford Studies in Comparative Education*, 5(2), pp. 7–9.

Risse, T. and Engelmann-Martin, D. (2002) 'Identity Politics and European Integration: The Case of Germany', in A. Pagden (Ed.) *The Idea of Europe: from Antiquity to the European Union*, pp. 287–316 (Cambridge, UK: Cambridge University Press).

Ross, A. (2000) 'Education for Citizenship and Identity within the Context of Europe', in R. Gardner, D. Lawton and J. Cairns (Eds.) *Education for Citizenship)*, pp. 183–199 (London: Continuum).

Ryba, R. (2000) 'Developing the European Dimension in Education: The Roles of the European Union and the Council of Europe', in E.S. Swing, J. Schriewer and F. Orivel (Eds.) *Problems and Prospects in European Education*, pp. 45–71 (London: Praeger).

Tulasiewicz, W. (1993) 'The European Dimension and the National Curriculum', in A.S. King and M.J. Reiss (Eds.) *The Multicultural Dimension of the National Curriculum*, pp. 240–258 (London: Falmer).

Weidenfeld, W. and Piepenschneider, M. (1990) *Junge Generation und europäische Einigung: Einstellungen, Wünsche, Perspektiven* (Bonn: Europa Union Verlag).

Woodard, S. (1998) 'Britain and Europe: History of a Relationship', in M. Fraser (Ed.) *Britain in Europe*, pp. 128–131 (London: Strategems).

# 13 Political Participation of Youth
## Young Germans in the European Context

*Wolfgang Gaiser and Johann de Rijke*

## INTRODUCTION

The question about young people's participation plays a central role in the public debate on the development of civil society, and key concepts of this are civil engagement, political participation and voluntary work. This was highlighted when the year 2001 was declared the 'international year of volunteers' by the UN plenary meeting.

The Eurobarometer on Young Europeans 2001 and 2007, the European Commission's White Paper on European Youth Policy, and the conclusions of the EU Council of Ministers of Youth of 25 November 2003, referring to the White Paper, all consider the issue of participation as a central topic. However, the polyvalence between the integration and relief functions of public institutions and the increasing control by state institutions remain untouched.

The discussion of young people's participation is not only relevant in relation to the social integration of the next generation, but also in relation to disintegration processes affecting the three main modes of integration of individuals into society, namely the welfare system, the labour market and democratic institutions (cf. Braun 2001). The young are confronted by multiple challenges: Firstly, the welfare state is undergoing changes towards a plural welfare model; secondly, the deregulation of the labour market is progressing, and thirdly, there are structural changes affecting the democratic order. This means that for the young, it is no longer just a question of needing to cope with the usual biographical tasks of youth to acquire socio-cultural and economic independence. In their transition to adulthood, today's young generation also needs to cope with dynamic social conditions, as they are faced by ever increasing demands for labour market flexibility, while at the same time there is the need for greater self-reliance in relation to welfare security and for increasingly active participation in the democratic process.

This chapter focuses on the wider spectrum of political participation, from membership in organizations or participation in informal groups to participation in public actions (e.g. demonstrations, collecting signatures). It draws on the Youth Survey carried out by the German Youth Institute

(DJI-Jugendsurvey) which studied the political orientations and participations as well as the living conditions of young people. The first two waves of the Youth Survey (in 1992 and 1997) employed face-to-face interviews of young people with German nationality between 16 and 29 years old in both parts of the Federal Republic of Germany. Both waves were designed to be representative for Germany, each including nearly 7,000 respondents (4,500 in West Germany, 2,500 in East Germany). The third wave of the survey in 2003 widened the group of respondents to include 12- to 15-year-olds as well as young residents without German nationality, thus expanding the sample to nearly 9,000 respondents. For more detailed information on the first wave, see Hoffmann-Lange (1995); for the second wave, see Gille and Krüger (2000); for the third wave, see Gille et al. (2006).

## EMPIRICAL RESULTS ABOUT THE PARTICIPATION OF YOUNG PEOPLE AND YOUNG ADULTS IN GERMANY

The discussions of social engagement often lack precision in the definition of their object. In the following analysis, we distinguish three forms of participation: These are closer to the concept of 'social capital' (see Robert D. Putnam 2000) than that of 'civil engagement' focusing on potential benefits or positive contribution to the community.

The first form of participation can be found within the institutionalized context of the 'intermediate system' of large organizations and associations. These organizations gather together interests and are structured in accordance with their functions; they view themselves as membership organizations. Membership and participation here imply long-term participation and loyalty, and instrumental relationships are considered to be strong. A different kind of participation is the involvement in informal groups, initiatives and alternative organizations such as ecological groups, freedom movements, citizens' initiatives, and self-supporting networks. These kinds of collectives, considered as forms of 'new social movements', developed during the 1970s and 1980s as movements outside the parliamentary sphere and established politics in connection with daily fields of action and public political targets. A third perspective involves forms that express particular participatory actions. These are temporary and concrete political actions, which serve the purpose of supporting or articulating specific political goals.

## MEMBERSHIP IN TRADITIONAL ORGANIZATIONS AND ASSOCIATIONS

To be part of an organization or association can be significant for adolescents and young adults in their identity development, social networking and also to assert their own claims. Membership in institutions is significant both for social integration of the individual and for the integration of society as a whole. At present, organizations and associations see their main problem in attracting new members (see Weßels 2001).

The low membership rate in the new Federal states—in the former East Germany—shows some specific traits. On the one hand, membership is less widespread among the population and has a shorter tradition. On the other hand, people in the new Federal states remain more sceptical towards trade unions and associations which they presume to be influenced by Western values.

Although membership represents a central form of participation, this still does not mean that each member actually participates in the activities and goals of the organization. The numbers of people who are active or passive members vary strongly between organizations. Whereas in trade unions, professional associations and political parties a relatively large proportion of members are passive, in sports clubs and in youth or student associations the proportion of passive participants is very low.

Membership in political parties is particularly important in the context of political participation. Political parties represent the most important

*Table 13.1*  Membership in Traditional Organizations and Associations, 1992, 1997 and 2003 (%)

| Member | 1992 | 1997 | 2003 |
|---|---|---|---|
| Sports associations/Sports clubs | 35 | 31 | 36 |
| Local tradition and citizens' associations | 2 | 8 | 10 |
| Other associations/unions or clubs | 8 | 7 | 9 |
| Other kinds of social organizations or social unions (bowling clubs etc.) | 8 | 10 | 9 |
| Trade unions | 17 | 7 | 8 |
| Religious associations and unions | 9 | 6 | 8 |
| Youth and student associations | 5 | 5 | 5 |
| Professional or trade associations/organizations | 4 | 3 | 4 |
| Political parties | 2 | 3 | 2 |
| Charitable institutions | 1 | 2 | 1 |
| Citizens' action groups/civil initiatives | 2 | 1 | 1 |
| Member of at least one organization | 58 | 49 | 57 |

Source: DJI-Jugendsurvey 1992, 1997 and 2003.
Note: The question was 'There are many ways to be active in your free time. One possibility is to be a member of an organization, association or club. Please look through this list and tell me for each organization, association and club if you are currently a member'. The respondents were 16- to 29-year-olds (German).

mediators in the political process, and this is specifically spelled out in the German Constitution (cf. Niedermayer 2005). Yet, although the number of members in political parties is, generally speaking, relatively low and declining, it is also true that the decline over recent decades has been mostly because younger generations are not joining in sufficient numbers. This 'political weariness of the young' leads to a 'loss of vitality' in political parties (Wiesendahl 2001). The 'ageing process' of parties is also seen to reflect the changing modes of participation. Thus, new and unconventional forms of political participation are mainly attractive to the young, while on the other hand they seem to have increasing difficulties in dealing with the organizational culture of traditional parties which is seen as obsolete.

## INFORMAL GROUPS WITH NEW MODES OF PARTICIPATION

Informal political associations, originally known as 'new social movements', raise specific social problems for discussion and allow action-oriented participation. They are against rigid and over-rationalized organizations and demand new forms of community life and new constructs of meaning. The specific nature of this type of group lies in the immediacy of social relationships between their 'members' and in their 'project-oriented mobilization', which differs from the classic pattern of long-term relationships tied to the social structure of large organizations (cf. Roth 1999).

Thus, informal groupings can be placed at an intermediate position between membership organizations and informal social entities in respect of their degree of organization. Because of their content, goals, forms of activity and flexible forms of participation, informal groups are highly attractive to young people.

Already in the first Youth Survey in 1992 we found that young people in the eastern part of Germany showed almost identical attitudes towards this type of association as their peers in the western states (cf. Schneider 1995). By 2003, young people in east and west Germany still showed a high acceptance of informal groups in terms not only of their emotional approval, but also their appreciation of the groups' substantive goals. Ecological groups and peace activists still enjoy the highest level of acceptance, followed by human rights initiatives. On the whole, young people in Germany are most attracted by groups which are concerned with ecological and social issues (e.g. ecological groups, peace and Third World initiatives, anti-nuclear activists, human rights activists and self-help groups).

Actual participation, as can be seen in the level of active involvement in the design and implementation of activities and attending meetings, is less developed (cf. Table 13.2). Nevertheless, the proportion of activists in ecological and pacifist movements and other locally active groups is

*Table 13.2* Participation in informal groups 1992, 1997 and 2003 (%)

| Groups | 1992 | 1997 | 2003 |
|---|---|---|---|
| Ecological groups | 13 | 11 | 8 |
| Peace activists | 10 | 6 | 8 |
| Third World initiatives | 5 | 6 | 6 |
| Human rights activists | 5 | 4 | 4 |
| Self-help groups | 4 | 4 | 3 |
| Women's/men's groups | 4 | 2 | 2 |
| Anti-nuclear activists | 5 | 4 | 2 |
| Active in at least one group | 21 | 19 | 19 |

Source: DJI-Jugendsurvey 1992, 1997 and 2003.
Note: Respondents were prompted as follows: 'In our society there are not only organizations which require continuous membership. There are also less stable associations and movements in which one can participate'. The figures encompass the following answers: 'I like it, I actively participate in it' and 'I like it, I sometimes participate in meetings/in activities'. The respondents were 16 to 29-year-olds.

similar in range to the proportion of participants in different membership organizations.

Though informal groups are able to mobilize roughly one in ten people at most, the proportion of members in at least one organization is still greater.

## DEVELOPMENT OF POLITICAL PARTICIPATION IN GERMANY

To provide a full picture of the political participation of adolescents and young adults, we must also consider specific forms of political articulation in relation to concrete topics (cf. Table 13.3). Such alternative forms of participation are relatively popular. Across Germany, about two thirds of young people have collected signatures on at least one occasion, while one third have participated in officially permitted demonstrations or public discussion forums.

Looking at the results, it becomes clear that a discrepancy exists between intentional and actual participation (cf. Table 13.4): Whereas 41 per cent of the respondents declared their readiness to participate in trade union strikes, in fact not even 5 per cent actually had taken part in this kind of activity.

About one tenth of young people aged 16–29 have participated at least once in political actions by sending letters to newspapers or politicians, or by giving donations. Likewise, no less than 10 per cent were at least on one occasion so convinced about their political ideas that they were prepared to break the law, for instance by taking part in illegal demonstrations.

*Table 13.3*   Political participation and political willingness, 1992, 1997 and 2003 (%)

| Participation | 1992 | 1997 | 2003 |
|---|---|---|---|
| **Conventional participation** | | | |
| Voter participation** | 93 | 92 | 92 |
| Letters to politicians | 28 | 31 | 31 |
| Donations for political purposes | 31 | 28 | 23 |
| Letters to newspapers | 35 | 39 | 31 |
| **Unconventional participation** | | | |
| Collection of signatures | 79 | 79 | 80 |
| Legal demonstrations | 65 | 62 | 60 |
| Trade union strike | 56 | 49 | 41 |
| Non-legal demonstrations | 29 | 27 | 21 |

Source: DJI-Jugendsurvey 1992, 1997 and 2003.
Note: The respondents were prompted as follows: 'Assuming that you want to have an influence or give your opinion on a political issue that is important to you'. First, a (long) list was presented introduced by the following question: 'Which of these options would you take into consideration and which not?' Then: 'Please go over all options again. In which of them have you already participated, in which not?' The respondents were 16- to 29-year-olds, with the exception of 'voter participation', for which only 18- to 29-year-old Germans were taken into consideration.

*Table 13.4*   Political participation, political willingness and political activities, 2003 (%)

| Participation | Youth Survey 2003 | |
|---|---|---|
| | Willingness | Have already done it |
| **Conventional participation** | | |
| Voter participation | 92 | 80 |
| Letters to politicians | 31 | 8 |
| Donations for political purposes | 23 | 7 |
| Letters to newspapers | 31 | 7 |
| **Unconventional participation** | | |
| Collection of signatures | 80 | 60 |
| Legal demonstrations | 60 | 32 |
| Trade Union's strike | 41 | 5 |
| Non-legal demonstrations | 21 | 7 |

Source: DJI-Jugendsurvey 1992, 1997 and 2003.
* The respondents were prompted as follows: 'Assuming that you want to have an influence or give your opinion on a political issue that is important for you'. First, a (long) list was presented introduced by the following question: 'Which of these possibilities would you take into consideration and which not?' The question to activities was: 'Please go over all possibilities again. In which of them have you already participated, in which not?'
The respondents were 16- to 29-year-olds, with the exception of 'voter participation', for which only 18- to 29-year-old Germans were taken into consideration.

# FACETS OF EXPLANATION

So far, the social participation of adolescents and young adults has been represented through three different areas: Firstly, membership in traditional organizations or associations, secondly, participation in informal groups, which imply a broader definition of politics, finally, specific political actions that are limited in time and directly related to particular situations. What kinds of relationships can be found among socio-economic indicators, indicators of value and political orientations, and deprivation indicators with respect to participation in membership organizations on the one hand, and participation in informal groups on the other?

*Region:* As far as membership in organizations is concerned, a clear difference between urban and rural settings in favour of rural regions is noted for some of the central associations. Activities in social and locally oriented associations are more pronounced in rural regions, and the same can be said for sports clubs, the associations with the highest membership. In contrast, participation in selective forms of political articulation (e.g. demonstrations) is slightly higher in urban settings. However, as far as overall participation in nongovernmental organizations is concerned, almost no difference between urban and rural settings is noticeable.

*Gender differences* can be found in the participation in informal groups in West Germany, where women do engage slightly more than men. However, the relationship is reversed when it comes to traditional associations, in which men are more active than women. This confirms the opposite trend concerning the engagement of both sexes with respect to traditional versus unconventional activities.

*The effect of education* becomes visible as well. Young people with Abitur (the German university entrance qualification) do engage more often than those with lower level certificates. This goes for both forms of participation.

Post-materialistic orientations play a certain role with respect to *value orientations*, although the effect is less intense: persons with post-materialistic attitudes are more likely to be active than those with materialistic orientations. (We follow here Inglehart's definitions: materialistic orientation is linked with traditional values, while post-materialistic orientation is typical for people who place more importance on individual self-realization and political participation; cf. Inglehart 1998).

Furthermore, there is a stronger tendency among members of informal groups to place themselves on the left of the political spectrum. This is likely to correspond to the self-perception of most groups belonging to the new social movements. Otherwise, this kind of political self-positioning plays no role regarding activities within the framework of traditional organizations.

The greatest impact on participation relates to the *political interest* in both activity forms. Obviously, political interest is a central motivational factor for engagement.

Still controversial is the issue of the extent to which social *deprivation* has an effect on participation. Does it promote mobilization, with the hope of improving the situation through engagement? Or does it paralyze and obstruct political action, because social disadvantage becomes associated with political marginalization? To answer these questions, it is possible empirically to contrast the group of unemployed people with other status groups. Thus, one can find a clear association among traditional organizations: unemployed people are less active than the employed.

Summing up, one can find some central indicators of features that explain political participation.

*Gender*: Girls and young women are more likely to participate in groups belonging to the new social movements. Boys and young men show a stronger interest in conventional politics. They engage more often in traditional organizations and associations.

*Education*: The higher the educational level, the higher is the level of engagement—whether this is the result of more insight and available resources, or a question of clearer principles or a better awareness of potential benefits.

It can be seen that political interest leads to the highest level of social and political participation. Even a person with a low level of education is able to engage in social political activity—if there is enough political interest. (For a more elaborate analysis of participation in formal organizations and informal groups, see Gaiser and de Rijke 2008).

## INTERIM RESULT

Social and political participation of adolescents and young adults show a multiplicity of aspects, some central features of which have already been discussed. There is evidence that active participation in traditional social organizations (associations, political parties etc.) is to some extent declining. Yet, traditional organizations are also changing and shifting. Thus, we cannot say that there is an outright refusal to participate among the young—although at the same time, politics cannot be seen as their central field of action. Participation in informal groups is at a constant level. This shows the prevailing sympathy for unconventional, flexible, and more decentralized and self-determined modes of action. There are selective forms of action for limited periods of time which do not require long-term commitment. These types of actions, especially if their issues are relevant for young people, are particularly able to mobilize the young. Modern communication media are likely to intensify these tendencies.

These facts should be taken into account more seriously by organizations interested in mobilizing the next generation. For instance, they could increase their attempts to combine their objectives, which need continuous organization, with more informal actions over a limited period of time, in order to take the target-oriented expectations of young people better into consideration.

There is evidence to suggest that adolescents and young adults see no contradiction between self-development and pro-social attitudes.

Faced with a multiplicity of necessities and possibilities, declining participation is more related to lack of time for additional commitment, since engaging in participation means a decision not only *for* something but also *against* something. Personal life, friends, partnership and family on the one hand, and education, career and work on the other hand, are highly valued by the young. In this sense, their lives are increasingly shaped by organizing, arranging and securing their social and economic participation. At the same time, young people's biographies are becoming more and more individualized: the links to social milieus are becoming weaker. Making bridges between different types of participation, e.g. from employment to engagement in trade unions, is no longer the norm.

On the other hand, young people's dissatisfaction with the types of opportunities for influencing politics, with co-determination in school and employment, show that their desire to assert themselves in society is not satisfied.

## ASPECTS OF PARTICIPATION WITHIN THE EUROPEAN CONTEXT

In this last part of the chapter, we will briefly examine the European context to gain a wider perspective. To do this, we ask a number of questions, such as: What variations can be found among the 27 European Member States? Are there specific variations between the 15 'old' (EU-15) and the 12 new Member States (NMS-12), and are the significant influences there the same as in Germany?

By comparing different European countries, we can often find great variations between the countries. However, it is not always easy to explain these variations. Other than evaluating dissimilarities of political participation and attitudes within one country, additional factors have to be considered when different countries are compared. This needs to be done from an awareness of the specifics which differentiate the countries under evaluation. Globally speaking, it is possible to distinguish a national level (e.g. with respect to influences on political attitudes and actions), an institutional level (e.g. the voting system or constitutionally structured political institutions), a field of concrete events and historical developments, an area of social structure and an area of political culture (cf. Gabriel and Kropp 2008, Braun and Mohler 2003). In the present chapter, we will need to limit our focus. Thus, we will first offer a brief descriptive overview of selected differences between European countries regarding political orientations and political participation.

By considering differences in political culture—roughly defined as orientations towards input, output and system of politics—we can distinguish groups of countries within the European context which show dissimilar levels of *democratic citizens' culture* (cf. Gabriel 2008). Here Denmark, Luxembourg, the Netherlands, Sweden, Finland and Greece are seen as countries where the citizens' political culture is developed, and support for democracy and political institutions is quite high. West Germany, Great Britain and Ireland show a more legalistic type of political culture with less satisfaction with the democratic process. And many new Eastern, postcommunist countries are more distant to political institutions, but Belgium, France and Portugal also show a more distant attitude to these institutions.

An examination of political participation issues shows similar groupings of countries with some differentiations (Gabriel and Völkl 2008). With respect to electoral participation (mean values between 2001 and 2006), one can find quite high levels of participation in northern, central and even southern European countries, with lower levels in Great Britain, Ireland and in France (in this context, it is necessary to remember that in some countries such as Greece, Italy, Belgium and Luxembourg voting in elections is compulsory; cf. Gabriel and Völkl 2008). Most new democratic countries from the former Eastern Bloc show a low level of electoral participation.

In the field of unconventional or protest forms of political participation, a similar but not fully identical picture can be seen. In northern Europe we find high rates of such activities, especially in Sweden with the highest value. In western central Europe rates are also high, with the exception of the Netherlands; France, for example, shows an even higher engagement in protest activities than most western European countries. (According to some other research, the acceptance of new social movements in France is rather low, although the willingness of young people to engage in, for instance, human rights initiatives must be considered as quite high, given that they receive two thirds of positive votes; cf. Muxel 2001: 134). Rates of engagement are also high in Great Britain, but not in Ireland. In the southern European countries, protest activities are relatively low, but countries of the former Eastern Bloc show the lowest rates now, even though at the beginning of the 1990s, '[m]any east Europeans had engaged in unconventional politics during the democratic transitions of the late 1980s and early 1990s, but these forms of action diminished after the transition in a kind of "post-honeymoon" effect' (Dalton and Klingemann 2007: 16).

All in all, combining the indicators of participation, we can see a clear scale from the most participative culture to the least: this scale is headed by northern European countries, followed by the Benelux countries, then west Germany and Austria, the western and southern European countries, with east European countries and Greece coming last (Gabriel and Völkl 2008: 285).

Having outlined these general differences, we would like to focus on the differences that seem to be specific to *younger age groups*, using data provided by the Flash Eurobarometer from 2007. In 2007, the European Commission (Directorate-General for Education and Culture, 'Youth' Unit) conducted a 'Flash Eurobarometer' as part of the Eurobarometer Special Surveys. This survey encompassed over 19,000 randomly selected young citizens aged between 15 and 30 in the 27 Member States (European Commission 2007).The area of political participation as described above can also be found in part. Therefore we will direct our attention towards the issues of 'membership in organizations', 'involvement in political life' and 'requested measures in order to improve participation'.

First, we offer some remarks on *the concept of organizational membership across Europe*. Membership in voluntary or other kinds of associations is usually considered an indicator of social integration. It can be tested relatively easily by means of surveys covering several countries, which permit the establishment of differences among countries or groups of countries. In this sense, Van Deth and Kreuter refer to European countries within the frame of World Values Surveys. They observe the percentage of interviewees (aged 18 and upwards) who are members of at least one organization in their country. As a result, Van Deth and Kreuter developed a list of 16 more or less structured organizations. On this basis, it is possible to determine clear national differences: the highest level of organization can be found in northern countries like Sweden, Denmark and Norway, but also in the Netherlands (each over 80 per cent). A middle group with a membership ratio of about 50–60 per cent comprises countries such as Ireland, the United Kingdom, Belgium, Austria and Germany (old Federal states). Finally, there is a group with low rates of membership comprising mostly southern European countries like Italy, Spain (only 23 per cent), Portugal but also France (38 per cent) (cf. van Deth and Kreuter 1998: 137f.)

These differences among countries can in part be described using characteristics of the context, e.g. specific national and cultural or political traditions of the respective countries. Nevertheless, Van Deth and Kreuter expound the problems regarding the summarization of the membership indicator, and thus try to grasp the structure of membership within organizations. As a result, they find that this structure is not the same in all countries. They conclude that an international comparison of participation in voluntary associations demands complicated theoretical and empirical conceptualizations, and that the simple method of additive measures is insufficient (van Deth and Kreuter 1998). However, this point of view cannot be taken into account in the following short overview.

In the Flash Eurobarometer 'Young Europeans 2007', young people are asked 'Are you a member of an organization?'.

The data on membership of organizations in the EU-27 shows the following (European Commission 2007: 20–26): In general, young people in the EU-27 are not very active in organizations or associations; only 22 per cent of young Europeans are members of an organization. Sports clubs are the most successful and are mentioned by just under one in two respondents

*Table 13.5*   Share of Young People (15–30) who are Members of at Least One
Organization in the EU-15 (%)

| | |
|---|---|
| Denmark | 47 |
| Germany | 46 |
| Sweden | 45 |
| Austria | 43 |
| Netherlands | 42 |
| Finland | 38 |
| Belgium | 35 |
| Luxembourg | 29 |
| Ireland | 28 |
| EU-15 | 26 |
| France | 23 |
| United Kingdom | 21 |
| Portugal | 14 |
| Italy | 13 |
| Spain | 12 |
| Greece | 11 |

Source: Flash Eurobarometer. Young Europeans 2007.

who report being a member of an organization. Smaller percentages (below
10 per cent) mention that they are members of a youth organization such as
the Scouts, a cultural or artistic association, a trade union, a hobby or special interest club; about 5 per cent or less are members of a political party,
a religious organization, an organization working for animal protection
and the environment, a human rights organization or a consumer organization. One in five respondents who reported membership is a member of
a type of organization other than those just mentioned. When comparing
membership rates between countries, we can see that young people in the
EU-15 (EU states without the 10 New Member States from 2004 and the 2
from 2007) are more likely to be members of an organization than young
people in the New Member States NMS-12 (26 per cent compared to 10
per cent).

Focussing only on the countries of the EU-15, a north-south divide
becomes evident, with the countries in the north having higher percentages
of membership than the countries in the south of Europe (cf. Table 13.5).
The highest percentage of those who are members of an organization are in
Denmark (47 per cent), followed by Germany (46 per cent) and Sweden (45
per cent). Portugal (14 per cent), Italy (13 per cent), Spain (12 per cent) and
Greece (11 per cent) have the lowest membership ratios.

With regard to country results for the New Member States, Malta has the highest percentage of respondents who are members of an organization (25 per cent). The smallest percentages of young people who are members of an organization are found in Poland (9 per cent), Romania (7 per cent) and Bulgaria (7 per cent).

We can also see that, in general, male respondents are more likely to be members of an organization than female respondents.

Considering the national similarities and differences in the type of organizations of which respondents are members, we find that sports clubs and associations are the most successful organizations among young people in almost all countries of the EU. Forty-nine per cent of those young people who are members of at least one organization mention sport clubs or associations. The next percentage is 8 per cent for youth organizations and cultural associations. The highest percentage of respondents who say that they are members of a sports club can be found in Germany (71 per cent). In Denmark and Finland, trade union membership is relatively high among young people, with 55 per cent of Danish respondents and 32 per cent of Finnish respondents replying that they are members of a trade union. Trade unions are also relatively successful among the young in Sweden and the United Kingdom.

Age differences can be found in some organizations: respondents in the youngest age category who report membership more often mention sports clubs and youth organizations. Older respondents who report membership, on the other hand, more often mention trade union membership and membership in a cultural or artistic association.

When asked 'Are you engaged in any voluntary activities?', only 16 per cent of all young people answer positively. Interestingly, almost 75 per cent of the young people state that more programmes encouraging voluntary work would be a good thing (see the end of this section). And whereas there were large differences in membership in organizations between the EU-15 and the NMS-12, only small differences can be found in the engagement in voluntary activities: 17 per cent of the young people in the EU-15 are engaged, and 13 per cent in the NMS-12.

In the Flash Eurobarometer 202, young people were asked about the ways in which they have been *involved in political life* during the last year (European Commission 2007: 47–49). The results tell us: 28 per cent of young adults signed a petition in the last year, 24 per cent presented their views in an online discussion forum, and 20 per cent took part in a public demonstration. Smaller percentages of respondents report that they have worked for an nongovernmental organization in the past year (11 per cent), were active in a trade union or were a member of a trade union (8 per cent), or worked for a political party (5 per cent). Differences in political involvement between the EU-15 and NMS-12 countries are evident: respondents in the former are in general more involved in political life than respondents in the latter.

246 Wolfgang Gaiser and Johann de Rijke

Again, in general young men are more politically active than young women. And highly educated respondents are more involved in political life than respondents with lower educational attainments.

Some aspects of participation can be expressed by membership in traditional organizations and associations and by engagement in voluntary work. Of course, the whole spectrum of participation possibilities is wider than this, and extends from state institutions and the educational system to private social networks of family and friends. While so far we have considered some aspects of actual participation, we will now take a brief look at the question relating to the priority of certain measures, intermediate channels and structures for young people with regard to social participation. To shed light on this, the Eurobarometer 2007 asked young people to choose from a given list of *those measures and norms which they considered particularly relevant to increasing participation of youth.*

The aim was to find out which measures would help to encourage young people's active participation in society (European Commission 2007: 36–38). Most respondents (81 per cent) suggest that young people should be consulted before any public decision concerning them was taken. About three out of four respondents (74 per cent) think that a good measure would be the availability of more programmes encouraging voluntary work, and 70 per cent of young Europeans think that the introduction of a compulsory educational programme about citizenship into schools would encourage the active participation of young people in society. Lowering the voting age as a measure to increase young people's active participation in society is mentioned by fewer than one in five respondents (19 per cent). This does not provide support for discussions on this subject which are ongoing in some countries, (e.g. in Germany the value is even somewhat smaller).


CONCLUSION

In the previous considerations, we found clear dissimilarities between different European countries. However, in general it was not possible to identify a constant and unambiguous ranking of results, or clear contrasts with reference to each comparison point.

Thus so far, explanations can only be formulated as plausible suppositions. As mentioned before, in order to conduct a more detailed analysis of data, several explanatory factors likely to derive from the institutional features of a country, historical events, social structure or political culture must be considered (for an example of such an analysis see Gerhards and Hölscher 2003).

If one intends to investigate these questions empirically, then appropriate explanatory features and indicators for each case should be integrated within the research. In this sense, the Eurobarometer represents a limited source of information. Nowadays, the research process should include more distinctions regarding the aspects of participation and their explanatory factors. At present, throughout Europe, there are two empirical research projects from which this could be expected. One of these research projects is the European Social Survey project, based on surveys among the population of more than 20 European countries (the first survey was carried out in 2002, the second in 2004, the third in 2006.[1] Another project, which puts more emphasis on the participation of young people, is "EUYOUPART—Political Participation of Young People in Europe—Development of Indicators for Comparative Research in the European Union". The latter project, from 2004, carried out empirical research among young people between 15 and 24 in eight countries of the European Union and accession candidates (http://www.sora.at/wahlen/EUYOUPART/). It refers to two aspects which must be taken into account when planning a pan-European survey and country-by-country comparison of the participation of young people: on the one hand, the range of indicators must be extended because new forms of information, mobilization and actual exertion of influence, such as the Internet and mobile phones, are becoming increasingly important and, on the other hand, new strategies of political articulation (strategic use of the consumer role, ethical consumption, boycotts of products and producers) are increasingly taken into consideration (cf. de Rijke, Gaiser and Waechter 2008). Using a comparative analysis of the country-specific structures of participation and qualitative interviews conducted with young citizens, this project also shows that individual political cultures must be taken into account, as activities, which may be identified as identical in terms of concept, may in fact have very different meanings in different societal contexts.

## NOTES

1. cf. http://www.europeansocialsurvey.org

## REFERENCES

Braun, S. (2001) 'Bürgerschaftliches Engagement—Konjunktur und Ambivalenz einer gesellschaftlichen Debatte', *Leviathan*, 1, pp. 83–109.
Braun, M. and Mohler, P. Ph. (2003) 'Background Variables', in J. A. Harkness, F.J.R. Van de Vijver and P.Ph. Mohler (Eds.) *Cross-Cultural Survey Methods*, pp. 101–115 (Hoboken, NJ: John Wiley & Sons).
Dalton, R. J. and Klingemann, H.-D. (2007) 'Citizens and Political Behavior', in R. J. Dalton and H.-D. Klingemann (Eds.) *The Oxford Handbook of Political Behaviour*, pp. 3–26 (New York: Oxford University Press).
de Rijke, J., Gaiser, W. and Wächter, F. (2008) 'Political Orientation and Participation—A Longitudinal Perspective', in R. Spannring, G. Ogris and W. Gaiser (Eds.) *Youth and Political Participation in Europe. Results of the Comparative Study EUYOUPART*, pp. 121–147 (Opladen & Farmington Hills: Barbara Budrich Publishers).
European Commission (2007) Directorate General for 'Education and Culture' ('Youth' Unit) *Flash Eurobarometer 202—The Gallup Organisation. Young*

*Europeans. A Survey among Young People aged between 15–30 in the European Union.* Analytical Report http://ec.europa.eu/public_opinion/flash/fl_202_en.pdf.

Gabriel, O. W. (2008) 'Politische Einstellungen und politische Kultur', in O.W. Gabriel and S. Kropp (Eds.) *Die EU-Staaten im Vergleich. Strukturen, Prozesse, Politikinhalte*, 3rd edition, pp. 181–214 (Wiesbaden: VS Verlag für Sozialwissenschaften).

Gabriel, O. W. and Kropp, S. (2008) 'Einleitung: Die EU-Staaten im Vergleich: Strukturen, Prozesse, Politikfelder', in O.W. Gabriel and S. Kropp (Eds.) *Die EU-Staaten im Vergleich. Strukturen, Prozesse, Politikinhalte*, 3rd edition, pp. 11–30 (Wiesbaden: VS Verlag für Sozialwissenschaften).

Gabriel, O. W. and Völkl, K. (2008) 'Politische und soziale Partizipation', O.W. Gabriel and S. Kropp (Eds.) *Die EU-Staaten im Vergleich. Strukturen, Prozesse, Politikinhalte*, 3rd edition, pp. 268–298 (Wiesbaden: VS Verlag für Sozialwissenschaften).

Gaiser, W. and de Rijke, J. (2008) 'Social and Political Participation of Adolescents and Young Adults in Germany', in R. Bendit and M. Hahn-Bleibtreu (Eds.) *Youth Transitions: Processes of Social Inclusion and Patterns of Vulnerability in a Globalised World*, pp. 195–228 (Leverkusen: Verlag Barbara Budrich).

Gille, M. and Krüger, W. (Eds.) (2000) *Unzufriedene Demokraten. Politische Orientierungen der 16- bis 29jährigen im vereinigten Deutschland* (Opladen: Leske + Budrich).

Gille, M., Sardei-Biermann, S., Gaiser, W. and de Rijke, J. (2006) *Jugendliche und junge Erwachsene in Deutschland. Lebensverhältnisse, Werte und gesellschaftliche Beteiligung 12- bis 29-JährigeR* (Wiesbaden: VS Verlag für Sozialwissenschaften).

Gerhards, J. and Hölscher, M. (2003) 'Kulturelle Unterschiede zwischen Mitglieds- und Beitrittsländern der EU. Das Beispiel Familien- und Gleichberechtigungsvorstellungen', *Zeitschrift für Soziologie*, 32(3), pp. 206–225.

Hoffmann-Lange, U. (Ed.) (1995) *Jugend und Demokratie in Deutschland* (Opladen: Leske + Budrich).

Inglehart, R. (1998) *Modernisierung und Postmodernisierung* (Frankfurt: Campus).

Muxel, A. (2001) *L'expérience politique des jeunes* (Paris: Presses de Sciences Po).

Niedermayer, O. (2005) *Bürger und Politik. Politische Orientierungen und Verhaltensweisen der Deutschen* (Wiesbaden: VS Verlag für Sozialwissenschaften).

Putnam, R. D. (2000) *Bowling Alone: The Collapse and Revival of American Community* (New York: Simon & Schuster).

Roth, R. (1999) 'Neue soziale Bewegungen und liberale Demokratie', in A. Klein, H.-J. Legrand and T. Leif (Eds.) *Neue soziale Bewegungen. Impulse, Bilanzen und Perspektiven*, pp. 47–63 (Opladen: Wiesbaden).

Schneider, H. (1995) 'Politische Partizipation—zwischen Krise und Wandel', in U. Hoffmann-Lange (Ed.) *Jugend und Demokratie in Deutschland*, pp. 275–335 (Opladen: Leske + Budrich).

van Deth, J. W. and Kreuter, F. (1998) 'Membership of Voluntary Associations', in J.W. Van Deth (Ed.) *Comparative Politics: The Problem of Equivalence*, pp. 135–155 (New York: Routledge).

Weßels, B. (2001) 'Vermittlungsinstitution und Interessenvertretung: Zur Performanz von Mitgliederorganisationen in Deutschland', A. Koch, M. Wasmer and P. Schmidt (eds) *Politische Partizipation in der Bundesrepublik Deutschland*, pp. 221–246 (Opladen: Leske + Budrich).

Wiesendahl, E. (2001) 'Keine Lust mehr auf Parteien. Zur Abwendung Jugendlicher von den Parteien', *Aus Politik und Zeitgeschichte*, 10, pp. 7–19.

# 14 Making a Difference?

## Political Participation of Young People in the United Kingdom[1]

*Martha Wörsching*

## INTRODUCTION

In mainstream media discourses in Britain today, children and young people are often depicted as a highly problematic and socially disruptive group. There is a widespread moral panic about the young who appear in headlines mainly in the context of violent street crime, binge-drinking, drug-taking, teenage pregnancy and homelessness. Unease about young people in the United Kingdom and their relationship to the older generation is also reflected in a report published by the left-leaning think tank, the Institute for Public Policy Research. The IPPR's director, Nick Pearce, is quoted in the following way: '[Young people] are not learning how to behave—how to get on in life'. According to Pearce, there is an 'increasing disconnect' between adults and children in Britain, as the young are mainly socialized in their own peer groups, without positive interaction between the generations (BBC Online 2006).

More recently, the UNICEF Report, 'Child poverty in perspective: An overview of child well-being in rich countries' (UNICEF 2007) has sparked off widespread debate in the media, as the report's findings seem to point to serious failure of past public policies:

> The UK finished in the bottom third of 21 industrialised countries in five out of six categories—material well-being; health and safety; educational well-being; relationships; behaviour and risks; and subjective well-being—ending up overall last, after the United States. The Netherlands, Sweden, Denmark and Finland topped the standings (Knight 2007).

At the time of writing, this report seems to have shocked the Labour government under Gordon Brown into activity to devise plans intended to lead to 'fitter, happier and better educated' young people (Curtis 2007). The concerns about British young people's relative lack of well-being on the one hand, and their perceived disruptive behaviour on the other have also led to questions as to why this generation seems to be little engaged with politics or in how far they are prepared to play an active role as citizens (Henn 2002; Henn and Weinstein 2004; Kimberlee 2002; O'Toole et al. 2003; White, Bruce and Ritchie 2000). The interest of young people in politics seems to be very low today; indeed, opinion polls suggest that in Britain 'the term and word "politics" has an extremely off-putting effect for young people' (Make Space Youth Review 2007: 92). Not surprisingly, the political class in Britain is seriously worried about the very low turnout of young people in elections and their generally low interest in conventional politics which, it is feared, will undermine the legitimacy of the political system itself. As a study of young people's political participation says:

> The government is . . . concerned. In 1997 it commissioned the Crick Report, *Education for Citizenship and the Teaching of Democracy in Schools*, which recommended that citizenship education should be compulsory for secondary school pupils, in order to tackle problems of declining political and civic participation among young people (O'Toole et al. 2003: 45).

Since then, the turnout of young people in elections has continued to decline, while 'media speculation and academic debate have been increasingly exercised over the alienation of young people from British political life' (White et al. 2000: 1).

This chapter will look at a number of recent studies to consider the political participation of young people in the United Kingdom, how they define politics themselves, what the reasons are for their disengagement with formal politics and in how far their distrust of politicians and parties, but also their attitudes towards wider political issues, may be seen as a form of civil commitment. It will consider further whether social inequality experienced by large numbers of young people and their feelings of public powerlessness and marginalization are responsible for the perceived political alienation of the young.

## YOUNG PEOPLE AND POLITICS IN THE
## UNITED KINGDOM—A SPECIAL CASE?

In international comparison, participation in elections, whether at national, local or European level, is relatively low in all age groups. According to the Electoral Commission, there is clear evidence that turnout in elections in the United Kingdom is declining among the population as a whole. Thus, in the 2001 General Election, the number of abstainers outweighed the number of people who cast their vote for Labour, the party elected to form the government. In the 2005 General Election, only 61.4 per cent of the electorate bothered to vote; this was slightly higher than in 2001, but it was 10 per cent lower than in 1997, itself a postwar low at the time (Electoral

Commission 2005). However, according to the Electoral Commission, the participation figures for young people—aged between 18 and 24—were only half as high as those for older people; according to Mori, only 37 per cent of young people voted in 2005, i.e. 2 per cent less than in 2001 (Electoral Commission 2005). Researchers working for the Electoral Commission believe that 'non-voting is the product of a broader political disengagement and that a section of the electorate are sceptical about the efficacy of voting at any election' (ibid.). However, this disengagement with parliamentary politics seems to be particularly true for the young.

When one considers the much better turnout of older age groups, one might hope that with increasing age, today's young people would also learn to become more interested in voting. However, researchers are less optimistic. They identify 'the apparent beginnings of a cohort effect with young age groups carrying forward the habit of non-voting into older age', and they assume that 'this suggests a very real risk that it will be even harder to mobilise turnout next time' (Electoral Commission 2005). Thus, young people's low interest in the formal political process and their low turnout—as an indication of the growing irrelevance of 'politics' to increasingly larger groups of the British population—can certainly alarm all those who see the legitimacy of representative democracy being eroded.

There are also serious discussions as to whether lowering the voting age from 18 to 16 might instil a more active feeling of citizenship in young Britons, turning them not just into 'citizens in the making' (Marshall 1950) but into 'citizens of today', leading to more active social and political participation. One might indeed ask why the young in Britain are deemed criminally responsible at the age of 10—and there are calls in the tabloid media even to lower this—while they are sexually competent at the age of 16, but not politically responsible until 18 (Matthews et al. 1999). The broad range of academic discussion on political participation and citizenship of the young sheds light on the issue from a range of different perspectives, but it does not provide simple solutions for the political class that sees the young as apathetic and elusive.

According to an international study which compared the political participation of young people in eight European countries—Austria, Estonia, Finland, France, Germany, Italy, Slovakia and the United Kingdom—the young in Britain seem to be more disengaged from institutional political life than any other age group, but also more than the young in most other European countries (Institute for Social Research and Analysis, Vienna 2005). This suggests that there may be particular factors affecting the young in Britain leading to especially high rates of disengagement.

The study, coordinated by the Institute for Social Research and Analysis at the University of Vienna, Austria, considered both participation *within* and *outside* the representative democratic system. It focused on attitudinal, behavioural and socio-demographic variables to identify the degree of and reasons for participation. Although the study's introduction underlines that there are limits to comparability because of differences in terminology, opportunity structures and political culture in the eight different countries, it nevertheless identifies clear differences in political participation between the countries—and on the whole the United Kingdom does not compare well.

The study shows the politicization of young people in graphs which plot Italy and Austria in the quadrant at the top left, corresponding to the highest levels of leftist and protest politicization; in contrast, the United Kingdom is located at the opposite end and is associated with a very low level of political participation and to very weak politicization (Institute for Social Research and Analysis 2005: 106). Similarly, in relation to parental politicization, the United Kingdom is seen by far as 'the country with the lowest level of politicisation. The same type of weak political socialisation and politicisation can also be observed with Estonia, Slovakia and Finland' (ibid.: 109).

Asked about their trust in political organizations or institutions, the UK sample has a distinctively low level of trust, namely only 6 per cent seem to trust political parties, while 9 per cent say they trust politicians, only 12 per cent trust the British government and the European Parliament, followed by 18 per cent for the UK Parliament, 33 per cent for Green Peace and 35 per cent for Amnesty International. Thus, institutions of formal politics rate much worse than informal organizations. Compared to other European countries, the study shows that the lowest party trust rates are found in Slovakia and the United Kingdom (ibid.: 130). Interestingly, at the European level, all countries show an overall higher level of trust in the European Commission than in their own national government, with the exception of Italy and the United Kingdom, where it is the other way round (ibid.: 135). The study also says that, in the United Kingdom, 'a remarkable number of young people does not make use of any mass media for political information' (ibid. 188), and adds: 'Significantly more young people in the UK (61%), in Slovakia (53%), Italy (53%) and France (46%) feel that politics is too complicated to understand' (ibid.: 229).

In the study's summary, it is highlighted that young people in Italy have the highest participation rate in elections, while the UK rate is lowest. It is also maintained here that '[t]he better educated young people are, the higher their voting rate and their perceived effectiveness of voting are' and adds that in 'Estonia and the UK membership as well as participation and volunteering are least common throughout all political organizations (ibid.: 244).

The UK national report of this study highlights again that young people in Britain are little interested in institutional politics and are much more involved with environmental and animal rights groups rather than political parties and trade unions (Moore and Longhurst 2005). In its summary the report concludes that fewer than 30 per cent of young people in Britain take an interest in political issues, and the interest that does exist is directed mainly at national events, with least attention given to European/EU-level politics (Moore and Longhurst 2005: 32). 'Over one third of young Britons (35%) felt politics is simply a game conducted by old men, with the vast majority of young people (75%) regarding "politics" as discussions conducted within parliament' (ibid.: 32). However, the authors see signs of optimism: 'Young people strongly believe that being politically active is important if the world is to become a better place, and very few believe that it is pointless to change the status quo' (ibid.: 32).

The low turnout in elections and the rejection of mainstream politics is also discussed in many other studies (for instance Henn and Weinstein 2004 or Kimberlee 2002). A qualitative study by White et al. and supported by the Joseph Rowntree Foundation explores the political views and behaviour of young people, consulting a cross-section of people aged 14–24 who come from diverse backgrounds. As the authors say, their aim is not to provide statistical evidence, but to show how young people themselves assess their interest in politics. The study demonstrates that different groups of young people are not uniform in their attitude towards politics, and it discusses the factors why young people are generally turned off politics. According to the authors, the research shows that young people in Britain feel that, firstly, politics are not interesting and accessible, secondly, that politicians are not responsive to their needs, and thirdly that there are not enough opportunities for them to enter the political process.

More specifically, when asking the question: 'What turns young people off politics?', the authors find that this age group feels that 'politics lack relevance to their lives at present' and that politics are 'for older and more responsible people whose lives are affected by politics' (White et al. 2000: 15); they feel that they do not have enough understanding about politics, and that the very language used in politics turns them off. The study also confirms the lack of trust in politicians and the feeling among young people that politicians are not interested in the views and concerns of the young (ibid.: 16).

The study is based on in-depth discussions with young people, and these show that they 'feel powerless and excluded from the political process' (ibid.: 34). Generally, the interviewees noted that there were not enough opportunities for them to participate in the political process. Especially the younger ones believed that there were no ways of participating until they were old enough to vote:

> Even where young people acknowledged there were opportunities to participate in the political process, either through conventional methods, such as voting or lobbying MPs, or less conventional methods, such as youth forums, they felt they lacked knowledge about the process of engagement. Underpinning this barrier was the perception that politics was a complex and alien subject, which they found hard to grasp and understand (White et al. 2000: 35).

They also said that only the views of those with money and status were listened to, while their own were dismissed by politicians as childish and unrealistic (ibid.: 35).

According to White et al., young people's reluctance to take part in elections was also due to their lack of trust in politicians and the fact that they felt ignored. Interestingly, other reasons why they felt that there was no point in voting was 'that a party was unlikely to win in a particular constituency where another party was dominant' and another reason was that 'there appeared to be so many similarities between the Conservative and Labour party; it was also believed that there was no opportunity to bring about change or make a difference to the way the country is governed' (ibid.: 39).

To be more responsive to the needs of young people, the interviewees felt that politicians would have to 'abandon the pomp and ceremony, removing the wigs and gowns' (ibid.: 42), and that they could represent young people much better if they were from a wider cross-section of society in terms of age, sex, ethnicity and class. There should be new opportunities for young people to participate more, by bringing them into contact with politicians who were less remote, by lowering the voting age and by empowering them to make their own decisions and giving them more control over more aspects of their own lives, so that they could learn about civic responsibility by practising it. Some young people warned that the introduction of new youth forums might raise expectations among the young which, if they could not be met, would lead to even more cynicism and apathy.

White et al. suggest that young people might develop more interest in politics with increasing age and changing life circumstances, but they believe that 'the age at which this is activated is now delayed, as a result of the changing social and economic environment in which young people now live' (White et al. 2000: 44).

According to White et al., issues that concern young people cover indeed a broad political agenda, even if they are not termed as such by them. The authors also believe that there is evidence that many of the young people already had engaged in a range of activities which can be seen as political, such as attending demonstrations and signing petitions, although they saw themselves being excluded from politics. It is suggested that an important factor discouraging more interest in politics is the narrow way in which young people conceive of politics as institutional and especially party politics. The teaching of citizenship at school is seen to be a step towards overcoming this, but the authors also feel that this would only work together with real empowerment in young people's everyday lives, within the family, at school and in the local community, thus listening and responding to their own needs and allowing them to practise their role as citizens.

Many of the previous findings are echoed in the study by Mahendran and Cook (2007), who say that 'young people in the UK report lower levels of political participation and engagement' (5) compared to other European

Union Member States, and they are the least likely to vote in elections to the European Parliament. However, they maintain that young people living in rich households with adults with higher educational qualifications were most likely to be interested in politics. In addition, they believe that early exposure to talk about politics has an important influence on young people's eventual interest in the subject (Mahendran and Cook 2007: 10). They also find that 'generally young people (15–24 year olds) claim to know less about the EU than older people. 43% state that they know nothing at all about it. . . . When young people are asked specific questions which test their knowledge, this relative ignorance is born out. For example, in 2005 only 22% of 15–24 year olds knew that the UK was holding the European Presidency, compared to 62% of over 55 year olds' (Mahendran and Cook 2007: 15).

## THE POLITICAL SYSTEM IN THE UNITED KINGDOM: A TURNOFF?

When comparing the political participation of young people in the United Kingdom with that in other European countries, it may not be too far-fetched to consider the particular institutional features of the political system and the political culture in which the individuals are socialized.

Despite more recent developments devolving political power to Scotland and Wales, Britain has been a highly centralized state where most decision making comes from London. The Thatcher years have certainly meant a reduction of decision making at the local level, and together with neo-liberal deregulation, the political accountability of democratically elected bodies has been greatly reduced.

The simple majority, first-past-the-post system for general elections works towards a two-party system, which means on the one hand that small parties have hardly any chance of influencing the democratic process, while on the other hand voters will be discouraged from voting for them, as this means wasting their vote. According to research by the Electoral Commission, there are:

> strong associations between turnout and people's perceptions of the importance, or otherwise, of the election and whether their vote will make a difference in some way. Our research after the 2005 general election found people reporting difficulties in deciding who to vote for, in part because of weakening political alignments but also because of the perceived similarities between the main parties (Electoral Commission 2005).

The feeling that casting one's vote will not make a difference may be particularly strong for young people who have not had any positive experience of having influenced any public matters. Also, in contrast to older people who may still identify with the fundamental ideological differences between the two main parties that existed in the past, the young today live in a culture where both Labour and the Conservatives exert themselves in scrambling for the so-called political middle ground. A populist homogenization of politics has taken place where both large parties try to 'modernize' themselves to gain the voters' attention. Blair's New Labour has certainly not left the Thatcherite neo-liberal path in terms of economic policy, while his successor as Labour prime minister, Gordon Brown, found it necessary to express his admiration for Lady Thatcher soon after he became head of government. The party politics of the past seem to have been turned upside down when the leader of the opposition, David Cameron, goes out of his way to show how 'touchy-feely', and socially and environmentally conscious the Conservative Party has become.

In addition to the blurring of party-political ideologies, one reason why parties and individual politicians in the United Kingdom have become distrusted by the electorate in general is the fact that the two-party system has during the last few decades led to the long duration of, first, the Conservative government (1979–1997) and then, the Labour government (1997 to date), thus providing ample potential for corruption and personal scandals. In addition to this, the 'expenses scandal' which broke in Spring 2009 and showed that many members of the House of Commons *from both main parties* had claimed for thousands of pounds for second homes they did not need or daily expenditure, by exploiting loop-holes in the law, have led to an all-time low in the respect for politicians among the public at large and the young in particular.

It is not surprising that the electorate as a whole, but especially the young, are confused about their ability to bring about real political alternatives in a political culture dominated by populism, where politicians vie with each other to base their public statements on the results of opinion polls and focus groups. This trivialization and personalization of politics may be seen as a reaction to the tabloidization of the media in Britain, but it is also actively engaged in by the politicians themselves and their media 'spin doctors'. Young people's low trust in parties and politicians may indeed be seen as a 'political' reaction, just as abstaining might be interpreted as a positive choice, especially when nonvoters may still behave as active citizens by taking part in other political activities (Todd and Taylor 2004).

If centralization, the two-party system without real alternatives, the growing erosion of respect for politicians and the trivialization of politics give young people the impression that they are remote from political decision making, then this is also compounded by the fact that Britain has no written constitution which might make the distribution of political powers more accountable and transparent. Many of the procedures of life at Westminster are run according to arcane rules, and the 'pomp and circumstance' of the opening of parliament are re-constructions of feudal medieval pageants which have not much to do with expressions of democratic governance. It may not baffle only the young as to why 'Her Majesty's government' needs to publish its new set of policies via a speech read out by the Queen! And the more recent 'reforms' of the House of Lords have only led to highlight the anachronism and lack of democratic legitimacy of this institution which—just like the buildings of the Houses of Parliament—hark back to the nineteenth century. It is difficult to imagine that the compulsory introduction of citizenship studies at school, including 'work on British values and national identity' (Woodward 2007), has managed to convince the young in general that they could have a say within this institutional system.

## THE YOUNG IN BRITISH SOCIETY: DISINTERESTED OR DISEMPOWERED?

Thus, the young themselves do not seem to believe that their voice counts for very much. Research into the views of first-time voters shows that they do not feel that they can influence the decision-making process (Henn and Weinstein 2003; Henn, Weinstein and Hodgkinson 2007; Make Space Youth Review 2007). Other studies conclude that:

> there is a growing recognition that within the UK young people are not given the respect or listened to with the seriousness that they deserve. . . . in contrast to Britain, in mainland Europe . . . there is ample evidence of effective ombudswork, national frameworks for the coordination of young people's affairs and well-established participatory structures which operate at grass-roots level. At a broader international scale, too, there is evidence that the Articles of the UNCRC are reaching out to incorporate growing numbers of young people world-wide. We suggest that the UK has much to learn from these experiences and until this happens, young people will remain largely invisible in public-policy making at all levels (Matthews, Limb and Taylor 1999: 10–11).

So what is it that seems to exclude young people in this country more than in other countries? Before we consider this question further, it should be worthwhile hearing more about the perceptions the young themselves have about their role as citizens.

An empirical, three-year-long study of young people between the ages of 16–23 set out to explore the way in which they understand themselves as citizens (Lister et al. 2003). The participants were stratified according to 'insider' and 'outsider' status, representing on the one hand the young person on the path to graduate-type employment, and on the other the person with few or no qualifications and a record of unemployment (ibid. 236). The researchers identified five models of citizenship in the discussions: (a) the universal status, (b) respectable economic independence, (c) constructive social participation, (d) social-contractual and (e) right to a voice. These models were not mutually exclusive. Overall, analysis showed that the 'universal' model dominated, but in the course of the study it became less important, while the 'respectable economic independence' and 'constructive social participation' types were emphasized more, 'with their invocation of economic and civic responsibility' (ibid.: 239).

The discussions on the meanings of citizenship showed the participants as a highly responsible group. The authors conclude that:

> [the] young people found it much easier to talk about responsibilities than rights and when they did identify rights they were more likely to be civil than political or social rights. . . . Few saw social security rights as unconditional. The young people also tended to place a high premium on constructive social participation in the local community. Such participation represented for many of them the essence of good citizenship and was one of two more responsibility-based models that emerged as prominent from general discussions of the meanings of citizenship. (ibid. 2003: 251) . . . Liberal rights-based and civic republican political participation-based models did not figure prominently in their discussions. This suggests that they have taken on board political messages about active citizenship and about responsibilities over rights (though not the related social-contractual model propounded by New Labour) that have become increasingly dominant over the past couple of decades in the UK. Similarly, the young people's image of the first class citizen is redolent of the successful citizen promoted by Thatcherism and to a degree under New Labour: economically independent, with money, own home and a family. For some of those classified as 'outsiders', this meant that they themselves identified with the label of 'second class citizen', below everyone else (ibid.: 251).

According to Lister et al., the potentially divisive and exclusionary character of the economic independence model is in conflict with the more inclusive universal membership model: 'Instead of challenging class divisions, the respectable economic independence model of citizenship reinforces them' (ibid. 251).

Thus, many of the 'outsiders' see themselves as 'second class citizens' without a say in public life. It would perhaps be surprising if the young in Britain—whether they are brought up in more privileged or deprived areas, thus segregated into educational establishments reflecting their parents' privileged or deprived status (see for instance: Curtis 2007a; Leaman 2008; Meickle 2007; Palmer 2007; Russell 2007)—were immune to the dominant ideology where both success and failure are seen to be the result of 'individual rational choice', instead of structural advantages and disadvantages. The 'winners' on the way to respectable economic independence may thus also feel more empowered to express their political voice, while the 'losers' feel that they deserve to be excluded. As Louise Vincent puts it in a critique of the ideologies dominating education today: 'Individual consumer choice and satisfaction rather than the world of political ideas, communities and social relationships are the benchmark against which success is measured' (Vincent 2004: 106).

Thus, the participation in public decision making is not something which the young in Britain experience very often in their everyday life in education, in training and in (un-)employment, and so it is not surprising that they see political decision making as an elite role to which only few aspire (Todd and Taylor 2004), especially as their experience of politics may be more likely to be that as objects of government policies.

## YOUNG PEOPLE AND SOCIAL INEQUALITY IN THE UK

This would also suggest that the young people growing up in today's neo-liberal climate are aware of the divisive forces in this society where all too early the young are sorted into 'insiders' and 'outsiders', 'winners' and 'losers', and this mainly according to the social background into which they were born and confined by an elitist education system that is all too keen to sort 'the wheat from the chaff', instead of fostering the capabilities of the many (Sennett 2008). Thus, research supported by the Sutton Trust reports:

> International comparisons of intergenerational mobility show that Britain, like the United States, is at the lower end of international comparisons of mobility. Also intergenerational mobility has declined in Britain at a time of rising income inequality. The strength of the relationship between educational attainment and family income, especially for access to higher education, is at the heart of Britain's low mobility culture (Blanden et al. 2005: 3).

A more recent report by the same team confirms again that bright children from poor backgrounds fall behind in their development within the first few years of their schooling (Curtis 2007b). Since the 1990s, child poverty in Britain has tripled, and despite efforts of the Labour government to reverse the trend, this has done little more than to stop the increase (Leaman 2008). Child poverty is measured as the proportion of children in households with incomes below 60 per cent of contemporary median income. Child poverty clearly hampers the development of the child and of course reflects the poverty in which the child and young person grows up; it is in many cases a reflection of the mother's, i.e. women's poverty—or the fact that in a country with an eroding welfare state, having children means risking poverty for all but the more comfortably off. According to a recent summary report by Middleton and Sandu on child poverty, 'by 2000 the

UK had the highest child poverty rate in the EU' (Middleton and Sandu 2006). The authors also identify a clear correlation between child poverty and lack of educational achievement, i.e. the potential for educational and also social exclusion as a result of poverty.

Nonetheless, despite the fact that official statistics show that more than three million children are in poverty in Britain, research undertaken for the Department for Work and Pensions shows that the population as a whole believes that there is 'very little poverty', and the researchers find that there is a view that 'the poor have themselves to blame' (Wintour 2007).

Thus, despite the clear evidence that Britain as a whole is a rich country, while a lot of its population—and many of them children and young adults—are deprived and marginalized, there is no general awareness of this. Many of the young people in this country have been poor all their lives, as they grow up in a society which is more unequal than most other EU countries. This is also reflected in the income inequality in Britain measured by the Gini Coefficient which shows that, among EU countries, only Latvia, Lithuania, Poland—three former Eastern Bloc countries—and Portugal—a country still characterized by its lack of a developed secondary and tertiary economic sector—have an even greater income inequality than the rich, developed United Kingdom (Poverty Organisation 2007). The government's own statistics show that '(i)ncome inequality still remains high by historical standards—the large increase which took place in the second half of the 1980s has not been reversed' (National Statistics Online 2007). As a result of economic restructuring and neo-liberal policies since the 1980s, Britain has become a polarized society. The same source informs us:

> The rate of male participation in the labour market has fallen, often in the households where there is no other earner. Conversely, there has been increased female participation among those with working partners. This has led to an increased polarisation between two-earner and zero-earner households. . . . (ibid.)

Deindustrialization in Britain over the last three decades has certainly also led to a geographical polarization between areas of thriving new service sector economies—mainly in the southeast around London but also in some other big cities—and declining areas of former industrial production where employment opportunities have become scarce. But there is also polarization within urban areas, with high unemployment and lucrative jobs side by side in the big cities where poor migrants and poor British people live in housing conditions reminiscent of the nineteenth century. As the Council of Race Equality (CRE) warns: 'The pace of change in Britain over the last few years has unsettled many, and caused people to retreat into and reinforce narrower ethnic and religious ties. Bonds of solidarity across different groups have reduced and tensions between people have increased' (CRE Report, quoted in Travis 2007).

Segregation between poor and rich communities is also a result of the housing policies of past governments, which are particularly problematic for the young. The extraordinarily steep increase in house prices over recent decades has led to overcrowding and homelessness for many families, especially for the young. In a country where home ownership was the norm for the majority of the population, young people in education and training are either forced to live with their parents or have to pay extortionate prices for sub-standard housing. Increasingly, it is middle-class young people at the beginning of their working life who are lucky enough to have parents prepared to share their housing wealth with them, while it is increasingly difficult for the young to get their foot on the ladder to home ownership (Sampson 2007).

This social inequality is disempowering and marginalizing many young people today, and if most of the research into political behaviour shows that better educated, more advantaged young people are more likely to take part in elections and believe that they can have a political voice, then this may reflect the fact that they can envisage the chance for a self-determined life within the existing system, as it allows them already the experience of agency, while the majority—and certainly the more marginalized groups—cannot imagine how they could exert real political power within a system that constantly confronts them with their own powerlessness.

## POLICIES FOR THE YOUNG?

So what can be done in an unequal society to overcome the 'political apathy' and the marginalization of the young? The government during the last ten years certainly has been under pressure to devise policies aiming towards a greater social inclusion of the young to promote their transition to adult citizenship. However, as Alan France finds in an article focusing on more recent government policies towards the young, the debate is largely influenced by a media-led moral crusade which sees in the young the single cause of panic for the adult population (France 2007). Core values such as self-reliance, economic independence, respect and civic responsibility are emphasized, with the aim of creating 'good citizens' who are able to take responsibility for their families and communities (Home Office 2006). A range of policy initiatives and programmes on education, training and employment have been introduced with the aim of targeting the most socially excluded young people. At the same time, New Labour has been keen to make benefits conditional on work, as part of a new 'social contract' (France 2007). The political climate determined by the right-wing media in which policies are shaped can be seen from an article in the *Sunday Telegraph*: Here, the authors comment on research commissioned by the Prince's Trust charity and carried out by the Centre for Economic Performance at the London School of Economics into the behaviour of young people who drop out of education, the so-called NEETs ('Not in Education, Employment or Training'). The paper claims that 'this "lost generation" is costing the country £3.65 billion a year—enough to fund a 1p cut in income tax. Indeed, the Government's own figures estimate that each new NEET dropping out of education at 16 will cost the taxpayer an average of £97,000 during their lifetime. The worst will cost more than £300,000' (Henrie and Goslett 2007). Thus the traditional political Right sees the young merely in terms of a danger to the public or cost to the tax payer, but certainly not as present or future citizens with a voice of their own.

That the mainstream adult population expects youth policies to be instruments of controlling and disciplining the young also becomes clear in the way that the idea of volunteering and 'active citizenship' is discussed, for instance in the *Daily Mail* where specific government plans are wel-comed in the following way: 'Premier Gordon Brown is keen to promote activities which encourage responsible citizenship, community service and volunteering and has already championed the spread of combined cadet forces to state schools' (Clark 2007).

Thus, according to France, New Labour policies aimed at overcoming exclusion are characterized by a strong moral agenda that is 'victim-blam-ing', while issues of structural inequality or lack of economic resources are ignored. 'Many of the risk factors identified as "causal" are related to failings by individuals, and therefore the problems are seen as being located in poor parenting, bad influences from peers, and lack of interest in school' (France 2007: 5). This individualizing of problems also means that individuals, families and whole communities are pathologized and seen to be in need of coercive intervention. As France says, 'social policy in educa-tion therefore has taken a regulatory and disciplinary function for those defined outside the parameters of middle-class social acceptability' (ibid.: 7). This, together with New Labour's continued commitment to a hard line on law and order towards the young, has led to the expansion of juvenile secure units and giving courts new powers to lock up children under the age of 15, while courts have been given increased powers to create Deten-tion and Training Orders for 12- to 17-year-olds (ibid.: 10–11). According to France, the government's policies to encourage greater social partici-pation through volunteering, leisure and sports activities are based on an agenda oriented towards the *employability* of the young, with the aim of providing the labour market with suitable 'human capital'. Questioning the effectiveness of such policies to overcome exclusion, France maintains that 'historical evidence shows that participation in these areas of social life has always been shaped by inequalities between different classes, genders and ethnicities' (ibid.: 14). The government's idea of 'good citizenship' is thus based on values reflecting a moral order which is white, male, Anglo-Saxon and middle class. 'To be included, young people must not only accept and conform to such values, but be seen to act upon them. Acting outside of this "normality" is then constructed as a "problem"' (ibid.: 15). Policies to promote forms of participation, while claiming to 'empower' young people, thus also have forms of social control built into them. As France maintains, the 'issue of power either between adults and young people or policy, professional practice and young people is rarely considered in debates about participation' (ibid.: 17). The young remain the passive objects of policies, and it is not surprising that this objectification does not encourage them to experience their own political agency, fostering the feeling that their actions might *make a positive difference* in a public context that goes beyond their own, individual private life.

So what should be done? In a study which aims to understand why young people in Britain today are politically disengaged, the researchers look at the relative effects of socio-economic location and social capital, to consider the potential of policies which might increase social engagement (Henn et al. 2007). The research was based on a nation-wide survey of 'attainers', young people who were voting for the first time. The complex study which considered political engagement, support for the democratic process, political efficacy and perception of political parties and professional politicians, came to the conclusion that government policies to mobilize social capital may encourage more civic engagement, while measures to improve socio-economic factors in general seem to be what is needed to make a real difference in terms of participation. Indeed, the recommendations are surprisingly direct, if challenging for a government that tries to appease the *Daily Mail* readers:

> Policy which succeeds in expanding educational participation, reducing social class differences and social exclusion, regenerating neighbourhoods and communities, strengthening local community networks and promoting social cohesion, and fostering volunteering and self-help, may contribute in helping to at least limit the drift towards political disengagement among youth in Britain (Henn et al. 2007: 475–476).

## CONCLUSION

As this discussion of recent research has shown, British young people are less politicized than most other young people in the EU, they are reluctant to take part in elections, have relatively little trust in parties and individual politicians, are not very interested in the EU and generally sceptical about formal, institutional politics, but they are more interested in general political issues and believe that being politically active is important if the world is to become a better place. However, they don't seem to see how they themselves could *make a difference* in the political world.

Their alienation from the formal political process can be explained in terms of the system itself—with its archaic and absurd procedures and its lack of real alternatives—not encouraging the participation of the young for whom political decision making is an elite occupation, but not part of their daily life where they could gain experience of their own political agency and learn about democratic processes. The feeling of being ignored by the politicians is particularly acute among the more disadvantaged young in a society which is materially very unequal, and where a large part of the young have grown up in relative poverty. As Leaman maintains, there is indeed 'strong evidence that the growth of inequality and the relative poverty that accompanies that process threatens the social stability of the welfare capitalism that characterized the post-war years. The strong correlation between levels of inequality and criminality should be a convincing indicator of the perils of promoting inequality á la neo-liberalism and seeking to manage that inequality á la New Labour' (Leaman 2008: 54) Past and present governments inspired by neoliberal policies have also intensified the experience of alienation and powerlessness of the young, especially as government policies to tackle exclusion have been predicated on objectifying children and young people, with the clear agenda of containing, disciplining and controlling them.

It seems, therefore, that the problem does not lie with the young, but with those who are in power in this socio-economic, political reality. Empowering the young to participate more in politics is a difficult task in a society that is becoming increasingly fragmented and polarized.

## NOTE

1   This is the revised version of an article published in Spanish with the title '¿Desafección y uniformidad? Participación política juvenile en el Reino Unido', in *Revista de Estudios de Juventud*, 81/2008: INJUVE Ministerio de Igualdad, Gobierno de España, with the permission of the journal's editors.

## BIBLIOGRAPHY

BBC Online (2006) 'UK Youth "Among Worst in Europe"', http://news.bbc.co.uk/1/hi/uk/6108302.stm (accessed 2 Nov. 2009).
Blackman, S.J. (2005) 'Youth Cultural Theory: A Critical Engagement with the Concept, Its Origins and Politics, from the Chicago School to Postmodernism', *Journal of Youth Studies*, 8 (1), pp 1–20.
Blanden, J., Gregg, P. and Machin, S. (2005) *Intergenerational Mobility in Europe and North America*, A Report Supported by the Sutton Trust, Centre for Economic Performance, April 2005, http://www.suttontrust.com/reports/IntergenerationalMobility.pdf (accessed 2 Nov. 2009).
Bradley, H. and Van Hoof, J. (Eds.) (2005) *Young People in Europe: Labour Markets and Citizenship* (London: Policy Press).
Buckingham, D. (2000) *The Making of Citizens: Young People, News and Politics* (London: Routledge).
Carle, J. (2003) Welfare Regimes and Political Activity among Unemployed Young People, in T. Hammer, (Ed.) *Youth Unemployment and Social Exclusion in Europe: A Comparative Study*, pp. 193–205 (Bristol: Policy Press).
Child Poverty Action Group (2006) 'Media Briefing: The Government's Child Poverty Target', http://www.cpag.org.uk/capaigns/media/CPAG_HBAI_2006_Media_Briefing.pdf (accessed 26 July 2007).

Clark, L. (2007) '"Out-of-control" British Teens Worst Behaved in Europe,' *The Daily Mail*, http://www.dailymail.co.uk/pages/live/articles/news/news.html?in_article_id=470919&in_page_id=17 (accessed 26 July 2007).

Cohen, N. (2005) 'Britain's Rich Kids Do Better Than Ever', *The New Statesman*, http://www.suttontrust.com/press056.asp (accessed 21 March 2005).

Curtis, P. (2007a) 'Study Reveals Stressed Out 7–11 Year-Olds', *The Guardian*, http://education.guardian.co.uk/primaryeducation/story/0,,2189589,00.html (accessed 13 October 2007).

Curtis, P (2007b) 'School Results Still Depend Heavily on Class', *The Guardian*, http://education.guardian.co.uk/schools/story/0,,2226589,00.html (13 December 2007).

Davies, I. and Evans, M. (2002) 'Encouraging Active Citizenship', *Educational Review*, 54 (1), pp. 69–78.

Denham, J. and Piatt, W. (2007) 'The Key to Unlocking Talent: Whose Job Is It, Universities or Government, to Transform the Educational Chances of Poor Children?', *The Guardian*, http://education.guardian.co.uk/egweekly/story/0,,2175931,00.html (accessed 25 September 2007).

Electoral Commission, Election (2005) 'Turnout. How many? Who and why?' http://www.electoralcommission.org.uk/files/dms/Election2005turnoutFINAL_18826-13874__E__N__S__W__.pdf (accessed 12 October 2007).

European Commission (2007) 'Directorate-General for "Education and Culture" ("Youth" Unit): Flash Eurobarometer 202—The Gallup Organisation, Young Europeans: Survey among Young People Aged 15–30 in the European Union, Analytical Report' http://ec.europa.eu/public_opinion/flash/fl_202_sum_en.pdf (accessed 13 October 2007).

France, A. (1998) '"Why Should We Care?" Young People, Citizenship and Questions of Social Responsibility', *Journal of Youth Studies*, 1 (1), pp. 97–112.

France, A. (2007) *Understanding Youth in Late Modernity* (Maidenhead: Open University Press).

Hall, T., Williamson, H. and Coffey, A. (1998) 'Conceptualizing Citizenship: Young People and the Transition to Adulthood', *Journal of Education Policy*, 13 (3), pp. 3001–3315.

Henn, M. (2002) 'A Generation Apart? Youth and Political Participation', in Britain, *The British Journal of Politics and International Relations*, 4 (2), pp. 167–92.

Henn, M. and Weinstein, M. (2003) 'First Time Voters' Attitude towards Party Politics in Britain, Nottingham Trent University', http://www.ess.ntu.ac.uk/esr-cyouth/ (accessed 13 December 2007).

Henn, M. and Weinstein, M. (2004) 'Politically Alienated or Apathetic: Young People's Attitudes towards Party Politics in Britain', in B. Linsley and E. Rayment (Eds.) *Beyond the Classroom: Exploring Active Citizenship in 11–16 Education*, pp. 89–98 (London: New Politics Network).

Henn, M., Weinstein, M. and Hodgkinson, S. (2007) 'Social Capital and Political Participation: Understanding the Dynamic of Young People's Political Disengagement in Contemporary Britain', *Social Policy and Society*, 6 (4), pp. 467–479

Henn, M., Weinstein, M. and Wring, D. (1998). 'Lowering the Age of Assent: Youth and Politics in Britain', *Fabian Review*, 110(4).

Henn, M., Weinstein, M. and Wring, D. (2003) 'Alienation and Youth in Britain', in G. Taylor and M. Todd (Eds.) *Democracy and Protest*, pp. 196–217 (London: Merlin Press).

Henrie, J. and Goslett, M. (2007) Meet the NEETS, *Sunday Telegraph*, http://www.telegraph.co.uk/news/main.jhtml?xml=/news/2007/04/15/neets15.xml (accessed 14 April 2007).

Home Affairs Committee (2006) Young Black People and the Criminal Justice System, CRE Submission, http://www.cre.gov.uk/downloads/youngblackpeople_cjs. pdf (accessed 13 December 2007).

Home Office (2006) 'Respect Drive Targets Troublesome Families', http://press. homeoffice.gov.uk/press-releases/Respect-drive (accessed 13 December 2007).

Institute for Social Research and Analysis, Vienna (2005) 'Political Participation of Young People in Europe—Development of Indicators for Comparative Research in the European Union (EUYOUPART), Deliverable 17: Final Comparative Report', http://www.sora.at/images/doku/euyoupart_finalcomparativereport. pdf (accessed 13 December 2007).

Kimberlee, R.H. (2002) 'Why Don't British Young People Vote at General Elections?', *Journal of Youth Studies*, 5 (1), pp. 85–98.

Leaman, J. (2008) 'Managing Poverty: Great Britain in Comparative Perspective', *Journal of Contemporary European Studies*, 16 (1), pp. 41–56.

Lister, R. and Smith, N. (2001) 'Negotiating Transitions to Citizenship', Report on Findings, CRSP 2389, http://www.post16citizenship.org/files/NegotiatingTransitions_to_Citizenship.pdf (accessed 14 December 2007).

Lister, R., Smith, N., Middleton, S. and Cox, L. (2003) 'Young People Talk about Citizenship: Empirical Perspectives on Theoretical and Political Debates', *Citizenship Studies*, 7 (2), pp. 235–253.

Lister, R., Smith, N., Middleton, S. and Cox, L. (2005) 'Young People as Real Citizens: Towards an Inclusionary Understanding of Citizenship', *Journal of Youth Studies*, 8 (4), pp. 425–443.

Mahendran, K. and Cook, D. (2007) 'Young People's Views on Participation & Their Attitudes Towards the European Union: Building Bridges Between Europe and its Citizen, Evidence Review Paper Three, Scottish Executive Social Research, Finance & Central Services Department', http://www.scotland.gov. uk/Resource/Doc/163788/0044575.pdf (accessed 14 December 2007).

Make Space Youth Review (2007) Transforming the Offer for Young People in the UK, London: 4Children, www.makespace.org.uk.

Marshall, T.H. (1950) *Citizenship and Social Class and Other Essays* (Cambridge, UK: Cambridge University Press).

Matthews, H. (2001) 'Citizenship, Youth Councils and Young People's Participation', *Journal of Youth Studies*, 4 (3), pp. 299–318.

Matthews, H. and Limb, M. (2003) 'Another White Elephant? Youth Councils as Democratic Structures', *Space and Polity*, 7 (2), pp. 173–192.

Matthews, H., Limb, M. and Taylor, M. (1999) 'Young People's Representation in Society', *Geoforum*, 30 (2), pp. 135–144.

Meickle, J. (2007) 'Third of Oxbridge come from 100 schools', *The Guardian*, http://education.guardian.co.uk/universityaccess/story/0,,2172797,00.html (accessed 20 September 2007).

Middleton, S. and Sandu, A. (2006) 'Child Poverty in the UK: The Headline Figures', http://www.crsp.ac.uk/downloads/publications/sues_papers/child_poverty_in_the_UK_the_headline_figures.pdf (accessed 14 December 2007).

Milbourne, L. (2002) 'Unspoken Exclusion: Experiences of Continued Marginalisation from Education Among "Hard to Reach" Groups of Adults and Children in the UK', *British Journal of Sociology of Education,* 23 (2), pp. 287–305.

Moore, C. and Longhurst, K. (2005) 'Political Participation of Young People in Europe, National Report: United Kingdom, EUYOUPART, WP 8/D15', http:// www.sora.at/images/doku/D15UKReport.pdf (accessed 13 December 2007).

National Statistics Online (2007) 'Income Inequality', http://www.statistics.gov. uk/cci/nugget.asp?id=332 (accessed 15 December 2007).

Osler, A. and Starkey, H. (2006) 'Education for Democratic Citizenship: A Review of Research, Policy and Practice 1995–2005', *Research Papers in Education*, 21 (4), pp. 433–466.

O'Toole, T., Lister, M., Marsh, D., Jones, S., McDonagh, A. (2003) 'Tuning Out or Left Out? Participation and Non-participation Among Young People', *Contemporary Politics*, 9 (1), pp. 45–61.

Palmer, S. (2007) 'League Tables Only Do Harm', *The Guardian*, http://education.guardian.co.uk/primaryeducation/story/0,,2222738,00.html?gusrc=rss&feed=8 (accessed 6 December 2007).

Park, A., Phillips, M. and Johnson, M. (2004) *Young People in Britain: The Attitudes and Experiences of 12 to 19 year olds*, Research Report RR564, Department for Education and Skills/National Centre for Social Research', http://www.dfes.gov.uk/research/data/uploadfiles/RR564.pdf (accessed 15 December 2007).

Poverty Organisation (2007) 'Income Inequality: Gini Coefficient, August 2007', http://www.poverty.org.uk/L14/a.jpg (accessed 15 December 2007).

Roker, D., Player, K., Coleman, J. (1999) 'Young People's Voluntary and Campaigning Activities as Sources of Political Education', *Oxford Review of Education*, 25 (1/2), pp. 185–198.

Russell, J. (2007) This Education System Fails Children by Teaching Them to Parrot, Not Think, *The Guardian*, http://education.guardian.co.uk/higher/comment/story/0,,2176606,00.html (accessed 25 September 2007).

Sampson, A. (2007) 'The Price of Housing Mania', *The Guardian*, 12 October 2007.

Sennett, R. (2008) *The Craftsman* (London: Penguin Books).

Shepherd, J. (2007) 'Breaking Free', in *Education Guardian*, 23 October, 2007.

Skelton, T. and Valentine, G. (2003) 'Political Participation, Political Action and Political Identities: Young D/deaf People's Perspectives', *Space and Polity*, 7 (2), pp. 117–134.

Smith, N., Lister, R., Middleton, S. and Cox, L. (2005) 'Young People as Real Citizens: Towards an Inclusionary Understanding of Citizenship', *Journal of Youth Studies*, 8 (4), 425–443.

Todd, M. J. and Taylor, G. (Eds.) (2004, *Democracy and Participation: Popular Protest and New Social Movements* (London: Merlin Press).

Travis, A. (2007) CRE Bows Out with Plea to Root Out Discrimination, *The Guardian*, http://www.guardian.co.uk/guardianpolitics/story/0,,2171441,00.html (accessed 18 September 2007).

UNICEF (2007) 'Child Poverty in Perspective: An Overview of Child Well-being in Rich Countries', *Innocenti Report Card* 7, 2007, UNICEF Innocenti Research Centre, Florence, http://www.unicef-icdc.org/presscentre/presskit/reportcard7/rc7_eng.pdf (accessed 15 December 2007).

Vincent, L. (2004) 'What's Love Got to Do with It? The Effect of Affect in the Academy', *Politikon*, 31 (1), pp. 105–115.

White, C., Bruce, S. and Ritchie, J. (2000) 'Young People's Politics: Political Interest and Engagement amongst 14–24 Year Olds, National Centre for Social Research, Joseph Rowntree Foundation', http://www.jrf.org.uk/bookshop/eBooks/1859353096.pdf (accessed 18 September 2007).

Wintour, P. (2007) Research Shows 41% of People Believe There Is Very Little Child Poverty, *The Guardian*, 11 December 2007.

Woodward, W. (2007) Slimmed-down School Curriculum Aims to Free Quarter of Timetable for Pupils Aged 11 to 14, *The Education Guardian*, 13 July 2007 http://education.guardian.co.uk/schools/story/0,,2125489,00.html (13 July 2007).

Wring, D., Henn, M. and Weinstein, M. (1999) 'Committed Scepticism or Engaged Cynicism? Young People and Contemporary Politics', in J. Fisher et al (Eds.) *British Elections and Parties Review*, 9 (London: Frank Cass).

# 15 Renouncing Violence or Substituting for It?

## The Consequences of the Institutionalization of *Alleanza Nazionale* on the Culture of Young Neo-Fascist Activists in Italy

*Stéphanie Dechezelles*

Italy's history was marked by a long period of violent mobilization in the post-1968 period, which clearly differentiates it from most European countries (Tarrow 1989). The so-called 'Years of Lead' between 1969 and 1980 were a period of violent political turmoil which caused the death of several hundred victims. After a long series of controversies and investigations, it seems incontrovertible today that most of these acts of deadly violence and terrorism were perpetrated by neo-fascist militants—the bombings of Piazza Fontana in Milan in 1969 and Piazza della Loggia in Brescia in 1974, the blowing up of the *Italicus* train in the rail tunnel between Bologna and Florence in 1974, and the 'Bologna Massacre' which destroyed the city's central railway station in 1980. This period was also marked by regular clashes between groups of young far-left and far-right activists, and several people were killed on these occasions. However, tension and violence have somewhat abated since then, in spite of sporadic bouts of verbal or physical violence—brawls in Parliament, the killing of several politicians and magistrates by the Mafia, Umberto Bossi's calls to take up 'Padan Kalachnikovs' (Padania is the name of an imaginary country in the north of Italy whose independence is claimed for by *Lega Nord*), the death of Carlo Giuliani, a young antiglobalization militant during the demonstrations against the G8 Summit in Genoa in July 2001, or the assassination of law professor Marco Biagi by members of the new Red Brigades in 2002. Admittedly, these acts were not committed by the activists of the main neo-fascist party[1], *Alleanza Nazionale,* or its youth organization, *Azione Giovani*, contrary to the previous decades which saw the historical and parent movement, *Movimento Sociale Italiano* (MSI) and its youth organization, *Fronte della Gioventù*, regularly hit the headlines on account of their violent clashes with political opponents (Ferraresi 1993)[2]. Today political violence mainly originates in a loose conglomeration made up of hooligan or neo-Nazi groups.

The evolution of *MSI*—which was the heir to the fascist movement— may be explained by the legitimation strategy adopted by the party, which became *Alleanza Nazionale* on the occasion of its 1995 Congress in Fiuggi, at the initiative of its leader, Gianfranco Fini[3]. He successfully turned *Alleanza Nazionale* into an institution which was more conservative and nationalist than radical or 'national-populist' (Kitschelt and McGann 1995)[4]. In spite of internal opposition, the party eventually rallied around this strategy. Those *MSI* members who were most hostile to the compromises deemed necessary to reach the highest spheres of power—the very same who saw themselves as the custodians of pure ideology—embarked on some secessionist initiatives which led to the creation of sub-movements closer to their aspirations (*MS-Fiamma Tricolore*, *Alternativa Sociale*, etc.) but eventually failed to attain electoral success. The main question for the *Alleanza Nazionale* militants was therefore to handle the passage from violent action—ranging from terrorism to violent confrontation with political opponents, a highly hierarchical vision of social relations, a nationalist ideology and the promotion of aggressive modes of action—to a strategy of conquest and exercise of power. How could activists, who belonged to a socialized political organization and shared a culture of violence, give up such time-honoured and deeply rooted practices? What were the alternative derivatives they could turn to, substituting for physical violence which had for long been regarded as the norm?

Sociological research work on political violence (Braud 2004) has mainly focussed on the concept of relative frustration (Gurr 1970) and the mobilization of resources. In the present chapter we have chosen to adopt a different perspective and focus on the culture of activist groups (Cefaï 2001), an approach partly inspired by research in the field of cultural anthropology (Geertz 1973). This approach makes it possible not only to address the question of violent action as a reference point, as a mode of justification and as the *modus operandi* of an activist organization, but also to deal with the consequences that the relinquishing of these reference points may have had on the militants and their political engagement—socialization, ideological corpus, careers. Our objective is indeed to propose a tentative explanation of the reasons and mechanisms of the 'disuse' of violence, of its obsolescence, so to speak, rather than study the mechanisms and reasons for the recourse to violence. In more precise terms, we will study in detail the case of the young *Alleanza Nazionale* militants and shed light on the modalities of the passage to a culture of nonviolence and on the consequences that such an apparent de-radicalization process may have had on the organization and institutionalization of players previously bent on violent activism (Sommier 1998).

There are many reasons for our specific interest in the young *Alleanza Nazionale* activists. They are defined as 'young' according to their status (the 14–30 age group) but also, and mainly, through the roles and positions—most often of secondary importance—assigned to them by the 'adults'. Focussing on the younger members of this political party thus implies taking into consideration the impact of generational dominance and symbolic violence exerted by the 'elders' who delegate to the youth organizations the honorific, rather than constraining, function of being the guardians of the party's ideological purity. The generational division of activist work accounts for the fact that party leaders, some of whom may occupy important positions that lead them to adopt more conciliatory and moderate stances, tend to entrust the 'young' militants with the task of conducting violent or risky operations. This sociological approach to the issue of age and generation in political issues is also a way to break free from the subjective and substantialist vision of 'youth' which has prevailed since the end of the Second World War (Bourdieu 1993). As a breeding ground for the future leaders (Recchi 2001), the youth organizations offer a vantage point for understanding the process of political professionalization, especially when it comes to analyzing political parties which have so far been excluded from governments. Finally, the study of a specific organization within a party—young activists in this case—has the great advantage of deconstructing the homogeneous and consensual image that party members often give of themselves.

The starting point of the present study is the objective fact that the main neo-fascist party—MSI first, then *Alleanza Nazionale*—has evolved in the space of a few years from political exclusion and marginalization to full participation in the exercise of power. The party first joined the coalition government with *Forza Italia* in 1994, then in 2001 with *Forza Italia*, *Lega Nord* and *UDC*, a coalition which later incorporated *Movimento per l'Autonomia* in 2008. Its secretary general was appointed Vice President of the Council by Silvio Berlusconi between 2001 and 2006, Italy's representative at the Convention for the European Constitutional Treaty and Foreign Affairs minister at the end of the mandate. Several ministers and many local and national elected representatives were party members (Morini 2007). We may uphold the hypothesis that such an institutionalization process has necessarily implied some cognitive problems of identity among its members socialized and politically trained in a culture of violence. The consequence of such an evolution is all the more important as party members, who shared this common culture, were traditionally exhorted to perpetuate the memory of the group, of its heroes and fallen martyrs. They have not all been able to compensate for or justify this new identity matrix, on account of their position in the sociogenerational hierarchy of the party and in spite of early political careers. Adapting to such changes with a view to acquiring greater political respectability has necessarily led to adopting new strategies in order to twist, alter and overthrow a culture imbued with physical violence[5].

## BOIA CHI MOLLA !⁶ THE ROLE OF VIOLENCE AND DEATH IN THE CULTURE OF YOUNG ALLEANZA NAZIONALE NEO-FASCISTS

Focussing on the cultural references of a political party—or a partisan youth organization in the case at hand—makes it possible to understand the founding and organizational principles of a party's relations of allegiance and loyalty (Dechezelles 2006). In that respect the analysis of the narrative (Jackson 2002) as constructed by the members of the *AN* youth organization reveals a dual pattern of affiliation—they see themselves both as members of a delegitimized order, the historical losers, and as the heirs to the fallen heroes of a glorious past.

## A 'Cemetery' Movement of Young Heirs

In the hierarchy of *Alleanza Nazionale*, the young must show respect, obedience and loyalty to the elders. There is thus much emphasis put on the recognition and celebration of sacrificed lives. Such a macabre fascination indeed originates in the fascist matrix, extolling self-sacrifice as the sign of civilizational renaissance and the 'natural' elimination of the 'soft-minded, introverted' and 'parasite' members of society. However, this feeling is typically shared by all political movements founded on revolutionary or elitist heroism and buttressed on the idea of a militant and active *avant-garde*, standing out from 'ordinary' men, which alone may go down in legend through its action. Though the celebration of glorious feats of arms is not specific to *AN*, it has played a fundamental role. Activism has significantly been associated with tragic and violent events that must be commemorated, so that the links between the young heirs and their courageous ancestors are perpetually revived (Dechezelles 2009). Whatever the historical references may be, the vocabulary used—the 'fallen', the 'martyrs', the 'heroes'—often echoes the lexis used to evoke the dead soldiers killed on the battlefields of past wars. The emotional dimension of such commemorations of the past thus hinges on nostalgia.

*Azione Giovani* may appear, in many respects, as a 'cemetery', full of heroes who sacrificed their lives for a worthy cause. Their courage and indefatigable devotion for the cause have made them true legends that the young militants have to emulate, in the image of Italy's Gabriele D'Annunzio⁷, Romania's Corneliu Codreanu⁸, France's Alain Escoffier⁹ or Jan Palach¹⁰ from Prague. In the *AN*'s pantheon are also to be found the young Italian activists in the occupied town of Trieste who were killed during the November 1953 riots¹¹ or the Hungarian students who revolted in Budapest in 1956. Policemen and soldiers are more particularly admired. In 2002, on the occasion of the 60th anniversary of the battle of El Alamein (Egypt), *AG* leadership launched a series of initiatives with a view to glorifying the courage of the soldiers of the *Fulgore* battalion who fought against British and American troops, though they were vastly outnumbered and poorly equipped[12]. *AG* activists have also more recently mobilized *in memoriam* of the Italian contingent in Afghanistan and Iraq, and published articles in their fanzines on advertiser Enzo Baldoni who was killed in August 2004 after being kidnapped by the Islam Army of Iraq, *Il Manifesto* journalist Guiliana Sgrena, humanitarian workers Simona Torretta and Simona Pari, secret service officer Nicola Calipari and private security guard Fabrizio Quattrocchi[13].

## Nostalgia for Violence: Memory as an Activist Imperative

Nostalgia is one of the main springs of the Italian far right's emotional economy and memory (Tarchi 1995; Cheles 1995), more particularly among the young *AN* activists (Germinario 2005). Nostalgia and thanatophilia are the two pillars of their militant culture. This trend which was first initiated in the 1970s has also been reinforced by recurrent references to Julius Evola and Ernst Jünger, two writers who celebrated the beauty of defeat and death. The persistent reactivation of the memory of a 'delegitimized' order against the 'oblivious' masses who blindly threw in their lot with the 'liberators' has been a distinctive feature of fascist nationalists since the end of the Second World War. The young *AG* activists see this duty to remember not only as the possibility of learning about the past but also as a means of creating an uninterrupted link between militants, past and present. The celebration of these values is best illustrated by an extract from one of their publications: '*If we give up, if we fall and do not stand up again, we shall not only betray ourselves but also the faith of those who came before us and the hope of those who will come after us*'[14].

The youth sections have regularly staged ceremonies to pay homage to the dead. We may quote the famous twenty-two *Fdg* young activists who were killed in the years 1970–1980 during violent clashes with far-left militants[15], or deliberately shot down[16]. Their portraits are hung on the walls of the local sections, especially when, as in the case of Giuseppe Mazzola and Graziano Giralucci, they came from the provincial section of Padua. In this militant pantheon, there are also the victims of the Trieste events in 1953[17], as well as the thousands of civilians who were exiled, deported, raped or executed by foreign armies—Yugoslavian, German—during the liberation of Istria, Dalmatia and Friuli between 1944 and 1945. Those so-called '*foibe*' victims (*foibe* are very deep karst sinkholes in northeast Italy) who were thrown down into these natural pits, sometimes alive, with their arms tied behind their backs and weighed down with heavy stones, are the object of special attention from the young neo-fascists[18]. They organize commemorations during which sprays of flowers are placed on the war memorial, the national anthem is played together with the last post in memory of the '*caduti d'Italia*' (the fallen of Italy) among nationalistic speeches and fascist salutes. These ceremonies usually take place in February[19], with the support of irredentist associations such as 'Lega Nazionale' and 'Continuità Adriatica—Norma Cossetto'. The duty to remember has often taken the form of disputes and lobbying activities with municipalities with a view to naming streets or squares after their 'fallen' heroes, as in Rome where a street was given the name of Paolo di Nella, who died in the city on 9 February 1983 after being hit on the head with a monkey wrench, or that of Sergio Ramelli, killed on 13 March 1975 in Verona—the street was officially inaugurated on 23 April 1988. The main idea is to create symbolic '*loci* of memory' which may contribute to their fight against the left-wing movements who also have their own memorial places for 'their' dead comrades (Isnenghi 2006). Indeed all these funeral ceremonies—marches, torchlight processions, death and commemoration notices posted on walls, leaflets, books with personal photos—and incantatory speeches on the 'never forget' theme have contributed to forging a collective memory and conferring on the neo-fascist movement the image of 'victims'—or even of 'martyrs'—of the barbarity of their enemies.

However, as the most violent period has seemingly ended, the objective is now to mobilize the young activists in favour of a more peaceful form of political struggle, even if references to violence are never totally forgotten.

## A SINUOUS PATHWAY FROM VIOLENCE TO NEW NARRATIVES AND ALTERNATIVE PATTERNS OF POLITICAL STRUGGLE

In spite of the relative pacification of political struggle from the mid-1980s onwards, the collective memory of past acts of violence has significantly contributed to sustaining the fighting spirit of the young neo-fascists and socializing the new recruits within an activist culture promoted by some players intent on preserving its 'movementist' dimension[20].

## Narratives of Violence as Catalysts of Collective Identity and Hierarchy

In spite of the changing environment and the alternative modes of militant action, the young activists of *AN* still adhere to the old slogans of *Fronte della Gioventù* and the heroic narratives of their 'elders'. Changes have indeed affected the 'adult' leadership of the party much more than the youth organization, led by former 'young adults' who were politically trained in the 1980s in a political culture of violent confrontation (Vignati 2001) and are today the custodians of a 'stainless culture' (Ignazi 1994: 89). In their view, hardship helps to turn boys into 'men', and thus into 'true militants'. Thanks to collective experience, the group has been constituted around a strong feeling of belonging and deeply rooted solidarity.

Past difficulties have conferred increased authority and legitimacy on those who have gone through them. For instance, Enrico, *AG* provincial secretary in Padua and a town councillor in a small town, is viewed as a local hero. As an *Fdg* member in 1987 when he was only fourteen—he actually lied about his age—the narrative of his early militant life is quite revealing. '*I was grabbed by eight members of Autonomia Operaia armed with hammers, and left lying in a pool of blood. Such things had already happened before to many young, some of them lost their lives; it either scared you away or made you stronger to go on.* [ . . . ] *I am proud today to have held out*'. When he speaks of the consequences of a violent clash in the late 1980s, he says that '*when they broke my head when I was 17, my mother's life changed, because I lay in bed, with no hair left on my head, vomiting my guts out, shaken with spasms, and the Communists would phone my mother at night, saying: your son is already dead, and stuff like that, and I was there with my head all smashed*'.

Fights against far-left, Communist or Anarchist activists are seen as so many rites of passage which have today progressively become less common and violent. They confer the aura of 'veterans' on those who took part in them, as evidenced by the scars they sport on their bodies. Galeazzo, a local leader in Emilia-Romagna and a town councillor in Bologna, recalls memories of his youth when he was a secondary school pupil in the 1990s: '*I was "the fascist" by antonomasia, that is to say that they would be waiting for me at the school entrance, push me against a wall and beat me up for no reason, the usual thing for the "fascists" as they called us at that time. We had to keep silent. They just hit you and that was it. I ended up four or five times in hospital. I also have a scar on the forehead because the Communists broke my head.*' The art of turning these events into glorious narratives, through various rhetorical devices—hyperbole, bombast, schoolboy pranks—is combined with the fascination that the young recruits may have for the old militants. Massimiliano, a braggart from Treviso, is a notable case: '*I had to be accompanied back home every evening because they had written: "Fascist, beware of your head!" In Padua, we had just lived through a period when there still was the anti-fascist week with people armed with iron bars, monkey wrenches, spiked clubs. They took on the first fascist they could lay their hands on and would just massacre him. I saw someone have one of his ears sawn off at incredible speed in Padua. I saw a guy who had 33 internal stitches and 30 external ones [ . . . ] I saw one of my best friends lose a testicle*'. Such narratives of past violence— either actually experienced or imagined—contribute to reinforcing the charisma of the 'elders' and creating a 'complex of posterity' among the younger militants. As they were not old enough to live through such glorious collective experiences, they tend to develop a feeling of frustration, which is perceptible in their interviews, and even the fear that they might be accused of opportunism for having joined the party after it became legitimate. The 'new recruits' are thus entrusted with the task of billposting, especially at night, to prove their audacity and virility. It is the same 'pacified' logic which prompts them to join sports clubs—rugby, fencing, martial arts or parachuting—in order to train physically for future confrontations while respecting the ideological code of the far right.

## Alternative Forms of Struggle

The young *AN* members have thus been forced to adopt new modes of militant action in an evolving environment marked by their party's new approach to political commitment and quest for power. The political, ideological and cultural context of the late 1980s and early 1990s contributed to the emergence of *MSI*, and *AN* some time after. It was at that time that far-right intellectuals started revisiting their ideological reference points, after the collapse of Communist ideology and governments. The '*Nouvelle Droite*' in France, whose main representative was Alain De Benoist, thus became a major reference in the corpus of the neo/post-fascist organizations (Germinario 2002). One of their main objectives was to initiate revisionist historiographical debates, hinging on the downgrading of the far left's collective mobilization movements and the reevaluation of the activities of the far right. Such a revisionist approach to history was indirectly legitimized by the research work on 'historical revisionism' conjointly conducted by some liberal historians and some members of the Italian 'left'[21]. Indeed Renzo De Felice[22] was at the origin of a controversy which spread after he published the biography of Benito Mussolini. His work on the fascist regime—together with that of other historians[23]—partly put an end to the taboo attached to this period and challenged the myth of a 'Resistance Nation' relayed by official historiography. As a consequence, his work—which in fact laid the blame on both Communism and fascism—was promoted within *AG* sections. Documents that referred to the main points of his research work on fascism and Mussolini could be found on the *AG*'s official site, a deliberate move by the party.

Young militants were also encouraged to defend the thesis according to which—contrary to the official, 'left-wing' vision of history—the Resistance fighters were not generous and heroic liberators but rather brutish killers whose crimes always surpassed the atrocities perpetrated by the Nazis and fascists. Their main target was Marxist 'cultural terrorism'[24].

This new strategy which originated in the concept of 'national pacification' adopted by *MSI* leader Giorgio Almirante as early as the late 1940s implied linking up the moral requirements of the National Liberation Committee and those of the fascist leaders of the Social Republic of Italy. From this perspective, Resistance fighters would be more to blame than the SS for having caused the death of an even higher number of civilians in Italy. Young militants took up this line of accusation, enriched by personal experience and family narratives—looting for food, brutality, rapes—deemed to be more 'credible' than the official version proposed in the history books written by Communist sympathizers. In the same vein they accused Yugoslav troops of having committed atrocities in northeastern Italy. Overall, all these historical events were deliberately mixed up, with a view to discrediting the antifascist political forces, gathering under the same umbrella term—*Partigiani*—both Italian Resistance fighters and Tito's Slavic troops, paralleling the supposed cowardice of the former with the acknowledged barbarity of the latter.

Such historiographical disputes originally aimed to strengthen and perpetuate the identity of the group, in spite of the pacification process in their relations with political opponents. However, the search for a common identity was weakened by the new strategy, developed by Gianfranco Fini, which aimed at achieving power. It also led to cleavages within the activist culture of the young militants. Indeed the *Alleanza Nazionale* activists, who shared a culture of political violence, were torn between worshipping their elders—for their glorious past achievements—and hating them—because they had betrayed the cause by accepting compromises with the government. They were at the same time satisfied with the strategy adopted by the party leadership, and by themselves in some cases, and sceptical about the future of the party and the real motives of the new members—were they mere opportunists or truly committed to the cause? The new ideology and the conflicting visions it engendered influenced in a contrasting manner these militants' approach to political activism (Bertolino and Chiapponi 2001). Confronted with changing political messages and new electoral configurations, the young party members who answered our questions have indeed expressed their scepticism and doubts, especially those who had joined the movement after the creation of *AN*, those who were local, municipal, provincial or regional elected representatives or those who were local or regional party leaders. Because of their political responsibilities and the coalition agreements made with *Forza Italia* first, then with *Lega Nord* and the Christian Democrats, they have been obliged to accept compromises, new alliances with political partners, the logic of majority rule and the respect of the freedom of expression of the opposition, especially when they belong to the local executive. As a consequence, the institutionalization of the party and its commitment in a multiparty government may have furthered the careers of some, but it has also led to criticism and defection. In spite of the existence of important resources, some young militants have still not accepted the transformations of the party and have decided to leave it.

## CONCLUSION

Whether they have been used by or imposed on the members of the party or of the groups defended by the party, the modes of violent action are essential reference points in the culture of the *AN* youth organization. Obliged as they have been to tone down their activism, they have engaged in alternative forms of political struggle. However, these changes have brought about cleavages within the group's activist culture. *AN*'s decision to be part of the government and its merger with *Forza Italia* into a single partisan organization have led to further distancing the party from the activist culture of the youth organization. Some have even gone so far as to take to the streets in September 2008—shortly after the election as mayor of Rome of Gianni Alemanno, a former representative of the *MSI* youth organization—claiming they would never be 'antifascist'.

## NOTES

1. The terms 'neofascist' or 'postfascist' (Ignazi 1994), used to describe *Alleanza Nazionale,* may sound somewhat inappropriate after the ideological U-turn made by Gianfranco Fini, a prominent political figure of the movement, in the mid-1990s, as exemplified by his declaration in Yad Vashem in November 2003 about Nazi atrocities and racial laws, his proposed bill to grant the right to vote to immigrants for local elections and to decriminalize the use of soft drugs in 2004, his tactical rapprochement with Christian-Democratic UDC, or his support for the referendum on assisted procreation in 2007. We may also refer to the change in rhetoric, 'nonconformism' and 'rebellion' substituting for 'revolution' or 'ideology'. However, the use of the adjective 'neo-fascist' is justified in so far as, from the culturalist approach we adopt in the present analysis, the references of the youth organizations are still today directly or indirectly inspired by the fascist ideological corpus of the first half of the twentieth century.
2. Since the parliamentary elections of spring 2008, AN has joined *Partito delle Libertà,* Silvio Berlusconi's new party, whose organization and mode of functioning remain uncertain.
3. There were some profound socio-political changes in Italy between the late 1980s and the early 1990s. Italians aged 15 to 30 developed political awareness in an ever evolving political environment. The organizations which had dominated political life at national and local levels after the war either disappeared or reorganized themselves—*Democrazia Cristiana* in the 'white' regions (Lombardy, Venetia, etc.) and *Partito Comunista* in the 'red' regions of Central Italy, particularly in Tuscany, Emilia Romagna and Umbria. They developed in a general context of political disenchantment towards the 'conventional' forms of affiliation—parties, unions and political elites. However, the number of militants remained conspicuously higher than in the rest of Europe during this period (Scarrow 2000; Muxel and Cacouault 2001).
4. Even though this move towards more legitimacy and moderation was perceptible before (Ignazi 1998), it was not before the Fiuggi Congress in 1995 that MSI split up between *Movimento Sociale-Fiamma Tricolore*, which stuck to the hard line, and *Alleanza Nazionale* which had opted for a political alliance with S. Berlusconi as early as 1994 and wanted to become a conservative 'right-wing' party.
5. The present chapter is based on the analysis of data collected for a doctoral thesis on the engagement of young activists within the main right-wing parties of Italy, *Forza Italia, Alleanza Nazionale* and *Lega Nord.* The corpus comprises 89 semi-directive interviews (39 with FI, 30 with AN and 30 with LN members) conducted between the end of 2001 and the end of 2002. Data

were collected during a one-year stay in the two northern regions of Venetia and Emilia Romagna, from ordinary militants, provincial or regional
leaders and young elected representatives. Some of the younger respondents
belonged to *Azione Giovani* (a youth organization linked to the party) and
*Azione Universitaria* or *Azione Studentesca* (students' and pupils' organizations). Data incorporate various propaganda documents (programmes, fanzines, leaflets, websites, songs, etc.) collected from the early 2000s onwards,
either directly or remotely. They all refer to the early months of the coalition
of the second Berlusconi government and thus do not encompass the total-
ity of the mandate. They concern a specific segment of the population, i.e.
members of youth organizations who live and militate in the north of Italy,
a region which is very different from the south and the islands of Sardinia
and Sicily in economic, social, cultural and political matters. Moreover the
northern regions of Italy do not provide as many electors, militants or elected
representatives as Latium, more particularly Rome, and the southern regions
of Calabria and Apulia where fascism still plays a significant role in industry
and agriculture and where war was less dramatically felt than in Toscana,
Emilia Romagna or Venetia.

6. 'Shame on those who give up!' This fascist slogan is said to have been coined
by Roberto Mieville when he was a prisoner in a US Prisoner of War camp
at the end of the war. It was in fact the slogan of *Raggrupamento Giovanile
Studenti e Lavoratori,* the youth organization of the newly created MSI. It
was mainly used during the 1970 riots in Reggio-Calabria. Some of the young
respondents use it to show the importance of loyalty and tenacity in difficult
periods or the difficulties they have to face in their militant activities.

7. Gabriele D'Annunzio was revolted by the fact that the Treaty of Versailles
did not provide for the annexation of some territories Italy claimed—Dalmatia and Albania—in spite of the high price paid by this country (650,000
dead, 950,000 wounded, a quarter of its budget) and though Italy was on
the side of the 'winners'. He decided to create an irregular force of some
1,000 men in 1919 and, from September 1919 onwards, occupied the city
of Fiume which had been given to Yugoslavia. This led a fifteen-month-long
siege during which he progressively lost the support of the local population.
In December 1920, the siege came to an end when he was forced to capitulate
by the Italian army (Mussolini annexed the city in 1924).

8. Corneliu Zelea Codreanu (1899–1938) was the founder of *the Legion of the
Archangel Michael,* while he was in prison in June 1927. His objective was
to 'save' the traditions of Romania from the capitalist threat. In 1930, he
founded the *Iron Guard,* a paramilitary group. He endeavoured to improve
the living conditions of farmers and workers by erecting dikes and collecting
funds. His electoral success (he was elected to the Chamber of Deputies in
1931) and his violent activities attracted the attention of the government who
outlawed him in 1934. In 1935, he gave new impetus to his movement whose
name he changed for *Totul Pentru Tara* ('Everything for the Fatherland')
and fiercely opposed King Corolus II. As a consequence he was arrested and
sentenced to ten years of hard labour. On the night of 29 November 1938,
as he was being transferred to another prison, he was strangled with thirteen
other legionaries. The underground movement was to continue its activities
under Communist rule up to the 1950s.

9. Alain Escoffier was a member of the far-right group *'Mouvement Action Jeu-
nesse'.* On 10 February 1977, he self-immolated before the offices of airline
company Aeroflot, to protest against the Soviet gulag.

10. Jan Palach was a Czech student who committed suicide by self-immolation
in front of a museum in Prague in January 1969. In a letter that he had left,

he declared he wanted to protest against the occupation of his country by the Soviet troops.

11. *La nuova Europa. 2000 anni di storia, di patrie, di eroi,* catalogue Ag and Au.
12. '60° Anniversario della battaglia di El Alamein', pamphlet Ag, 2002.
13. 'This is how an Italian dies. [ . . . ] We side with the heroes. We side with all those men, Italians, military personnel and civilians, who, thanks to their action in the world, stand for *Patria*. [Fabrizio Quattrochi] died as a hero [ . . . ] because he showed pride and dignity in spite of the horrible circumstances of his death', *IdeAzione. Periodico di informazione ed attualità di Azione Giovani Padova,* March–April 2004.
14. *Azione ! Temi e principi utili per colui che vuol liberarsi dai falsi miti della società contemporanea,* catalogue Ag, 2002.
15. Ugo Venturini (Genoa, 18/04/1970), Angelo Pistolesi (Rome, 28/12/1977), Carlo Falvella (Salerno, 07/07/1972), Franco Bigonzetti (Rome, 07/01/1978), Stefano et Virgilio Mattei (Rome, 16/04/1973), Francesco Ciavatta (Rome, 07/01/1978), Giuseppe Santostefano (Reggio Calabria, 31/07/1973), Stefano Recchioni (Rome, 07/01/1978), Manuele Zilli (Pavie, 03/11/1973), Alberto Giaquinto (Rome, 10/01/1979), Giuseppe Mazzola (Padoue, 17/06/1974), Stefano Cecchetti (Rome, 10/01/1979), Graziano Giralucci (Padua, 17/06/1974), Francesco Cecchin (Rome, 29/05/1979), Mikis Mantakas (Rome, 28/03/1975), Angelo Mancia (Rome, 12/03/1980), Sergio Ramelli (Milan, 29/04/1975), Nanni De Angelis (Rome, 05/10/1980), Mario Zicchieri (Rome, 29/10/1975), Paolo Di Nella (Rome, 02/02/1983), Enrico Pedenovi (Milan, 29/04/1976).
16. On 25 February 1975, during the trial of some members of *Potere Operaio* who were accused of arson, which caused the death of the two sons—aged 8 and 22—of the secretary of the MSI section, three activists of *Autonomia Operaio* broke into the headquarters of the party and shot down Mikis Mantakas, a Greek student who had joined FUAN. The main suspect, Alvaro Lojacono who had also been condemned in absentia to sixteen years' imprisonment for the assassination of Aldo Moro, was arrested in Corsica in June 2000. '25 anni senza giustizia', pamphlet Ag, 2000.
17. '*Pietro Addobbati, Emilio Bassa, Leonardo Manzi, Saverio Montano, Francesco Paglia and Antonio Zavadil.* [ . . . ] *are a precious testimony of our city and evidence without any doubt its deeply-rooted Italian identity. [they] are the last Martyrs of national Risorgimento*', 'L'irredentismo giuliano-dalmata e i ragazzi del '53', Ag and Au.
18. On *Azione Giovani*'s official website, there are many documents presenting the main events, the topographical list of foibe, several testimonies from eye-witnesses, extracts from coroners' legal reports, as well as a collection of songs which can be downloaded.
19. *AN* managed to push Act 92 through Parliament (30 March 2004) which instituted 10 February as the official commemoration date for the 'foibe' victims.
20. The distinction between 'fascism movement' and 'fascism regime' was first made by historian Renzo De Felice. The history of *MSI*—and of *AN* later on—was marked by a strong polarization process between the two main trends within the party: the old *RSI* militants with Pino Rauti who were closer to the tradition of the historical '*arditi*' movement (Francesco Storace, Gianni Alemanno) and the more pragmatic and less ideological group led by Giorgio Almirante whose objective was less to promote loyalty to fascist ideology than to secure a place for the party in a coalition government (Gianfranco Fini).

21. The successive presidents of the Republic, Francesco Cossiga in 1992 and Carlo Azeglio Ciampi in 2002, the president of the Chamber of Deputies, Luciano Violante in 1996 and singer Francesco De Gregori in 2000, respectively sent signals in favour of such a sacrificial approach.
22. Until he published *Intervista sul fascismo* in 1975, R. De Felice had been regarded as a 'left-wing' or 'anti-fascist' historian by *MSI*. There was a fierce controversy among academics, and some went so far as to accuse him of producing an 'a-fascist' historiography.
23. Claudio Pavone, *Una guerra civile. Saggio storico sulla moralità della Resistenza*, Turin, Bollati Boringhieri, 1991; Pietro Scoppola, *25 Aprile. Liberazione*, Turin, Einaudi, 1995; Nicola Tranfaglia, *Un passato scomodo : fascismo e postfascismo*, Rome-Bari, Laterza, 1995; Gian Enrico Rusconi, *Resistenza e postfascismo*, Bologna, Il Mulino, 1995.
24. The fascist party and its youth organization published 'counter-manuals' with excerpts deemed seditious from 'politically oriented' books, as, for example, Annalisa Terranova, *La Riforma come origine della modernità*, Rimini, Il Cerchio, 2000; Mariano Vezzali (dir.), *Scoprire l'Ottocento. Politica e storia del secolo lungo*, Rimini, Il Cerchio, 2000; Rutilio Sermonti, *L'Italia nel XX secolo. Storia dell'Italia moderna per gli studenti che vogliono la verità*, Parma, All'insegna del Veltro, 2001.

# BIBLIOGRAPHY

Bertolino, S. and Chiapponi, F. (2001) 'L'identità alla prova', in R. Chiarini and M. Maraffi (Eds.) *La destra allo specchio. La cultura politica di Alleanza nazionale*, pp. 84–117 (Venice: Marsilio).

Bourdieu, P. (1993) 'Youth is Just a Word', in *Sociology in Question*, pp. 94–102 (London: Sage).

Braud, P. (2004) *Violences politiques* (Paris: Seuil).

Cefaï, D. (Ed.) (2001) *Cultures politiques* (Paris: PUF).

Cheles, L. (1995) 'Nostalgia dell'avvenire: The Propaganda of the Italian Far Right between Tradition and Innovation', in L. Cheles, R. Ferguson, M. Vaughan (Eds.), *The Far Right in Western and Eastern Europe*, pp. 41–90 (London: Longman).

Dechezelles, S. (2006) *Comment peut-on être militant ? Sociologie des cultures et des (dés)engagements. Les jeunes militants d'Alleanza Nazionale, Lega Nord et Forza Italia face au pouvoir*, PhD thesis, Sciences Po Bordeaux (France).

Dechezelles, S. (2009) Mémoires militantes, histoire nationale et émotion. Héritiers fascistes et orphelins padans en Italie, in C. Traïni (Ed.), *Emotion . . . Mobilisation!*, pp. 217–235 (Paris: Presses de Sciences Po).

Ferraresi, F. (1993) *Threats to Democracy: The Radical Right in Italy after the War.* (Princeton, NJ: Princeton University Press).

Geertz, C. (1973) *The Interpretation of Cultures* (New York: Basic Books).

Germinario, F. (2002) *La destra degli dei. Alain de Benoist e la cultura politica della Nouvelle Droite* (Torino: Bollati Boringhieri).

Germinario, F. (2005) *Da Salò al governo. Immaginario e cultura politica della destra italiana* (Torino: Bollati Boringhieri).

Gurr, T. (1970) *Why Men Rebel* (Princeton, NJ: Princeton University Press).

Ignazi, P. (1994) *Postfascisti? Dal Movimento Sociale Italiano ad Alleanza Nazionale* (Bologna: Il Mulino).

Ignazi, P. (1998) *Il polo escluso. Profilo storico del Movimento Sociale Italiano* (Bologne: Il Mulino).

Isnenghi, P. ed (2006) *L'Italie par elle-même, lieux de mémoire italiens de 1848 à nos jours* (Paris: Editions Rue d'Ulm).

Jackson, M. (2002) *The Politics of Storytelling: Violence,Transgression, and Intersubjectivity* (Copenhagen: Museum Tusculanum Press—University of Copenhagen).

Kitschelt, H. and McGann, A. J. (1995) *The Radical Right in Western Europe* (Ann Arbor, MI: The University of Michigan Press).

Morini, M. (2007) 'Movimento Sociale Italiano—Alleanza Nazionale', in: L. Bardi, P. Ignazi and O. Massari (Eds.) *I partiti italiani ? Iscritti, dirigenti, eletti*, pp. 149–174 (Milan: Università Bocconi Editore).

Muxel, A. and Cacouault, M. (2001) *Les jeunes d'Europe du sud et la politique. Une enquête comparative France, Italie, Espagne* (Paris : L'Harmattan).

Recchi, E. (2001) L'entrée en politique des jeunes italiens: modèles explicatifs de l'adhésion partisane. *Revue Française de Science Politique*, 51 (1–2), pp. 155–175.

Scarrow, S. (2000) 'Parties without Members ? Party Organization in a Changing Electoral Environment', in D. J. Russell and M. P. Wattenberg (Eds.) *Parties Without Partisans*, pp.79–101 (Oxford: Oxford University Press).

Sommier, I. (1998) *La violence politique et son deuil. L'après 68 en France et en Italie* (Rennes: PUR).

Tarchi, M. (1995) *Cinquant'anni di nostalgia. La destra italiana dopo il fascismo* (Milan: Rizzoli).

Tarrow, S. (1989) *Democracy and Disorder. Protest and Politics in Italy, 1965–1975* (Oxford: Clarendon Press).

Vignati, R. (2001) 'La Memoria del Fascismo', in R. Chiarini and M. Maraffi (Eds.), *La destra allo specchio. La cultura politica di Alleanza nazionale*, pp.43–83 (Venice: Marsilio).

# Contributors

**Mathias Albert** is Professor of Political Science at the University of Bielefeld, Germany. His current research interests are theories of globalization and world society, global governance and youth research.

**Andreu López Blasco** is Professor of Sociology at the Departamento de Investigación Sociológica, Valencia, Spain. Since 1996, he has been a co-founder and member of the European Group for Integrated Social Research (EGRIS), and he is the scientific director of the research group AREA concerning the family and young people in Europe. He has published widely in the context of contemporary youth studies.

**Rachel Brooks** is a reader in social policy in the Department of Politics at the University of Surrey, co-convenor of the British Sociological Association's Youth Study Group and co-editor of the *International Journal of Lifelong Education*. She has published widely in a variety of journals and has written two books: *Friendship and Educational Choice* (Palgrave, 2005) and *Researching Young People's Lives* (Sage, 2009, with Sue Heath, Elizabeth Cleaver and Eleanor Ireland) and an edited collection: *Transitions from Education to Work: New Perspectives from Europe and Beyond* (Palgrave, 2009).

**Johann de Rijke** is a Senior Researcher in the Centre for Long-Term Observation and Methods at the German Youth Institute, Munich, Germany. He has published widely in the context of young people in Germany and Europe today.

**Daniel Faas** is Lecturer in Sociology at Trinity College Dublin. His research interests include migration and education, European integration and globalization, citizenship and identity politics, multiculturalism and social cohesion, ethnicity and racism, and curriculum and policy developments. He has been involved in a number of European and transatlantic research projects in these fields. He is author of *Negotiating Political Identities: Multiethnic Schools and Youth in Europe* (Ashgate, 2010).

**Stéphanie Dechezelles** is Lecturer in Political Science at the Political Studies Institute of Aix-en-Provence (France). Her PhD thesis examined the political cultures and involvement of young rightist activists in contemporary Italy. Her primary areas of research interest include right-wing extremism, youth and party political culture, political sociology, comparative politics and Euroscepticism. She will co-edit a special issue on "Populism or Scepticism? Parties and the Europeanization of Political Competition' for *Perspectives on European Politics and Society* [forthcoming, June 2010].

**Alan France** is Professor of Social Policy Research in the Centre for Social Policy Research at Loughborough University, United Kingdom. He has published widely in the area of youth studies and has recently published the book *Understanding Youth in Late Modernity* (Open University Press 2007).

**Wolfgang Gaiser** is Senior Researcher in Comparative Youth Studies at the German Youth Institute, Munich, Germany. He has published widely in the context of young people in Germany and Europe today.

**Gavin Hales** is Senior Reseach Fellow at Institute of Criminal Justice Studies at the University of Portsmouth, United Kingdom. He is at present seconded to the Metropolitan Research Group. He researches on gun crime, statistics and cannabis use.

**Terry Hanley** is a Lecturer in Counselling at the School of Education, Manchester University, United Kingdom. His work focuses on the development of online counselling services for young people in the United Kingdom. He has recently guest-edited a special edition of the British Association for Counselling and Psychotherapy Research Journal (*Counselling and Psychotherapy Research*) and published more generally in this field.

**Kairi Kasearu** is a Senior Researcher in the Family and Social Networks Research Group at the Faculty of Social Sciences, University of Tartu, Estonia. She has been involved in a number of European research projects in relation to transition societies and intergenerational transmission of poverty and published in this field.

**Peter Kraftl** is Lecturer at the Centre for Children and Youth in the School of Social Sciences at the University of Northampton, UK. His main areas of research are children's geographies and utopia and utopian geographies, and he has published extensively in these fields.

**Dagmar Kutsar** is Professor of Social Policy at the University of Tartu; she has also been head of the Unit of Family and Welfare Studies since 1991. Her research interests are family, childhood and welfare and associated policies, social indicators and social reporting. She has published widely in these areas, and is author of *Living Conditions in Estonia Five Years Later.*

**Jeremy Leaman** is Senior Lecturer in German and European Political Economy at the Department of Politics, History and International Relations at Loughborough University, United Kingdom. For many years he has been joint editor of the *Journal of Contemporary European Studies* and has published widely in the areas of Political Economy.

**Chris Lewis** is Senior Research Fellow and visiting professor in the Institute of Criminal Justice Studies at the University of Portsmouth, United Kingdom. He was Chief Statistician at the Home Office and head of the OCU Research Unit from 1976–2003. He researches on crime, organized crime and comparative studies.

**Gudrun Quenzel** is a Research Associate in the Bielefeld School of Public Health at the University of Bielefeld, Germany. Her research and publication areas include youth and cultural studies and the construction of identity.

**Magdalena Rek** is a junior researcher in the Department of Sociology at the University of Łódź, Poland. She worked as a research assistant in the recent EC 6FP project 'Policy Responses Overcoming Factors in the Intergenerational Inheritance of Inequalities' (PROFIT), a study of young adults in eight European countries.

**Ewa Rokicka** is Professor of Sociology at the Department of Sociology at University of Łódź, Poland. She acted as second coordinator of the recent EC 6FP project 'Policy Responses Overcoming Factors in the Intergenerational Inheritance of Inequalities' (PROFIT), a study of young adults in eight European countries.

**Daniel Silverstone** is Senior Lecturer at Institute of Criminal Justice Studies at the University of Portsmouth, United Kingdom. He researches on drugs, gun crime, Vietnamese organized crime, and covert operations.

**Barbara Stauber** is Professor of Sociology at the Institute of Education, University of Tübingen, Germany. Her research interests are in the field of youth and gender studies, and she has published widely on gender, participation and motivation in the phase of transition between school and employment.

**Liz Sutton** is a Research Associate at the Centre for Social Policy Research at Loughborough University, United Kingdom. She has been involved in conducting a number of qualitative studies into lifestyles and living standards, welfare services and social exclusion. Her areas of interest and experience are in childhood inequality and social exclusion, childhood and youth policy, qualitative and participatory methodology, and research with children and families.

**Avo Trumm** is a Lecturer in the Unit of Family and Welfare Studies at the Departments of Sociology, University of Tartu, Estonia. He has been involved in a number of European research projects in relation to transition societies and intergenerational transmission of poverty and published in this field.

**Andreas Vossler** is a Lecturer in Psychology in the Psychology Department, Faculty of Social Science, at The Open University, Milton Keynes, United Kingdom. He is a Chartered Scientist, Psychological Psychotherapist and trained systemic family therapist. His research interests and main publications are in the areas of counselling and psychotherapy and community psychology, with a special focus on systemic theory and practice, technology-based counselling forms and participation of children and adolescents.

**Amanda Waring** is a Research Associate at the Centre for Social Policy Research at Loughborough University, United Kingdom. She has a wide range of research interests including health and physical activity, lifestyle, social capital and social exclusion. Her research experience includes focus groups with adults and young people, interviews and observations.

**Wielisława Warzywoda-Kruszyńska** is Professor of Sociology and Head of the Department of Sociology at the University of Łódź, Poland. She has been involved in numerous European research projects and was the main coordinator of the recent EC 6FP project 'Policy Responses Overcoming Factors in the Intergenerational Inheritance of Inequalities' (PROFIT), a study of young adults in eight European countries.

**Johanna Waters** is a lecturer in human geography at the University of Liverpool. She has published on migration and education in a range of Geography and interdisciplinary journals including: *Transactions of the Institute of British Geographers; Global Networks; Antipode; Social and Cultural Geography; The Canadian Geographer;* and *Environment and Planning A.* Her research monograph entitled *Education, Migration and Cultural Capital in the Chinese Diaspora* was recently published by Cambria Press. She is currently conducting a research project with Dr Maggi Leung, funded by the ESRC, on transnational education in Hong Kong.

**Martha Wörsching** is a Lecturer in German and European Studies at the Department of Politics, History and International Relations, Loughborough University, United Kingdom. She has been a member of the editorial board of the *Journal of Contemporary European Studies* and its reviews editor for many years. Her main publications are in the area of cultural, media and gender studies as well as youth and sports studies.

# Index

An environmentally friendly book printed and bound in England by www.printondemand-worldwide.com

PEFC Certified

This product is
from sustainably
managed forests
and controlled
sources

www.pefc.org

PEFC/16-33-415

www.fsc.org

MIX
Paper from
responsible sources
FSC® C004959

This book is made entirely of chain-of-custody materials; FSC materials for the cover and PEFC materials for the text pages

#0044 - 101212 - C0 - 229/152/16 [18] - CB